Exploring Complexity in Legal Translation and Discourse Analysis

Mansour Amini
https://orcid.org/0000-0003-2149-4604
Universiti Sains Malaysia, Malaysia

Shuangjiao Wu
https://orcid.org/0009-0001-2144-7173
Zhejiang Yuexiu University, China

Qiufen Wang
Kashi University, China

IGI Global
Scientific Publishing
Publishing Tomorrow's Research Today

Vice President of Editorial	Melissa Wagner
Director of Acquisitions	Mikaela Felty
Director of Book Development	Jocelynn Hessler
Production Manager	Mike Brehm
Cover Design	Jose Rosado

Published in the United States of America by
IGI Global Scientific Publishing
701 East Chocolate Avenue
Hershey, PA, 17033, USA
Tel: 717-533-8845 | Fax: 717-533-7115
Website: https://www.igi-global.com E-mail: cust@igi-global.com

Library of Congress Cataloging-in-Publication Data

Names: Amini, Mansour, 1984- editor | Wu, Shuangjiao, 1987- editor | Wang, Qiufen, 1995- editor

Title: Exploring complexity in legal translation and discourse analysis / Mansour Amini, Shuangjiao Wu, Qiufen Wang.

Description: Hershey : IGI Global Scientific Publishing, 2027. | Includes bibliographical references and index. | Summary: "Legal translation is widely recognized as one of the most challenging domains within translation studies, operating at the intersection of linguistic precision, comparative law, and cultural specificity. Unlike general translation, legal translation involves the transposition of concepts between incongruent legal systems, where a singular term can carry vast historical, judicial, and systemic weight. This book dissects the multifaceted nature of legal texts through the lens of discourse analysis. It moves beyond the traditional focus on terminology management to investigate how legal discourse functions as a system of power, persuasion, and obligation. By applying critical discourse analysis (CDA), corpus linguistics, and genre analysis, this book uncovers the underlying structures that make legal texts difficult to translate and to propose methodological frameworks for overcoming these challenges"-- Provided by publisher.

Identifiers: LCCN 2026024279 (print) | LCCN 2026024280 (ebook) | ISBN 9798337391793 hardcover | ISBN 9798337391809 paperback | ISBN 9798337391816 ebook

Subjects: LCSH: Language and languages--Law and legislation | Translating and interpreting--Law and legislation | Discourse analysis | Machine translating | Corpora (Linguistics) | Artificial intelligence--Linguistic applications

Classification: LCC K487.L38 E97 2027 (print) | LCC K487.L38 (ebook)

LC record available at https://lccn.loc.gov/2026024279

LC ebook record available at https://lccn.loc.gov/2026024280

British Cataloguing in Publication Data
A Cataloguing in Publication record for this book is available from the British Library.

This volume is dedicated to the brilliant minds and tireless researchers who continually push the boundaries of translation studies and applied linguistics.

To my esteemed co-editors, colleagues and collaborators and beyond, whose intellectual rigor and unwavering support have been the cornerstone of my academic journey. Your dedication to advancing the intersection of technology and language has been a constant source of inspiration in the development of this work.

To my exceptional graduate students and mentees. Your curiosity, resilience, and commitment give me immense hope for the future of our field. Mentoring such dedicated scholars remains the most rewarding aspect of my career, and your hard work continually motivates me to explore new pedagogical frontiers.

Finally, to the countless legal translators, interpreters, and educators navigating the increasingly automated landscape of global communication. Your daily efforts to preserve human agency, linguistic equity, and the performative force of law in the face of rapid technological disruption are the true heartbeat of this discipline. You are the ultimate guardians of justice in our multilingual world.

Editorial Advisory Board

Table of Contents

Detailed Table of Contents

This chapter investigates how semiotic and multimodal elements converge to shape meaning, authority, and accessibility in legal texts. It argues that law functions as a multimodal artefact, in which linguistic content interacts with visual, spatial, and performative cues, such as seals, emblems, typography, layouts, and digital interfaces. Drawing on semiotic theory, systemic functional linguistics, and multimodal critical discourse analysis, the chapter demonstrates how these resources signal institutional power, legitimacy, and obligation, influencing interpretation across jurisdictions and media. Methodological implications include multimodal corpora, annotation schemes, and accessibility standards, while practical recommendations address translator training and institutional drafting policies. Ultimately, recognising law's multimodal nature is essential for preserving legitimacy and promoting inclusivity in legal communication.

Legal discourse poses challenges for EFL learners, yet teaching-oriented studies rarely engage deeply with discourse complexity. Most approaches treat complexity as a barrier to remove rather than a phenomenon to understand. This chapter analyzes how complexity in legal discourse is negotiated through a genre-informed lens in EFL contexts. Using genre-based analysis of contracts, statutes, and case summaries, plus learner data from an EFL legal English classroom, it distinguishes potential complexity (text-internal features) from actualized complexity (learner errors). Findings show errors reveal which features are most opaque. The chapter reframes complexity as negotiated, not static, and positions the EFL classroom as a site for observing meaning construction under partial knowledge. Genre-informed approaches engage with complexity without oversimplification, offering both theoretical and methodological contributions.

The difficulty of bilingual laws and the authority of the statutory texts in the Malaysian setting make it necessary that the translators focus more on legal precision rather than common lexical correspondence. The legal translator must thus know the precedence of the legal sources and the authority of the words in statutory law in translating legal works to a different language. This paper discusses the concept of "terminological priority" in the translation of Malaysian legal documents, particularly statutory instruments. It states that in the interpretation of laws like the Employment Act 1955, the meaning adopted in the Act should be given priority rather than the meaning of the words in the general dictionaries or even the style. For example, when the statute uses the word "hendaklah" to signify the mandatory nature of "shall," the statutory formulation must take precedence over any other possible equivalents suggested by authoritative sources, such as the dictionaries published by Dewan Bahasa dan Pustaka.

This chapter examines the growing role of Artificial Intelligence (AI) in legal translation and multilingual legal governance, with particular focus on the relationship between technology, language, constitutionalism, and institutional power. The chapter argues that legal translation is not merely a technical process of linguistic conversion but an interpretive exercise shaped by legal culture, procedural context, and constitutional values. Through an interdisciplinary socio-legal and doctrinal analysis, the chapter explores how AI-driven translation systems influence access to justice, linguistic equality, democratic participation, and legal interpretation in multilingual constitutional democracies such as India. It further analyses challenges relating to algorithmic bias, low-resource languages, data colonialism, and technological centralization, demonstrating how AI systems often reproduce existing linguistic hierarchies.

The integration of artificial intelligence (AI) in legal translation has created a critical analytical blind spot: the "illusion of accuracy," where linguistic fluency masks the erosion of legal fidelity. This chapter argues that AI systems do not merely transfer meaning but reconstruct discourse, often sacrificing specialized legal nuance for statistical probability. Utilizing Systemic Functional Linguistics (SFL) and Critical Discourse Analysis (CDA), the study examines how algorithmic mediation weakens modal obligations and flattens syntactic complexity, thereby threatening institutional authority. To address this, the chapter proposes the AI–Legal Discourse Transformation Model (ALDTM), a three-layer diagnostic framework that maps transformations across input, processing, and output stages. By shifting the focus from surface-level correspondence to functional-discursive integrity, this research provides essential insights for AI governance and multilingual legal communication, ensuring that automated systems responsibly uphold the performative force of law.

The growing use of neural machine translation and large language models has improved the speed and consistency of legal translation, but fluent output may conceal errors in legal meaning, ambiguity, and normative force. This chapter examines AI through algorithmic mediation, understood as the active shaping of meaning by computational systems between source and target texts. Drawing on critical discourse analysis, genre theory, and systemic functional linguistics, it argues that legal meaning depends on conventions, intertextuality, deontic modality, and jurisdiction-specific concepts rather than lexical equivalence alone. It develops a fourfold taxonomy of lexical, syntactic, pragmatic, and systemic ambiguity and shows how AI may silently resolve or erase such indeterminacy. The chapter also considers authority, accountability, minority-language risks, and the responsibilities of certified translators. It concludes that AI should support, not replace, professional judgement through disclosure, human review, ambiguity-aware design, and responsibility for legal outcomes.

This study aims to analyze the translation of institutional and honorific expressions in the courtroom records of the IMTFE from 5 and 6 August 1947. By analyzing the three texts – the English source text, the published Chinese translation, and the machine-translated Chinese version – the study intends to discuss the most salient types of such expressions and the degree to which the two Chinese versions preserve their interpersonal meanings in terms of tenor and interpersonal equivalence. Results reveal that institutional role labels, historical official titles, and courtroom honorifics are among the most salient categories. It is also found that interpersonal meanings are generally better preserved in the published translation.

Foreword

Legal translation has long been acknowledged as one of the most rigorous and consequential areas of professional translation. In an era defined by globalization, cross-border trade, and complex supranational governance, the demand for precise legal communication across linguistic boundaries has never been greater. Yet, the field is undergoing a profound transformation. The rapid integration of Artificial Intelligence and neural machine translation into legal workflows has introduced unprecedented efficiencies, alongside significant conceptual and ethical risks. It is within this dynamic and challenging landscape that Exploring Complexity in Legal Translation and Discourse Analysis emerges as a timely and indispensable resource.

This volume distinguishes itself by moving beyond traditional, purely lexical approaches to legal translation. Instead, it embraces a comprehensive discourse analysis perspective, recognizing that legal meaning is constructed through complex layers of genre, power, and semiotic resources. The chapters within this book meticulously dissect how legal authority is negotiated and transferred, offering profound insights into the structural and pragmatic hurdles that practitioners and scholars face today.

Particularly commendable is the foundational exploration of meaning-making presented in the early chapters. By examining law as a multimodal artefact, the text provides a sophisticated framework for understanding how visual and performative cues interact with linguistic content to signal institutional legitimacy. This theoretical depth is brilliantly complemented by pedagogical insights, offering a genre-informed lens that reframes how legal discourse complexity can be effectively navigated in English as a Foreign Language contexts.

Furthermore, the collection excels in its application of these theories to diverse, real-world jurisdictions. The detailed case studies ranging from the critical examination of terminological priority in Malaysian statutory instruments to the corpus-assisted analysis of conceptual asymmetry in Hong Kong bilingual legal texts and the nuanced translation of personal data legislation in Greek contexts ground the broader theoretical discussions in vital empirical evidence. These contributions highlight the indispensable role of the human expert in deciphering the normative force embedded within specific legal cultures.

Perhaps the most critical contribution of this volume is its unflinching examination of technological disruption. As the authors astutely point out, the fluency of modern Artificial Intelligence can often mask a dangerous erosion of legal fidelity. By critically analyzing algorithmic mediation, the flattening of syntactic complexity, and the shifting dynamics of institutional power, this book confronts the critical blind spots of automated translation. The culmination of these insights into a proposed human-in-the-loop framework provides a forward-looking, pragmatic solution for integrating machine efficiency with necessary human oversight.

Exploring Complexity in Legal Translation and Discourse Analysis is a rigorous, thought-provoking, and deeply necessary addition to the literature. It bridges the gap between theoretical discourse analysis and practical translation strategy, making it an essential text for doctoral students, professional translators, legal practitioners, and policymakers navigating multilingual legal systems. I highly recommend this publication to anyone committed to preserving the accuracy, authority, and equity of legal communication in our increasingly automated world.

Davoud Amini
Azarbaijan Shahid Madani University, Tabriz, Iran

Preface

OVERVIEW OF THE SUBJECT MATTER

Legal translation is widely recognized as one of the most intellectually demanding and consequential areas of professional translation practice. It is an intricate discipline that requires rigorous expertise in linguistic structures, comparative law, and deeply embedded cultural contexts. Unlike general translation, legal translation involves the highly sensitive task of transferring binding concepts between distinct legal systems, where terms, procedures, and interpretations frequently lack direct equivalents across jurisdictions. Legal language remains notoriously difficult to navigate due to its specialized terminology, technical precision, complex syntactic structures, and the profound real-world consequences attached to every clause.

Exploring Complexity in Legal Translation and Discourse Analysis is a comprehensive volume that dissects the multifaceted nature of legal texts through the rigorous lens of discourse analysis. Moving deliberately beyond the traditional focus on terminology management, this publication investigates how legal discourse functions fundamentally as a system of power, persuasion, and obligation. By applying critical discourse analysis, corpus linguistics, and genre analysis, the research presented herein uncovers the underlying linguistic and systemic structures that render legal texts inherently resistant to straightforward translation. Through the exploration of semiotics, multimodality, multilingual legal frameworks, and pedagogical strategies, this volume proposes robust methodological frameworks for overcoming the profound challenges inherent in legal communication.

THE TOPIC IN THE MODERN WORLD

The themes addressed in this publication occupy a position of critical urgency in contemporary global society. As globalization aggressively expands the volume of international trade, cross-border litigation, migration, and human rights initiatives, the fundamental need for accurate and reliable legal translation has escalated exponentially. We are operating in an era where domestic legal systems are increasingly intertwined with supranational governance, requiring constant and precise cross-lingual mediation to maintain the rule of law.

Simultaneously, the global translation ecosystem is experiencing a seismic technological disruption. The rapid deployment of Large Language Models and the evolving nature of the Human-Algorithm Interface represent a profound paradigm shift. While neural machine translation and artificial intelligence offer unprecedented processing speed, they introduce severe, often concealed risks to legal fidelity. Algorithms frequently flatten the deontic modality of legal texts, stripping away the nuanced obligations and prohibitions that give the law its performative force. This technological mediation risks creating an illusion of accuracy, where grammatically flawless outputs mask deep conceptual failures and algorithmic biases. Consequently, this book situates itself at the crucial intersection of traditional legal fidelity and modern technological efficiency, addressing how linguistic inequality and institutional power are actively reshaped in the digital age.

TARGET AUDIENCE

Given the interdisciplinary nature of the subject matter, this book is designed as a fundamental resource for a diverse and specialized readership. It provides vital theoretical and methodological grounding for graduate and doctoral students engaging in translation studies, applied linguistics, and discourse analysis. Professional translators, interpreters, and legal localization experts will find the practical frameworks and empirical case studies directly applicable to their daily workflows.

Furthermore, this publication is highly relevant for educators and researchers operating in English as a Foreign Language contexts, offering them genre-informed strategies for teaching highly complex legal materials. Beyond academia and the translation industry, the insights contained within these chapters are indispensable for legal practitioners, attorneys, judges, notaries, court administrators, and judicial professionals who regularly interact with multilingual legal frameworks. Finally, policymakers and developers of artificial intelligence systems will benefit immensely from the critical analyses of algorithmic mediation, utilizing these perspectives to design more responsible, ambiguity-aware governance tools.

THE IMPORTANCE OF CHAPTER SUBMISSIONS

1. Semiotics and Multimodality in Legal Translation

This opening chapter is fundamentally important because it dismantles the traditional view that legal meaning is exclusively textual. By investigating how semiotic and multimodal elements converge to shape meaning, authority, and accessibility, the research establishes that law functions as a highly complex multimodal artefact. The chapter explores how linguistic content interacts dynamically with visual, spatial, and performative cues, such as seals, emblems, typography, and digital interfaces. This contribution is vital for the field because it demonstrates how these non-linguistic resources actively signal institutional power and legitimacy. The practical recommendations for translator training and institutional drafting policies set a new standard for preserving legitimacy and promoting true inclusivity in cross-jurisdictional legal communication.

2. Legal Discourse Complexity: A Genre-Informed Perspective on Teaching Legal Texts in EFL Contexts

The significance of this chapter lies in its pedagogical innovation. Teaching legal discourse in English as a Foreign Language environments poses severe challenges, yet current approaches often oversimplify the material, treating complexity merely as a barrier to be eradicated. This chapter fundamentally reframes complexity as a negotiated, dynamic phenomenon rather than a static obstacle. By utilizing genre-based analysis of contracts, statutes, and case summaries alongside actual learner data, the author provides a critical distinction between text-internal features and actualized learner errors. This research is essential because it positions the classroom as a living laboratory for observing meaning construction under partial knowledge, offering educators theoretically sound methods to engage with legal complexity without compromising its integrity.

3. Source Hierarchy and Terminological Priority in Malaysian Legal Translation

This chapter provides a crucial intervention in the debate over lexical correspondence versus legal precision. Focused on the Malaysian legal setting, the research highlights the absolute necessity for translators to understand the precedence of legal sources and the strict authority of statutory words. The concept of terminological priority is explored in depth, demonstrating that in statutory interpretation, the specific meaning adopted within an act must absolutely supersede general dictionary definitions. This contribution is of paramount importance to practitioners and scholars because it meticulously outlines how authoritative statutory formulations dictate translation outcomes, thereby preventing catastrophic legal misinterpretations that could arise from relying on generalized linguistic resources.

4. Exploring False Friend Risk in Hong Kong English-Chinese Bilingual Legal Texts: A Corpus-Assisted Study on Legal Terminology

The profound importance of this chapter stems from its rigorous empirical analysis of conceptual asymmetry in bilingual law. By examining the Hong Kong English-Chinese legal environment, the study tackles the insidious nature of false friend risks. Utilizing corpus retrieval tools to analyze marriage and family laws, the research reveals that translation risks in legal contexts rarely manifest as obvious, overt mistranslations. Instead, they present as highly dangerous implicit conceptual risks hidden beneath standardized terminology. This chapter is vital for the advancement of translation studies because it conceptualizes these risks as incomplete conceptual equivalence, fundamentally deepening our structural understanding of the hidden dangers in cross-linguistic legal reconstruction.

5. Legal Translation: The Case of Personal Data Translations from Greek into English

This chapter is highly significant due to its timely focus on the intersection of legal translation and rapid technological regulation. The translation of personal data legislation involves extreme conceptual density and powerful normative force. By examining the linguistic, conceptual, and pragmatic difficulties inherent in translating documents like the EU General Data Protection Regulation from Greek into English, this research addresses a critical pressure point in modern supranational governance. The importance of this study lies in its detailed mapping of how translators must navigate complex rights-based frameworks across languages, ensuring that the protection of fundamental privacy rights is not lost or distorted through the process of cross-border linguistic mediation.

6. Artificial Intelligence, Legal Translation, and Linguistic Complexity: A Critical Study of Technology, Meaning, and Power in Multilingual Legal Systems

The contribution of this chapter is absolutely critical for understanding the macro-level socio-legal implications of technological integration. It boldly argues that automated translation is not a neutral technical process but a highly subjective interpretive exercise heavily shaped by procedural context and constitutional values. By conducting a doctrinal analysis of multilingual constitutional democracies, the author exposes how AI-driven systems actively influence access to justice and democratic participation. This chapter is essential reading because it bravely confronts the darker realities of algorithmic mediation, including low-resource language marginalization, data colonialism, and the reproduction of historical linguistic hierarchies by modern technological centralization.

7. The Illusion of Accuracy: How AI Reshapes Discourse and Authority in Legal Translation

This chapter presents a groundbreaking diagnostic approach to one of the most dangerous phenomena in modern translation practice. The author identifies the illusion of accuracy, demonstrating how the polished linguistic fluency of artificial intelligence systems frequently masks the severe erosion of underlying legal fidelity. By utilizing Systemic Functional Linguistics and Critical Discourse Analysis, the study proves that AI reconstructs discourse based on statistical probability, systematically weakening modal obligations and flattening crucial syntactic complexity. The proposal of the AI-Legal Discourse Transformation Model is a vitally important contribution, providing a structured diagnostic framework that shifts the industry focus away from dangerous surface-level correspondence toward the preservation of functional-discursive integrity.

8. Algorithmic Mediation in Legal Translation: Discourse, Ambiguity, and Authority

The importance of this chapter is anchored in its profound analysis of legal ambiguity and machine mediation. While neural networks improve translation speed, this study reveals how fluent computational outputs actively conceal vital errors in normative force. By developing a comprehensive fourfold taxonomy of lexical, syntactic, pragmatic, and systemic ambiguity, the author demonstrates how artificial intelligence frequently and silently erases legal indeterminacy. This research is deeply important because it directly addresses the systemic risks to authority and accountability, ultimately concluding with a powerful argument for ambiguity-aware design and the absolute necessity of maintaining professional human judgment in all legally binding translation processes.

9. A Comparative Analysis of Human and Machine Translation of Institutional and Honorific Expressions in the IMTFE Courtroom Records

This chapter is highly valuable for its unique historical and empirical approach to interpersonal meaning in legal contexts. By analyzing the 1947 courtroom records of the IMTFE, the study provides a meticulous comparison between historical human translations and modern machine outputs of the same source text. Focusing on institutional role labels and courtroom honorifics, the research uncovers the specific areas where machine translation fails to grasp the nuances of tenor and interpersonal equivalence. This chapter is an essential historical anchor for the book, proving empirically that the preservation of interpersonal meaning and institutional hierarchy remains a distinct advantage of human cognition over automated processing.

10. Toward a Human-in-the-Loop Framework for AI-Assisted Legal Translation: A Case Study in Deontic Modality

Serving as a powerful and pragmatic conclusion to the themes of the book, this chapter is indispensable for the future of translation practice. By rigorously evaluating how prominent commercial language models render deontic modality in commercial contracts across multiple languages, the study identifies consistent, systemic failures in automated legal drafting. The immense value of this chapter lies in its proposed solution, a comprehensive four-stage workflow that mandates jurisdictional profiling, controlled AI drafting, and expert legal post-editing. This framework is crucial for the advancement of the field, establishing the definitive institutional measures and human-in-the-loop competencies required to harness machine efficiency without surrendering legally consequential decisions to automated systems.

CONCLUSION AND IMPACT ON THE FIELD

Exploring Complexity in Legal Translation and Discourse Analysis constitutes a definitive intervention in the fields of applied linguistics, critical discourse analysis, and specialized translation. This volume fundamentally redefines the act of legal translation, shifting the paradigm away from mechanical linguistic substitution toward a nuanced understanding of translation as a high-stakes arena of discursive, cultural, and institutional negotiation. By treating legal texts not as static documents but as dynamic artifacts of governance, this collection asserts that effective translation requires rigorous engagement with the socio legal contexts that construct meaning.

By systematically addressing the theoretical foundations of multimodal meaning making alongside the most pressing modern challenges of algorithmic mediation, this book bridges a critical gap in contemporary academic literature. It actively contributes to the evolving discourse surrounding the Human-Algorithm Interface in translation, providing scholars and practitioners with an unyielding critical vocabulary to interrogate the illusion of machine accuracy. Furthermore, it offers concrete, actionable frameworks designed to ensure that human expertise and the human lead remain unequivocally central to legal interpretation. These frameworks are particularly vital as localization practices become increasingly complex and deeply embedded within automated workflows.

The research presented in this volume also charts a new trajectory for future scholarship in Multimodal Translation Studies. It demonstrates that as legal communication increasingly relies on digital platforms, formatting, and visual semiotics, translators must be equipped to navigate beyond traditional text based paradigms. This requires a profound pedagogical shift, one that prepares future professionals to critically assess algorithmic outputs and maintain the precise deontic modality that gives legal texts their binding authority.

Ultimately, this publication empowers the next generation of researchers and legal communicators to safeguard linguistic equity, preserve the performative force of law, and maintain the integrity of justice. In an increasingly complex, multilingual, and technologically mediated world, relying solely on automated systems risks severe conceptual asymmetry and the dangerous erosion of legal rights. By championing a model of human machine collaboration that prioritizes critical oversight, this book ensures that the fundamental principles of justice are accurately localized and fiercely protected across all global jurisdictions.

Mansour Amini
Universiti Sains Malaysia, Malaysia

Acknowledgment

The publication of this edited book, Exploring Complexity in Legal Translation and Discourse Analysis, is the result of a collaborative effort involving many dedicated individuals. We would like to express our deepest gratitude to everyone who contributed their time, expertise, and support to bring this project to fruition.

First and foremost, we extend our sincere thanks to the contributing authors. Your insightful research into artificial intelligence, linguistic inequality, multimodal translation, and the evolving dynamics of legal discourse forms the core of this volume. We deeply appreciate your dedication, intellectual rigor, and patience throughout the detailed revision phases managed via the eEditorial Discovery platform. Your willingness to refine your work through multiple rounds of feedback has ensured the high scholarly standard of this book.

We are equally grateful to the peer reviewers who generously volunteered their time and expertise. Your critical evaluations, constructive feedback, and meticulous reviews played an indispensable role in shaping the quality and direction of each chapter. The rigorous evaluation process succeeded because of your commitment to academic excellence.

Special thanks are due to the editorial and development teams at IGI Global Scientific Publishing. Your professional guidance, technical support, and continuous assistance throughout the book production process have been invaluable in transforming this collection of research into a cohesive published reality.

Finally, we acknowledge the institutional support from Universiti Sains Malaysia to undertake and complete this editorial project. To our colleagues, and particularly Professor Dr. Hazri Jamil, the dean of School of Languages, Literacies and Translation, Universiti Sains Malaysia thank you for your unwavering encouragement throughout this journey.

Introduction

The intersection of law and language represents one of the most pivotal domains of human interaction. Legal systems are fundamentally constructed, maintained, and enforced through linguistic expression. Consequently, the act of transferring legal concepts across linguistic boundaries is never merely a mechanical substitution of vocabulary. It is a profound negotiation between differing cultural philosophies, historical precedents, and institutional power structures. As global integration accelerates, the demand for absolute precision in cross border legal communication has surged, revealing critical inadequacies in traditional, equivalence based translation models. Exploring Complexity in Legal Translation and Discourse Analysis emerges from the urgent need to address these inadequacies by offering a sophisticated, multidimensional approach to the discipline.

Historically, legal translation has often been treated as an exercise in advanced lexicography, where the primary goal was to locate the closest corresponding term in a target language. However, the contributors to this volume demonstrate that such an approach strips the law of its performative force. Meaning is not housed exclusively within individual words but is generated through complex discursive structures. By adopting critical discourse analysis, systemic functional linguistics, and genre theory as primary investigative lenses, this book uncovers the hidden mechanisms that give legal texts their authority and binding nature. The research presented here shifts the academic focus toward the systemic environments in which legal discourse operates, treating the text as a living artifact rather than a static document.

The architecture of this book is deliberately designed to guide the reader through an expanding conceptual landscape. The initial investigations challenge the boundaries of textual analysis by introducing multimodal and semiotic perspectives. Recognizing that legal authority is often communicated through visual layouts, institutional seals, and digital interfaces is a crucial step in understanding modern legal literacy. This theoretical foundation naturally extends into the pedagogical realm, exploring how educators can effectively guide learners through the dense, specialized genres of legal English without reducing the material to overly simplified exercises. Teaching these texts requires an acknowledgment of their inherent complexity, transforming the classroom into a dynamic space for observing how meaning is constructed.

Following these foundational chapters, the text grounds its theoretical frameworks in highly specific regional and functional realities. The detailed examinations of statutory precedence in Malaysia, conceptual asymmetry in Hong Kong, and supranational data privacy regulations in Greece serve as empirical proof of the challenges facing today's practitioners. These studies illustrate that even when dealing with standardized bilingual laws, hidden conceptual risks and structural mismatches threaten the integrity of legal interpretation. Translators must constantly balance lexical correspondence against rigid statutory hierarchies, making consequential decisions that protect the legal rights of individuals and institutions alike.

Finally, the introduction of automated technologies represents the most significant disruption to the field in recent history. The latter portions of this work rigorously interrogate the deployment of neural networks and algorithmic models in legal workflows. While these systems offer remarkable speed, they fundamentally alter the discursive structure of the law, frequently flattening deontic obligations and erasing vital ambiguities. The authors critically assess the geopolitical and institutional implications of this shift, arguing that unchecked algorithmic mediation reproduces systemic biases and threatens the foundation of multilingual justice. By mapping these technological transformations, this introduction sets the stage for a comprehensive exploration of how human expertise must be strategically positioned to govern the future of legal communication.

Mansour Amini
Universiti Sains Malaysia, Malaysia

Shuangjiao Wu
Zhejiang Yuexiu University, China

Qiufen Wang
Kashi University, China

Section 1
Theoretical and Pedagogical Perspectives

Chapter 1
Semiotics and Multimodality in Legal Translation

Imelda Hermilinda Abas
http://orcid.org/0000-0002-1328-436X
Shinawatra University, Thailand

Maryam Alipour
http://orcid.org/0000-0002-7084-7114
Shinawatra University, Thailand

Lina Fathi Sidig Sidgi
http://orcid.org/0000-0002-6687-6625
Aliraqia University, Iraq

Ebrayek Deen Hamed Aljheme
Sebha University, Libya

ABSTRACT

This chapter investigates how semiotic and multimodal elements converge to shape meaning, authority, and accessibility in legal texts. It argues that law functions as a multimodal artefact, in which linguistic content interacts with visual, spatial, and performative cues, such as seals, emblems, typography, layouts, and digital interfaces. Drawing on semiotic theory, systemic functional linguistics, and multimodal critical discourse analysis, the chapter demonstrates how these resources signal institutional power, legitimacy, and obligation, influencing interpretation across jurisdictions and media. Methodological implications include multimodal corpora, annotation schemes, and accessibility standards, while practical recommendations

DOI: 10.4018/979-8-3373-9179-3.ch001

address translator training and institutional drafting policies. Ultimately, recognising law's multimodal nature is essential for preserving legitimacy and promoting inclusivity in legal communication.

INTRODUCTION

This chapter situates semiotics and multimodality in legal texts at the convergence of legal translation and discourse analysis. Legal translation has traditionally sought to be faithful not merely to linguistic meaning but also to the institutional and normative frameworks that govern legal indicators across many languages and jurisdictions. Academic debate emphasises that translation must consider visual and other semiotic elements, such as layout, typography, and symbols, particularly in digital and multimodal contexts, where meaning is conveyed through several modes (Pau, 2017). Concurrently, discourse-analytic approaches have shown the limitations of monomodal studies, demonstrating that legal, statutory, and contractual texts often rely on non-verbal indicators, such as images, diagrams, and physical objects (Wang, 2017).

Legal texts are complex in a unique way, mobilising verbal, visual and material aspects to signal authority, legality and procedure. Law has been shown to be a multimodal semiotic system by the significant contributions of Jackson (1985, 1988) and Kevelson (1987, 1988), who have demonstrated that legal meaning is constructed through the interplay of textual, visual and symbolic codes. In line with that study, this chapter discusses the application of semiotic and multimodal analysis in the context of translator training and presents a systematic framework for multimodal semiotic auditing in legal translation. Legal authority is based not only on spoken language but also on formatting, seals, and institutional symbols (Heritier, 2023), which are likewise embedded in statutes, contracts, and judgments. Courtroom practices and digital legal portals demonstrate that multimodal resources affect interpretation and accessibility, while the formation of borders and identity is supported by identifying papers and legal visuals (Heritier, 2023). Kozhevnikov (2022) indicates that the semiotic frameworks comprise legal reasoning techniques, which are deductive, inductive, and deontic. This shows the law's dependence on signs at all levels of practice and norms. This complexity creates problems for translation, as the semiotic differences between languages and cultures can hide responsibilities or change the apparent legitimacy of legal documents. It further complicates discourse analysis by requiring consideration of how multimodal features support or challenge power relations (Wang, 2017).

This chapter examines: How do semiotic and multimodal elements work together to create meaning, authority and accessibility in legal texts? Theoretical perspectives, empirical illustrations and methodological consequences are also addressed throughout the chapter. This chapter starts by considering how signs, symbols and cultural codes generate meaning in legal writings. Following sections then provide the theoretical scaffolding by reviewing semiotics and multimodality in law to justify the need for a systematic framework for translator training. The following part brings these notions together, explaining through examples how semiotic and multimodal views meet in legal writing. Then, the chapter discusses the implications of legal translation. Using discourse-analytic frameworks, it explores how power, ideology and accessibility are negotiated across multiple forms. The practical part provides translators with ideas for training teachers, and techniques to clarify multimodal legal information. The original contribution of this chapter is to offer a systematic framework for multimodal semiotic auditing in legal translation, for the purposes of translator training and curriculum development. The framework conceptualises the translator as more than a linguistic mediator. The translation is also an auditor of semiotic authority and accessibility across multimodal legal texts. The conclusion brings all these ideas together to show how semiotic and multimodal factors combine to alter meaning, authority, and access in law.

The chapter uses a literature review and comparative document analysis. The study does not generate new primary data but builds on existing analyses of multimodal legal texts, including judicial decisions, multilingual contracts and digital legal websites. Sources were selected from peer-reviewed publications and scholarly monographs in the fields of legal semiotics, multimodal discourse analysis, and translation studies, published between 2000 and 2025. In the review process, we identified repeating multimodal characteristics (e.g., seals, multilingual headers, logos, typography and accessibility icons) and investigated how they have been documented in legal contexts. Then, a comparative analysis was conducted to identify translation issues and strategies across jurisdictions. This methodological decision not only grounds the ideas advanced in this chapter in documented, replicable evidence but also opens the possibility of designing a pedagogical framework for multimodal semiotic auditing in translation training. The analysis clarifies its evidence base and locates the chapter inside a systematic review design to distinguish it from purely conceptual positioning articles. This study does not present new primary data, but rather a methodical synthesis of prior assessments of multimodal legal texts. Such limitations on empirical scope are deliberate: the chapter's contribution is to consolidate existing findings into a pedagogical framework for multimodal semiotic auditing. This could be further developed in the future by applying the approach to corpora of decisions, contracts or institutional documents to develop replicable case studies.

SEMIOTICS IN LEGAL TEXT

Defining Semiotics in the Legal Domain

To ground the proposed framework, this section surveys the application of semiotics to law and highlights the sign processes that translators must examine. In significant contributions, Jackson (1985, 1988) and Kevelson (1987, 1988) established law itself as a semiotic system in which meaning is generated through signs, narratives, and interpretive procedures. In this chapter, we extend their ideas by operationalising them in a translator-training context and by presenting a systematic paradigm for multimodal semiotic auditing in legal translation.

Semiotics provides a systematic tool to analyse how signs function in legal texts, such as statutes, case law, contracts, judgments, and legal images. Semiotics, scholars argue, explains how meaning is conveyed in dynamic systems, and is relevant to the interpretive procedures and normative force of law (Reifman, 2022). Legal sign processes include textual language, linguistic signs, visual signs such as emblems, seals, and layouts, and material signs like physical papers and artefacts that create meaning-making systems (Heritier, 2023; Reifman, 2022). This perspective supports the general argument that law employs varied sign modalities for the implementation, communication, and enforcement of norms (Krimpas, 2023; Olteanu & Ongstad, 2024). Tiersma's Legal Language (1999) likewise highlighted the linguistic aspect of legal semiotics and demonstrated how specialised legal language combines with visual and material cues to create authority. His study shows that translation must consider not only terminology but also the semiotic environment in which legal language functions.

Jackson's Semiotics and Legal Theory (1985) created the field of legal semiotics, while Law, Fact and Narrative Coherence (1988) showed how narrative elements underlie legal interpretation. The ideas guide the focus of this chapter on semiotic auditing, in which narrative consistency is considered a multimodal resource in translation. Jackson observed that the semiotic groups and sign-creating activities that are built into law affect legal reasoning and discourse. He argued for a legal meaning generated through sign processes spanning linguistic, rhetorical, and culturally situated semiotics, rather than a purely textual conception of law (Gorlée, 2005). Jackson, in his work on legal semiotics and the semiotic movement in jurisprudence, underscored the role of law as a field where signs bear social and moral significance. Various sign systems, linguistic, visual and procedural, interact with the context and audience to produce meaning (Chodkiewicz, 2004).

Kevelson's The Law as a System of Signals (1988) and Peirce, Science, Signs (1996) applied Peircean semiotics to law, reading legal discourse as a multimodal system of signals and logics. In this chapter she expands her argument that law is translated across modalities, operationalising it in duties of translator training. Kevelson systematised the concept that law is a system of signals and constructed a Peircean-informed framework to interpret legal language. She maintained that legal communication involves translation between sign systems and logics (deductive, inductive, abductive, deontic, and even rhetorical logics of questions and responses) with sign relations crossing many modalities. Her work made law interdependent with other social sign systems, and stressed interpretation, discovery and the pragmatic manufacture of meaning in legal contexts (Cacciaguidi Fahy & Mooney, 2009; Gorlée, 2005; Chodkiewicz, 2004). Throughout Kevelson's publications, including her explorations of Peircean speculative rhetoric and the cross-modal nature of legal discourse, the idea that "law is a system of signs" is key.

The Peircean tradition provides a valuable framework for understanding law by modelling signs as triadic processes. A triadic process consists of three components: the sign itself (representamen), the object to which it refers, and the meaning generated for the interpreter (interpretant) (Bor & Könczöl, 2019; Deacon & Rączaszek-Leonardi, 2019; Nöth, 2021). This model illustrates that meaning in law is not solely derived from the text but arises from the interaction of various elements. A seal on a document signifies institutional authority and conveys legitimacy to the reader. Bor and Könczöl (2019) present a three-tiered framework consisting of surface, basic, and deep levels, in which habit serves as a mediator between stylistic form and interpretive patterns. This explains the roles of diction, rhetoric, and typographic design as semiotic resources that influence interpretation and reinforce cultural practices in legal contexts. Deacon and Rączaszek-Leonardi (2019) advocate moving beyond coding metaphors to a triadic framework of semiosis, thereby elucidating the functioning of legal signs within communities of practice. These approaches position law as a domain in which sign-making, interpretation, and context are fundamentally interconnected (Nöth, 2021).

Law can be conceptualised as a dual semiotic system, governed by linguistic rules and legal norms that structure interpretation. This perspective underscores essential insights in legal semiotics, indicating that the assignment of meaning is influenced by internal linguistic structures and the normative framework of the legal system, encompassing concepts such as canonicity and the distinctions between langue and parole (Brenner, 2015; Frantsuzova, 2019). Semiotics offers methodologies for examining the emergence of legal meaning at the convergence of language, doctrine, and practice.

Social semiotics enhances this analysis by situating sign-making within social and cultural contexts. Language selections, arrangement, and imagery establish authority and accountability within legal proceedings (Rashid, 2023; Wang, 2017). In contexts where law operates as a social practice, semiotic resources signify social positions, ideologies, and institutional power, influencing readers' orientations toward legal claims and procedures (Heritier, 2023; Rashid, 2023; Wang, 2017).

Semiotics is highly relevant in digital and multimodal legal contexts. Legal meaning is conveyed through text, images, video, and interface design in online portals, courtrooms, and multimedia exhibits, creating multimodal semiotic ecologies. Scholars contend that comprehending legal texts in digital media requires examining the interaction between multimodal configurations of signs and linguistic meaning (Heritier, 2023; Jones, 2012; Pau, 2017; Rashid, 2023). Semiotics facilitates the descriptive analysis of contemporary legal discourse and provides practical guidance for translation and interpretation within multimodal contexts (Jones, 2012; Pau, 2017; Rashid, 2023).

Law functions through systems of signs and codes; therefore, translation and discourse analysis should consider multimodal semiotics in addition to linguistic equivalence. Accurate translation necessitates the careful negotiation of visual and material signs to maintain authority and functionality across diverse languages and cultures (Duan, 2024; Nikioporietz et al., 2024). In discourse analysis, employing a semiotic lens facilitates comprehensive examinations of power and legitimacy through the interaction of images, layouts, and other sign modes with verbal discourse (Heritier, 2023; Rashid, 2023). Semiotics in law is defined as the examination of sign processes across linguistic, visual, and material modalities within social-institutional contexts. This definition establishes a coherent framework for analysing the production and negotiation of meaning in legal texts (Bor & Könczöl, 2019; Frantsuzova, 2019).

This field contains areas of contention. Caution is advised against reducing law to sign-based processes, as normative and institutional dimensions may resist semiotic abstraction (Bor & Könczöl, 2019). A balanced approach integrates Peircean structural analysis and social semiotics to prevent reductive interpretations of legal meaning (Heritier, 2023; Rashid, 2023). There is an ongoing debate over whether law should be conceptualised as a quasi-logical code or as a practice integrated into communities of sign use. The integration of canonicity and context-sensitive interpretations accounts for cross-jurisdictional variation and the adaptive characteristics of legal semiotics (Brenner, 2015; Reifman, 2022).

Legal Symbols and Authority

Seals, emblems, and institutional insignia serve as material semiotics that convey authority beyond verbal communication. They function as sign systems that communicate legitimacy, official status, and procedural traceability in legal processes. Their presence in documents, courtrooms, and institutional settings serves as a non-verbal indicator that the artefact is endorsed by a legitimate authority and that its content holds significance within the legal framework (Goodrich, 1998; Peters, 2020). Scholars characterise seals as integral to the "visual economy" of legal institutions, indicating trust, authenticity, and consequence through their appearance and placement (Peters, 2020). Insignia direct readers towards authority by visually associating texts with established legal powers and historical juridical practices (Goodrich, 1998; Peters, 2020). Douzinas and Nead's *Law and the Image* (1999) emphasised the aesthetic and visual dimensions of law, demonstrating how images and artistic representations reinforce legal authority. Their analysis complements the semiotic role of seals and emblems by showing that visual culture is integral to the legitimacy of legal discourse.

Recent work within this paradigm directly links textual, visual, symbolic, and material cues from legal documents such as contracts, statutes, institutional visuals, and identity items. The collaborative function of modalities in the construction of meaning, the establishment of legitimacy and adherence to rules in legal contexts has been highlighted by several studies (Bennett, 2019; Havelka, 2024). The multimodal lens has also made its way into legal education and translator training. Here, auditors and learners evaluate the interaction of non-textual semiotics (images, layout, icons) with textual provisions to ensure legal effect and understanding of users across cultures (Heritier, 2023; Rey, 2019). The semiotic functions of legal symbols and the greater multimodal scope of law show that authority is not only communicated through spoken provisions but also through visual symbols, material and spatial clues.

These symbols also establish legal identity and jurisdictional affiliation. Emblems representing national or institutional authority on documents, signage, or certificates indicate that the content reflects a specific legal framework and normative system. Studies of logos and insignia within organisational settings illustrate their role in shaping perceptions of legitimacy and adherence to formal regulations, leveraging culturally ingrained associations with authority and expertise (Goodrich, 1998; Peters, 2020). The reproduction of these signs across various media, such as print, digital platforms, or courtroom videos, reinforces a consistent semiotic ecology that is acknowledged as legitimate governance indicators. Spatial semiotics enhances this function by demonstrating how symbols in signage, architecture, and urban landscapes contribute to legal order and sovereignty, thereby embedding law within material environments (Goodrich, 1998; Prathap & Kabaleeswaran, 2025).

Legitimacy is reinforced in legal discourse through these sign systems. Institutional theory delineates the regulative, normative, and cultural-cognitive pillars of legitimacy, each represented by seals and emblems (Heritier, 2023). They indicate conformity with legal statutes, alignment with professional standards, and adherence to common legal principles. Semiotic theory elucidates the encoding of authority through symbols, indexes, and icons: symbols denote sovereignty, indexes indicate procedural authority, and icons invoke normative ideals like justice (Goodrich, 1998; Peters, 2020). They collectively establish a semiotic ecology that facilitates the communication and auditing of legitimacy among various audiences. The standardisation of these devices across courts and registries improves recognizability and trust, facilitating cross-jurisdictional comprehension when legal texts are disseminated internationally (Peters, 2020). In digital contexts, seals and insignia accompany text, video, and interface cues, thereby extending authority into multimodal environments while also prompting inquiries regarding misapplication or symbolic ambiguity (Heritier, 2023; Rashid, 2023).

Scholars advise against considering symbols solely as indicators of legal content. Symbols play a crucial role in the construction of legality and can generate effects that extend beyond their textual interpretations. This necessitates a balance between formal symbol analysis and an examination of discursive practices, power dynamics, and institutional histories (Goodrich, 1998; Prathap & Kabaleeswaran, 2025). There is an ongoing debate regarding the contexts in which symbols confer legitimate authority. In certain instances, there is a risk of becoming ritualised or commodified, resulting in hollow connotations unless supported by enforceable practices and transparent procedures (Peters, 2020; Nicolini et al., 2021).

In translation, it is crucial to recognise seals and insignia as elements that convey meaning. Translators should evaluate how these devices express authority within target cultures, ensuring that both prestige and procedural cues are maintained or suitably modified (Duan, 2024; Rashid, 2023). In discourse analysis, legal symbols serve as a focal point for examining the performance and legitimisation of power through visual and material modalities (Heritier, 2023; Peters, 2020; Rashid, 2023). Their deployment highlights the mechanisms by which institutions establish credibility, regulate audiences, and delineate jurisdictional boundaries beyond mere textual arguments.

The definition of semiotics in legal contexts, particularly in relation to seals, emblems, and insignia, underscores how authority is expressed through integrated systems of textual, visual, and material signs. These symbols serve as enduring semiotic resources that convey legitimacy, provenance, and procedural authority, while embodying the principles of law and justice. A multimodal semiotic perspective demonstrates the performance of legitimacy through sign content and institutional artefacts, providing a solid foundation for analysis in translation, jurisprudence, and discourse studies.

Intertextuality and Cultural Codes

Intertextuality is a fundamental mechanism in law, in which contemporary meanings are understood through the frameworks of prior texts, legal traditions, and culturally significant symbols. Statutes and rulings frequently rely on precedent, established doctrines, or significant legal symbols that reflect enduring cultural perceptions of legitimacy and authority. Intertextuality is conceptualised by scholars as a mechanism that facilitates both continuity and change, connecting contemporary arguments to established cultural memes and legal myths that audiences recognise and utilise (Heritier, 2023; Pau, 2017; Rashid, 2023). In multimodal contexts, intertextual references encompass not only text but also logos, emblems, and institutional visuals that signal to audiences historical lineage or jurisdictional authority.

Cultural codes influence the criteria for legitimate interpretation. Legal symbols obtain their authority from the collective interpretations associated with them, including the scales of justice, seal colours, and court insignia, which align with cultural narratives of fairness, impartiality, and sovereignty. When texts are translated across languages and media, the codes may be recontextualised to align with the expectations of the target culture, thereby influencing perceptions of authority and legitimacy (Peters, 2020). Law is not merely a formal code; it is a culturally situated practice whose semiotics are co-constructed with readers and institutions over time (Frantsuzova, 2019; Heritier, 2023; Olteanu & Ongstad, 2024).

Historical context further shapes intertextual effects. The same legal symbol or reference may carry different implications across different historical periods or professional communities. Changes in constitutional interpretation, modifications in evidence law, and evolving standards of transparency alter the comprehension and contestation of intertextual cues. This temporal dimension corresponds with cultural semiotics, highlighting that meaning is generated within a historically evolving semiosphere, where texts circulate and transform over time (Bor & Könczöl, 2019; Frantsuzova, 2019; Reifman, 2022).

Examples demonstrate how culturally embedded signs function within legal contexts. Seals on official documents indicate provenance and authority, utilising established iconography and ritualised practices, while ensuring recognizability across various media (Goodrich, 1998; Peters, 2020). Symbols such as the scales of justice or Lady Justice's blindfold represent cultural concepts of fairness and due process, connecting modern texts to historical discourses (Peters, 2020). National emblems and institutional logos serve as intertextual links between legal content and broader political narratives, shaping interpretations of authority in multilingual or multinational contexts (Peters, 2020). Legal discourse repurposes motifs across various genres and media, encouraging readers to align new texts with established frameworks (Jones, 2012; Pau, 2017; Rashid, 2023). In digital contexts, hyperlinks, embedded seals, and layout configurations integrate with verbal text to form cohesive semiotic environments that convey legitimacy and authority.

There are debates regarding the extent of intertextuality. Caution is advised against considering all legal signs as derivatives of previous texts, as certain semiotic resources exhibit autonomous functions that defy intertextual mapping. A balanced approach recognises both dependencies and the capacity for signs to produce new meanings via ritual, practice, or institutional reform (Brenner, 2015; Bor & Könczöl, 2019; Frantsuzova, 2019). Cross-cultural translation complicates intertextual effects, as culturally loaded references may possess divergent associations, necessitating careful negotiation of equivalence and adaptation (Nikioporietz et al., 2024; Pau, 2017).

In translation, it is crucial to consider intertextual references and cultural codes to maintain function and legitimacy within target contexts. Translators are required to recognise underlying intertexts, such as precedents, symbols, and canonical phrases, and determine whether to render them transparently, adapt them, or annotate them to preserve authority and align with the audience (Nikioporietz et al., 2024; Pau, 2017). Intertextuality in discourse analysis serves as a framework for examining the production and legitimisation of legal meaning. Analysts can delineate sign relationships across texts and media to comprehend the construction of authority, the orientation of audiences toward legal positions, and the ways in which cultural codes either reinforce or challenge justice outcomes (Heritier, 2023; Peters, 2020; Rashid, 2023).

Intertextuality and cultural codes are essential for comprehending legal meaning. Legal texts reference previous documents, symbolic representations, and culturally ingrained scripts that influence interpretation, legitimacy, and authority. A culturally informed multimodal semiotic analysis demonstrates how legal signs function across various cultures and historical contexts, establishing a basis for research in translation, discourse analysis, jurisprudence, and legal communication.

The multimodal approach indicates that translation and legal interpretation should consider intermodal interactions, rather than just linguistic equivalence. This viewpoint underlies the methods of translation as intersemiotic transfer, in which sign potentials travel between modes, with consideration of jurisdictional semiotics and audience expectations. Foundational researchers suggest frameworks for multimodal semiotic auditing in legal translation to identify and correct incompatibilities between textual and non-textual semiotics (Bennett, 2019; Havelka, 2024; Matulewska, 2019; Nikiporets et al., 2024).

There is broad consensus among law scholars that law is intrinsically multimodal, i.e., that meaning is produced through interaction among sign systems (Bennett, 2019; Havelka, 2024; Nikioporietz et al., 2024; Novak, 2021; Rey, 2019). However, subtleties persist concerning the relative weight of textual vs visual cues and the methodological obstacles of operationalising auditing in training. Some sources emphasise the cyclical, evolving nature of legal semiotics, indicating that symbols and practices change with culture and technology. Others cite the challenge of trans jurisdictional alignment of semiotic conventions. These perspectives support integrating semiotic auditing into translation education as a systematic, evidence-based process.

The foundational works of Jackson (1985, 1988), Kevelson (1988, 1996), Douzinas & Nead (1999), and Tiersma (1999), along with other scholars cited above, establish legal semiotics and legal language as mature fields of inquiry, and recent scholarship extends these insights into multimodal and digital contexts. What has remained largely underexplored, and what this chapter tackles, is the integration of these traditions into a systematic pedagogy for multimodal semiotic auditing in legal translation.

MULTIMODALITY IN LEGAL TEXT

Beyond the Written Word

This section extends the background by examining multimodality in legal texts and provides the conceptual basis for the translator-training framework developed later. Multimodality enhances legal interpretation by incorporating visual, spatial, and performative elements into legal discourse. Visual symbols, including emblems, seals, logos, and court insignia, serve as markers of institutional origin and legitimacy, conveying established authority across various languages and media (Goodrich, 1998; Heritier, 2023; Peters, 2020). Visuals in digital portals and courtroom artefacts coexist with text to create cohesive semiotic environments that affect credibility assessments and interpretive results (Heritier, 2023; Jones, 2012; Pau, 2017; Rashid, 2023). Iconic imagery such as scales of justice, Lady Justice, and gavels symbolises fairness and sovereignty, connecting modern texts to historical discussions on justice while fostering recognition and trust across print, online, and video formats to establish a consistent semiotic ecology that facilitates cross-jurisdictional interpretation (Peters, 2020).

Spatial organisation conveys meaning as well. Statutory, judicial, and contractual layouts indicate hierarchy and procedural order via indentation, headings, and column formats, facilitating reader navigation through intricate arguments (Jones, 2012; Rashid, 2023). Institutional spaces, including courtrooms and legislative chambers, manifest power dynamics through their seating configurations, podium placements, and signage. The architecture and design serve to reinforce notions of legitimacy and solemnity (Goodrich, 1998; Prathap & Kabaleeswaran, 2025). Digital interfaces expand spatial semiotics into navigable environments, utilising layout, colour coding, and iconography to organise information and indicate procedural status, thereby influencing confidence in the digital mediation of law (Rashid, 2023).

The performative dimensions enhance the embedding of meaning within legal frameworks. Legal processes are executed through verbal communication, nonverbal cues, visual attention, and multimedia presentations, thereby establishing authority and accountability in real time (Heritier, 2023; Rashid, 2023). Typography and formatting, including capitalisation, bold headings, and typographic hierarchy, serve as rhetorical devices that communicate emphasis, urgency, and normative hierarchy (Nikioporietz et al., 2024; Szarkowska, 2010). Audience reception is influenced by multimodal cues that shape interpretations of evidence, credibility, and legitimacy across various cultures and media (Heritier, 2023; Rashid, 2023; Wang, 2017).

Translation in a multimodal context necessitates preserving linguistic meaning while also accounting for visual, spatial, and performative cues that exert normative influence. Translators are required to modify or annotate layout, typography, seals, and icons to ensure functional equivalence across languages and media (Jones, 2012; Pau, 2017; Rashid, 2023). Discourse analysis is enhanced by a multimodal perspective that reveals the role of non-verbal signs in shaping interpretive authority, legitimacy, and the distribution of power within legal cultures (Heritier, 2023; Rashid, 2023; Wang, 2017). With the ongoing shift of legal communication to digital platforms, it is essential for researchers to utilise computational tools and annotation frameworks that can effectively manage multimodal corpora, integrating text, images, video, and interface data to accurately model meaning in current practices.

Although written language is fundamental, non-linguistic dimensions are essential to the formation of legal meaning. Visuals, layouts, and performances operate in conjunction with text, and their impacts differ among jurisdictions. An effective analysis combines multimodal resources with linguistic content to encompass the complete semiotic ecosystem of law. Multimodality broadens the comprehension of law beyond textual representation, illustrating how authority and justice are performed through integrated semiotic systems across various languages, cultures, and media.

Multimodal Genres of Law

Statutes, contracts, judgments, and digital legal platforms demonstrate the role of multimodality in shaping legal meaning by integrating textual precision with visual, spatial, and interactive elements. Statutes, while rich in text, rely on layout, typographic conventions, and numbering to indicate hierarchy, scope, and enforceability, with bold headings for mandatory provisions or italics for definitions serving as paratextual scaffolds that guide readers on normative force and procedural implications (Duan, 2024; Jones, 2012; Rashid, 2023). Contracts combine textual provisions with graphical components, including tables, clause diagrams, and typographic emphasis, where devices such as bullet points, shaded boxes, and highlighted risk notices serve as semiotic resources that elucidate responsibilities and remedies, thereby improving understanding and enforceability (Duan, 2024). Judgments integrate argumentative writing with structured formatting, headnotes, and official insignia that signify authority and origin. Layout cues, including indented quotations and numbered sections, assist readers in navigating reasoning and dispositive findings, thereby enhancing legitimacy and promoting cross-jurisdictional comprehension (Heritier, 2023; Rashid, 2023; Wang, 2017). Digital legal platforms enhance multimodality by integrating text, navigational design, icons, and interactive elements. Hyperlinks, colour codes, and dashboards represent procedural states and direct user actions, influencing perceptions of transparency and efficiency within digital frameworks (Jones, 2012; Pau, 2017; Rashid, 2023).

Courtroom practice illustrates performative multimodality, in which spoken language, gesture, gaze, and exhibits converge to create meaning and shape outcomes. Attorneys align verbal communication with nonverbal signals, integrating oral arguments with visual aids like timelines or graphics to emphasise evidence and ensure narrative consistency. Multimodal performances collaboratively generate credibility and persuasion within the context of judicial decision-making (Matoesian & Gilbert, 2018). Performative multimodality encompasses gaze, posture, and prosody, which influence audience interpretation and reinforce legitimacy. The interaction of oral advocacy and visual elements forms composite sign systems that enhance perceived authority and credibility (Basu et al., 2025; Matoesian & Gilbert, 2018).

Translation within these genres necessitates a focus on multimodal equivalence. The translation of statutes, contracts, judgments, and digital interfaces requires maintaining linguistic precision, as well as the visual and spatial indicators that denote hierarchy, obligation, and procedural status. Translators must adapt or annotate these features to preserve functional meaning in target cultures (Duan, 2024; Jones, 2012; Pau, 2017; Rashid, 2023). Discourse analysis enhances understanding by mapping how multimodal signs, such as encompassing text, gesture, space, and interface, either support or challenge legal claims. Analysing courtroom practices alongside written genres reveals the enactment of power and epistemic authority through multimodal assemblies (Basu et al., 2025; Matoesian & Gilbert, 2018; Rashid, 2023). With the increasing multimodal complexity of digital mediation, it is essential for researchers to utilise integrated annotation schemes that encompass textual, visual, interface, and performative cues to effectively model meaning within modern legal ecosystems.

A nuanced analysis recognises that although statutes, contracts, and judgments adhere to established conventions, their multimodal expressions differ across jurisdictions and media. Visual and performative signs engage with text in varied ways depending on institutional context, whereas digital platforms emphasise interface cues as the primary conveyors of meaning. Recognising this variation prevents over-generalisation and emphasises the interdependence of textual and performative signs in legal communication (Basu et al., 2025; Heritier, 2023; Matoesian & Gilbert, 2018; Pau, 2017; Rashid, 2023). Multimodal genres of law represent a convergence of textual precision, visual rhetoric, spatial layout, and performative practices that collectively produce authority and legitimacy across languages, cultures, and technologies.

Multimodality and Accessibility

Multimodality is essential in shaping accessibility in legal texts, either facilitating or obstructing public comprehension through the design of visual, spatial, and interactive elements. Effective visual hierarchies, readable typography, organised layouts, and user-friendly digital interfaces enable readers to efficiently identify obligations, rights, and procedures. Icons, colour-coding, and semantic diagrams mitigate cognitive load and enhance interpretation, especially in intricate statutes or contracts necessitating cross-referencing (Duan, 2024; Jones, 2012; Pau, 2017; Rashid, 2023). Juridical documents incorporating audio-visual materials, including video summaries or annotated exhibits, enhance comprehension by accommodating various learning preferences and increasing engagement (Mendonca, 2021; Reisberg, 2018).

Simultaneously, multimodality may present obstacles. Inconsistent visuals, dense layouts, and non-standard typography can hinder comprehension, particularly for individuals with cognitive or visual impairments or those utilising assistive technologies (Mendonca, 2021). Inaccessible PDFs, graphics lacking alt-text, and the exclusive use of colour to convey distinctions compromise usability and exclude individuals from legal proceedings. Implementing these principles in legal texts, through alt-text, meaningful reading order, keyboard navigation, and accessible colour contrast, enhances inclusivity in legal communication (Mendonca, 2021).

Case-based contrasts exemplify these dynamics. Accessible statutes may incorporate hierarchical headings, plain-language definitions, icons alongside text, and responsive interfaces that accommodate screen readers and high-contrast modes (Jones, 2012; Pau, 2017; Rashid, 2023). Inaccessible examples, conversely, exhibit dense text devoid of headings, diagrams lacking captions, or platforms that do not support assistive technology, resulting in misinterpretations and exclusion (Mendonca, 2021). Research highlights the need for culturally informed multimodal design to ensure accessibility, as legal signs transcend languages and jurisdictions. In translation, multimodal equivalence is essential. Translators are required to maintain not only the linguistic meaning but also the visual, spatial, and interactive indicators that denote authority and obligation, including restyling, utilising alternative formats, or providing annotated guidance to ensure functional equivalence across cultures (Duan, 2024; Jones, 2012; Pau, 2017). This complexity underscores the value of discourse analysis, when combined with mixed-methods approaches such as usability testing and comprehension assessments, in enhancing the iterative design of accessible legal materials by investigating how design choices impact comprehension and inclusion, thereby identifying optimal practices through comparisons of accessible and inaccessible configurations (Mendonca, 2021; Reisberg, 2018).

Accessibility is contingent on context and influenced by user requirements, technological devices, and cultural norms. Inclusive methodologies require adaptability in delivering content across textual, auditory, and visual media while maintaining legal accuracy. Balancing simplification with accuracy necessitates collaboration among legal drafters, designers, and accessibility specialists. Multimodality has the potential to enhance participation and trust in legal processes, provided that accessibility principles are intentionally incorporated into statutes, contracts, judgments, and digital platforms.

THE INTERSECTION OF SEMIOTICS AND MULTIMODALITY

Semiotic Reading of Multimodal Legal Texts

Semiotics enhances multimodal analysis in law by providing a systematic framework for understanding how signs function across verbal, visual, spatial, and performative dimensions. Sign theory elucidates the production of meaning through the relationships between the signifier and the signified, as articulated in Saussurean terms, and between the representamen, the object, and the interpretant, as defined in Peircean terms. This enables analysts to investigate the convergence of statutes, emblems, and courtroom gestures in the enactment of rights, duties, and authority (Matoesian & Gilbert, 2018; Olurotimi, 2022). Peirce's triadic model effectively illustrates the influence of habitual sign relations on legal practice and precedent, while Saussurean insights emphasise the relationship between the systemic structures of law (langue) and their application in texts and discourse (Bor & Könczöl, 2019; Deacon & Rączaszek-Leonardi, 2019; Kozhevnikov, 2022).

Social semiotics contextualises these processes within cultural and institutional frameworks, illustrating how layouts, typography, seals, and visuals convey legitimacy that transcends linguistic content. This viewpoint emphasises power, identity, and cultural norms, elucidating how readers position themselves in relation to legal claims across various communities of practice (Durant & Davis, 2018; Heritier, 2023; Novak, 2021). Semiotic analysis highlights the importance of multimodal integration, in which design elements such as colour, spacing, and icons interact with textual semantics to affect comprehension and trust. This is particularly pertinent in digital platforms, where interface indicators influence perceptions of transparency and procedural legitimacy.

Cross-cultural and cross-media perspectives illustrate how intertextuality and iconography traverse languages and jurisdictions. Analysts can predict misinterpretations or discrepancies by aligning signs with cultural repertoires, thereby maintaining cultural relevance in translation and discourse analysis (Hakimzadeh, 2020; Rashid, 2023). Examples include seals and insignia that certify provenance and enforceability (Goodrich, 1998; Peters, 2020), iconic imagery such as the scales of justice that anchor ideals of fairness (Peters, 2020), and digital semiotics where icons and navigational cues influence perceptions of accessibility (Pau, 2017; Rashid, 2023).

Semiotics underscores inherent tensions. Signs are inherently biased, embedding power and ideology, which necessitates that analysts examine whose interests are upheld or contested (Hakimzadeh, 2020; Heritier, 2023). Jurisdictional variation indicates that sign repertoires vary across legal cultures, underscoring the need for cross-cultural semiotic analysis (Heritier, 2023; Olteanu & Ongstad, 2024). Researchers advise against excessive dependence on sign theory, advocating for its integration with pragmatics and discourse analysis to prevent simplistic interpretations (Bor & Könczöl, 2019; Frantsuzova, 2019).

In translation, semiotic-informed practice extends beyond lexical equivalence. It involves accurately rendering multimodal signs, adjusting visuals, layout cues, and institutional symbols to maintain authority and readability (Duan, 2024; Jones, 2012; Pau, 2017). Semiotics in discourse analysis facilitates comprehensive examinations of persuasion, legitimacy, and audience alignment by integrating visual and material signs into interpretive frameworks (Heritier, 2023; Rashid, 2023; Wang, 2017). The combination of semiotic analysis with multimodal discourse and corpus-assisted approaches effectively illustrates the evolution of law across languages and technologies, modelling the interactions among text, image, layout, and interface within contemporary legal ecosystems. The intersection of semiotics and multimodality offers a thorough framework for examining the production, legitimisation, and contestation of legal meaning across various signs, genres, and cultures, highlighting the influence of semiotic and multimodal elements on authority and accessibility in the legal domain.

Research in this area is collecting evidence that court decisions and the related legal documents include multimodal components in addition to plain text. Research consistently demonstrates the presence of official seals, multilingual headers, logos, watermarks, and typographic standards that have legal significance and authority (Bennett, 2019; Havelka, 2024; Novak, 2021; Nikiporets et al., 2024). These are semiotic resources that index legitimacy and guide interpretation, and translators are required to adopt processes that preserve textual and multimodal integrity. Textual analysis of civil judgments shows that seals and multilingual introductions function as markers of authority and audience cues. The academic community advises reproducing seals as images whenever possible, providing regulated transcriptions of inscriptions, and presenting bilingual headers with parallelism to enhance scannability and jurisdictional clarity (Matulewska, 2019). Researchers examining bilingual case captions and marginalia highlight the importance of retaining layout rules and typographic cues in order to preserve the integrity of cross-references and interpretive cues in translation (Bennett, 2019). Further studies extend the scope to include attestations at the end of the document, signature blocks and digital seals, highlighting the need for translators to balance accuracy and jurisdictional requirements. Scholars argue that signature blocks and attestations should be copied with absolute fidelity to names, titles and cultural allusions; seals may need transliteration or explanatory notes to preserve their semiotic meaning (Havelka, 2024). The complexity of translation in digital environments is further increased by multimodal features such as multilingual notices, accessibility icons, and infographic summaries, which require approaches that adapt colour semantics, iconography, and layout to different audiences (Heritier, 2023).

Studies on intersemiotic translation increasingly illustrate the use of legal contracts and verdicts in infographics and hybrid media. The results suggest that translators have to match textual needs with visual cues and colour codes, and to maintain legal correctness. Parallel textual representations have been proposed for legal validity across several formats (Novak, 2021). The analyses presented here jointly show law as a multimodal semiotic system and thus call for multimodal auditing in translation training and practice.

IMPLICATIONS FOR LEGAL TRANSLATION

Translating Semiotic and Multimodal Complexity

Legal translation is characterised by semiotic complexity and multi-modality. Translators have to make sense of authority and cultural marks such as seals, emblems and jurisdictional indicators, and to adjust visual and material elements such as bilingual headings, typography and layout rules. These are markers of validity and guides to interpretation across languages and cultures.

Šarčević's New Approach to Legal Translation (1997) characterised legal translation as a special act of intercultural and interlingual communication, in which the normative function and the legal implications of texts had to be preserved. Translation is not a matter of linguistic equivalency, she stressed, but of parity of legal outcomes and interpretive purpose and thus requires juridical skill as well as linguistic ability. Her functionalist position is oriented towards the content and not the form and sees legal translation as a bilateral transfer of legal and linguistic sign-systems. This is in line with multimodal semiotic auditing, which holds that legal meaning is mediated by jurisdiction-specific semiotics, not just by language in texts, and that translators should replicate legal consequences rather than literal meaning.

In Translating Law (2007), Cao retained and developed Šarčević's functionalist focus on the foregrounding of the professionalisation of legal translation and the curricular needs of translator training. She stressed that legal translation is not just a matter of language transfer but also requires a deep understanding of legal systems, terminology, and procedures. Translators need to address the bicultural and multilingual nature of law and be aware that translation has legal implications and requires specialist competences. In extending this training-oriented multimodal auditing approach, Cao has formalised the competences associated with legal cultures and with institutional procedures, which contributes to the educational side of translation education.

In Communication in the Legal Universe, Madsen (1997) describes law as a communicative system in which meanings are communicated through textual, visual, and procedural modes. He stressed the importance, from a sociological and performative perspective, of understanding how law functions in social and institutional settings in legal communication. Madsen's emphasis on law as a communication cosmos is not simply a treatise on translation but an invitation to a multi-modal reading of legal texts. It highlights the importance of audience, context and sign systems rather than plain English. This broader perspective supports the views of Šarčević and Cao by placing translation in the sociological context of law and thereby justifying the kind of training that considers legal culture, audience consciousness and intersemiotic considerations.

At the same time, multimodal features encoded in legal texts, logos, watermarks, marginal remarks and accessibility indicators pose a problem for translation. To preserve their semiotic burden, techniques other than language equivalence are needed. Visual hierarchy, typographic emphasis and layout cues have to be recognisable in the target language, and culturally unique standards have to be adapted when needed. This requires an awareness of textual authenticity and multimodal authority, as well as the tension between legal correctness and accessibility to diverse audiences.

Legal translation is not just a matter of one language to another. It is a systematic approach to the semiotic and multimodal features that confer authority, validity, and usability. Symbols, images and formatting, from seals, emblems, logos, typography, layout conventions, colour coding and digital symbols, convey meanings and institutional status that are culturally anchored and cannot be fully expressed through language (Heritier, 2023; Olurotimi, 2022; Rashid, 2023). If these parts are not carefully translated, the result may be a diminished sense of legitimacy and procedural clarity in the target culture. Depending on the kind of sign, the translator faces different problems.

Seals, logos and other visual signs give provenance and validity. When symbolic repertoires differ between jurisdictions, they are usually carefully adapted, localised or annotated with explanations (Goodrich, 1998; Peters, 2020). Normative iconography, such as scales of justice and gavels, can have different meanings across cultures and require context-sensitive decisions about whether to retain, substitute or augment with captions (Peters, 2020). Legal duties and processes are governed by layout and typographic standards such as numbering, headings, line length and emphasis and thus must be preserved or carefully adapted to provide clarity and avoid misinterpretation (Olurotimi, 2022).

In digital contexts, this process is even more complicated as interactive icons, progress indicators, and accessibility components such as alt-text are important in indicating workflow and eligibility (Rashid, 2023). The differences in time and jurisdiction further complicate the challenges. Symbols may mean different things in different historical periods or legal cultures. Translators need to be aware of context and the audience's expectations when deciding whether to copy or change (Reifman, 2022).

In multilingual and multinational documents, the localisation of symbols or the use of explanatory notes is often important to preserve intended meaning and clarity (Olteanu & Ongstad, 2024). Therefore, a pre-translation semiotic audit is required to identify indicators of normative relevance and evaluate their potential adaptation needs (Heritier, 2023; Rashid, 2023) to address these problems efficiently. Cultural sign mapping refers to the association of source and target semiotic repertoires by means of parallel references, captions or culturally appropriate substitutes in the absence of direct equivalents (Kozhevnikov, 2022). Annotations and parallel indicators can reduce the risk of misinterpretation, especially when the original is not readily available (Jones, 2012). Any reform of symbolic formatting should be carried out in collaboration with legal and design experts to ensure effective symbolism and compliance with local conventions (Novak, 2021; Pitkäsalo & Kalliomaa-Puha, 2019).

According to Mendonca (2021), digital legal content should include features such as alt text, keyboard navigation, and proper contrast to ensure accessibility. It should also log the semiotic decisions made during the translation process, thereby ensuring transparency, quality assurance, and future audits. These could include altering or adding a local emblem and caption to a statute's national seal, preserving the iconography such as the scales of justice but adding an explanatory note, or replacing the iconography with local imagery; reformatting the definition tables and risk boxes in contracts to the conventions of the target language; and localising icons and accessibility features in digital portals (Bennet, 2019; Rashid, 2023).

Another example was found in another study on translation focusing on strategies in text/translation analysis, solutions, and problems. Wan et al. (2018) identified structural/semantic and cultural difficulties in translating three Malay traditional stories into English. Structural concerns include polysemous terms, assertions without literal equivalents, and awkward literal translations that sound odd in English, while cultural concerns involve proper names, titles, and Malay-rooted idioms with no direct English equivalents. To solve these problems, the translators used various solutions and strategies such as literal translation, amplification (adding words for clarity), reduction (removing redundancies), correspondence/equivalence (using natural English expressions instead of the original terms), loan/borrowing, explicitation, modulation, particularisation (choosing a more specific meaning), and transposition (changing grammatical structures for better flow). Translation analysis procedures involved comparing source and target texts to identify semantic and cultural inconsistencies, and adjusting sentence-level solutions using translation-theory frameworks, direct and oblique translation approaches, and Pym's concept of "prosodic effects" (Wan et al., 2018). These strategies could be taught in translator training classrooms so that novice translators can theorise and implement flexible solutions rather than relying solely on literal translation.

It is compulsory upon translators to balance fidelity and readability in all situations, and all changes must be explained to maintain the sense (He et al., 2024). They should also consider ethical and legal issues that may affect the authenticity of the translations (Matoesian & Gilbert, 2018; Olurotimi, 2022). Corpus analysis can potentially complement these methods in providing insights into the operation of symbols across jurisdictions and media (Jones, 2012). The translation of legal writings, in terms of language and legal systems, essentially consists of procedures that are delicate, context-sensitive, and entail semiotic and multimodal auditing, localisation, annotation, accessibility, and documentation. These strategies are closely related to the key role that semiotic and multimodal aspects play in preserving legal meaning in translation, particularly in maintaining authority, legitimacy, and clarity.

These semiotic and multimodal features highlight the complex nature of legal translation. They talk about the necessity of systematic techniques that combine semiotic analysis with multimodal auditing. The conceptual tools introduced here set the basis for the pedagogical framework elaborated in the next section, where these insights are operationalised as a structured workflow for translator training.

Multimodal Semiotic Auditing Framework

The framework proposed here draws on seminal works in legal translation (Šarčević, 1997; Cao, 2007; Madsen, 1997) and elaborates on their focus on functional equivalence, legal consequences and communicative practice into a systematic multimodal semiotic auditing model for translator training. Šarčević (1997), Cao (2007) and Madsen (1997) share the view that legal translation is not a trivial linguistic transfer but a professional activity requiring specific skills. A common focus on functional equivalence, legal repercussions and communicative context provides a basis for multimodal semiotic auditing in translator education. These insights can be used to develop curriculum to teach students how to identify legal sign equivalences across languages and cultures, including intersemiotic manoeuvres such as diagrams, infographics and bilingual headings.

While the language and conceptual dimensions of legal translation have been extensively researched, the systematic incorporation of multimodal semiotic into translator training has been far less explored. This section synthesises those documented analyses into a pedagogical framework for translation education, drawing on the theoretical underpinnings. The framework is intended to train translators not just as language mediators, but also as auditors of multimodal authority and accessibility. It provides a systematic workflow to help practitioners to identify semiotic resources, assess authority cues, adapt multimodal characteristics across languages and cultures, and validate accessibility in translated legal documents. The framework, presented in Table 1, serves as a Multimodal Semiotic Auditing Framework for translation training programs.

Translating multimodal legal texts requires strategies that preserve authority, clarity, and usability across diverse languages and jurisdictions. Effective methods begin by considering multimodal signs, such as seals, icons, colour codes, layout hierarchies, and interactive elements, as integral to meaning rather than ancillary features. Translators should integrate a semiotic checklist into their process to ensure that every non-textual cue in the source text is properly represented in the target version (Jones, 2012; Rashid, 2023). Initiating a semiotic audit enables the systematic cataloguing of signs, their purposes, and audience expectations, thereby informing decisions related to replication, replacement, annotation, or redesign (Heritier, 2023).

Literal reproduction should give way to functional equivalence. In instances where cultural or legal factors obstruct direct symbol equivalency, translators are required to employ culturally relevant substitutions or annotations to convey the intended effect, such as illustrating obligation or authority (Kozhevnikov, 2022; Novak, 2021). Annotated translations are crucial for transparency, as they reveal the choices regarding meaning and the rationale behind them. Collaboration among attorneys, artists, and accessibility specialists is crucial for maintaining the functionality and clarity of multimodal signage in appropriate contexts (Pitkňalo & Kalliomaa-Puha, 2019). Monitoring updates, including adding comments or modifying photographs, facilitates review and enhances learning across projects.

Examples of adaptation illustrate the application of these strategies. A culturally appropriate substitute seal, along with an explanation of its origins, may be incorporated into existing legislation that already features a national seal. This upholds the rule of law and honours regional traditions (Goodrich, 1998; Peters, 2020). Icons, such as scales of justice, may be replaced with symbols more pertinent to the region or accompanied by explanatory labels to ensure comprehension among all individuals (Bennet, 2019). Contracts may require reformatting to include risk-notice boxes and numbered sections, in accordance with the target language's requirements. Bilingual glossaries and culturally appropriate formatting are employed to enhance message comprehension (Duan, 2024; Jones, 2012). Digital portals featuring progress bars and icons should include visible tooltips for all users, provide localised translations for specific regions, and ensure compatibility with assistive technology (Rashid, 2023).

Semiotic decision trees and sign-adaptation matrices serve as effective workflow tools that help translators make systematic translation decisions. Translators utilise decision trees to identify relevant signals, select appropriate functions, and decide whether to replicate, replace, or annotate a sign. Adaptation matrices enable translators to evaluate the benefits and drawbacks of each sign type and their potential impact on readers. Translator notes elucidate the functioning of signs, their usage, and associated legal implications, while standardised annotation guidelines promote consistency. Quality assurance requires establishing review criteria to assess the integrity of function, readability, accessibility, and enforceability (Novak, 2021). Nuances encompass context-dependence, indicating that optimal strategies differ across jurisdictions, mediums, and audiences (Duan, 2024; Jones, 2012). Translators must balance opacity and transparency, avoiding excessive annotation that makes text harder to read while keeping it clear for non-expert audiences (Novak, 2021). Ethical considerations are highly significant, as changes in symbols may alter rights or obligations; thus, translators should consult legal authorities (Olurotimi, 2022). Translating multimodal legal texts requires systematic, collaborative, and context-sensitive strategies. Utilising semiotic audits, functional equivalence, annotated translations, and comprehensive quality assurance enables translators to maintain symbolic meaning while ensuring that authority, legitimacy, and usability are retained across diverse languages and cultures. This directly addresses the research question by demonstrating the necessity of managing semiotic and multimodal features to maintain legal meaning in translation. The following table synthesises key strategies for translating multimodal legal texts, combining practical approaches with illustrative examples to show how authority, clarity, and accessibility can be preserved across languages and jurisdictions.

Table 1 presents the components of the proposed Multimodal Semiotic Auditing Framework. It organises the workflow into step-by-step strategies for translator training, showing how semiotic resources, authority cues, and accessibility features can be systematically audited in legal translation.

Table 1. Components of multimodal semiotic auditing framework

Steps/Components	Description	Application in Translation	Pedagogical Implications
Semiotic Checklist	Treat multimodal signs (seals, icons, colour codes, layout, interactive elements) as integral to meaning.	A statute with a national seal is checked for symbolic load before translation.	Ensures that authority signals are preserved or appropriately adapted.
Pre-translation Semiotic Audit	Catalogue signs, their functions, and audience expectations before translation begins.	Audit identifies seals, icons, and layout cues in a multilingual contract.	Guides adaptation decisions, reducing the risk of misinterpretation.
Functional Equivalence	Preserve the intended effect of signs rather than literal reproduction.	Scales of justice icon retained with explanatory caption or replaced with a locally resonant symbol.	Maintains interpretive alignment across cultures.
Annotated Translations	Document semiotic decisions and rationale transparently.	Translator notes explain why a seal was substituted with a neutral emblem.	Provides transparency and supports future reviews.
Collaborative Review	Involve legal drafters, designers, localisation experts, and accessibility specialists.	Risk-notice boxes in contracts redesigned with culturally recognisable formatting.	Preserves enforceability and improves user comprehension.
Documentation of Adaptations	Maintain a record of all semiotic decisions for traceability.	Digital portal icons localised with tooltips and accessibility features, documented in translator notes.	Ensures auditability and consistency across projects.

DISCOURSE ANALYSIS OF MULTIMODAL LEGAL TEXTS

Analytical Frameworks

Critical discourse analysis (CDA) has long been employed to examine how language shapes ideology, authority, and legal frameworks. This approach has evolved to encompass multimodal discourse analysis (MCDA), which acknowledges that images, diagrams, typography, colour schemes, layouts, and interface cues collectively contribute to the construction of legal meaning alongside verbal language (Duan, 2024). These multimodal resources interact with legal arguments to either reinforce or challenge authority, paralleling how social semiotics and systemic functional linguistics investigate the construction of rights and obligations across different modalities.

The MCDA analytical approach is grounded in semiotic social theory, particularly Kress and van Leeuwen's (2020) notion of visual grammar, which illustrates how images and design elements function like language by adhering to rules and structures that shape meaning. The arrangement of objects, application of colour, and orientation of gaze can indicate authority, significance, or relationships, analogous to how grammar structures meaning in sentences. This framework emphasises that visuals in legal texts, such as seals, diagrams, and layouts, possess communicative significance and influence interpretation rather than serving merely decorative purposes. Halliday and Matthiessen's (2013) systemic functional linguistics (SFL) provides an analysis of how language choices reflect social roles, attitudes, and power dynamics. SFL reveals how words express obligation, authority, or stance, while visual grammar delineates how design choices fulfil analogous functions in non-verbal modes. They offer a cohesive approach to the analysis of multimodal legal texts, enabling researchers to examine the interplay between text and image in the construction, support, or challenge of legal authority (Mackay, 2015).

Methodologically, MCDA involves how legal texts operate across multiple modalities, selecting corpora that integrate text, images, and interface elements, and categorising multimodal resources based on their communicative functions, such as conveying authority, risk, or procedural information (Duan, 2024). Analysts then assess how these multimodal cues collectively shape institutional power and audience perceptions, while also considering ethical concerns such as accessibility and potential bias (Bennett, 2019; Nikiporietz et al., 2024). The integration of semiotics and multimodality into discourse studies foregrounds law as a multimodal artefact. Social semiotics demonstrates how authority and risk are signalled across languages and media, situating sign-making practices within institutional and cultural contexts (Goodrich, 1998; Heritier, 2023). By treating documents, seals, and digital interfaces as communicative acts, multimodal discourse analysis emphasises the coordination of modalities and alignment with audience expectations (Duan, 2024; Jones, 2012; Torresi, 2013). This approach clarifies how readers interpret, negotiate, and contest legal meanings in various contexts, including courtroom discourse, legislative drafting, contractual agreements, and digital platforms, thereby enabling cross-genre and cross-media analysis (Jones, 2012; Rashid, 2023).

Methodological implications include the development of annotation schemes that capture cross-modal codes, the construction of multimodal corpora integrating text, visuals, and interfaces, and the presentation of findings through multimodal descriptions that illustrate the interaction between diagrams, layouts, colour coding, and textual provisions. Analysts must also address challenges in interpreting signs by balancing structured semiotic models, contextual variability, and audience reception (Mackay, 2015). Considerations of cross-cultural validity require attention to jurisdictional differences in sign repertoires, while ethical concerns encompass privacy and accessibility.

Figure 1 below illustrates the MCDA framework, showing how Semiotic Social Theory integrates Systemic Functional Linguistics and Visual Grammar to analyse legal texts such as statutes, contracts, and digital portals, in terms of their construction of authority, legitimacy, and accessibility.

Figure 1. MCDA analytical framework

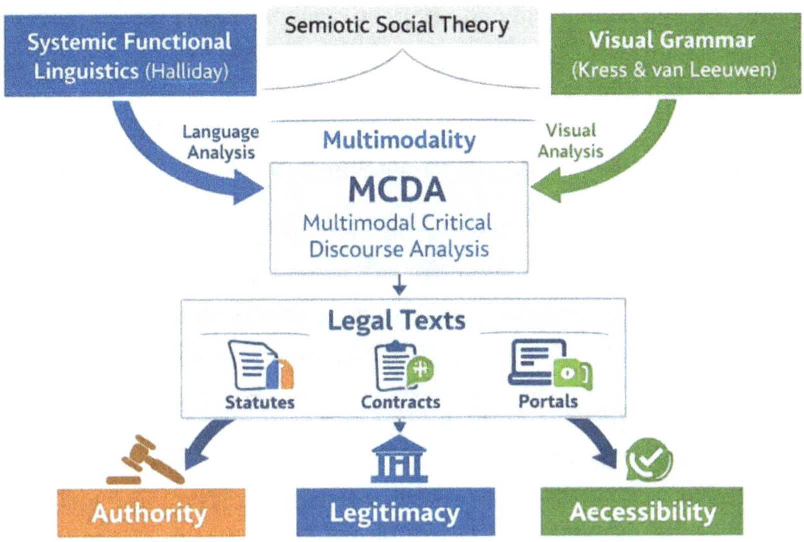

Figure 1 represents the analytical framework discussed in the section. It shows how Semiotic Social Theory informs Multimodal Critical Discourse Analysis (MCDA) by combining Halliday's Systemic-Functional Linguistics with Kress and van Leeuwen's Visual Grammar. The two analytical strands of language and visual analysis meet in multimodality to explore how legal materials, such as statutes, contracts, and internet portals, convey meaning. The figure substantiates the paragraph's assertion that MCDA systematically relates verbal and visual semiotic techniques to interpret how authority, legitimacy, and accessibility in law are conveyed through multimodal aspects. The text and image together suggest that multimodal discourse analysis offers a holistic view of how legal communication works across modes to construct interpretation and institutional power.

Power and Ideology in Legal Multimodality

The interplay of visual, textual, and digital signs in multimodal legal discourse clarifies the dynamics of power and ideology, shaping constructs of authority and legitimacy. Seals, emblems, typography, and colour schemes function as indicators of institutional power, conveying prestige and procedural authority that extend beyond the written text. Multimodal resources facilitate reader trust and compliance across various languages and media, thereby reinforcing institutional endorsement and enforceable legitimacy (Goodrich, 1998; Peters, 2020). Layout elements like headings, callouts, and marginalia structure perceived significance and urgency, directing readers toward particular interpretations and priorities in statutes, contracts, or judgments. In digital environments, interactive elements and status signals such as "sealed," "confidential," or "public" enhance formal power relations by influencing user access and compliance with processes (Jones, 2012; Rashid, 2023).

Ideology operates through multimodal signs, integrating cultural and political values into legal discourse. Iconography, including the scales of justice and national emblems, conveys concepts of fairness, sovereignty, and legitimacy that differ across cultures and jurisdictions (Olurotimi, 2022; Peters, 2020). Legal texts utilise intertextual references to previous rulings and doctrines, with visual and layout cues connecting contemporary claims to established authority and institutional memory (Bor & Könczöl, 2019; Frantsuzova, 2019). Multimodal design can either highlight or conceal marginalised voices; the presence of accessibility features and the inclusivity of interfaces influence which perspectives are visible and how dissenting arguments are framed (Mackay, 2015).

Empirical analysis of multimodal evidence demonstrates the mechanisms through which power is enacted and legitimised within legal contexts. In courtroom discourse, verbal arguments are complemented by gestures, gaze, and digital exhibits, collectively generating authority that impacts credibility and outcomes (Matoesian & Gilbert, 2018). Statutory and contract design incorporates ideological assumptions via the organisation of provisions and visual risk indicators, thereby encoding norms of responsibility and fairness (Kozhevnikov, 2022; Novak, 2021). Digital legal portals enhance access to rights and procedures, utilising dashboards and progress indicators to influence user participation and transparency (Duan, 2024).

Methodological reflection necessitates a balance between critique and fidelity. Analysts should differentiate between authentic authority signalling and manipulative or exclusionary design, examining whether multimodal cues contribute to comprehension or perpetuate inequality (Torresi, 2013). Cross-cultural caution is crucial, as symbols and layouts possess varying meanings across different jurisdictions; comparative analysis mitigates overgeneralization and emphasises contextual variation (Heritier, 2023; Olteanu & Ongstad, 2024). Ethical reflexivity is fundamental to credible interpretation, safeguarding privacy and consent in the analysis of courtroom visuals and protecting vulnerable audiences.

Attention to multimodal authority is essential for translation. Translators are required to maintain or elucidate the institutional significance of seals, icons, and layouts, employing annotations to clarify jurisdictional implications and power relations (Duan, 2024; Olurotimi, 2022). A power-aware multimodal lens in discourse analysis reveals the construction and contestation of authority across genres, thereby contributing to wider discussions on justice and accessibility (Heritier, 2023; Wang, 2017). MCDA training should incorporate an understanding of power relations, promoting the documentation of how sign choices affect interpretation and legitimacy (Havnen, 2019; Mackay, 2015).

Multimodal signs are inherently biased, as they convey power and ideology through intentional design decisions. A single visual cue can convey distinct meanings depending on the context; for instance, a seal may denote sovereignty in one jurisdiction and institutional authority in another, while colour schemes may indicate different levels of confidentiality or urgency. Understanding these contextual differences is essential for maintaining the accuracy, ethics, and responsiveness of discourse analysis in multimodal legal texts, particularly regarding the construction of authority and ideology through multimodal communication in law.

Accessibility and Equity

Accessibility and equity in multimodal legal discourse demonstrate that design choices can either reduce barriers or perpetuate exclusion. Visual hierarchies, plain-language glosses, and accessible layouts facilitate the rapid identification of rights and obligations for lay readers, non-native speakers, and individuals with diverse literacy levels (Duan, 2024). Multilingual typography and explicit cross-references diminish cognitive load, facilitating navigation of complex statutes and contracts (Jones, 2012; Pau, 2017). Digital interfaces enhance accessibility by providing interactive features such as search facets, annotated examples, and user-friendly dashboards, enabling various audiences to customise their engagement with legal texts beyond conventional print formats. Inclusive iconography, accessible colour schemes, and alternative text for graphics support readers with disabilities and diverse cultural backgrounds, thereby aligning legal communication with accessibility standards (Mendonca, 2021).

Notwithstanding these advantages, multimodal design can create inequity. Symbols and visuals can encode culturally specific power dynamics, favouring professional communities and marginalising wider audiences (Goodrich, 1998; Olurotimi, 2022). Poorly designed digital portals, inaccessible PDFs, and visuals lacking textual alternatives can exclude users with disabilities or limited digital literacy, thereby undermining open justice (Mendonca, 2021). Language and cultural discrepancies present challenges, as multimodal cues may convey different meanings across jurisdictions, necessitating meticulous localisation and inclusive translation practices.

Case-focused analysis demonstrates the potential of multimodality to either democratise or limit participation. Video exhibits, graphics, and timelines in courtroom settings can improve understanding for jurors and the public; however, if not designed inclusively, they risk perpetuating exclusionary practices (Olurotimi, 2022). Statutes and contracts in multilingual contexts are enhanced by visual aids and colour-coded risk notices that align with cultural reading habits and legal traditions, thereby promoting equitable understanding (Olurotimi, 2022). Digital portals that provide information on rights and case statuses can reduce barriers to justice if they follow inclusive design standards and ensure multilingual accessibility, but if usability gaps remain, they risk reinforcing existing hierarchies.

Researchers should methodically collect multimodal corpora encompassing text, visuals, layout, and interface data across various languages and media. It is essential to document context and audience to comprehensively assess accessibility (Heritier, 2023; Jones, 2012; Rashid, 2023). Annotation schemes should encompass readability, visual cues, layout signals, and interface affordances. Additionally, participatory evaluation must include a diverse range of readers, such as individuals with disabilities and non-experts, in usability testing and comprehension tasks (Mendonca, 2021).

Guidelines for practice underscore the importance of designing with both universality and locality, integrating accessibility principles while honouring cultural repertoires (Mendonca, 2021; Olurotimi, 2022). Practitioners need to annotate sign decisions to maintain transparency and foster interdisciplinary collaboration among legal drafters, translators, designers, and accessibility experts. This approach ensures that materials are precise, culturally appropriate, and accessible. Accessibility in multimodal legal discourse represents a continuous obligation rather than a singular accomplishment. Equity necessitates more than mere adherence to standards; it requires active consideration of language inclusivity, cultural significance, and substantive engagement. Ethical considerations such as privacy and consent are fundamental when analysing courtroom visuals or user interactions, ensuring that multimodal legal communication fosters justice and inclusion.

PRACTICAL APPLICATIONS AND RECOMMENDATIONS

Guidelines for Legal Translators

The concepts are applied by the legal translators working with multimodal materials to the practical translation process. This section translates those notions into actionable items for professional translators and educators. Following the audit stage described in Table 1, legal translators conduct a pre-translation semiotic audit to identify all non-textual signs in the source document, including seals, emblems, logos, icons, diagrams, layout structures, typography, colour conventions, and digital cues (Jones, 2012). Each sign requires assessment of its function, whether it denotes authority, facilitates navigation, or enhances accessibility, and must be evaluated for jurisdictional and cultural relevance, enabling translators to identify signs that certify provenance or enforceability, guide readers through procedures, and necessitate alternative access features (Rashid, 2023).

Upon identification, translators organise signs according to their functions within a sign-function matrix. Translators subsequently determine whether to reproduce, adapt, or annotate each sign. Reproduction is suitable when equivalents are present and legal contexts are consistent; adaptation is required when cultural or legal discrepancies occur; annotation is employed when reproduction would alter the intended meaning (Pitkäsalo & Kalliomaa-Puha, 2019). All decisions should be recorded with appropriate justification, citations of relevant standards, and an explanation of their expected impacts on the audience, thereby promoting transparency and accountability in translation practices (Novak, 2021).

Consistent with the multimodal semiotic framework in Table 1, the treatment of visuals, layout, and typography needs to be handled precisely. Seals and emblems must be reproduced in high resolution when legally allowed, or replaced with culturally relevant alternatives that include captions (Peters, 2020). Additionally, typography should align with conventions in the target language to enhance clarity and readability. Accessibility considerations are crucial; integrating alt-text for images, ensuring adequate colour contrast, ensuring screen-reader compatibility, and providing text-based equivalents for interactive elements are necessary to ensure equitable access (Rashid, 2023).

Annotation and documentation practices enhance fidelity and transparency. Translator notes must elucidate the purpose and rationale for each adaptation, whereas a centralised sign dossier documents all semiotic choices and their potential legal consequences. Captions must connect visuals to relevant textual provisions, and accessibility documentation should detail the accommodations made for audit purposes. These practices maintain multimodal fidelity and enhance the trustworthiness of the translated text (Pau, 2017; Novak, 2021). Assurance necessitates multimodal fidelity checks to verify that authority, obligation, risk, and navigation signals are preserved. Testing with lay audiences, professionals, and individuals with disabilities evaluates comprehension and perceived legitimacy. Legal drafters and localisation specialists conduct stakeholder reviews to ensure adherence to local norms. Ethical validation is essential; adaptations should not misrepresent or modify rights and responsibilities, and it may be necessary to consult with local council (Pitkäsalo & Kalliomaa-Puha, 2019; Rashid, 2023).

Translators utilise decision heuristics in their practice. Signs must be reproduced when direct equivalents are available, substituted in cases of incompatibility, annotated when reproduction may distort meaning, and redesigned when layout or typography necessitates adjustments for readability. All decisions should be guided by inclusivity and cultural respect, avoiding stereotypes and ensuring transparency through comprehensive documentation (Olurotimi, 2022; Kozhevnikov, 2022). The deliverables must include the localised document, a semiotics appendix, translator notes, and accessibility-compliant versions of the visual components. Integrating workflow requires incorporating the semiotics checklist into translation processes, including audits at project initiation, regular evaluations, and final fidelity assessments (Heritier, 2023). These guidelines ensure that multimodal legal translation maintains authority, legitimacy, and accessibility, while also respecting cultural variation and ethical standards (Jones, 2012; Rashid, 2023).

Legal translators should engage with multimodal texts through systematic audits, precise adaptation, and clear documentation. The integration of fidelity checks, participatory evaluation, and ethical reflexivity in translation practice ensures the preservation of the authority of legal texts while enhancing accessibility and equity across jurisdictions. This directly addresses the research question by demonstrating how multimodal translation strategies protect legitimacy and inclusivity in legal discourse (Goodrich, 1998; Novak, 2021; Olurotimi, 2022). Figure 2 summarises the step-by-step process for legal translators, outlining how semiotic auditing, adaptation, documentation, and ethical validation work together to ensure that multimodal legal translations preserve authority, clarity, and accessibility across jurisdictions.

Figure 2. Legal translation semiotics checklist

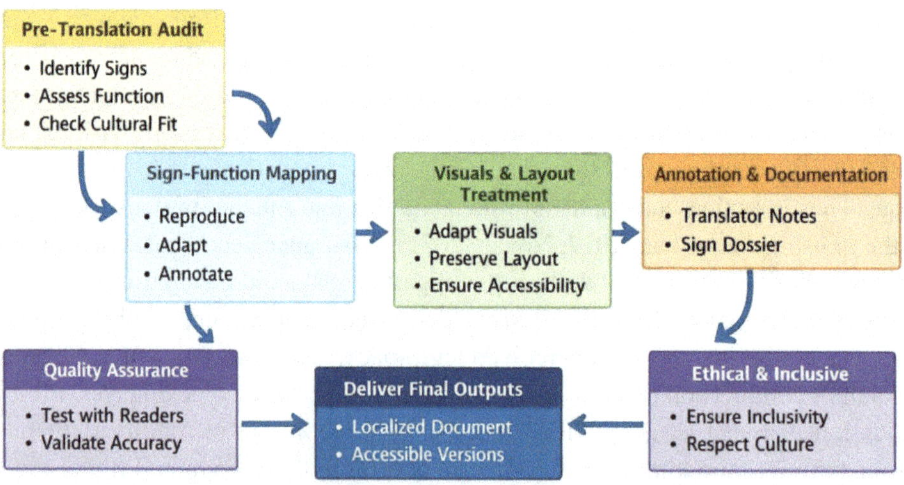

The conceptual and methodological insights presented are translated into professional practice. Translators "embed" fidelity checks, participatory evaluation, and ethical reflexivity into the workflow, ensuring that multimodal legal texts maintain authority and inclusivity across jurisdictions. This move from theoretical understanding to framework design to applied guidance illustrates how multimodal semiotic auditing can be incorporated into translator training and institutional standards.

Pedagogical Implications

Legal translator training guidelines highlight the importance of cultivating multimodal literacy as an essential professional skill. The objective is to assist translators in reading and interpreting non-textual signs such as seals, emblems, icons, colour codings, and layout hierarchies, and assessing their legal functions, including authority, obligation, and risk signalling, across jurisdictions (Goodrich, 1998; Olurotimi, 2022). Translators must practice transferring or adapting these cues to maintain or clearly convey their meanings in the target culture (Wang et al., 2025), utilising annotations when direct reproduction is impractical (Jones, 2012; Rashid, 2023). Accessibility and inclusivity are essential components of this training, guaranteeing that multimodal translation is comprehensible and functional for a wide range of readers, including individuals with disabilities (Mendonca, 2021; Reisberg, 2018).

The curriculum integrates theoretical principles with practical skill development. Initial modules cover semiotics in law, multimodal discourse analysis, and accessibility principles (Torresi, 2013; Novak, 2021). Subsequent modules emphasise semiotic auditing, localisation labs, and accessibility integration, in which students conduct audits of sample texts, modify visuals and layouts, and develop alt-text and colour-contrast evaluations (Heritier, 2023). Engagement in peer review and collaboration with designers and legal editors replicates real-world workflows and improves multimodal fidelity (Pitkäsalo & Kalliomaa-Puha, 2019).

The program prioritises active, hands-on learning using authentic materials, including statutes, contracts, and digital portals. Assessment rubrics assess adherence to function, readability, accessibility, and cultural relevance, rather than focusing solely on linguistic accuracy. Collaboration among translators, designers, and accessibility specialists reflects professional practice, while reader-centred evaluation via usability testing collects empirical feedback on comprehension and perceived legitimacy (Mendonca, 2021; Reisberg, 2018). The assessment criteria evaluate sign fidelity and function (30%), readability and navigability (25%), accessibility compliance (20%), cultural and jurisdictional alignment (15%), and documentation quality (10%). These metrics guarantee that translations maintain authority and clarity while adhering to accessibility and cultural standards (Heritier, 2023; Rashid, 2023).

Resource development facilitates ongoing education via repositories of legal sign conventions, open educational materials, and professional workshops focused on semiotics and accessibility. Challenges, including the balance between fidelity and legibility, jurisdictional variation, and scalability, are addressed through annotated captions, localised sign mapping, and progressive project scaling. The evaluation of outcomes encompasses post-course feedback on confidence and competence in multimodal translation, employment-readiness metrics, and scholarly contributions through case studies and publications.

Institutional Recommendations

Recommendations for multimodal legal drafting emphasise integrating clear policies, standardised practices, and accountability mechanisms to maintain authority, legitimacy, and accessibility. Drafting policies must acknowledge that meaning derives from both linguistic content and multimodal elements, such as visuals, layout, and digital interfaces, and include guidelines clarifying how these cues communicate authority and obligation (Jones, 2012; Rashid, 2023). Standardised sign inventories for statutes, contracts, and judgments should include seals, emblems, icons, and colour codes, each linked to its function and cultural implications (Goodrich, 1998; Kozhevnikov, 2022). Accessibility must be a fundamental drafting criterion, requiring text alternatives, keyboard operability, and colour-contrast compliance (Mendonca, 2021).

Implementation involves structured steps: adopting policies through style guides and exemplar documents (Pau, 2017), creating a centralised Sign Handbook with symbol sets and localisation guidance (Olurotimi, 2022), and integrating design reviews into workflows with interdisciplinary sign-off points (Novak, 2021). Translation protocols should standardise procedures for reproducing, annotating, or redesigning non-textual cues, supported by translator notes (Novak, 2021). Training programs must build staff competency in multimodal literacy and accessibility through case studies and practical exercises (Rashid, 2023).

Quality assurance requires multimodal conformity audits to verify fidelity and accessibility (Jones, 2012), reader-centred validation with diverse groups (Reisberg, 2018), and documentation practices that enhance transparency (Novak, 2021). Ethical and governance considerations include attention to linguistic diversity and cultural variation (Torresi, 2013), licensing and sovereignty in the use of seals and emblems (Peters, 2020), and public accountability through clear explanations of multimodal elements (Rashid, 2023). Table 2 summarises the institutional recommendations for multimodal legal drafting, organising them into key areas: policy, implementation, quality assurance, ethics, and deliverables, to provide a concise and accessible overview.

Table 2. Institutional recommendation

Area	Key Recommendation
Policy Drafting	Recognise meaning as both linguistic and multimodal; establish sign inventories.
Implementation	Adopt policies via style guides; create Sign Handbook; integrate design reviews.
Quality Assurance	Conduct multimodal audits; validate with diverse readers; maintain documentation.
Ethics & Governance	Ensure inclusivity; respect cultural diversity; manage symbol licensing.
Deliverables	Drafting guidelines, signing dossiers, and accessibility compliance reports.

Deliverables include drafting guidelines, signing-dossier templates, and accessibility compliance reports. Case illustrations demonstrate application, such as bilingual seals requiring annotated captions, contracts with colour-coded risk notices, and digital portals with accessible icons and tooltips.

CONCLUSION

This chapter has shown that law is a multimodal semiotic system in which textual, visual, and material signs interact to construct meaning, authority, and accessibility. The discussion contextualised semiotics and multimodality in the field of legal translation and discourse analysis, and highlighted the importance for legal translators of considering not only language equivalence but also the semiotic environment in which legal texts are utilised.

The chapter brings together the current scholarship into a pedagogical framework for multimodal semiotic auditing through comprehensive literature review and comparative analysis. This theory constructs the translator as an auditor with semiotic authority whose task is to mediate visual, spatial and symbolic clues with verbal information. In doing so, it extends the well-established traditions in legal semiotics and translation studies into digital and multimodal environments, where new challenges of accessibility and legitimacy arise.

The contribution's originality lies in bringing to the fore the digital-multimodal dimension of law and in suggesting ways of translator training that operationalise semiotic auditing. Although the work does not produce new primary data, it provides a replicable analytical basis that could be used to analyse corpora of judgments, contracts, and institutional documents in future research. Finally, the chapter argues that translation in law is not only linguistic mediation but a multimodal process that preserves authority and accessibility across jurisdictions. This paradigm introduces semiotic and multimodal perspectives into translation education so that practitioners are prepared to critically interact with the changing semiotic ecologies of law in order that legal meaning stays coherent, legitimate and accessible across a range of cultural and technological contexts.

REFERENCES

Basu, S., Prakash, S., Barge, A. M., Jaiswal, S. D., Dash, A., Ghosh, S., & Mukherjee, A. (2025). Judging by appearances? Auditing and intervening vision-language models for bail prediction. *arXiv*. https://doi.org//arXiv.2510.00088DOI: 10.48550

Bennett, K. (2019). The new iconicity: Challenges for translation theory and practice. *Translation Matters, 1*(2), 1–8. DOI: 10.21747/21844585/tm1_2int

Bor, B., & Könczöl, M. (2019). Towards a semiotic theory of style in law: A Peircean approach. *International Journal of Law in Context, 15*(3), 263–273. DOI: 10.1017/S1744552319000272

Brenner, J. E. (2015). Three aspects of information science in reality: Symmetry, semiotics and society. *Information (Basel), 6*(4), 750–772. DOI: 10.3390/info6040750

Cacciaguidi-Fahy, S., & Mooney, A. (2009). The Promise of Legal Semiotics. *International Journal for the Semiotics of Law - Revue Internationale De Sémiotique Juridique, 22*(4), 381–386. DOI: 10.1007/s11196-009-9123-7

Cao, D. (2007). *Translating law* (Vol. 33). Multilingual Matters.

Chodkiewicz, C. (2004). Review of La Langue de La Common Law by Anne Wagner. *International Journal of Speech Language and the Law, 11*(1), 0146–158. DOI: 10.1558/ijsll.v11i1.150

Deacon, T. W., & Rączaszek-Leonardi, J. (2019). Abandoning the code metaphor is compatible with semiotic process. *The Behavioral and Brain Sciences, 42*, e216. DOI: 10.1017/S0140525X19001419 PMID: 31775915

del Rey, J. T. (2019). The proper place of localization in translation curricula. In Sawyer, D.B., Austermühl, F., and Raído, V.,E. (Eds.), *The Evolving Curriculum in Interpreter and Translator Education. Stakeholder perspectives and voices* (pp. 229–258). John Benjamins Publishing. DOI: 10.1075/ata.xix.11tor

Douzinas, C., & Nead, L. (1999). *Law and the Image*. University of Chicago Press.

Duan, M. (2024). A study of subtitle translation from the perspective of multimodal discourse analysis: A case of *My People, My Country. Journal of Social Sciences and Humanities, 6*(10), 24–32. DOI: 10.53469/jssh.2024.6(10).05

Durant, A., & Davis, J. (2018). Linguistic analysis in trade mark law: Current approaches and new challenges. In L. Solan & P. Tiersma (Eds.), *The Oxford handbook of language and law* (pp. 287–320). https://doi.org/DOI: 10.1515/9781614514664-014

Frantsuzova, A. D. (2019). Communication failure in court interpreting within a linguosemiotic approach: A mismatch of expectations. In *Proceedings of the International Scientific and Practical Conference "Individual and Society in the Modern Geopolitical Environment"* (pp. 214–219). Atlantis Press. https://doi.org/ DOI: 10.2991/ismge-19.2019.38

Goodrich, P. (1998). Signs taken for wonders: Community, identity, and "A history of sumptuary law.". *Law & Social Inquiry*, *23*(3), 707–728. DOI: 10.1086/492655

Gorlée, D. L. (2005). Hints and guesses: Legal modes of semio-logical reasoning. *Sign Systems Studies*, *33*(2), 239–272. DOI: 10.12697/SSS.2005.33.2.01

Hakimzadeh, S. (2020). Reclaiming the commons: Law, rhetoric, and C. S. Peirce's pragmatic philosophy. *Law, Culture and the Humanities*, *19*(3), 603–623. DOI: 10.1177/1743872120935934

Halliday, M. A. K., & Matthiessen, C. M. I. M. (2013). *Halliday's introduction to functional grammar* (4th ed.). Routledge., DOI: 10.4324/9780203431269

Havelka, I. (2024). Interpreting intercepted communication: From talk to evidence. *The International Journal of Translation and Interpreting Research*, *16*(1), 17–37. DOI: 10.12807/ti.116201.2024.a02

Havnen, R. (2019). Multimodal and interactional aspects of sight translation – A critical review. *FITISPos-International Journal*, *6*(1), 91–106. DOI: 10.37536/FITISPos-IJ.2019.6.1.206

He, H., Amini, M., Ganapathy, M., & Lah, S. C. (2024). The application of Juliane House's translation quality assessment model in the English translation of Yu Hua's 'Yanre de xiatian.'. *Cogent Arts & Humanities*, *11*(1), 2386781. DOI: 10.1080/23311983.2024.2386781

Heritier, P. (2023). Understanding legal semiotics. In *Research handbook on legal semiotics* (pp. 11–31). Edward Elgar Publishing., DOI: 10.4337/9781802207262.00010

Jackson, B. S. (1985). *Semiotics and legal theory*. Routledge & Kegan Paul.

Jackson, B. S. (1988). *Law, fact and narrative coherence*. Deborah Charles Publications.

Jones, R. H. (2012). Multimodal discourse analysis. In *The encyclopedia of applied linguistics*. Wiley-Blackwell., DOI: 10.1002/9781405198431.wbeal0813

Kevelson, R. (1987). *Law and semiotics* (Vol. 1). Plenum Press., DOI: 10.1007/978-1-4613-0959-8_1

Kevelson, R. (1988). *The law as a system of signs*. Springer. DOI: 10.1007/978-1-4613-0911-6

Kevelson, R. (1996). *Pierce, science, signs* (Vol. 9). Peter Lang.

Kozhevnikov, V. V.Vladimir Valentinovich Kozhevnikov. (2022). Legal semiotics. *Matondang Journal*, *2*(1), 36–46. DOI: 10.33258/matondang.v2i1.807

Kress, G., & van Leeuwen, T. (2020). *Reading images: The grammar of visual design* (3rd ed.). Routledge., DOI: 10.4324/9781003099857

Krimpas, P. G. (2023). Semiotics in matters legal. *Punctum International Journal of Semiotics*, *9*(2), 241–245. DOI: 10.18680/hss.2023.0029

Mackay, R. R. (2015). Multimodal legitimation: Selling Scottish independence. *Discourse & Society*, *26*(3), 323–348. DOI: 10.1177/0957926514564737

Madsen, D. (1997). Towards a description of communication in the legal universe: Translation of legal texts and the Skopos theory. *Fachsprache (1990), 19*(1-2), 17-27.

Matoesian, G., & Gilbert, K. E. (2018). Let the fingers do the talking: Language, gesture and power in closing argument. In Leung, J. H. C., & Durant, A. (Eds.), *Meaning and power in the language of law* (pp. 137–163). Cambridge University Press., DOI: 10.1017/9781316285756.007

Matulewska, A. (2019). Legal and LSP Linguistics and Translation: Asian Languages' Perspectives. *International Journal for the Semiotics of Law - Revue Internationale De Sémiotique Juridique, 32*(1), 1–11. DOI: 10.1007/s11196-019-09602-x

Mendonca, M. (2021). *Access denied: Exploring web accessibility standards and their implications for users with cognitive impairments* [Master's thesis, Toronto Metropolitan University]. https://doi.org/DOI: 10.32920/ryerson.14655063.v1

Nicolini, D., Reinecke, J., & Ismail, M. A. (2021). *You're grounded! Toward a theory of enactive legitimation, materiality and practice. Research in the Sociology of Organizations.* Emerald Publishing Limited., DOI: 10.1108/S0733-558X20200000071004

Nikioporietz, S., Kulish, L., Magas, L., Melnik, M., & Piddubchak, S. (2024). Utilizing the semiotic model to enhance semantic adequacy in translation processes. *Вісник науки та освіти, 3*(21), 47–62. https://doi.org/DOI: 10.52058/2786-6165-2024-3(21)-47-62

Nöth, W. (2021). Linguistics and semiotics in the framework of sciences in general. *Cahiers du Centre de Linguistique et des Sciences du Langage, 65*, 29–50. https://doi.org/DOI: 10.26034/la.cdclsl.2021.1360

Novak, M. (2021). Visual as multi-modal argumentation in law. *Bratislava Law Review*, *5*(1), 91–110. DOI: 10.46282/blr.2021.5.1.187

Olteanu, A., & Ongstad, S. (2024). Utterance-genre-lifeworld and sign-habit-Umwelt compared. *Biosemiotics*, *17*(2), 523–546. DOI: 10.1007/s12304-024-09561-2

Olurotimi, T. S. (2022). Semiotics: A transdisciplinary quest for meaning. *International Journal of Linguistics. Literature and Translation*, *5*(8), 117–124. DOI: 10.32996/ijllt.2022.5.8.14

Pau, C. C. (2017). *Localization as multimodal-cultural translation: A comparative case study* [Master's thesis, Nanyang Technological University]. https://doi.org/ DOI: 10.32657/10356/72421

Peters, T. D. (2020). Daredevil as legal emblem. *Law. Technology and Humans*, *2*(2), 198–226. DOI: 10.5204/lthj.1656

Pitkäsalo, E., & Kalliomaa-Puha, L. (2019). Democratizing access to justice: The comic contract as intersemiotic translation. *Translation Matters*, *1*(2), 30–42. DOI: 10.21747/21844585/tm1_2a2

Prathap, S., & Kabaleeswaran, D. (2025). *The construction of identities and resistance through film narratives*. Sociology Lens., DOI: 10.1111/johs.70013

Rashid, B. N. (2023). Multimodality in the courtroom in American and British criminal cases. *IJPS*, *16*(1), 1–8. DOI: 10.37648/ijps.v16i01.001 PMID: 36998925

Reifman, D. (2022). Canonicity as a defining feature of legal and religious discourse. In *The Cambridge handbook of law and humanities* (pp. 151–170). https://doi.org/ DOI: 10.1017/9781108760997.007

Reisberg, L. (2018). Interpretation of undefined legal concepts and fulfilling of legal gaps in Juri Lotman's semiotic framework. *Juridica International*, *27*, 3–11. DOI: 10.12697/JI.2018.27.01

Szarkowska, A. (2010). Between text and image: Updating research in screen translation. *International Journal of Translation Studies*, *22*(2), 363–368. DOI: 10.1075/target.22.2.11sza

Tiersma, P. M. (1999). *Legal Language*. University of Chicago Press. DOI: 10.7208/chicago/9780226854809.001.0001

Torresi, I. (2013). *The photographic image: Truth or sign?* Springer., DOI: 10.1007/978-90-481-9322-6_6

Wan, S. Y. C., Abu Bakar, A., Amini, M., & Rafik-Galea, S. (2018). Problems and solutions in English translations of Malay short stories. *The Journal of Social Sciences Research, 6*(Special Issue), 1158–1166. https://arpgweb.com/pdf-files/spi6.3.2.1158.1166.pdf

Wang, H. (2017). Multimodal discourse of criminal courtroom discourses. *ICPEL Proceedings*. https://doi.org/DOI: 10.2991/icpel-17.2017.56

Wang, Q., Amini, M., & Tan, D. A. L. (2025). Strategies, errors, and challenges in translating Culture-Specific Items in Chinese-English literary works: A systematic review. *JURNAL ARBITRER, 12*(2), 259–273. https://arbitrer.fib.unand.ac.id/index.php/arbitrer/article/view/591

ADDITIONAL READING

Amini, M., Alavi, S., & Wu, S. (2026). From Tradition to Innovation: Understanding the Shifts in Translation Pedagogy and Practice. In Amini, M. (Ed.), *Bridging theory and practice in translation: Perspectives, challenges, and innovations* (pp. 1–34). IGI Global., DOI: 10.4018/979-8-3373-3705-0

De Carvalho, E. M. (2010). *Semiotics of international law: Trade and translation* (Vol. 91). Springer Science & Business Media.

Goodrich, P. (1996). *Law in the courts of love: Literature and other minor jurisprudences*. Routledge.

Jackson, B. S. (2017). A Journey into Legal Semiotics. *Actes Sémiotiques*, (120). https://doi.org/DOI: 10.25965/as.5669

Lloyd, H. A. (2021). How to Do Things with Signs: Semiotics in Legal Theory, Practice, and Education. *University of Richmond Law Review. University of Richmond, 55*(3). https://scholarship.richmond.edu/lawreview/vol55/iss3/6?utm_source=scholarship.richmond.edu%2Flawreview%2Fvol55%2Fiss3%2F6&utm_medium=PDF&utm_campaign=PDFCoverPages

Novak, M. (2021). Visual as Multi-Modal Argumentation in Law. *Bratislava Law Review, 5*(1), 91–110. DOI: 10.46282/blr.2021.5.1.187

Robertson, C. D. (2016). *Multilingual law: A framework for translation and interpretation*. Routledge. DOI: 10.4324/9781315596280

Silva, T., Verde, D., Paiva, S., Barreto, L., & Pereira, A. I. (2023). Accessibility strategies to promote inclusive mobility through multi-objective approach. *SN Applied Sciences*, *5*(5), 150. DOI: 10.1007/s42452-023-05349-0

Wang, B. (2018). Exploring Approaches to Interpreting Studies: From semiotic perspectives to multimodal analysis. *Chinese Semiotic Studies*, *14*(2), 149–161. DOI: 10.1515/css-2018-0010

Zhang, C., & Wang, Z. (2025). Meaning transformation and recontextualization: From multimodal courtroom discourse to legal judgments. *Humanities & Social Sciences Communications*, *12*(1), 1640. DOI: 10.1057/s41599-025-05861-1

KEY TERMS AND DEFINITIONS

Accessibility and Equity in Multimodal Legal Discourse: Accessibility and equity in legal discourse are achieved through inclusive design practices that ensure legal texts are understandable and usable for diverse audiences, including those with disabilities.

Intertextuality and Cultural Codes in Law: Intertextuality in legal texts means that meaning comes from references to laws, past court decisions, and cultural symbols like emblems or scales of justice. Recognising these references during translation is important to keep the legal message clear and valid across different languages and countries.

Multimodality in Legal Texts: It refers to the integration of various semiotic modes, i.e., textual, visual, spatial, and performative, within legal documents and digital platforms. This approach highlights how legal meaning is constructed through the interplay of these modes, which can affect interpretation, accessibility, and the negotiation of power and ideology.

Power and Ideology in Multimodal Legal Discourse: The interplay of visual, textual, and digital signs in legal discourse shapes power dynamics and ideological constructs, influencing how authority and legitimacy are perceived.

Semiotic and Multimodal Auditing in Translation Training: Integrating semiotic and multimodal auditing into legal translation training equips translators with the skills to identify, analyse, and adapt the visual and symbolic elements of legal texts.

Semiotic Auditing Framework: A semiotic auditing framework for legal translation is a systematic process that evaluates the semiotic elements (seals, emblems, typography, layout, and digital cues) of legal texts to ensure they accurately convey authority, legitimacy, and accessibility across different languages and cultures.

Semiotics in Legal Context: Semiotics in the legal domain involves analysing how signs, symbols, and visual elements convey meaning within legal texts, such as statutes, judgments, and contracts. This approach recognises that legal authority is not solely conveyed through language but also through visual and material cues that establish legitimacy and procedural norms across different jurisdictions.

Chapter 2
Legal Discourse Complexity:
A Genre-Informed Perspective on Teaching Legal Texts in EFL Contexts

Saber Alavi
http://orcid.org/0009-0009-0331-8229
Payap University, Thailand

Siripa Thanyaphaisan
http://orcid.org/0009-0004-8442-6750
Phuket Rajabhat University, Thailand

Maryam Alipour
http://orcid.org/0000-0002-7084-7114
Shinawatra University, Thailand

ABSTRACT

Legal discourse poses challenges for EFL learners, yet teaching-oriented studies rarely engage deeply with discourse complexity. Most approaches treat complexity as a barrier to remove rather than a phenomenon to understand. This chapter analyzes how complexity in legal discourse is negotiated through a genre-informed lens in EFL contexts. Using genre-based analysis of contracts, statutes, and case summaries, plus learner data from an EFL legal English classroom, it distinguishes potential complexity (text-internal features) from actualized complexity (learner errors). Findings show errors reveal which features are most opaque. The chapter reframes complexity as negotiated, not static, and positions the EFL classroom as a

DOI: 10.4018/979-8-3373-9179-3.ch002

site for observing meaning construction under partial knowledge. Genre-informed approaches engage with complexity without oversimplification, offering both theoretical and methodological contributions.

INTRODUCTION

The expansion of English as the dominant language of international law, arbitration, and commerce has generated increasing demand for legal literacy beyond law specialists (Northcott, 2008; Tessuto, 2011). Lawyers, corporate professionals, and EFL learners preparing for legal studies now require reading and interpretive competence in legal genres ranging from contracts to judicial opinions (Bhatia, 2023). This demand extends across civil and common law jurisdictions, where English functions as a lingua franca even in domestic legal contexts. Consequently, legal English pedagogy has emerged as a specialized domain within English for Specific Purposes (ESP), distinct from general academic English instruction (Sierocka, 2014). Unlike business or medical English, legal discourse is embedded in institutional practices and reasoning conventions that are not transparent to outsiders (Hoffman, 2011). This chapter addresses how genre-informed pedagogy can help EFL learners negotiate the particular complexities of legal texts.

Legal texts present multiple, interacting sources of difficulty for EFL learners (Alavi, 2024). At the syntactic level, legal English employs long nominal phrases, multiple embeddings, passive constructions, and conditional chains that exceed the complexity of general academic prose (Bhatia, 1983; Kim, 2018; Xu, 2020). Lexically, legal discourse is dense with specialized terminology, terms of art, archaic expressions, and Latinate phrases that rarely appear outside legal contexts (Voskanyan, 2018). Pragmatically, legal texts are constrained by institutional authority, intertextual dependence on statutes and precedents, and the need for precision that often overrides readability (Candlin et al., 2002). EFL learners struggle not only with individual vocabulary items but more fundamentally with discursive organization and meaning construction (Park, 2014). Research on L2 legal writing has documented persistent difficulties with modality interpretation (e.g., Wu et al., 2025b), embedded clause processing, and genre-appropriate reasoning (Kothalawala et al., 2023; Xu et al., 2023). These challenges suggest that legal English pedagogy requires more than vocabulary lists or grammar exercises.

EFL pedagogy for legal English has tended to focus on simplification and direct instruction rather than treating complexity as a discourse phenomenon. Bhatia (1983) distinguished between simplification, reducing textual complexity, and easification, providing pedagogical support while maintaining authentic texts, yet much classroom practice still favors the former. Candlin et al. (2002) critiqued legal writing materials that prioritize lexis and sentence patterns while neglecting genre structure and interpretive processes. Breeze (2015) demonstrated a corpus-driven approach to teaching legal vocabulary, showing that frequency-based selection can prioritize high-yield terms for learners, but cautioned that lexical instruction alone does not address syntactic or pragmatic complexity. Tessuto (2011) argued that legal English pedagogy often treats legal discourse as monolithic, ignoring jurisdictional variation and the specific conventions of genres such as the Legal Problem Question. Xu et al. (2023) observed that plain English instruction, while valuable for accessibility, may conflict with the syntactic elaboration expected in academic legal writing, a tension that pedagogical research has rarely addressed systematically. Girón García (2016) reported on online legal English instruction, noting that digital environments can support self-paced engagement with authentic texts but cannot replace mediated discussion of interpretive procedures. More broadly, Hoffman (2011) contended that legal English teaching remains under-theorized, relying on intuition rather than discourse analysis. While existing research has recognized that complexity is reader-dependent (e.g., the distinction between textual difficulty and learner difficulty), these insights have not been systematically applied to legal discourse in EFL contexts. What is missing is a framework that conceptualizes complexity not as a barrier to be removed but as a negotiated phenomenon that learner engagement can illuminate within the specific domain of legal English pedagogy.

Furthermore, the rapid digitization of legal practice means that EFL learners increasingly encounter legal texts not as static paper documents but as interactive digital artifacts: online contracts with click-to-accept interfaces, legislative databases with hyperlinked cross-references, and case law repositories with embedded headnotes and annotations. These multimodal and hypertextual environments (Alavi, 2026) introduce new dimensions of complexity, navigation, hyperlink integration, and screen-based reading, that are not addressed in traditional legal English materials. This chapter focuses on printed-style legal texts, but the implications for genre-informed pedagogy extend to digital contexts, where genre awareness may also help learners navigate non-linear document structures.

This chapter aims to analyze how complexity in legal discourse is structured and negotiated through a genre-informed lens in EFL contexts. It addresses three research questions:

1. How is complexity realized in selected legal genres (contracts, statutes, case summaries)?
2. How do EFL learners negotiate and interpret this complexity in comprehension and translation tasks?
3. How can genre analysis inform pedagogical mediation without resorting to oversimplification?

This chapter conceptualizes complexity as a discourse phenomenon, distinguishing linguistic features from interpretive processes. Legal Discourse and Genre examines legal discourse through genre theory, identifying sources of complexity across three genres. The Methodology section presents the research design, including data selection criteria and unit of analysis. Analysis: Complexity in Legal Texts analyzes complexity in legal texts themselves (potential complexity). Analysis: Negotiating Complexity in EFL Contexts analyzes how EFL learners negotiate that complexity (actualized complexity). Pedagogical Mediation derives analytical implications for pedagogical mediation. The Discussion section discusses theoretical contributions and limitations.

The chapter develops the theoretical and methodological framework necessary to analyze learner data; learner examples appear in Analysis: Negotiating Complexity in EFL Contexts. While this delay is intentional, the framework must be established first to interpret the data meaningfully, a brief preview may be helpful. Consider one example from the dataset analyzed in Analysis: Negotiating Complexity in EFL Contexts. An EFL learner, when asked to translate the contract phrase "the Seller shall replace the non-conforming goods", produced "the seller will replace the goods", substituting a future prediction for a binding obligation. This is not merely a grammar error; it reveals that the learner applied everyday English intuitions about shall (rare, old-fashioned, future-oriented) rather than the genre-specific legal interpretation (mandatory duty). This chapter argues that such errors are diagnostic data, not deficiencies to be corrected and forgotten. The following sections build the framework for analyzing such examples systematically.

CONCEPTUALIZING COMPLEXITY IN LEGAL DISCOURSE

Complexity in discourse is not a single measurable property but a constellation of linguistic features that interact with reader expertise, task demands, and genre expectations (Xu et al., 2023).

Operationalizing Complexity: Four Linguistic Dimensions

For the purposes of this chapter, complexity is operationalized across four linguistic dimensions. First, syntactic complexity refers to structural elaboration: subordination, embedding, passive constructions, and clause chaining that increase processing load (Kim, 2018). Second, lexical density encompasses specialized terminology, nominalization (turning processes into nouns), and low-frequency vocabulary that requires domain-specific knowledge. Third, modality and hedging involve the use of modal verbs (shall, may, must) and other markers of obligation, permission, or probability, which in legal contexts carry binding force (Kim, 2018). Fourth, ambiguity and indeterminacy arise when linguistic form underdetermines meaning, requiring interpretive principles to resolve (Bhatia, 2023). These dimensions are not exhaustive but provide a tractable framework for analyzing legal texts and learner engagement with them. Critically, complexity is not inherently problematic; it serves communicative purposes such as precision, authority, and contingency coverage (Candlin et al., 2002).

The Discursive Construction of Legal Complexity

Legal discourse is often described as inherently complex, but this claim risks circularity if complexity is treated as a mere label. The question is not whether legal language is complex but how that complexity is discursively constructed and institutionally maintained (Bhatia, 2023). Legal texts operate under a fundamental tension between precision and interpretability. Precision requires anticipating contingencies, covering all possible scenarios, and using consistent terminology. Interpretability requires that readers, judges, lawyers, clients, can actually determine what the text means. This tension is managed not through linguistic simplification but through specialized interpretive canons that constrain how ambiguity is resolved (Tessuto, 2011).

Legal-Linguistic Constraints as Interpretive Tools

Three legal-linguistic constraints illustrate this discursive construction. Contra proferentem is the principle that ambiguous clauses in a contract are interpreted against the drafter. This canon does not eliminate ambiguity but allocates its risk, thereby shaping how drafters write (Bhatia, 2023). Ejusdem generis (of the same kind) is a canon of statutory interpretation providing that general words following specific ones are interpreted as limited to the same class. This principle transforms what looks like vagueness into structured interpretive guidance. The canon against surplusage requires that every word in a legal text be given effect; no provision is treated as redundant (Hoffman, 2011). This canon forces readers to treat apparent repetition or unusual phrasing as meaningful, a significant source of complexity for EFL learners unfamiliar with the assumption.

These constraints demonstrate that legal complexity is not a failure of clarity but a product of institutionalized interpretive procedures. Legal texts are complex not because lawyers write poorly but because the legal system has developed specific tools for managing precision-interpretability trade-offs (Northcott, 2008).

A Discourse-Oriented Perspective on Meaning Construction

From a discourse-oriented perspective, meaning is not located solely in the text but is socially and institutionally constructed through interpretive practices (Bhatia, 2023). Legal texts do not carry fixed meanings that readers simply extract; rather, meanings are negotiated within the constraints of legal doctrine, precedent, and professional norms (Candlin et al., 2002; Northcott, 2013). This perspective shifts attention from decontextualized linguistic features to the interpretive procedures that readers use to resolve indeterminacy (Hafner & Candlin, 2007). For EFL learners, this means that comprehending a legal text requires more than vocabulary knowledge; it requires acculturation into the discourse community's ways of reading (Park, 2014; Shamonina & Kostova, 2025). Discourse analysis provides tools for making these interpretive procedures visible, including examination of cohesive devices, presuppositions, and intertextual references (Novikova et al., 2020). This chapter adopts this discourse-oriented stance, treating learner difficulties not as evidence of inadequate language proficiency (Alavi & Amini, 2026) alone but as windows into the interpretive demands of legal genres.

Beyond discourse analysis, research in second language acquisition and cognitive load theory provides complementary insights into why legal texts pose particular challenges for EFL learners. Lin et al. (2023) examined syntactic complexity in translated legal texts, demonstrating that even when lexical items are accessible, structural complexity independently increases processing difficulty. Litvishko et al. (2025) argued that English legal discourse is difficult to understand not primarily because of vocabulary but because of the interaction between syntactic elaboration, textual conventions, and reader expectations. From a cognitive load perspective, legal texts require learners to hold multiple conditional dependencies in working memory while simultaneously resolving lexical ambiguities and tracking genre-specific interpretive canons. This multi-factor processing demand distinguishes legal reading from general academic reading and suggests that pedagogical interventions must address not only linguistic knowledge but also cognitive strategies for managing competing demands.

Genre analysis provides a principled framework for mediating between the linguistic features of legal texts and the interpretive procedures required to understand them (Bhatia, 2023). Within the English for Specific Purposes tradition, genres are conceptualized as structured responses to recurring communicative purposes within discourse communities (Bhatia, 1993; Swales, 1990). This chapter assumes familiarity with foundational genre concepts: moves (functional units of rhetorical action), steps (strategies realizing moves), and the relationship between communicative purpose and lexico-grammatical realization (Kothalawala et al., 2023).

Genre analysis is particularly suited to legal discourse because legal genres are highly conventionalized. Contracts, statutes, and judicial opinions each follow predictable organizational patterns that reflect their distinct communicative purposes: binding agreements, prospective rules, and reasoned resolutions of disputes (Bhatia, 2023; Kim, 2018). As Hyland (2022) argued in his disciplinary variation framework, genre conventions are not merely stylistic preferences but respond to the epistemological and social practices of specific discourse communities. Legal English, medical English, and engineering English are not variations on a common academic template; they are fundamentally different discourse systems with distinct assumptions about evidence, authority, and argumentation. For the EFL learner, this means that genre knowledge acquired in one professional domain (e.g., business English) does not automatically transfer to legal contexts. Legal genre instruction must therefore attend to the specific interpretive conventions of legal discourse rather than assuming generic ESP strategies suffice.

Complexity as Negotiation of Meaning: A Refinement

Before proceeding, a terminological clarification is necessary. This chapter uses the term "negotiation" in two related but distinct senses. First, in legal interpretive practice, "negotiation" refers to the institutionalized procedures, such as canons of construction like contra proferentem and ejusdem generis, through which legal professionals resolve ambiguity and assign meaning to texts (Bhatia, 2023). Second, in EFL learner processing, "negotiation" refers to the adaptive strategies, simplification, rephrasing, omission, and metalinguistic repair, that learners deploy when encountering complexity, they cannot fully resolve (Hoffman, 2011). The first sense is normative and professional; the second is cognitive and developmental. The chapter's argument is that these two senses are not unrelated: learner breakdowns often occur precisely where the professional interpretive procedures have not yet been acquired. The distinction is maintained throughout the analysis: The Discursive Construction of Legal Complexity and Legal-Linguistic Constraints as Interpretive Tools focus on the professional sense; Analysis: Negotiating Complexity in EFL Contexts focuses on the learner sense.

The distinction proposed here is not entirely new. Applied linguistics has long recognized that difficulty is not a fixed property of texts. Corder (1967) distinguished between input (what is available to the learner) and intake (what is actually processed), while more recent work has distinguished textual complexity from learner difficulty (see review in Xu et al., 2023). What this chapter does is refine and apply this distinction to legal discourse, where it has not been systematically explored. Accordingly, this chapter proposes a refinement rather than a breakthrough: from treating complexity as a static property of texts to understanding it as negotiation of meaning between text, reader, and institutional context (Hafner & Candlin, 2007). The contribution lies in the contextual application and operationalization of this distinction within legal EFL pedagogy, not in the invention of a new construct.

From this perspective, what EFL pedagogy often calls "difficulty" is better understood as a breakdown in the interpretive procedures that legal readers use routinely. When an EFL learner misreads a modal verb, interpreting shall as a future tense marker rather than an obligation, this is not merely a grammar error. It reveals that the learner has not yet acquired the genre-specific interpretive convention that in legislative texts, shall signals a binding duty (Xu et al., 2023). Similarly, when a learner omits a subordinate clause in translation, this may indicate not laziness but an inability to hold the syntactic structure in working memory while resolving lexical ambiguities (Kothalawala et al., 2023).

Treating complexity as negotiation has three analytical advantages for this chapter. First, it directs attention to processes rather than products: to how learners engage with complexity, not just whether they get the right answer (Hoffman, 2011). Second, it reframes errors as evidence of the interpretive demands that legal texts impose, providing diagnostic information for pedagogical mediation (Candlin et al., 2002). Third, it positions the EFL classroom as a site for observing complexity in action, not merely delivering instruction (Northcott, 2008). Before turning to how learners negotiate complexity, it is necessary to examine the generic landscape of legal discourse itself. The following section identifies the characteristic features of legal language across genres, then focuses on three specific genres, contracts, statutes, and case summaries, to establish a typology of genre-specific complexity sources that will inform the analysis.

For the classroom teacher, the theoretical distinctions above have a practical implication: before deciding that a legal text is "too difficult" for EFL learners, analyze which dimension of complexity (syntactic, lexical, modal, or ambiguity) is causing the difficulty. A learner who misreads *shall* needs a different intervention than a learner who cannot track conditional chains. The remainder of this chapter demonstrates how to make this diagnostic distinction systematically.

Legal Discourse and Genre

Legal discourse exhibits several distinctive characteristics that distinguish it from general academic or professional English. Formality is evident across lexical, syntactic, and pragmatic levels: legal texts avoid colloquialisms, employ technical terminology, and adhere to prescribed textual conventions (Bhatia, 1983, 2023). Precision is a driving force behind many seemingly redundant features, definitions are spelled out exhaustively, modifiers are stacked to narrow reference, and synonyms are repeated to ensure coverage of all contingencies (Tessuto, 2011). This precision, however, creates constraint: legal language is designed to limit interpretive flexibility, binding readers to specific obligations or prohibitions (Northcott, 2008).

Repetition and redundancy are pervasive but serve identifiable functions. Formulaic expressions (e.g., null and void, terms and conditions) ensure consistent interpretation across contexts; restatements of the same concept in different words (e.g., give, devise, and bequeath) reflect historical layering of English, French, and Latin vocabulary (Voskanyan, 2018). Interdiscursivity, the mixing of genre conventions, is increasingly common as legal texts incorporate promotional, narrative, or explanatory elements (Kothalawala et al., 2023). These characteristics are not arbitrary; they respond to the institutional demands of legal practice, including the need for precedential stability, resistance to unilateral amendment, and accountability to multiple interpretive communities (Sierocka, 2014).

This chapter focuses on three legal genres selected for their prominence in EFL legal education and their distinct profiles of complexity: contracts, statutes, and case summaries. Contracts are legally binding agreements between parties, structured around offer, acceptance, consideration, and an array of boilerplate provisions (Alasmary, 2019). They are characterized by conditional logic (if X, then Y), performative language (hereby agrees), and extensive use of defined terms (Kothalawala et al., 2023). Statutes are legislative enactments that establish rules of general application. They exhibit high nominalization, obligatory modality (shall), and complex referencing patterns both internal (cross-references among sections) and external (to regulations or case law) (Kim, 2018). Case summaries (or judicial opinions) are retrospective accounts of disputes and their resolutions. They integrate narrative, procedural, and analytical discourse, moving between statements of fact, legal rules, and their application (Hoffman, 2011). These three genres represent a range of communicative purposes, binding private parties, governing public behavior, and justifying legal decisions, and therefore impose different interpretive demands on EFL readers.

Genre analysis identifies the rhetorical organization of legal texts in terms of moves (functional units) and steps (strategies within moves). This section provides a schematic overview of each genre's structure without offering an extended primer on genre theory (see Bhatia, 1993, 2023; Swales, 1990).

Contracts typically follow a recognizable structure: title and parties, recitals (background and intent), definitions, operative provisions (rights and obligations), representations and warranties, covenants, conditions, boilerplate clauses (e.g., governing law, dispute resolution), and signatures (Kothalawala et al., 2023). The communicative purpose is to create enforceable obligations; every move serves either to establish the scope of the agreement, to specify what parties must or must not do, or to allocate risk in case of breach (Alasmary, 2019).

Statutes follow a legislative macrostructure: title, preamble or purpose section, definitions, operative sections (often organized as a series of shall or may provisions), exceptions and qualifications, penalties or remedies, and administrative provisions (Kim, 2018). Unlike contracts, which bind specific parties, statutes address indefinite classes of actors; their rhetorical organization prioritizes general applicability and delegations of authority to administrative bodies (Northcott, 2008).

Case summaries (judicial opinions) exhibit a reasoning-oriented structure. In common law jurisdictions, the standard organization includes case caption, procedural history, statement of facts, legal issue(s), rule of law, application of rule to facts (analysis), holding, and disposition (Tessuto, 2011). This structure embodies the IRAC (Issue-Rule-Application-Conclusion) framework common in legal education, which teaches students to separate descriptive, prescriptive, and analytical discourse (Novikova et al., 2020).

Each legal genre generates complexity from different sources, reflecting its distinct communicative purpose. For EFL learners, recognizing these genre-specific patterns is a prerequisite for effective negotiation of meaning.

Clause chaining in contracts produces extreme syntactic complexity. Contracts frequently embed conditions within conditions, using multiple subordinate clauses linked by logical operators (provided that, subject to, notwithstanding, unless) (Candlin et al., 2002). A single contractual sentence may run several hundred words, containing a main clause, several conditional protases, and multiple exceptions. The complexity is functional: it allows drafters to specify precise sets of circumstances under which obligations arise, are suspended, or terminate (Alasmary, 2019).

Conditional logic in statutes operates differently. While statutes also use conditionals, their complexity lies in nested hierarchies of applicability. A statute may state a general rule (shall), then carve out exceptions, then provide exceptions to the exceptions, then specify which governmental actor has authority to determine whether an exception applies (Bhatia, 2023). This layered structure reflects legislative compromise and the need to balance general rules with special cases (Hoffman, 2011). EFL learners frequently misinterpret statutory conditionals by collapsing the hierarchy, treating an exception as the main rule, or missing the scope of a qualifying clause (Park, 2014).

Argumentation in case law presents a different order of complexity: not syntactic or lexical but rhetorical and inferential. Judicial opinions are retrospective justifications of decisions; they construct a coherent narrative from disputed facts, select which precedents are relevant, analogize or distinguish those precedents, and apply them to the case at hand (Novikova et al., 2020). The complexity lies in following the judge's reasoning path, which may include dicta (non-binding statements), dissents (alternative analyses), and reversals of lower court reasoning (Wu et al., 2025a; Wu et al, 2026). For EFL learners, case law complexity is not primarily about decoding long sentences but about reconstructing a chain of reasoning that is only partly explicit in the text.

METHODOLOGY

Research Design

This study adopts a qualitative, discourse-analytic research design. The objective is not to measure learner proficiency against a norm but to examine how complexity in legal discourse is realized textually and how EFL learners engage with that complexity through interpretation and translation (Hafner & Candlin, 2007). The design is exploratory and descriptive, prioritizing analytical depth over generalizability (Sierocka, 2014). Data consist of legal text excerpts and corresponding learner outputs, analyzed through the genre-based framework developed in Conceptualizing Complexity in Legal Discourse and Legal Discourse and Genre.

Data Selection

Legal texts were selected according to three criteria. First, text length is restricted to 200–400 words per excerpt. This range allows for meaningful analysis of genre structure and complexity features while remaining manageable for learner engagement in a single session (Kothalawala et al., 2023). Second, authenticity is maintained: texts are unaltered but excerpted from publicly available sources (contract templates, legislative databases, judicial opinion repositories). No pedagogical simplification or adaptation is applied, preserving the complexity features that are the object of analysis (Candlin et al., 2002). Third, no glosses are provided at initial exposure, ensuring that learner outputs reflect unassisted negotiation of complexity rather than mediated comprehension (Park, 2014).

Complexity features are divided into preselected and emergent categories. Preselected features, modal verbs (shall, may, must), conditional structures (if, provided that, unless), and nominalizations, are drawn from the operationalization in Operationalizing Complexity: Four Linguistic Dimensions (Bhatia, 2023). Emergent features are identified inductively during analysis (e.g., unusual anaphoric references, intertextual signals). Learner outputs consist of written interpretations (open-ended comprehension responses), translations (into the learner's L1), and summaries (condensed restatements of content). These three output types capture different levels of interpretive engagement (Tessuto, 2011).

Analytical Framework

The analytical framework integrates genre-based analysis (Bhatia, 2023) with the complexity indicators operationalized in terms of syntactic embedding, lexical density/nominalization, modality/hedging, ambiguity/indeterminacy. Genre analysis provides the macrostructure for identifying communicative purposes and move structures. Complexity indicators provide the microstructure for locating specific features that pose interpretive challenges for EFL learners (Alavi, 2024). The framework is applied consistently across all three legal genres examined.

Data Collection Context

Data were collected in an EFL classroom setting at the university level, with learners enrolled in a legal English course as part of an international law program. The instructional context is not treated as a site for evaluating teaching effectiveness but as an observational context for documenting how learners negotiate complexity when encountering authentic legal texts (Northcott, 2008). Learners are advanced EFL speakers (CEFR B2–C1) with foundational knowledge of legal concepts in their L1 but limited prior exposure to English legal genres. Tasks were administered individually under timed conditions (30 minutes per text excerpt) to capture initial interpretive responses rather than polished, edited outputs (Park, 2014). The researcher was present to give task instructions but did not provide linguistic or conceptual support during the task, ensuring that outputs reflect unassisted learner negotiation (Sierocka, 2014). Translation has been underexploited as a diagnostic tool in legal English pedagogy, yet recent work in translation studies offers frameworks for analyzing learner outputs systematically. He et al. (2024) applied Juliane House's Translation Quality Assessment model to literary translation, demonstrating that shifts in modality, cohesion, and register provide evidence of interpretive decision-making. Wan et al. (2018) identified recurring problems in English translations of short stories, including omission of embedded clauses and simplification of logical relationships, patterns that closely mirror the learner errors documented in Analysis: Negotiating Complexity in EFL Contexts of this chapter. Wang et al. (2025) further systematized the analysis of translation strategies, errors, and challenges, offering a typology that distinguishes between obligatory shifts (required by L1-L2 structural differences) and optional shifts (reflecting translator choice). This chapter adopts an adapted version of this typology in Translation as Evidence of Negotiation, treating translation not as an exercise in fidelity but as a window into how learners negotiate legal complexity under conditions of partial knowledge.

Analytical Procedures

Unit of analysis is specified at three levels, each aligned to a different dimension of complexity. At the clause level, syntactic complexity, embedding, subordination, clause chaining, is analyzed (Kim, 2018). At the move level, genre structure, functional units within each legal genre, is identified following the schemas in Legal Discourse and Genre Section (Kothalawala et al., 2023). At the learner output level, each interpretation, translation, or summary is treated as a record of negotiation, preserving both successful comprehension and points of breakdown (Hafner & Candlin, 2007). Analytical procedures follow four steps:

a) Identify genre structure of each legal text excerpt, mapping clauses to moves (e.g., operative provision, definition, exception) using the genre schemas established in Legal Discourse and Genre Section.
b) Locate complexity features within each move, distinguishing preselected features (modals, conditionals, nominalizations) from emergent features identified during close reading.
c) Align each text feature with learner output, comparing the original text's linguistic realization to the learner's interpretation, translation, or summary. Alignment is performed at the clause level for syntax and at the move level for genre structure (Candlin et al., 2002).
d) Analyze mismatch patterns where learner output diverges from plausible expert reading, categorizing mismatches by type (modality error, conditional misreading, omitted embedding, genre misidentification) (Kothalawala et al., 2023).

Table 1. Illustration of alignment analysis (sample learner outputs)

Original Text Feature	Learner Output	Alignment Analysis	Mismatch Type
***"The Seller shall, at the Buyer's option, either (i) replace... or (ii) refund..."* (contract, obligation)**	*"The seller will replace the goods or give a refund."*	Learner omitted the Buyer's option and changed *shall* (obligation) to *will* (future prediction).	Modality error + omission
***"For the purposes of this Act, 'undue influence' means the improper exercise of any form of persuasion, pressure, or control..."* (statute, definition)**	*"Undue influence means wrongly forcing someone to agree."*	Learner captured core meaning but lost the three-part legal categorization (*persuasion/pressure/control*).	Lexical simplification (loss of precision)
***"Provided that the Buyer has given written notice... and provided further that the non-conformity substantially impairs the value..."* (contract, conditional chain)**	*"The buyer gives notice within 14 days. The goods have a serious problem. Then the seller will replace."*	Learner broke the long sentence into three independent clauses but lost the dependency structure (both conditions required).	Conditional misreading (AND → implied sequence)

This table demonstrates how alignment moves from text feature to learner output to mismatch categorization. Without such illustration, readers must rely on the author's interpretations alone. The examples above are representative of the patterns discussed in Analysis: Negotiating Complexity in EFL Contexts Section.

ANALYSIS

Complexity in Legal Texts

This section establishes potential complexity; the linguistic description of text-internal features that may pose interpretive challenges for EFL learners. It does not assume that all identified features will cause difficulty; rather, it provides the textual baseline against which learner negotiation (Analysis: Negotiating Complexity in EFL Contexts Section) will be analyzed. Each subsection draws on authentic excerpts from the three focal genres: contracts, statutes, and case summaries.

Syntactic Complexity

Syntactic complexity in legal discourse is most visibly realized through long sentences and embedding. Bhatia (1983) noted that legal sentences routinely exceed fifty words, with some extending to several hundred. This length is not stylistic excess; it serves the functional need to specify conditions, exceptions, and qualifications within a single syntactic unit, avoiding fragmentation that might create unintended gaps in coverage (Kim, 2018).

A typical commercial contract's operative provision illustrates this syntactic configuration. Such provisions commonly delay the main obligation, for example, a seller's duty to replace non-conforming goods or refund the purchase price, by first establishing conditions precedent: the buyer must have given written notice of non-conformity within a specified timeframe, and the non-conformity must substantially impair the goods' value. The main clause then presents alternatives, each with additional temporal and qualificatory phrases, such as the timeframe for performance and any deductions attributable to the buyer's prior use of the goods.

Clause-level analysis reveals multiple layers of embedding. The main clause (the Seller shall...) is delayed by two conditional protases (*Provided that..., provided further that...*). Each protasis contains its own embedded structures: the first includes a temporal clause, the second a causal-condition clause. The main clause then presents two alternatives, each with additional temporal and qualificatory phrases (Bhatia, 2023).

This syntactic configuration creates processing demands. The reader must retain the main clause's obligation (the Seller shall) through two conditions, then manage a binary choice between replacement and refund, each with distinct cost allocations and timeframes (Kothalawala et al., 2023). Statutory syntax follows similar patterns but with nested hierarchies of applicability (Kim, 2018). Case law, while generally less syntactically dense than contracts or statutes, exhibits embedding in statements of legal rules, where multiple precedents are cited within a single long sentence (Tessuto, 2011).

Lexical Density and Terminology

Lexical complexity in legal texts operates through two interconnected phenomena: specialized terminology (terms of art) and nominalization (transforming processes into nouns). It has been documented that the high frequency of low-occurrence legal terms in judicial case reports, noting that terms such as *apprehend*, *purport*, and *whereas* carry specialized meanings distinct from their everyday usage.

A typical statutory definition illustrates these features. Consider how a statute might define a concept such as "undue influence." The definition would characteristically pack multiple legal constraints into a single sentence: the improper exercise of persuasion, pressure, or control; the impairment of independent judgment; and mental state categories such as intentional, reckless, or negligent conduct. The definition operates through a tripartite formula, a substantial impairment threshold, and multiple qualifying conditions.

Lexical density is evident in the concentration of content words per clause. The definition compresses multiple legal constraints into a dense nominal structure: improper exercise, persuasion/pressure/control (a tripartite formula), independent judgment, substantially impaired, and the three mental state categories (intentionally, recklessly, negligently) (Voskanyan, 2018).

Nominalization compounds this density. Where everyday English would use verbs (*to influence, to persuade, to control*), legal texts nominalize (*exercise* becomes a noun, *persuasion* stands for the act of persuading). Bhatia (2023) observed that nominalization serves two functions: it allows precise modification (e.g., *improper exercise* vs. *exercise improperly*) and it reifies actions as stable legal categories. For the EFL learner, however, nominalization obscures agency and temporality, it becomes unclear who did what to whom and when (Candlin et al., 2002).

Case law presents different lexical demands. Judicial opinions use specialized terms of argumentation (*analogous, distinguishable, dicta, holding, overruled*) that are rare outside legal discourse (Novikova et al., 2020). These terms are not definitions that can be memorized in isolation; they function relationally within a network of precedent-based reasoning (Xu et al., 2023).

Ambiguity and Modality

Paradoxically, legal texts designed for precision also generate ambiguity, not as a flaw but as a structured feature that interpretive canons are designed to resolve (Bhatia, 2023). Modal verbs are a primary site of this tension. In legal English, *shall*, *may*, and *must* carry specific deontic meanings that differ from their everyday usage.

Consider a typical contract containing three modal constructions: a representation clause where the seller warrants that goods *shall* conform to specifications, an inspection clause stating that the buyer *may* inspect prior to delivery, and a notice provision requiring that the carrier *must* provide notice of damage within a specified period. Each modal carries a distinct legal force.

Under standard legal interpretation, *shall* signals a mandatory obligation: the Seller has no discretion (Kim, 2018). *May* signals permission or discretion: the Buyer may choose to inspect or not (Alasmary, 2019). *Must* signals an absolute requirement, often with penalties for non-compliance (Xu et al., 2023). For the EFL learner, however, these distinctions are non-transparent. In everyday English, *shall* is rare (except for suggestions: *Shall we go?*); *must* often expresses strong advice rather than legal duty; *may* expresses possibility rather than permission (Park, 2014). Filipović (2016) demonstrated experimentally that non-native English speakers systematically misinterpret the evidential and deontic force of modal verbs like *may* and *might*, with measurable consequences for legal judgment. Her findings suggest that even advanced EFL learners may not infer the same degree of obligation or permission as native readers, a gap that persists even when learners can correctly define the modals in isolation.

Statutory modality introduces further complexity. Legislative texts frequently use *shall* to impose duties on public officials, but interpretive canons may convert *shall* to *may* in certain contexts (e.g., when the duty is owed to the public rather than an identifiable individual) (Bhatia, 2023). This context-sensitivity means that modality in legal texts cannot be read off the modal verb alone; the reader must apply genre-specific interpretive principles.

Case law modulates modality differently. Judicial opinions use *may* to indicate holdings that are not binding precedent (*dicta*), *should* to suggest preferred interpretations, and *must* to indicate logical entailments from established rules (Novikova et al., 2020). For the EFL learner, tracking these evidential distinctions across a single opinion is cognitively demanding (Xu et al., 2023).

Genre-Specific Patterns

While all three genres exhibit syntactic, lexical, and modal complexity, the profile of complexity differs systematically. This subsection provides a contrastive overview, not an exhaustive inventory.

Table 2. Genre-specific complexity profiles across contracts, statutes, and case summaries

Complexity Dimension	Contracts	Statutes	Case Summaries
Syntactic	Clause chaining with multiple conditions and exceptions	Nested hierarchies of applicability	Moderate, argument structure, not clause length
Lexical	Defined terms, performance verbs (warrant, indemnify)	Abstract categories, delegations of authority	Precedent terminology (distinguish, overrule, analogize)
Modal	*Shall* (obligation), *may* (discretion)	*Shall* (binding duty), *may* (agency authorization)	*May* (possibility), *must* (logical necessity)
Primary interpretive demand	Tracking condition-obligation dependencies	Reconstructing layer-cake applicability	Following analogical reasoning chain

Contracts prioritize condition-obligation dependencies. The reader must track which obligations are triggered by which conditions, and how exceptions modify those triggers (Bhatia, 2023). Failure to manage these dependencies, holding an obligation as absolute when it is conditional, constitutes a major error in legal reading (Wu et al., 2025a).

Statutes prioritize hierarchical applicability. A statutory provision may state a general rule, then carve out exceptions, then qualify those exceptions, then specify which administrative body has authority to determine whether an exception applies (Kim, 2018). The reader must reconstruct this hierarchy without visual aids (indentation, numbering). EFL learners frequently collapse the hierarchy, treating an exception as canceling the rule entirely rather than limiting its scope (Park, 2014).

Case summaries prioritize analogical reasoning chain. Unlike contracts and statutes, which are prescriptive (telling readers what to do), case law is justificatory (explaining why a decision was reached) (Tessuto, 2011). The reader must follow the court's reasoning from facts to rule to application, attending to which precedents are treated as binding, which are distinguished, and which are overruled (Shamonina & Kostova, 2025). Syntactic complexity in case law is generally lower than in contracts or statutes, but the inferential load is higher: the reader must supply missing premises and evaluate analogical mappings (Hafner & Candlin, 2007).

These genre-specific patterns establish the potential complexity baseline. The section Analysis: Negotiating Complexity in EFL Contexts examines how EFL learners actually negotiate these features, identifying points of successful engagement and recurring breakdown.

Negotiating Complexity in EFL Context

This section analyzes actualized complexity; how EFL learners engage with, misinterpret, repair, or circumvent the complexity features identified in Analysis: Complexity in Legal Texts Section. Given the small dataset (n=15) and the specific instructional context, the following findings are presented as exploratory illustrations of how complexity negotiation can be observed, not as statistically generalizable claims. The patterns reported below are intended to generate hypotheses for future research rather than to establish population-level prevalence.

Learner Interpretation Strategies

When confronted with authentic legal texts, EFL learners in this study deployed three recurrent interpretive strategies: simplification, rephrasing, and omission. These strategies are not errors per se but adaptive responses to processing overload.

Simplification involved reducing syntactic complexity by breaking long sentences into shorter independent clauses. For the contract excerpt in 5.1 (the conditional obligation chain), one learner wrote: *"The buyer must give notice within 14 days. The goods must have a serious problem. Then the seller will replace the goods or give a refund."* This response preserves the core conditional logic but loses the temporal precision (*within thirty days of receiving such notice*) and the cost allocation (*at the*

Seller's expense). Simplification trades precision for comprehensibility, a rational trade-off in unassisted reading but a potential source of legal risk in professional contexts (Xu et al., 2023).

Rephrasing involved substituting everyday vocabulary for legal terminology. For the statutory definition in 5.2 (*undue influence*), one learner rephrased *"improper exercise of any form of persuasion, pressure, or control"* as *"wrongly forcing someone to agree."* This rephrasing captures the core meaning but loses the three-part categorization (*persuasion/pressure/control*) that has specific legal significance in case law (Voskanyan, 2018).

Omission was the most common strategy when learners encountered features they could not resolve. In the contract excerpt, six of fifteen learners omitted the phrase *"less any amount attributable to the Buyer's use of the goods prior to notice"* entirely from their summaries. Omission is not laziness; it reflects cognitive triage when working memory is exceeded. These strategies will be revisited in Section Translation as Evidence of Negotiation through translation data.

Points of Breakdown

Beyond adaptive strategies, learners exhibited systematic points of breakdown, features where interpretation diverged from plausible expert readings (Hoffman, 2011). Two categories predominated: misinterpretation of modality and misreading of embedded clauses.

Misinterpretation of modality was most pronounced for *shall*. In the statute excerpt from section Ambiguity and Modality, the provision stated: *"The carrier must provide notice of any damage within seven days."* In this sample, eight of fifteen learners interpreted *must* as a strong suggestion rather than an absolute requirement, suggesting a pattern worth investigating. This tentative pattern aligns with Xu et al.'s (2023) finding that plain English instruction may inadvertently weaken learners' sensitivity to deontic modality in legal texts. For *may*, misinterpretation ran in the opposite direction: four learners read *"The Buyer may inspect the goods prior to delivery"* as *"The buyer must inspect"*, confusing permission with obligation (Bhatia, 2023).

Misreading of embedded clauses occurred most frequently in the statute excerpt's hierarchical structure (section Genre-Specific Patterns). The original text presented a general rule, an exception, and a qualification of that exception. However, only three of fifteen learners accurately reconstructed this hierarchy. The majority collapsed it, producing interpretations such as "The rule does not apply." The correct reading was more nuanced: "The rule applies except in specified circumstances, and those circumstances are further limited" (Tessuto, 2011). One learner's response is particularly revealing: *"First it says X, then it says not X, so I don't know which one is the law.*" This comment explicitly names the breakdown, the learner recognized the contradiction but lacked the genre-specific interpretive framework (hierarchical reading, canon against surplusage) to resolve it (Hoffman, 2011).

Translation as Evidence of Negotiation

Translation from English into the learner's L1 provided the richest evidence of negotiation because it forces explicit decisions that paraphrasing can avoid. Where a summary might gloss over ambiguity, a translation must commit to a specific reading (Kothalawala et al., 2023).

Shifts in meaning were most evident in translations of modal verbs. For the contract excerpt's *shall* (Ambiguity and Modality), six learners used a future tense marker in their L1 rather than an obligation marker. This shift changes the legal effect: a future prediction (*the seller will do X*) is not a binding promise (*the seller shall do X*). When asked to explain their choice in a debriefing, these learners reported that *shall* "feels old-fashioned" or "looks like future", importing everyday English intuitions into legal reading (Kim, 2018).

Loss of precision occurred systematically in the translation of conditional chains (Section Syntactic Complexity). The contract excerpt's two *provided that* clauses and their relationship to the main clause were frequently collapsed. One learner translated both conditions as simple *if* clauses attached to the same verb, losing the dependency structure entirely. The original text specified that *replacement* is contingent on both conditions; the learner's translation made replacement contingent on either condition, a legally material difference (Alasmary, 2019).

Gain of precision was rare but instructive. Two learners added explicit logical connectives in their L1 translations that were absent in the English original, inserting *"only if"* to clarify a conditional relationship, or adding *"respectively"* to disambiguate a paired list. These additions suggest that these learners had developed metalinguistic awareness of ambiguity and were actively repairing it (Hoffman, 2011). Rather than merely reproducing English syntax, they were constructing meaning for a target legal audience in their L1.

This "gain of precision" finding is theoretically significant because it reverses the typical direction of analysis in learner translation research. Most studies (including earlier sections of this chapter) focus on loss, omission, or distortion, what learners cannot do. The gain of precision phenomenon, however, shows learners adding interpretive structure that the original text lacks. Two observations are worth highlighting.

First, both learners who gained precision added logical connectives that made conditional or sequential relationships explicit. In the original English contract, the conditional relationship between notice, non-conformity, and replacement was signaled through syntactic embedding (clause chaining) rather than explicit logical markers like "only if." The learners' insertion of "only if" suggests they recognized the logical dependency but found the English syntax insufficiently transparent for their L1 legal audience. This is not a failure of comprehension but a metalinguistic repair.

Second, these learners were not the most proficient in the cohort by standardized measures (both were B2, not C1). This suggests that metalinguistic awareness, the ability to reflect on ambiguity and repair it, may be partially independent of overall language proficiency. Learners who actively construct meaning for an audience may develop different skills than learners who focus on decoding the text for themselves. This hypothesis requires further research but opens a new direction for pedagogy: training learners to translate for a target audience, not just for comprehension checks.

The gain of precision finding thus offers diagnostic insight that error analysis alone cannot provide. It reveals not only what learners know (they recognized a logical dependency) but also what they value (precision for a legal audience). Future research should examine whether such metalinguistic repair can be cultivated through explicit instruction.

Role of Genre Awareness

This subsection reports a finding that emerged from the data, not a pre-existing claim. Learners were not systematically trained in genre analysis prior to the task, but a subset (n=5 of 15) had previously completed a short module on legal genre structure in a different course. Their performance was compared to learners without such exposure (n=10). It should be noted that this comparison involves unequal group sizes (n=5 vs. n=10) and potential confounding variables (e.g., learners with genre exposure may have differed in prior legal knowledge or motivation). The following observations are therefore presented as exploratory rather than conclusive, and future research with balanced groups is needed to validate these patterns. The comparison reveals differential outcomes related to genre awareness (Tessuto, 2011).

Within this exploratory dataset, learners with genre-structure labels (e.g., "operative provision," "definition," "exception clause," "holding") showed two tentative advantages. First, they identified the locus of obligation more accurately in the contract excerpt. When reading the contract excerpt (5.1), all five genre-aware learners correctly located the main obligation in the *Seller shall* clause, whereas five of ten genre-unaware learners focused on the conditional protases as if they contained the primary obligation (Sierocka, 2014).

Second, genre-aware learners were more likely to flag unresolved ambiguity rather than guess in their written responses. In the statute excerpt (section Ambiguity and Modality), three of five genre-aware learners explicitly noted in their responses: *"The exception and the rule seem to conflict, I would need to know which canon applies"* or *"This section delegates authority but does not specify the procedure."* No genre-unaware learner produced such metalinguistic comments (Shamonina & Kostova, 2025).

However, genre awareness did not eliminate modality misinterpretation. Even genre-aware learners misread *shall* as future tense at rates similar to their unaware peers. These tentative observations suggest that genre knowledge supports macro-structural comprehension (move identification) but does not automatically transfer to lexico-grammatical precision (modal interpretation) (Xu et al., 2023). Nevertheless, given the small and unequal groups (n=5 vs. n=10), these observations require replication with larger, balanced samples before firm conclusions can be drawn.

What does learner behavior reveal about legal discourse complexity itself? Three insights emerge from the analysis above.

First, complexity is not a uniform barrier but a layered phenomenon. Learners successfully negotiated some features (e.g., identifying main clauses) while breaking down on others (e.g., modality, hierarchical conditionals). This dissociation suggests that different dimensions of complexity, syntactic, lexical, modal, impose different cognitive demands and may require different pedagogical responses (Bhatia, 1983).

Second, learner errors are diagnostically informative. A learner who collapses a conditional hierarchy is not simply "wrong"; she is revealing that the text's logical structure is not transparent to a reader without legal-interpretive training (Park, 2014). The error points to a specific gap in genre-specific interpretive procedures, not a general deficit in language proficiency (Hafner & Candlin, 2007).

Third, negotiation is not binary (success vs. failure). Learners who omitted challenging clauses, rephrased imprecisely, or added logical connectives were actively constructing meaning, not passively failing. The translation data (section Translation as Evidence of Negotiation) showed learners making trade-offs between precision and comprehensibility, trade-offs that expert legal readers also make, albeit with different resources (Tessuto, 2011).

These findings, together with the genre-awareness comparison (section Role of Genre Awareness), suggest that complexity in legal discourse is not an obstacle to be removed but a feature to be mediated. The section on Pedagogical Mediation will explore what kind of pedagogical mediation, analytical, not prescriptive, follows from this view.

PEDAGOGICAL MEDIATION

From Teaching to Mediation

The findings in Sections Analysis: Complexity in Legal Texts and Analysis: Negotiating Complexity in EFL Contexts support a reconceptualization of the teacher's role in legal English instruction: not as a transmitter of simplified content but as a mediator of discourse complexity (Hoffman, 2011). The term "mediation" is chosen deliberately to distinguish this role from traditional pedagogical functions. Where teaching implies transmission of established knowledge, mediation implies facilitating learners' engagement with authentic texts while making visible the interpretive procedures that expert readers deploy automatically (Northcott, 2008).

This reconceptualization treats the pedagogy as a research site rather than merely a delivery mechanism (Sierocka, 2014). The learner errors and strategies documented in Section Analysis: Negotiating Complexity in EFL Contexts are not evidence of failed instruction but data about how complexity operates in real-time interpretive contexts (Park, 2014). From this perspective, the classroom becomes a setting for observing the gap between text-internal complexity (Section Analysis: Complexity in Legal Texts) and learner negotiation (Section Analysis: Negotiating Complexity in EFL Contexts), and for identifying which aspects of genre-specific interpretive competence are most opaque to learners (Tessuto, 2011). Mediation, therefore, is not about eliminating difficulty but about providing principled access to it.

A critical perspective raised by Flowerdew (2011) warrants acknowledgment. The ESP tradition, while excellent at describing text structure, tends to treat genres as neutral objects, focusing on helping learners master the conventions of professional genres without questioning whether those conventions are fair, accessible, or serve whose interests. Legal genres are not neutral; they are products of institutional power structures that may systematically disadvantage non-native readers. This chapter does not resolve this tension, but it acknowledges that teaching EFL learners to negotiate legal complexity involves more than skill transmission. It also involves making visible the power asymmetries embedded in legal discourse, for instance, that contracts are typically drafted by one party (the offeror) and impose interpretive burdens on the other, or that statutory language reflects legislative compromises that may not be democratically accountable. Future research should examine whether genre-informed pedagogy can simultaneously develop interpretive competence and critical awareness of legal discourse as a site of institutional power.

What Learner Negotiation Data Implies for Instructional Design

Methodological guardrail: Each principle below is directly traceable to a finding in Sections Analysis: Complexity in Legal Texts or Analysis: Negotiating Complexity in EFL Contexts; none is presented as a validated teaching technique. These are analytical implications, not prescriptive recommendations.

Principle 1: Making Genre Structure Visible as an Interpretive Tool (Traceable to Sections Genre-Specific Patterns and Role of Genre Awareness).

The genre-aware learners in Section Role of Genre Awareness demonstrated improved ability to locate the locus of obligation in contracts and to flag unresolved ambiguity in statutes. This finding implies that explicit visual mapping of genre structure, distinguishing operative provisions from definitions, exceptions, and boilerplate, may reduce the cognitive load of macro-structural orientation. The implication is not that teachers should provide genre taxonomies to memorize, but that learners benefit from seeing how move identification (e.g., "this is an exception clause, not the main rule") constrains interpretive possibilities (Bhatia, 2023). The data show that genre-unaware learners collapsed hierarchical structures (Section Points of Breakdown) not because they lacked language proficiency but because they lacked a framework for distinguishing rule from exception. Making genre structure visible addresses that specific gap.

Principle 2: Focusing Instruction on Points of Recurrent Breakdown (Traceable to Section Analysis: Negotiating Complexity in EFL Contexts).

The data identify three features as recurrent breakdown points: modality (especially *shall* vs. *may* vs. *must*), embedded conditional hierarchies, and the distinction between rule and exception in statutes. These features are not obscure or marginal; they appear in every legal genre examined. The implication is that pedagogical mediation should prioritize these high-leverage features over exhaustive coverage of legal vocabulary. Learners who misread *shall* as future tense (Section Translation as Evidence of Negotiation) do not need more vocabulary lists; they need explicit contrastive work on the deontic function of modals in legal versus everyday registers (Xu et al., 2023). Similarly, learners who collapse conditional hierarchies (Section Points of Breakdown) need practice in mapping condition-obligation dependencies, a skill that transfers across contracts and statutes. The implication is not to drill grammar but to design tasks that require learners to track dependencies across clause boundaries.

Principle 3: Using Translation as Diagnostic Evidence (Traceable to Section Analysis: Negotiating Complexity in EFL Contexts)

Translation forced explicit decisions that paraphrasing did not. Learners who could produce a coherent English summary still produced translations that revealed modality errors or omitted clauses. The implication is that translation into the L1 functions as a diagnostic tool for surfacing interpretive gaps that comprehension questions may miss (Kothalawala et al., 2023). This is not an argument for grammar-translation pedagogy (Alavi et al., 2026) but for using translation as occasional evidence, not exercise. The data show that translation reveals the learner's interpretive commitment in ways that multiple-choice or open-ended comprehension questions do not. Mediation, therefore, can include structured comparison between learner translations and expert translations to make visible what was lost, added, or shifted (Novikova et al., 2020). Taken together, these three principles, making genre structure visible, focusing on recurrent breakdown points, and using translation diagnostically, share a common orientation: they treat learner errors as data rather than deficits, and they prioritize authentic texts over simplified ones. This orientation has broader implications for how legal English pedagogy is conceptualized in EFL contexts, to which Section Implications for EFL Contexts now turns.

Implications for EFL Contexts

The three principles above converge on a broader implication for legal English pedagogy in EFL contexts: developing interpretive competence requires different priorities from general English instruction.

First, interpretive competence is genre-specific. Learning to read contracts does not fully transfer to reading statutes or case law (Section Genre-Specific Patterns). EFL programs must decide which genres are most relevant to learners' target professional contexts and focus mediation accordingly (Sierocka, 2014). Second, interpretive competence requires tolerating unresolved ambiguity. In Section Role of Genre Awareness, genre-aware learners flagged ambiguities they could not resolve; genre-unaware learners guessed or omitted. The ability to recognize ambiguity as ambiguity, rather than as incomprehensibility, is a professional skill that can be mediated (Shamonina & Kostova, 2025).

Third, and most critically, avoiding oversimplification is not a luxury but a necessity. Simplified texts (Bhatia's 1983 critique) remove the very features, conditional chains, modal distinctions, nested exceptions, that learners need to learn to negotiate.

The data show that learners can engage with authentic complexity, albeit with gaps and errors. The goal of mediation is not to eliminate those gaps but to make them visible and systematic (Xu et al., 2023). Oversimplification forecloses that diagnostic opportunity. EFL legal English instruction, therefore, should prioritize authenticity of text over completeness of learner comprehension, trusting that partial, effortful negotiation is more educative than flawless performance on simplified materials.

From Principles to Practice: Sample Classroom Tasks

The three principles articulated in Section What Learner Negotiation Data Implies for Instructional Design, making genre structure visible, focusing on recurrent breakdown points, and using translation as diagnostic evidence, require concrete instantiation in classroom materials. Below are three sample tasks, each derived directly from a finding in Sections Analysis: Complexity in Legal Texts and Analysis: Negotiating Complexity in EFL Contexts. These are not prescriptive curricula but illustrative examples of how mediation can be operationalized.

The tasks below assume familiarity with basic genre concepts (moves, steps, communicative purpose). Instructors who are new to genre theory need not master the full framework before using these tasks. The following minimal scaffolding is sufficient:

Move = a functional unit of a text that serves a specific purpose (e.g., "defining a term," "stating an obligation," "carving out an exception").

Genre = a conventionalized text type (contract, statute, case summary) with predictable moves.

Genre awareness = recognizing which move a passage belongs to, which constrains how it should be interpreted.

For instructors who wish to deepen their genre knowledge, foundational sources include Swales (1990) and Bhatia (1983, 2023). However, the tasks below can be implemented using only the move labels provided in each task (e.g., "operative provision," "definition," "exception"). The key insight, that legal texts are not random but organized, does not require full genre theory training.

Task 1: Genre Mapping (traceable to Sections Genre-Specific and Patterns Role of Genre Awareness)

Goal: Help learners distinguish operative provisions from definitions, exceptions, and boilerplate.

Materials: An unmodified contract excerpt (200-300 words) with move boundaries obscured.

Procedure: Provide learners with a list of move labels (e.g., "operative obligation," "definition," "exception," "condition precedent," "boilerplate"). Ask them to draw boxes around each move and label it. Then, provide a color-coded expert version for comparison. Debrief by asking: *"How did you know where the exception ended and the main rule resumed?"*

Diagnostic use: Learners who place exception language inside the operative obligation box reveal a failure to distinguish rule from exception, a pattern documented in Section Points of Breakdown.

Task 2: Modal Contrastive Analysis (traceable to Sections Ambiguity and Modality and Points of Breakdown)

Goal: Develop sensitivity to legal modality (*shall* vs. *may* vs. *must*).

Materials: Three parallel sentences showing the same action expressed with different modals:

The buyer shall inspect the goods within seven days.

The buyer may inspect the goods within seven days.

The buyer must inspect the goods within seven days.

Procedure: Ask learners to translate each sentence into their L1, then compare translations. Facilitate a discussion: *"What is the legal consequence if the buyer does not inspect?"* (Shall = breach; May = no consequence; Must = absolute requirement, often with penalty). Then, ask learners to write a fourth sentence using a different modal and exchange with a peer, who must identify the legal effect.

Diagnostic use: Learners who translate *shall* as future tense (Section Translation as Evidence of Negotiation) benefit from explicit contrast between legal and everyday registers.

Task 3: Translation for Two Audiences (traceable to Section Translation as Evidence of Negotiation)

Goal: Develop metalinguistic awareness and audience-sensitive translation.

Materials: A conditional chain from a contract (e.g., the excerpt in Section Syntactic Complexity).

Procedure: First, ask learners to translate the excerpt for themselves (comprehension check). Second, ask them to translate the same excerpt for a legal client who needs to know their exact obligation. Then, compare the two translations. Ask: *"What did you add, omit, or change for the client version? Why?"*

Diagnostic use: Learners who add logical connectives (e.g., "only if") in the client version are demonstrating metalinguistic repair. Learners who produce identical translations may need support in audience awareness.

Task 4: Error as Data (traceable to Sections Points of Breakdown and Role of Genre Awareness)

Goal: Reframe errors as diagnostic evidence for both teacher and learner.

Materials: Anonymous learner errors drawn from the class (or from the examples in Section Analysis: Negotiating Complexity in EFL Contexts).

Procedure: Present an error (e.g., *"The seller will replace the goods"* for *"The seller shall replace the goods"*). Ask learners: *"What would this error mean in a real contract? Would it be enforceable?"* Then ask: *"What might the learner have been thinking?"* Facilitate a discussion that treats the error as a window into interpretive procedures, not as a mistake to be ashamed of.

Diagnostic use: This task shifts classroom culture (Wang et al., 2026) from error avoidance to error analysis, aligning with the theoretical stance of Section Complexity as Negotiation of Meaning: A Refinement.

These tasks are not exhaustive. They are designed to show how the analytical findings in Sections Analysis: Complexity in Legal Texts and Analysis: Negotiating Complexity in EFL Contexts translate into classroom practice. Teachers should adapt the complexity level (text length, modal difficulty) to their learners' proficiency. The core principle remains authentic texts, explicit mediation, and diagnostic use of errors.

DISCUSSION

This chapter's primary theoretical contribution is refinement rather than a revolution. It reconceptualizes complexity in legal discourse as interactional and interpretive rather than text-internal and static, building on existing insights from applied linguistics (input/intake, textual vs. learner difficulty) but extending them to the underexplored context of legal EFL pedagogy.

This reconceptualization contributes to discourse analysis in three ways. First, it provides an empirical method for distinguishing between complexity dimensions that are genuinely problematic versus those that learners navigate successfully, a distinction that purely text-internal measures cannot make (Xu et al., 2023). Second, it reframes errors as diagnostic data about interpretive procedures, not merely as evidence of deficient proficiency (Candlin et al., 2002). Third, it positions the EFL classroom as a legitimate site for observing discourse processing under conditions of partial knowledge, a perspective that has been underexploited in legal discourse studies (Northcott, 2008). The genre-aware learner data in Section Role of Genre Awareness further suggest that even partial genre knowledge alters interpretive behavior, a finding with implications for theories of genre acquisition (Bhatia, 2023).

A second contribution is methodological: this chapter demonstrates how teaching can function as an analytical lens rather than merely a site for applying research findings. Most applied linguistics research treats pedagogy as the destination, research informs teaching. This chapter inverts that relationship. The classroom is treated as an observational context that reveals dimensions of legal discourse complexity that text analysis alone cannot capture.

The translation data in Section Translation as Evidence of Negotiation exemplifies this inversion. Text analysis alone (Section Analysis: Complexity in Legal

Texts) can identify that contracts contain conditional chains; it cannot reveal which conditional relationships are most vulnerable to misinterpretation, or what kinds of trade-offs learners make between precision and comprehensibility (Xu et al., 2023). Learner outputs provided that missing evidence. Similarly, the genre-awareness comparison in Section Role of Genre Awareness would be impossible without an instructional context that produced learners with differential exposure to genre labels (Sierocka, 2014).

This bidirectional relationship, from discourse analysis to pedagogy and from pedagogy back to discourse analysis, is the chapter's distinctive methodological contribution. It suggests that legal discourse studies need not choose between linguistic rigor and pedagogical relevance; the two can inform each other when teaching is treated as an analytical site (Northcott, 2008).

Limitations and Future Research

Several limitations constrain the generalizability and scope of this study. First, the dataset is small, comprising approximately 15 learner outputs per text excerpt across three genres, and findings are context-bound to a specific instructional setting and learner proficiency profile (B2–C1). This limits statistical generalizability but is appropriate for qualitative discourse-analytic inquiry focused on identifying patterns of negotiation rather than measuring prevalence (Sierocka, 2014). Consequently, the findings reported in Analysis: Complexity in Legal Texts and Analysis: Negotiating Complexity in EFL Contexts are presented as exploratory illustrations of how complexity negotiation can be observed, not as generalizable claims about EFL legal learners as a population. Replication across different jurisdictions and learner populations is necessary to assess broader applicability (Shamonina & Kostova, 2025). Second, the absence of longitudinal data means this study captures initial negotiation of complexity rather than developmental trajectories. Xu et al. (2023) demonstrated that complexity negotiation changes over time with instruction; this study does not claim to address such change. The finding that genre awareness did not eliminate modality errors (see Role of Genre Awareness) further suggests that some dimensions of complexity may require extended instructional time to shift, a hypothesis that requires longitudinal designs to test (Sierocka, 2014). Third, the study focused on comprehension and translation, not production. Whether learners' genre awareness would manifest in their own legal writing remains an open question (Alasmary, 2019). Additionally, learner outputs are written only; oral think-aloud protocols or retrospective interviews might reveal additional dimensions of negotiation not captured in written responses (Hafner & Candlin, 2007). Fourth, the genre-awareness comparison in Role of Genre Awareness, while suggestive, involves an imbalance (n=5 vs. n=10) and possible confounding variables (learners with genre exposure may have differed in other ways). Future research should employ larger datasets with controlled comparisons to validate the observed patterns (Tessuto, 2011). Finally, cross-linguistic and cross-jurisdictional comparison is urgently needed. The learners in this study shared an L1 from a civil law jurisdiction; their errors may reflect specific transfer effects (e.g., how modality is expressed in their L1 legal system). Replication with learners from different L1 backgrounds and different target legal systems (common law vs. civil law) would distinguish universal complexity features from language- or jurisdiction-specific ones (Shamonina & Kostova, 2025). Future research should also examine how learners from common law backgrounds negotiate civil law texts written in English, a growing context in international legal education.

Where learner outputs include responses to simplified or glossed texts (none in the primary dataset), such deviations are noted and treated as separate analytical observations rather than conflated with unassisted negotiation data.

CONCLUSION

This chapter began with a problem that legal discourse is linguistically and structurally complex, and EFL learners struggle with it. But the preceding analysis has argued for a reconceptualization of that problem. Legal discourse complexity is not merely a barrier to be removed or simplified away; it is a negotiated phenomenon that learner engagement makes visible. Section Complexity as Negotiation of Meaning: A Refinement introduced this shift from "difficulty" to "negotiation of meaning." Sections Analysis: Complexity in Legal Texts and Analysis: Negotiating Complexity in EFL Contexts operationalized it by distinguishing potential complexity (text-internal features) from actualized complexity (learner uptake, errors, and repairs). Section Role of Genre Awareness's finding that genre-aware learners flagged ambiguities while unaware learners guessed, and Section Translation as Evidence of Negotiation's evidence that translation forced interpretive commitments that paraphrasing did not, together demonstrate that complexity is not a static obstacle but a dynamic interaction between text, reader, and interpretive procedures.

The chapter's primary contribution is methodological and theoretical. EFL contexts reveal how meaning is constructed and contested in legal discourse precisely because learners lack the automaticity of expert readers. Their errors are not noise to be filtered out but data about which features of legal texts are most opaque and which interpretive procedures are most in need of explicit mediation. The genre-aware learner comparison (Section Role of Genre Awareness) showed that even partial genre knowledge alters interpretive behavior, but does not eliminate modality errors, suggesting that different dimensions of complexity require different forms of mediation. This bidirectional relationship, from discourse analysis to pedagogy and from pedagogy back to discourse analysis, reframes teaching as an analytical lens rather than merely a site for applying research findings.

The final implication is principled rather than prescriptive. Genre-informed approaches provide a way to engage with complexity without resorting to simplification.

Making genre structure visible (Principle 1), focusing on points of recurrent breakdown (Principle 2), and using translation as diagnostic evidence (Principle 3) are not teaching tips but analytical implications derived directly from learner negotiation data. They do not constitute a curriculum; they constitute a stance: that complexity is to be mediated, not eliminated; that authentic texts are to be engaged with, not replaced by simplified versions; and that learner errors are to be analyzed, not merely corrected.

Legal English pedagogy in EFL contexts faces a choice. It can continue to simplify, to gloss, to pre-digest legal texts for learner consumption, thereby removing the very features that define legal discourse as a professional genre. This chapter argues for treating the classroom as a site for observing and mediating complexity, using genre-informed analysis to make interpretive procedures visible. The data suggest this approach is both possible and productive.

REFERENCES

Alasmary, A. (2019). Lexical bundles in contract law texts: A corpus-based exploration and implications for legal education. *International Journal of English Linguistics*, *9*(2), 244–257. DOI: 10.5539/ijel.v9n2p244

Alavi, S. (2024). Challenges of lecturers in material selection to foster EFL university students' self-regulation. *LEARN Journal: Language Education and Acquisition Research Network, 17*(1), 514-537. Retrieved from https://so04.tci-thaijo.org/index.php/LEARN/article/view/270425

Alavi, S. (2026). Multimodality meets translation in TESOL: A scoping review of emerging pedagogies. In M. Amini. *Multimodality and Translation in Audiovisual Media* (pp. 249-288). IGI Global Scientific Publishing. DOI: 10.4018/979-8-3373-5717-1.ch009

Alavi, S., & Amini, M. (2026). Interdependencies of proficiency, motivation, and strategy: A quantitative study within a socio-cognitive framework for TESOL postgraduate curriculum design. *Community and Social Development Journal*, *27*(2), 115–127. DOI: 10.57260/csdj.2026.286722

Bhatia, V. K. (1983). Simplification v. easification—The case of legal texts1. *Applied Linguistics*, *4*(1), 42–54. DOI: 10.1093/applin/4.1.42

Bhatia, V. K. (2023). Designing English for legal communication programmes: Exploiting legislative genres. *International Journal for the Semiotics of Law*, *36*(4), 1883–1896. DOI: 10.1007/s11196-022-09968-5

Breeze, R. (2015). Teaching the vocabulary of legal documents: a corpus-driven approach. *ESP Today, 3*(1), 44-63. https://www.esptodayjournal.org/pdf/current_issue/2015/3.%20RUTH%20BREEZE%20-%20full%20text.pdf

Candlin, C. N., Bhatia, V. K., & Jensen, C. H. (2002). Developing legal writing materials for English second language learners: Problems and perspectives. *English for Specific Purposes*, *21*(4), 299–320. DOI: 10.1016/S0889-4906(01)00029-1

Filipović, L. (2016). May vs. Might in native vs. non-native English: Implications for inference and judgement in legal and educational contexts. *Applied Linguistics Review*, *7*(2), 181–201. DOI: 10.1515/applirev-2016-0008

Girón García, C. (2016). Teaching and learning EFL successfully through an online environment: An experimental study with "Legal English" students. *Journal of Electronics and Communication Engineering Research, 3*, 01-11. https://www.questjournals.org/jecer/papers/vol3-issue5/A350111.pdf

Hafner, C. A., & Candlin, C. N. (2007). Corpus tools as an affordance to learning in professional legal education. *Journal of English for Academic Purposes, 6*(4), 303–318. DOI: 10.1016/j.jeap.2007.09.005

He, H., Amini, M., Ganapathy, M., & Lah, S. C. (2024). The application of Juliane House's translation quality assessment model in the English translation of Yu Hua's 'Yanre de xiatian.'. *Cogent Arts & Humanities, 11*(1), 2386781. Advance online publication. DOI: 10.1080/23311983.2024.2386781

Hoffman, C. (2011). Using discourse analysis methodology to teach "Legal English." *International Journal of Law, Language & Discourse, 1*(1), 1-19. https://scholarship.law.georgetown.edu/cgi/viewcontent.cgi?article=2341&context=facpub

Kim, N. Y. (2018). Chatbots and Korean EFL Students' English Vocabulary Learning. *Journal of Digital Convergence, 16*(2), 1.

Kothalawala, C., Kothalawala, T., & Pereira, S. S. (2023). *Move analysis of Sri Lankan legal letters of demand for teaching English for specific purposes.* ESP., DOI: 10.4038/ouslj.v18i1.7583

Litvishko, O. M., Shiryaeva, T. A., Golubovskaya, E. A., & Mekeko, N. M. (2025). Why English Legal Discourse is Difficult to Understand. [IJAES]. *International Journal of Arabic-English Studies, 25*(1), 403–430. DOI: 10.33806/ijaes.v25i1.675

Northcott, J. (2008). Language education for law professionals. In Gibbons, J., & Turell, M. T. (Eds.), *Dimensions of forensic linguistics* (pp. 27–46). John Benjamins. DOI: 10.1075/aals.5.04nor

Northcott, J. (2013). Teaching legal English: Contexts and cases. In Paltridge, B., & Starfield, S. (Eds.), *The handbook of English for specific purposes* (pp. 471–487). Wiley-Blackwell.

Novikova, E. R., Polyakov, O. G., & Hausmann-Ushkova, N. V. (2020). Teaching English to law students by means of discourse analysis on the basis of C. Hoffman's comprehensive approach. *Pedagogy. Theory into Practice, 5*(5), 652–657. DOI: 10.30853/ped200166

Park, J. "The Multidimensional Prospects for L2 English Legal Writing" (2014). Open Access Theses. 363. https://docs.lib.purdue.edu/open_access_theses/363

Shamonina, G., & Kostova, B. (2025). Pravnite tsennosti kato kulturno-znachimi orientiri v obuchenieto po chuzhd ezik na studenti-yuristi [Legal values as culturally significant landmarks in foreign language training of law students]. *Chuzhdoezikovo Obuchenie, 51*(4). Advance online publication. DOI: 10.53656/for2025-04-07

Sierocka, H. (2014). *Curriculum development for legal English programs*. Cambridge Scholars Publishing.

Swales, J. M. (1990). *Genre analysis*. Cambridge university press., DOI: 10.1075/z.184.513swa

Tessuto, G. (2011). Nationalising English legal language pedagogy in L2 genre-based writing: Legal problem question in the UK loci of law. Implications and challenges for the pluricentricity of a legal English pedagogy. *ESP Across Cultures*, *8*, 7–28. DOI: 10.1016/j.esp.2011.05.001

Voskanyan, R. (2018). Legal English: Lexical competence and curriculum design. *The ESP Journal*, *SI-2*, 57–73. Advance online publication. DOI: 10.46991/AFA/2026.SI-2.57

Wang, Q., Amini, M., Yang, C., & He, Q. (2026). Translating Culture-Specific Items in The True Story of Ah Q: A comparative evaluation of GPT-4o, KIMI, and Google Translate under multimodal prompts. *SAGE Open*, *16*(1), 21582440251412225. Advance online publication. DOI: 10.1177/21582440251412225

Wu, S., Amini, M., & Mahfoodh, O. H. A. (2025a). A corpus-based analysis of modality shifts in English-to-Chinese courtroom translation. *Eurasian Journal of Applied Linguistics*, *11*(1), 152–166. https://ejal.info/menuscript/index.php/ejal/article/view/995/364

Wu, S., Amini, M., & Mahfoodh, O. H. A. (2025b). Exploring challenges and solutions in English-to-Chinese courtroom translation: Insights from the Tokyo Trial and implications for translator training. *SAGE Open*, *15*(4). Advance online publication. DOI: 10.1177/21582440251385865

Wu, S., Amini, M., & Wang, Y. (2026). Negotiating institutional hierarchy: Power, politeness, and meaning construction in English-to-Chinese courtroom translation. *SAGE Open*, *16*(1), 1–14. DOI: 10.1177/21582440261421582

Xu, W., Geluso, K., & Staples, D. (2023). Navigating complexity in plain English: A longitudinal analysis of syntactic and lexical complexity development in L2 legal writing. *Journal of Second Language Writing*, *62*, 101059. Advance online publication. DOI: 10.1016/j.jslw.2023.101059

Xu, Y. (2020). *Second Language Writing Complexity in Academic Legal Discourse: Development and Assessment under a Curricular Lens*. Linguistics. hdl.handle.net/10822/1060758

ADDITIONAL READINGS

Al-Tarawneh, A., & Al-Badawi, M. (2024). The impact of translation on contractual clarity and legal interpretation in corporate settings. In *Frontiers of Human Centricity in the Artificial Intelligence-Driven Society 5.0* (pp. 1311–1320). Springer Nature Switzerland., DOI: 10.1007/978-3-031-73545-5_122

Alhalalmeh, A. H., Al-Tarawneh, A., & Al-Badawi, M. (2025). Navigating the complexities of translation studies in the legal field. In *From Machine Learning to Artificial Intelligence: The Modern Machine Intelligence Approach for Financial and Economic Inclusion* (pp. 1-12). Cham: Springer Nature Switzerland. DOI: 10.1007/978-3-031-76011-2_1

Anthony, L. (2018). *Introducing English for specific purposes*. Routledge., DOI: 10.4324/9781351031189

Basturkmen, H. (2015). *Developing courses in English for specific purposes*. Springer., DOI: 10.1057/9780230290518

Botezat, O. (2012). The complexity of legal translation: Social and cultural Bounds aspects. *Contemporary Readings in Law and Social Justice*, *4*(1), 641–647.

Hafner, C., & Miller, L. (2018). *English in the disciplines: A multidimensional model for ESP course design*. Routledge., DOI: 10.4324/9780429452437

Hyland, K. (2022). English for specific purposes: What is it and where is it taking us? *ESP Today-Journal of English for Specific Purposes at Tertiary Level*, *10*(2), 202–220. DOI: 10.18485/esptoday.2022.10.2.1

Kobyakova, I., & Habenko, M. (2020). The challenges of legal texts translation in terms of European integration. *Philological Treatises, 9*(4), 39–45. Retrieved from https://tractatus.sumdu.edu.ua/index.php/journal/article/view/211

Lin, X., Afzaal, M., & Aldayel, H. S. (2023). Syntactic complexity in legal translated texts and the use of plain English: A corpus-based study. *Humanities & Social Sciences Communications*, *10*(1), 17. DOI: 10.1057/s41599-022-01485-x

Paltridge, B., & Starfield, S. (Eds.). (2013). *The handbook of English for specific purposes* (Vol. 592). Wiley-blackwell.

KEY TERMS AND DEFINITIONS

Actualized complexity: How learners engage with complexity, evidenced by interpretations, translations, errors, and repairs. This concept captures the gap between what a text makes possible (potential complexity) and what learners actually do when trying to understand it.

Complexity: Four linguistic dimensions in legal texts: syntactic embedding, lexical density (including nominalization), modality (*shall*, *may*, *must*), and ambiguity. Treated here as negotiated, not static. This means complexity is not an inherent property of a text but emerges from the interaction between textual features and a reader's interpretive resources.

Easification: Pedagogical support for authentic texts without simplifying the language itself. Contrasts with simplification. Examples include glossing difficult terms, providing structural organizers, or highlighting move boundaries while keeping the original text intact.

Genre awareness: Metacognitive knowledge of genre structures. In this study, genre-aware learners identified obligations more accurately and flagged ambiguities more often. This awareness helps readers distinguish main rules from exceptions and locate the locus of legal authority within a text.

Genre: A conventionalized text structure responding to a communicative purpose. Contracts, statutes, and case summaries each have distinct moves and organizational patterns. Recognizing a text's genre helps readers predict its rhetorical organization and apply appropriate interpretive conventions.

Interpretive competence: The ability to construct meaning from legal texts using genre-specific reading conventions. Develops through engagement with authentic complexity, not simplified versions. It includes knowing how to resolve ambiguity, track conditional dependencies, and apply canons of construction appropriate to the legal genre at hand.

Mediation: The teacher's role in making interpretive procedures visible. Treats the classroom as a research site, not just a delivery mechanism. Mediation focuses on helping learners notice and name the strategies expert readers use rather than transmitting simplified content.

Modality (legal): Deontic meanings of modal verbs: *shall* (obligation), *may* (discretion /permission), *must* (absolute requirement). Unlike everyday English, where these modals often express probability or suggestion, in legal contexts they carry binding force that determines rights and duties.

Negotiation: The interpretive work readers perform to resolve ambiguity and infer meaning. Learner errors signal breakdowns in negotiation, not just language deficits. In this framework, negotiation includes both professional interpretive canons (e.g., *contra proferentem*) and the adaptive strategies learners use when facing unresolved complexity.

Potential complexity: Text-internal features (syntactic, lexical, modal) that may challenge readers. The baseline for analysis. It describes what a text contains independently of any particular reader's encounter with it.

Chapter 3
Source Hierarchy and Terminological Priority in Malaysian Legal Translation

Yoke Lian Lau
http://orcid.org/0000-0002-7949-7683
Universiti Malaysia Sabah, Malaysia

ABSTRACT

The difficulty of bilingual laws and the authority of the statutory texts in the Malaysian setting make it necessary that the translators focus more on legal precision rather than common lexical correspondence. The legal translator must thus know the precedence of the legal sources and the authority of the words in statutory law in translating legal works to a different language. This paper discusses the concept of "terminological priority" in the translation of Malaysian legal documents, particularly statutory instruments. It states that in the interpretation of laws like the Employment Act 1955, the meaning adopted in the Act should be given priority rather than the meaning of the words in the general dictionaries or even the style. For example, when the statute uses the word "hendaklah" to signify the mandatory nature of "shall," the statutory formulation must take precedence over any other possible equivalents suggested by authoritative sources, such as the dictionaries published by Dewan Bahasa dan Pustaka.

DOI: 10.4018/979-8-3373-9179-3.ch003

INTRODUCTION

In Malaysia, the legal translation field is in a decidedly bilingual legal system where both Malay and English are used as languages of law, administration and adjudication. This duality, both enshrined at the constitutional level and in the substance itself, is a continuing difficulty that legal translators face especially in matters of precedence of sources and hierarchy of terms. Unlike general translation there are normative imperatives in the legal translation; precision, approval and the authenticity of legal texts are given a primary importance. Deviation from source order prescribed may give rise to substantive legal consequences: misinterpretation, procedural kinks or the charge of invalidity.

The underlying principle on the basis of Malaysian legal translation is that sources do not have equal authority. Statutory documents, the judgments of courts of justice and texts sanctioned by authorities stand above dictionaries, glossaries and stipulations of style. Trained translators thus have to rely as much as possible on primary sources, including Acts of Parliament, subsidiary legislation, gazetted texts, and authoritative court usage (Syameel, 2025b), through reference to secondary sources such as general dictionaries or precedent trades. Consequently, the translator's freedom of choice is enclosed within the boundaries of legal requirement to reproduce authoritative wording even when linguistically logical forms may seem to be preferable.

This dynamic is also strengthened through Malaysia's statutory regime of language. The Malay language text of federal and state enacted statutes are considered as authoritative versions, unless section 6 of the National Language Act 1963/67 states otherwise whereupon a clear legal precedence exists between linguistic versions and their translation. Accordingly, the translator of legal instruments, states, pleadings, affidavits, contracts, has to base the term choice upon the real text of the legislative or judicial act, and not lexical equivalency (Mokhtar, 1983).

Judicial usage also has the effect of giving terminological priority. Expressions such as “ia merupakan undang- undang mapan”(It is trite law that …), ” preseden Mengikat “(binding precedent) or “keputusan ringkas”(summary judgment) are not a product of lexicographic but of court usage as prevailing in Malaysian case law. Disagreements between the meaning of a dictionary and the professional terms borrowed from the judiciary are corrected by judicial precedent, more specifically in the form of law reports and written judgments (Syameel, 2025c).

Beyond the matter of terminology there are formal linguistic elements, judicial honorifics and means of address, which are subject to hierarchical and institutional rules. Misapplication can cause incorrect translation and consequent compromise in the propriety of a procedure and the professional reputation of a translator. Such considerations highlight that legal translation goes beyond the frame of linguistic transfer, it implies institutional and cultural aspects of the legal institution (Syameel, 2025a).

This forthcoming paper argues that for effective legal translation in Malaysia, there is a need to adopt systematics in the hierarchy of the sources. Translators must be aware of the sequence of sources, and explicate justification for prioritising some sources over others, before making any decisions of terminology. Drawing on practical training material, professional practise and a collection of legal documents, the study considers source hierarchy as a disciplinary structure of terminological choice guaranteeing consistency, legal predictability and institutional coherence in the framework of bilingual legal discourse. This contributes to the explanation of a principled concept of the legal translator's role in Malaysia, where the translator is no longer seen as a simple intermediary in the linguistic process, but is instead a mediator of legal power.

This research synthesises the knowledge of the current state of theoretical and empirical research in relation to source hierarchy and terminological priority in legal translation in Malaysia. It discussed the role of legal source hierarchy and language policy, considered and discussed theoretical frameworks and methodological approaches, assessed the issues and solutions in managing terminologies, and reviewed the gaps and possible directions to take in future study. The structure is propelling from basic context toward practical implications toward recommendations.

LITERATURE REVIEW

Malaysia's legal system is a linguistically and legally complex setting, comprised of a constitutional preponderance of the Malay language and the continued viability in the senior courts, law education and professional legal practise of the English language. This bilingual setup in the context of a plural legal system, which has statutory law, common law and Islamic jurisprudence elements, creates permanent problems for legal translation sometimes in the fields of hierarchy of sources, terminological precedence, and cohesion of doctrines (Bidin, 1995; Powell & Saw, 2021). Accordingly, the translation of the law in Malaysia works at the intersection of language, law and practise in the political institutions, where a concern with accuracy and consistency is the basis of legal certainty and accessibility.

It is crucial to understand how Malaysian's bilingual legal system has developed historically to understand why there are certain institutional logics that exist at the level of hierarchical terminologies. After gaining independence from Britain in 1957, the transition to using Malay as the dominant language of both law and government was codified with the National Language Act of 1963/67 (Act 32) which made Bahasa Malaysia the sole official language of the Federation. Section 6 of this Act establishes a legislative hierarchy based on language versioning of laws; making the Malay version the definitive version of Federal and State legislation unless stated otherwise in Parliament. As such, this will affect how translations occur: when an approved version of the law exists in Malay in statute it takes on legally enforceable status and cannot be replaced by a definition provided in a dictionary nor can it be replaced by preference of translator (Mokhtar, 1983). From the late 1960s onwards, there were many examples of Malay-medium legal documents being produced on an increasing scale leading eventually to the first published bilingual law report via the Malayan Law Journal (MLJ-BM); and, to further create specialized legal terms by Dewan Bahasa dan Pustaka (DBP). In addition to creating a complex multi-layered environment for terminological development within the legal profession, these developments also create confusion regarding what sources should take precedence, and therefore require a structured approach to make decisions about sources versus substituting words and phrases ad-hoc.

Empirical studies of legal practise in Malaysia, a bilingual society, suggest that the interaction between two languages (Malay and English) is a dynamic interaction and not hierarchical. Powell and Saw (2021) show that the bilingualism of both languages has created an indigenised common law discourse, especially in the training of professionals. Their findings complement the fact that terminological asymmetries may emerge when a single lexical item stands for a multiple number of legal concepts when languages exist (Bidin, 1995; Goh & Harjit Singh, 2015), highlighting the risks of inconsistency and semantic drift. Ramalingam et al. (2022) also criticizes linguistic uniformity assumptions by exposing differences in judicial language concerning West and East Malaysia, thus noting the need to make analysis more contextualised.

From a theoretical perspective, the prevailing issues for discussion on legal translation are polysemy, conceptual mismatch, and system-bound meanings. Foundational contributions by Šarčević (1997) and Cao (2010) highlight the importance of legal effect and institutional function in legal translation as pertaining to law which must be given priority over the issue of linguistic equivalence. Recent empirical studies provide further support for the existence of these challenges in the context of technologically-mediated environments; Meenal and Govindarajan (2023) and Nan (2026) provide relevant examples of the challenges which machine translation systems experience regarding issues of legal ambiguity and contextual interpretation; as such, they strengthen the need for human legal expertise in translation tasks.

Professional and institutional dimensions influence more the quality of the legal translation. Sulaiman et al. (2024) observe that the absence of formal accreditation, ethical regulation, and institutional governance are some of the weaknesses of the translation and interpreting sector in Malaysia. These findings are in line with Bajčić and Basaneže (2016) statement that legal translation is a higher responsibility institutional activity, which is essential for the protection of procedural fairness and access to justice. Hsieh (2018) complement to this perspective is bringing legal translation to an economic and regulatory activity, where translating mistakes may cause legal and financial risk.

Kusik (2024) places legal translation in broader projects to promote better inter-jurisdictional legal communication, while Scott (2017) examines the legal translation market as one where there is information asymmetry. Methodological contributions of Zweigert and Kötz (1983) and Graziadei (2024, 2025) also show that the principle of comparative legal analysis should focus more on functional and doctrinal equivalence and less on terminological similarity.

Prieto Ramos (2020) and Prieto Ramos and Cerutti (2021) show that institutional legal translation is regulated by conventions which prioritise the accomplishment of semantic accuracy, intertextual coherence, and consistency among the authoritative texts. Turaeva (2020) and Cosmulescu (2021) maintain that semantic loss is unavoidable in translation, but the use of linguistic, legal and pragmatic considerations is a solution that reduces it.

Many organised models have been suggested to direct legal-translation practise. Kocbek (2015, 2012) develops multi stage models combining the functionalist translation theory, comparative law and legal linguistics. Cao (2010) makes a difference between legislative translation in bilingual jurisdictions and informational translation in monolingual cases. Corpus-based and terminology-focused research also constitutes an empirical evidence of translation practises and inconsistencies (Sopjani & Hamiti, 2022; Biel and Kockaert, 2023; Huong & Anh, 2024).

Contemporary scholarship gradually tends to interdisciplinarity and cognition. Engberg (2020) conceptualises legal translation as a process of legal knowledge construction whereas Termorshuizen-Arts (2008) detects shared interpretive roots between law, translation and psycholinguistics. Additional studies of Orozco and Sánchez-Gijón (2011), Cheng and Sin (2008), Sun and Chen (2024), Heylen and Steurs (2014). Alwazna (2018) reaches the position that legal translation is a cognitively demanding, institutionally constrained, and professionally specialised activity.

Within the theoretical backdrop, Bajčić (2014) offers an important terminological and onomasiological framework, contention of which holds that legal translation needs to be based on conceptual structures shaped by institutional context and judicial interpretation. In conjunction with Bajčić and Basaneže (2016), these works provide the conceptual basis for term oriented, hierarchy sensitive approaches to legal translation and thus inform the current study.

The growth of use of machine translation and artificial intelligence-based tools in legal settings has generated increased research interest in Malaysia and in broader Southeast Asia legal translation literature. Research by Meenal & Govindarajan (2023) and Nan (2026), indicate that all automated systems have failed to identify legal polysemes, terms relevant only to jurisdictions, and the contextually dependent nature of bilingual statutory documents. Although these failures are technically based, they carry an institutional significance. When machine produced translations are used without expert review in Malaysian legal settings, the resulting terminological inaccuracies can result in a number of potential problems including, but not limited to; representing incorrect procedural stages, conflating different doctrines, creating formulations which do not possess institutional recognition necessary for proper legal communication. As this type of risk is particularly great in a legal environment utilizing two languages, where the authority of terminology comes from its certification via either statute or judicial practices. The above referenced studies confirm the necessity of source hierarchy awareness as a professional skill for legal translators who work in the Malaysian setting.

METHODOLOGY

Term-Oriented Doctrinal Comparative Method

This study uses Term-Oriented Doctrinal Comparative Method (TODCM), a hybrid methodology designed for investigation English-Malay legal translation in the Malaysian situation. TODCM is a combination of two traditionally established methodological traditions. The initial one is the tradition of doctrinal legal research, which involves defining the meaning of legal provisions on the basis of such authoritative instruments as legitimate statute and judicial pronouncements. The second tradition is term which oriented legal translation analysis according to which legal lexical items are not simply a part of ordinary language - they are regional units of meaning.

TODCM sees individual legal terms and concepts as the relevant and basic analytic unit. By focusing on a carefully chosen universe of terms, the methodology isolates basic legal concepts which may seem linguistically similar in different jurisdictions but which have different doctrinal connotations. This narrowed approach allows an accurate analysis of correspondence in terminology without hiding behind mere visual linguistic agreement the conceptual differences.

Each of the chosen terms is the subject of doctrinal scrutiny against the background of its legal environment. The process consists in analysing authoritative sources (such as legislation, judicial decisions and relevant scholarly literature) with the aim of determining the way the term is defined, interpreted and used in practise. The analysis goes beyond the official definitions and considers interpretive principles, judicial reasoning as well as the normative framework that governs the operation of the word. Later a systematic comparative assessment of the doctrinal meanings of in different legal contexts is undertaken, the points of similarity and differences are identified and the extent of functional equivalence is assessed. Contextual variations arising from legal culture, policy goals or basic values are considered explicitly, and thus conceptual clarity is ensured and equivocation avoided.

The combination of doctrinal analysis and term-based translation allows TODCM to (i) identify the authoritative legal meaning of a term using doctrinal methods, and (ii) evaluate the Malay translation equivalents from a system sensitive and authority-based perspective with a primary agenda to place importance on the legal effect and institutional validity, rather than on the purely semantic or stylistic equivalent. This methodology is in accordance with the current methodology in legal translation and comparative law, namely the focus on conceptual equivalence and legal functionality (Šarčević, 1997; Zweigert & Kötz, 1983; Graziadei, 2024).

The dataset is based on actual Malaysian legal documents extracted from the e-Hakim database, as it includes written judgement, ground of judgement and reported and unreported case law from courts in Peninsular Malaysia. Sabah and Sarawak are excluded in order to avoid confusion of two different constitutional and judicial regimes (Ramalingam et al.,2022). Texts have been selected on the basis that terminological decisions undertaken in them have an unmistakable doctrinal or procedural significance.Corpus Selection Process: Explicit Criteria Used to Select Texts

Firstly, all documents containing both English and Malay legal terminology from the same document or as close to it as possible by way of the bilingual pairing of documents were chosen. This allowed us to compare legal terms, using a common base where institutional use is authorized.

Secondly, used purposive sampling to select texts representing different levels of courts: Magistrates' Courts, Sessions Courts, High Courts and Courts of Appeal. By doing so, we captured variations in terminology across different judicial environments.

Thirdly, only those terms appearing in at least two separate judgments were selected into our data set to provide a basis upon which to evaluate consistency and stability in judicial usage.

Coding Procedure Used Three Analytical Categories for Each Term:

(a) Source Classification, Representing Four Tier Hierarchy (Statutory/Judicial/Lexicographical/Informal)
(b) Determination of Accuracy, Based Upon Alignment with Established Benchmark of The Court
(c) Functional Equivalence Assessment of Whether Translation Preserved Doctrinal Role and Procedural Effect of the Source Term

Due to the single-researcher design of the study, inter-coder reliability was not formally evaluated. The analysis happened in three successive stages. First of all, core legal terms relevant for the research objectives were identified and extracted from the corpus. Second, the second branch of this work consisted of analysing each term in relation to a hierarchical array of sources such as statutory provisions, judicial usage, lexicographical references, and secondary materials based on the principles expounded by Prieto Ramos (2020), Bajčić (2014), and Engberg (2020). Third, term-based decision tables were developed using the competing translation alternatives in evaluating the translation discovered that most satisfies legal function, institutional authority, and interpretive stability in determining the terminological choice.

Conceptual Framework: A Hybrid Foundation for the Term-Oriented Doctrinal Comparative Method

The hybrid framework can be based on two complementary insights pertaining to law-as-text and law-in-use. First, comparative- law theory (Graziadei, 2025; Šarčević, 1997), any legal system is a composite of several "legal formants", such as for example: judicial reasoning, institutional practise, implicit professional knowledge, etc. (Sacco, 1991) that might diverge, or even be in conflict with each other, this means that any comparison must not envisage a single unified meaning, "the correct", and on the contrary, must bring out dissociations between what rules say and how they act in practise. This same approach is also focused on "cryptotypes", i.e. silent, implicit dimensions of the legal world knowledge, which become distinctly noticeable when law travels across languages and conceptual grids (Graziadei, 2024).

Second, legal-translation theory according to Šarčević (1997) is a receiver-oriented act of communication within "the mechanism of the law", in which the decisive criterion is not the stylistic similarity but the way that parallel texts will be interpreted and applied in legal institutions (particularly courts). In this view, authenticated translations are not "mere translations" but work as originals with legal force, thus translators have to expect the reception of interpretation and strive for equivalence in legal effects rather than surface meaning (Šarčević, 1997).

Terminological choices have a kind of "signal" to the courts: choosing a functional equivalent might effectively steer interpretation towards one conceptual system as opposed to another; and judges might interpret that choice as an intentional indication (Zweigert & Kötz, 1983). The method is comparative terminological analysis aided by results of validation of the choice of the legal term maps according to the unity and intended operation of the legal instrument in the actual reception.

Procedure of Research

Begin with building a hierarchy of sources specific to Malaysian bilingual legal translation, which clearly identify (a) authoritative or (b) interpretive and operational sources. Then, justify as to why "terminological priority" is not a purely linguistic preference, but a mechanism of governance: Because terminological conflicts prove a major trigger for divergent interpretation, translators are compelled to consider each lexical decision in its relation of foreseeable paths of interpretation, and possible misreading in the various legal settings.

The next step is to operationalise the method using a term dossier workflow. Select a defensible set of high-impact. For each term, prepare a dossier to record (1) occurrences in light of authoritative bilingual texts, (2) and extract any clausal definitions along with cross-references, (3) doctrinal treatment in the judgments (ratio of judgments and interpretive moves), and (4) operational usage. This step is Sacco (1991) pluralism: one views each layer as a potentially distinct formant, and overtly allows for dissociation between the "paper rule" and operative rule (Graziadei, 2025). At the same time, remain analysis receiver-oriented: consider to what extent a proposed terminological preference is likely to stabilise interpretation as far as the direct receivers empowered to apply the instrument are concerned (Šarčević, 1997).

Finally, one needs to make terminological priority rule explicit and testable. A good example of a linguistically conscious doctrine is: The preference is to have a terminological option that best preserves equal legal effect across use within the bilingual instrument. (Šarčević, 1997). In the analysis part, demonstrate this rule at work, through case studies of close reading magnification i.e. term centres close reading and demonstration of contestants as there would be different options of the cue, result in different path of interpretation, also argue from source hierarchy and formant triangulation why one option would better assure uniform application in Malaysia legal practice This is directly in line with the argues that Šarčević (1997) also raises that "function - only" generalisations are not sufficient, the crucial criteria must be derived from the communicative and institutional situation in which the legal text is going to be received and used. Figure 1 shows the Conceptual Framework Flow, Term-Oriented Doctrinal Comparative Method. Figure 1 illustrates the conceptual framework flow of the study.

Figure 1. Conceptual framework flow, term-oriented doctrinal comparative method

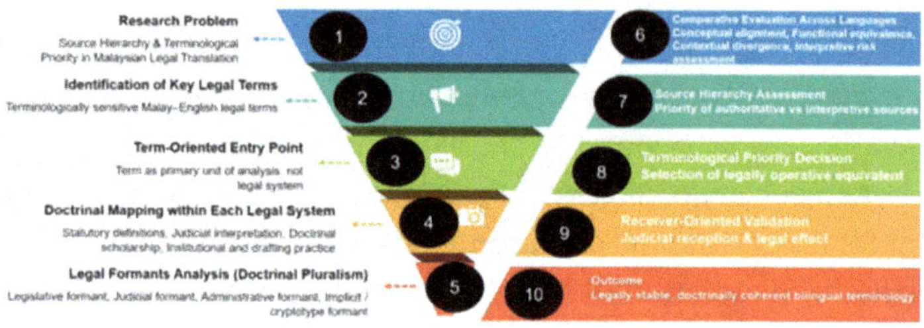

Table 1 shows the hierarchy of the sources that control the decisions of legal translation in the present study. It picks up a scenario-based multiple-choice framework aimed at the operationalisation of source hierarchy and terminological priority in the Malaysian legal context. Each row is organised according to a concrete case of translation from authoritative legal surroundings, specifically statutory instruments, contractual instruments, judicial decisions and reported case law as represented in MLJ - BM. The multiple-choice option a - d our competing translation strategies or source-based solutions one of these choices will be the terminologically and doctrinally more desirable choice: preference is based on institutional legal practise and not, say, on stylistic or lexical convenience.

Table 1. Prioritise sources

No	Scenario	a	b	c	d
1	You must translate section 10 of the *Employment Act 1955*. Where do you copy the wording from?	Dictionary	Law-firm precedent	Act	MLJ commentary
2	The text in an Act says "**hendaklah**" but a DBP dictionary suggests "**harus**" for "**shall**". Which do you use?	"harus"	"hendaklah"	Either (stylistic)	Combine both
3	A contract quotes an entire section from the Companies Act. You can't locate the Malay Act online. What do you do?	Paraphrase	Order an official reprint from AGC / use the gazette library	Use Google-translate	Rely on blog
4	The MLJ-BM report shows "penghakiman terus"; DBP glossary offers "penghakiman segera". Which wins?	DBP	MLJ-BM (court usage)	Either	Coin new term

continued on following page

Table 1. Continued

No	Scenario	a	b	c	d
5	"Assignor" appears in a deed. Oxford Law says "pencantum", DBP glossary says "penyerah hak". Which?	pencantum	Penyerah hak	Either	"pengalih milik"
6	A term isn't in DBP or Acts. Interactive Terminology for Europe (IATE) lists an EU equivalent. Next step?	Use IATE term	Check Malaysian case-law for local usage	Invent	Skip term
7	Gazette punctuation seems wrong. Firm precedent has ";". Action?	Follow precedent	Keep gazette punctuation; add translator note if critical	Fix silently	Ask editor
8	Translation of a court order must include judge's seal. Source?	Omit seal	Draw new seal	Insert "sealed" notation or image	Mention in note only
9	Conflicting meanings in Black's vs local FC case. Choose?	Black's	Federal-Court case	Dictionary average	Whichever clearer
10	You're unsure if a loan term exists in Malay. First search?	Blogs	Bilingual banking regulations / BNM circulars	Social media	Translator forum
11	Which of these is not primary law?	State Ordinance	Federal Regulation	DBP glossary	Act of Parliament

(Syameel, 2025b)

There is a limitation to translating legal texts that is determined by institutional authority and legal hierarchy, and not by the general linguistic rules (Šarčević 1997; Cao 2010; Prieto Ramos 2020). In accordance with the legal research of doctrinal law, primary law has preference over secondary and informal references. Statutory texts have a top-standing in hierarchy, because statuary texts do have a binding legal force and normative power. Consequently, where authorised Malay formulations are contained in Acts or subsidiary legislation, such formulations must be retained in translation in order to ensure legal validity and consistency of application (Bidin 1995; Šarčević 1997). The next highest level of authority is judicial, especially when referring to judicial reasoning, procedural stages and evidentiary standards. Established court formulations, in the form MLJ and written grounds of judgement, triumph over dictionary definitions or explanatory glosses as this represents how legal meaning is construed, stabilised and applied in practise (Engberg 2020; Termorshuizen-Arts 2008).

Table 1 goes on to operationalise insights gained from institutional legal translation research which shows that translation norms are created based on organisational conventions and legal hierarchies and are not solely created following the lexicographic norm (Prieto Ramos, 2020; Prieto Ramos & Cerutti, 2021). Dictionaries, including DBP resources, are therefore considered to work as an auxiliary reference tool rather than as an authoritative reference tool. Their role is therefore limited to helping in comprehension where guidance is not found in statute or in judicial decisions, the interpretation is over-ridden where its institutional usage suggests a different legal meaning. This hierarchy is based on findings in the area of both the EU and comparative legal translation research that stresses on intertextual coherence and consistency between the authoritative texts (Biel & Kockaert 2023).

At functional and linguistic level, the principle of the primacy of legal function in terminological choice is also demonstrated on Table 1, which show that legal function is more important than semantic, literal equivalence. Legal terms are analysed as system specific conceptual units, getting their meaning from their place in the legal framework rather than from surface lexical similarity (Bajčić 2014; Kocbek 2012; Engberg 2020). Translators are hence required to focus more on doctrinal correctness, procedural effect and institutional recognisability rather than on semantic proximity.

Finally, Table 1 uses the need to have recourse to official gazetted texts or authorised reproductions of those texts where it is not possible to have access to the original Malay versions, under the principles of legal certainty and institutional legitimacy (Šarčević 1997; Graziadei, 2024). By putting the translation decisions into hierarchical and well-defined, scenario-based structure, Table 1 is a transparent and replicable analytical tool that illustrates how terminological priority is established in practise under the Term-Oriented Doctrinal Comparative Method. Not only could the criteria for decision making be made clearer but the perception of legal translation as an integral part of legal interpretation in institutional legal communication could also be reinforced.

Data

Most of the empirical legal data used in this study could be obtained from e-Hakim Malaysia, which is the official electronic database of the judgments developed and maintained by the Malaysian Judiciary. The corpus is made up with the judicial materials downloaded directly from the portal and reflecting the authoritative record of the adjudication across the Malaysian courts. By using only this institutional source the study achieves the authenticity of the doctrine as well as consistency of the methodology, as the materials examined comprise the written articulation of the law on the courts' behalf rather than secondary summaries or editorialised reports.

The documents retrieved consist of both reported and unreported judicial decisions, both written judgments (penghakiman bertulis) and grounds of judgement (alasan penghakiman). These texts are the factual background of cases, the parts of the law that the court determined were the issue of the case, the way that the court interpreted the laws using the statutory and common law versions of the law, and then the final decisions that the court made. From a linguistic point of view, such documents are highly valuable inasmuch as they document how the legal terminology is operationalised in 'real' legal discourse, that is, in judicial discourse, including patterns of terminological choice, conceptual framing and intertextual reference in the authoritative legal reasoning.

In addition, the dataset also contains case law records administered from the Malaysian courts, which cumulatively record the evolution and stabilisation of legal meanings through judicial interpretation. These records form a solid doctrinal foundation for examining the construction of legal terms, their domination and hierarchical origin in practise. For the purposes of this study, e - Hakim judgments function as more than illustrative examples since they serve as primary linguistic-legal evidence which allows the study of terminological usage and interpretive authority in Malaysia's bilingual and hybrid legal system on a systematic basis.

The study has been purposefully limited to court rulings from Courts in Peninsular Malaysia and therefore does not include the judgments of Courts in Sabah and Sarawak. In terms of methodology, this limitation can be justified based on differences in constitutional arrangements; statutes and practices of judges that apply in East Malaysia which may result in differences in terminology usage and/or interpretation. By restricting the data base in such a manner, the analytical component of the research will retain its integrity with respect to analysis and avoid confounding the doctrinal/linguistic patterns generated from juridically disparate legal systems. Consequently, all conclusions and generalizations presented in this chapter have been specifically restricted to Peninsular Malaysian judicial practice. A separate analysis and study, taking into consideration the unique constitutional status of Sabah and Sarawak as defined by the Malaysia Agreement 1963 and their continuing application of pre-federation ordinances along with divergent uses of judicial language as described by Ramalingam et al. (2022), would be necessary if the TODCM framework were to be applied to Sabah and Sarawak. Future studies should address this jurisdictional gap to provide a complete national assessment of the hierarchy of terms used in Malaysian bilingual legal translations. Table 2 presents the Hierarchy-Driven Selection of Legal Terminology in Malaysian Judicial Translation.

Table 2. Hierarchy-driven selection of legal terminology in malaysian Judicial Translation

No.	Legal Term	Source A Statutory Authority	Source B Judicial Authority (MLJ-BM)	Source C Lexicographical / Reference Sources	Source D Non-authoritative / Informal Sources	Hierarchy Answer
		Acts / Parliament / Legislation	Judgments / Grounds / Reported Cases	DBP Dictionary / DBP Legal Glossary / Oxford Law Dictionary	Google Translate / Blogs / ChatGPT / Coined Terms	
1	**Abuse of process**	—	**penyalahgunaan proses mahkamah penahanan salah / penahanan menyalahi undang-undang** *(Ketua Pengarah Laut v Straits Bunker & Trading Sdn Bhd [2020] para. 35)*	—	penyalahgunaan proses (Google Translate)	court (functional equivalence)
2	**Acquitted and discharged**	—	**dilepaskan dan dibebaskan** *(Pendakwa Raya v Syed Akmar bin Syed Othman [2026] para 1.4; Public Prosecutor v Mohd Idham bin Mokhtar [2026], para. 2; Ketua Pengarah Laut v Straits Bunker & Trading Sdn Bhd [2020], para. 41; Pendakwa Raya lwn Mohd Jairulnizam bin Mohd Nordin dan satu lagi [2020], para. 1)* **Dilepaskan/dibebaskan** *(Pendakwa Raya v. Aliff Syukri bin Kamarzaman [2026], para. 68; Pendakwa Raya v Sarimah binti Abdul Rahman [2026], para. 5)*	dibebaskan dan dilepaskan (DBP)	dibebaskan dan dilepaskan (Google Translate)	court
3	**Aggra-vating factors**	—	**rayuan pemberatan** *(Pendakwa Raya v Mohamad Sukry bin Wahab & Muhammad Hafiszan bin Naser [2026] paras 59–64)* **hujahan pemberatan** *(Pendakwa Raya v Viknshpran [2026] para 8; Pendakwa Raya v Viknshpran a/l Batu Malai [2026], para. 8)*	—	faktor yang memburukkan (Google Translate)	court
4	**Beyond reasonable doubt**	—	**melampaui keraguan munasabah** *(Pendakwa Raya v Syed Akmar bin Syed Othman [2026], para 58; Pendakwa Raya v Mohamad Sukry bin Wahab & Muhammad Hafiszan bin Naser [2026], para 58; Che Mohd Faiz [2026], para 3; Pendakwa Raya v Mohamad Zakir Husim bin Mohd Alwi [2026], para. 3; Che Mohd Faiz bin Che Zulkifle v Pendakwa Raya [2026], para. 3; Pendakwa Raya v Mustapha bin Ibrahim [2026], para. 6)* **Keraguan munasabah** *(Pendakwa Raya v Mohd Nazuli bin Mohd Nazari [2026], para. 3)*	melampaui keraguan munasabah (DBP)	di luar keraguan munasabah (Google Translate)	court
5	**Burden of proof**	—	**beban pembuktian** *(Pendakwa Raya v Syed Akmar bin Syed Othman [2026], para 28; Pendakwa Raya v Mohamad Sukry bin Wahab & Muhammad Hafiszan bin Naser [2026], para 28; Pendakwa Raya v Aminuddin [2026], para 32; Pendakwa Raya v. Aliff Syukri bin Kamarzaman, 2026, para. 6; Pendakwa Raya v Mohamad Zakir Husim bin Mohd Alwi [2026], para. 10; Pendakwa Raya v Ibrahim bin Harun [2026], para. 7; Pendakwa Raya lwn Mohd Jairulnizam bin Mohd Nordin dan satu lagi [2020], para. 12)*	beban membukti (DBP)	beban pembuktian (Google Translate)	court

continued on following page

Table 2. Continued

No.	Legal Term	Source A Statutory Authority	Source B Judicial Authority (MLJ-BM)	Source C Lexicographical / Reference Sources	Source D Non-authoritative / Informal Sources	Hierarchy Answer
6	**Called to enter defence**	—	**dipanggil membela diri** *(Pendakwa Raya v Syed Akmar bin Syed Othman [2026], para 6.2; Pendakwa Raya v Akhil Mursyid [2026], para 11; Pendakwa Raya v Aminuddin [2026], para 3; Pendakwa Raya v Akhil Mursyid bin Nor Hisham [2026], para. 11; Pendakwa Raya v Ibrahim bin Harun [2026], para. 8; Pendakwa Raya v Mohd Nazuli bin Mohd Nazari [2026], para. 3; Pendakwa Raya lwn Mohd Jairulnizam bin Mohd Nordin dan satu lagi [2020], para. 12)*	—	dipanggil untuk memasuki pertahanan (Google Translate)	court
7	**Consecutive sentence**	—	**Hukuman berturut-turut** *(Hisyamudin bin Ahmad v. Pendakwa Raya [2020], para. 1)*	—	ayat berturut-turut (Google Translate)	court
8	**Conviction**	sabitan	**menyabitkan** *(Pendakwa Raya v Mohamad Sukry bin Wahab & Muhammad Hafiszan bin Naser [2026] para 58)* **disabitkan** *(Pendakwa Raya v Viknshpran [2026], para 3; Che Mohd Faiz [2026], para 3)* **Sabitan** *(Pendakwa Raya v. Aliff Syukri bin Kamarzaman, [2026], para. 5; Mohd Izaq Fikhry bin A. Rahim v. Pendakwa Raya, [2026], para. 34–36; Pendakwa Raya v Mohamad Sukry bin Wahab & Muhammad Hafiszan bin Naser [2026], para. 58; Che Mohd Faiz bin Che Zulkifle v Pendakwa Raya [2026], para. 3; Pendakwa Raya v Mustapha bin Ibrahim [2026], para. 6; Pendakwa Raya v Mohd Nazuli bin Mohd Nazari [2026], para. 4)* **Kesalahan jenayah** *(Mustafa 'Afifi Ab Halim et al. [2013], p. x; Hisyamudin bin Ahmad v. Pendakwa Raya [2020], para. 2; Pendakwa Raya lwn Mohd Jairulnizam bin Mohd Nordin dan satu lagi [2020], para. 12)*	kesalahan (DBP)	sabitan (Google Translate)	Act / court
9	**Cross-appeal**	—	**rayuan silang** *(Hisyamudin bin Ahmad v. Pendakwa Raya [2020], para. 2)*	rayuan balas (DBP)	rayuan balas (Google Translate)	court
10	**Grounds of judgment**	—	**alasan penghakiman** *(Pendakwa Raya v Syed Akmar bin Syed Othman [2026] heading; Pendakwa Raya v Mohamad Sukry bin Wahab & Muhammad Hafiszan bin Naser [2026] heading; Pendakwa Raya v Viknshpran [2026] heading; Pendakwa Raya v Akhil Mursyid [2026] heading; Pendakwa Raya v. Mohamad Zakir Husim bin Mohd Alwi [2026] heading)*	—	alasan penghakiman (Google Translate)	court

continued on following page

Table 2. Continued

No.	Legal Term	Source A Statutory Authority	Source B Judicial Authority (MLJ-BM)	Source C Lexicographical / Reference Sources	Source D Non-authoritative / Informal Sources	Hierarchy Answer
11	**Ingredient of offence**	unsur kesalahan	**inti pati kesalahan / inti pati pertuduhan** *(Pendakwa Raya lwn Mohd Jairulnizam bin Mohd Nordin dan satu lagi [2020], para. 21)* **elemen pertuduhan** *(Pendakwa Raya v Syed Akmar bin Syed Othman [2026]. paras 29–30; Pendakwa Raya v Mohamad Sukry bin Wahab & Muhammad Hafiszan bin Naser [2026]. paras 29–30; Pendakwa Raya v Aminuddin [2026] paras 24–25)* **elemen-elemen** *(Pendakwa Raya v Akhil Mursyid [2026], para 12)*	—	ramuan kesalahan (Google Translate)	court
12	**Inherent jurisdiction**	—	**bidang kuasa mahkamah** *(Ketua Pengarah Laut v Straits Bunker & Trading Sdn Bhd [2020], para. 21)*	—	bidang kuasa yang wujud (Google Translate)	—
13	**It is trite law that ...**	—	**ia merupakan undang-undang mapan** *(Phillvin Guachin v. Pendakwa Raya, [2026], para. 9)* **Undang-undang yang mantap** *(Hisyamudin bin Ahmad v. Pendakwa Raya [2020], para. 15)*	—	Ia adalah undang-undang basi itu (Google Translate)	court
14	**Leave to appeal**	—	**rayuan** *(Pendakwa Raya v. Tee Wei Xuan [2026], para. 1; Pendakwa Raya v Mustapha bin Ibrahim [2026], para. 1; Pendakwa Raya v Firdaus Rizal bin Abdul Manan [2026], para. 1.3; Pendakwa Raya v Hazmi Ruzaini bin Azlihudin [2026], para. 7; Hisyamudin bin Ahmad v. Pendakwa Raya [2020], para. 14)*	—	biarkan untuk merayu (Google Translate)	court
15	**Maximum evaluation**	penilaian maksimum	**penilaian yang maksima** *(Pendakwa Raya v Syed Akmar bin Syed Othman [2026] para 6.1; Che Mohd Faiz [2026] para 20)* **penilaian maksimum** *(Pendakwa Raya v Akhil Mursyid [2026] para 20; Pendakwa Raya v Akhil Mursyid bin Nor Hisham [2026], para. 20; Pendakwa Raya v Ibrahim bin Harun [2026], para. 7; Pendakwa Raya v Sarimah binti Abdul Rahman [2026], para. 3)* **penilaian maksima** *(Pendakwa Raya lwn Mohd Jairulnizam bin Mohd Nordin dan satu lagi [2020], para. 15)*	—	penilaian maksimum (Google Translate)	Act / court

continued on following page

Table 2. Continued

No.	Legal Term	Source A Statutory Authority	Source B Judicial Authority (MLJ-BM)	Source C Lexicographical / Reference Sources	Source D Non-authoritative / Informal Sources	Hierarchy Answer
16	**Mitigation**	—	**mitigasi** *(Hisyamudin bin Ahmad v. Pendakwa Raya [2020], para. 10)* **rayuan pemberatan** *(Pendakwa Raya v Mohamad Sukry bin Wahab & Muhammad Hafiszan bin Naser [2026], paras 59–64)* **rayuan mitigasi** *(Pendakwa Raya v Viknshpran [2026], para 7; Pendakwa Raya v Viknshpran a/l Batu Malai [2026], para. 7)* **hujahan mitagasi** *(Pendakwa Raya v Firdaus Rizal bin Abdul Manan [2026], para. 2.2; Pendakwa Raya v Ku Mahamad Isa bin Jaafar [2026], para. 6)*	hukuman diringankan (DBP)	mitigasi (Google Translate)	court
17	**Plea of guilty**	—	**mengaku salah** *(Pendakwa Raya v Viknshpran [2026], para 3)* **pengakuan salah** *(Pendakwa Raya v Viknshpran a/l Batu Malai [2026], para. 3; Pendakwa Raya v Firdaus Rizal bin Abdul Manan [2026], para. 1.2; Pendakwa Raya v Ku Mahamad Isa bin Jaafar [2026], para. 4; Pendakwa Raya v Hazmi Ruzaini bin Azlihudin [2026], para. 2)* **Pengakuan bersalah** *(Hisyamudin bin Ahmad v. Pendakwa Raya [2020], para. 2)*	menyatakan seseorang itu bersalah (DBP)	pengakuan bersalah (Google Translate)	court
18	**Prima facie case**	—	**kes prima facie** *(Pendakwa Raya v Syed Akmar bin Syed Othman [2026], paras 6.1–6.2; Pendakwa Raya v Mohamad Sukry bin Wahab & Muhammad Hafiszan bin Naser [2026], para 41; Pendakwa Raya v Akhil Mursyid [2026], para 11; Pendakwa Raya v Aminuddin [2026], para 32; Che Mohd Faiz [2026], para 18; Pendakwa Raya v. Aliff Syukri bin Kamarzaman, [2026], para. 7–8; Pendakwa Raya v Akhil Mursyid bin Nor Hisham [2026], para. 11; Pendakwa Raya v Mohamad Zakir Husim bin Mohd Alwi [2026], para. 3; Pendakwa Raya v Ibrahim bin Harun [2026], para. 8; Public Prosecutor v Mohd Idham bin Mokhtar [2026], para. 2; Pendakwa Raya v Sarimah binti Abdul Rahman [2026], para. 3; Pendakwa Raya lwn Mohd Jairulnizam bin Mohd Nordin dan satu lagi [2020], para. 12)*	kes prima facie (DBP)	kes prima facie (Google Translate)	court
19	**Public interest**	—	**kepentingan awam** *(Pendakwa Raya v Viknshpran [2026] para 10; Pendakwa Raya v Viknshpran a/l Batu Malai [2026], para. 10; Mustafa 'Afifi Ab Halim et al. [2013], p. vii; Hisyamudin bin Ahmad v. Pendakwa Raya [2020], para. 18; Ketua Pengarah Laut v Straits Bunker & Trading Sdn Bhd [2020], para. 40)*	kepentingan umum (DBP)	kepentingan awam (Google Translate)	court

continued on following page

Table 2. Continued

No.	Legal Term	Source A Statutory Authority	Source B Judicial Authority (MLJ-BM)	Source C Lexicographical / Reference Sources	Source D Non-authoritative / Informal Sources	Hierarchy Answer
20	**Sentence (criminal)**	hukuman	**hukuman penjara** *(Pendakwa Raya v Mohamad Sukry bin Wahab & Muhammad Hafiszan bin Naser [2026], para 66; Pendakwa Raya v Viknshpran [2026] para 11; Che Mohd Faiz [2026], para 4; Che Mohd Faiz bin Che Zulkifle v Pendakwa Raya [2026], para. 4; Pendakwa Raya v Hazmi Ruzaini bin Azlihudin [2026], para. 6; Hisyamudin bin Ahmad v. Pendakwa Raya, 2020, para. 2)* **hukuman** *(Mohd Izaq Fikhry bin A. Rahim v. Pendakwa Raya [2026], para. 25–26; Pendakwa Raya v Ku Mahamad Isa bin Jaafar [2026], para. 2)*	menghukum (DBP)	hukuman (Google Translate)	Act / court
21	**Writ habeas corpus**	—	**writ habeas corpus** *(Ketua Pengarah Laut v Straits Bunker & Trading Sdn Bhd [2020], para. 41)*	writ habeas corpus (DBP)	writ habeas corpus (Google Translate)	Malaysian courts do not translate this term fully. It is treated as a Latin legal term and retained in its original form.

Note: DBP = Dewan Bahasa Dan Pustaka; MLJ-BM = Malayan Law Journal (Bahasa Malaysia). Bold entries in Source B indicate the court-attested term; citations in italics provide evidentiary support.

Source: Author

Hierarchy-Based Priority in Legal Term Translation

In the field of translation of legal terms, priority has been adjudged according to the law rather than language preference. Statutory authority is at the top of this hierarchy, followed by the way words are used by judges, and secondary to these three by lexicographical evidence itself. Informal sources are completely set aside for consideration. Where there is statutory wording then that trumped any other source and would exclude any stylistic substitution. In the absence of statutory guidance, judicial usage takes precedence and thus reflects the way in which legal meaning is assumed and essentialized as practice. Lexicographical resources may only help in the vacuity of authoritative legal formulations.

This hierarchy scheme ensures the existence of legal certitude, doctrinal stability and institutional consistency in a bilingual legal system. It is also consonant with ethic duties incumbent to the legal translator for whom the goal is not linguistic elegance and stylistic variation, but rather to maintain legal effect.

Functional Equivalence in Legal Translation

In the area of legal translation, the term "functional" refers to a translation decision that is based primarily on the legal status, impact and consequences of a term in the destination legal context rather than its literal semantic content or (apparent) linguistic similarity. A functional methodology asks not the words of a term but what function it plays in the legal system, looking at its doctrinal, procedural and institutional operations. Such an approach is consistent with the existing theory of legal translation according to which legal terminology is a system of conceptual entities whose meanings are defined by normative models as well as interpretive conventions.

Category I: Statutory Body (Acts of Parliament and Subsidiary Legislation)

Statutory authority is the most dominant authority in the of hierarchy governing the translation of legal terminology. Any deviation from the authorised statutory language can be seen to risk a change of legal meaning, the weakening of normative force or the creation of interpretive ambiguity. As Wan Mahmud (2026) highlights, legal texts are not simple communication artefacts but legal effect conferencing tools, for which translators are ethically and professionally committed to preserve the legal meaning of the original text without modification or embellishment. Dictionaries and explanatory materials may be considered for the purpose of clarifying but cannot under any circumstances supersede the wording of the statute.

Category II Judicial Authority (Written Judgment of Courts and Report)

Judicial authority comes from the usage of the courts, the language used by judges in the written judgements, grounds of the decision and in the reasoning by appellate courts. Although there are law reports such as the Malayan Law Journal which acts as the reporting vehicles, the law language's authority lies not with the publisher but in the authorship of the judges. When a term is repeatedly and consistently used by courts, especially that is used across the context of written judgments and reported cases, that use gains institutional power and becomes a stabilised expression of legal meaning.

Category III: Lexicographical and Reference Materials (DBP and Legal Dictionaries)

Lexicographical sources such as DBP dictionaries, DBP legal glossaries and specialised dictionaries of law such as Oxford Dictionary of Law occupy a secondary and supportive position in the hierarchy. These resources are descriptive in nature: they explain generic meaning, usages, or recommended equivalents of the disabilities or unjustness surrounding a particular ground - but they in no way create binding legal norms.

Category IV: Non-Authoritative and Informal Sources

Non-authoritative sources include outputs of machine translation, informal online commentary, blogs, unverified websites, and coined or invented terms. These sources have the lowest level of hierarchy and are given no legal authority. Wan Mahmud (2026) warns that uncritical use of automated tools or accessed information from informal sources may underpin accuracy, subtlety, and responsibility for legal accountability, which require intensive verification of the process of information or knowledge by a rigorous human pursuant to supportive cross checking or authoritative sources of law.

Analysis

This study discusses legal translation in Malaysia by focusing especially on source hierarchy and terminological authority by considering that legal terms are doctrinally embedded conceptual units instead of simple lexical items. Consistent with term-oriented strategies in legal translation the analysis brings forward as primary determinants of legal meaning authoritative legal sources, i.e. statutes and judicial rulings (Šarčević 1997; Bajčić 2014). Thus, the criteria used to make translation decisions in relation to legal texts emphasises the achievement of legal function, institutional validity and interpretive stability in the Malaysian context over resemblance in meaning.

It is an important analytical concern that the judicial usage supports the stabilisation of legal meaning, in particular. We analyse recursive formulations in written judgement and legal reports as institutionalised formulations and they function as procedural and doctrinal signals. In accordance with the institutional and cognitive approaches to legal discourse, judicial language is one site of the interpretation, consolidation, and reproduction of legal meaning through practise (Engberg, 2020; Termorshuizen-Arts, 2008). When disconcerts are found between the definitions in the dictionaries and the real use of the language in practise, the judicial practise is considered authoritative and thus becomes the operationalisation of the legal norms in adjudication (Prieto Ramos, 2020).

Finally, the analysis brings into the foreground of the professional communication strategies functional equivalence and professional competence as the key determinants on terminological selection. Legal terms have been evaluated on the basis of their place of function in the legal system, not on their surface linguistic similarity, by borrowing from the comparative and functionalist approach to legal translation (Cao 2010; Kocbek 2012; Graziadei 2024). Such a functional orientation is a great indicator of the challenges of using either only linguistic or automatic translation methodologies and the need for both legal knowledge and institutional awareness in the course of legal translation practices (Bajčić & Basaneže 2016; Meenal & Govindarajan 2023). Through this multi-layered analysis, this study shows that legal translation at a certain level engages in the norm-governed interpretive activity in the context of legal institutions and judicial decision-making. Table 3 shows the Quantitative Analysis of Accuracy of DBP and Google Translate Against Judicial Usage.

Table 3. Quantitative analysis of accuracy of DBP and Google translate against judicial usage (n = 21)

Source	Accurate (n)	Accurate (%)	Not Accurate (n)	Not Accurate ((%)
DBP (Dictionary / Legal Glossary)	12	57.1%	9	42.9%
Google Translate	3	14.3%	18	85.7%

The accuracy of the translation of legal terms produced by Dewan Bahasa dan Pustaka (DBP) resources and Google Translate system were evaluated using a relative, hierarchy-based evaluation developed on framework as presented in Table 3. Judicial usage (Source b) was accepted as one controlling benchmark (CW) in the assessment of accuracy on the basis that judicial language is the main mechanism in the institutionalisation of legal terminology, the stabilisation and operationalisation of legal terminology within the Malaysian legal system. Language used by courts in written judgments, as well as the grounds of judgement, is a manifestation of authoritative legal meaning, as it is used in practise, and not just a description at the lexical level. As a result, judicial usage was accepted as the normative point of reference with reference against which alternative translations were considered.

For the purpose of analysis, each outcome of the translation was dichotomously determined to be either accurate or not accurate. A translation that was coded as accurate was the equivalent that DBP or Google Translate gave that was consistent with, or functionally consistent with terminology used repeatedly and systematically in judicial decisions. Functional alignment was not only determined and measured according to the degree of semblance in linguistics, but also whether the translated term contained doctrinal meaning and procedural role, as well as institutional effect within the Malaysian legal context. A translation was classified as not accurate if it was semantically vague, legally misleading, not juridical in style or as rejected in favour of a stabilised judicial formulation. This distinction reflects the basic distinction between descriptive, lexical meaning, and legally sanctioned institutional meaning.

To ensure methodological consistency and to avoid the disproportionate weighting of frequently cited expressions, for the purpose of statistical analysis the fencible legal terms that appear in Table 3 (n= 21) were counted once only according to the number of judicial examples in which each one appeared, irrespective of its frequency. This approach guarantees that the level of terminological reliability considered is not measured by frequency of occurrence but by the level of difference between legal concepts, and it therefore allows for a balanced and transparent comparison of different sources.

RESULTS

Comparability of Accuracy of DBP and Google Translate

The data show that the DBP resources have reasonable accuracy based upon a standard scale of judgment. In comparison to most of the procedural terminology (which are mostly used at high frequency) and all other general doctrinal nouns that have relatively comparable Malay equivalents (such as "beban pembuktian", "kes prima facie", "hukuman penjara", "kepentingan awam" and "sabitan"), the DBP has proven to be somewhat accurate. This is due to the fact that these terms appear in statute, judicial decisions, and references; this allows dictionary entries to provide fairly precise descriptions of how the terms are being utilized by the courts. However, DBP translations become progressively unreliable when an expression's interpretation depends upon the formulation of a traditional idiomatic expression, or its functional/doctrinal nuances are critical factors in determining what the court will determine. For example, "dipanggil membela diri" takes its semantic value from its position within the procedural context and customary practice of judges rather than through the use of general linguistic semantics. Conceptually rich expressions such as abuse of process, similarly do not lend themselves to straightforward lexicographic representation. Additionally, the many common law terms that remain in Latin ("writ habeas corpus") present similar challenges.

In contrast, Google Translate has a generally low level of accuracy in translating legal terminology. Acceptable outputs are limited to rare situations when legal terms overlap with the usage of the vernacular Malay language and do not contain much doctrinal content such as "hukuman", "kepentingan awam" when used generally in a non-technical way. Beyond these instances, Google Translate has an overall systematic failure in dealing with procedural expressions, doctrinal concepts or formulaic judicial language. Terms like "dipanggil membela diri" demand knowledge of criminal procedure and expressions like abuse of process demand knowledge of institutional and doctrinal limitations one cannot extract from general knowledge of language. The inability of the system to recognise conventionalised legal phrasing or institutional function leads to legally misleading, stylistically inappropriate, or conceptually inaccurate output. This accounts for the high rate of 85.7% lack of accuracy, and proves that Google Translate is structurally unfit for the selection of legal terms for professional or doctrinal purposes. Theoretical explanations for these systematic errors are found in the structure of legal authority itself. Machine translation models train on distributional patterns within large corpora of text and therefore optimize statistical frequency of word co-occurrence over normative validity. However, legal terminology does not gain its meaning from the general usage frequency of terms but from their authorization through institutional sources; that is an act of Parliament, a judicial formulation or a professionally recognized convention. A term such as "dipanggil membela diri" has been certified by courts to be used as the procedural marker which indicates the transition from prosecutor to defense in criminal trials under the Criminal Procedure Code. No distributional model trained on general language data will be able to capture this normatively-directed dimension without specific encoding of the hierarchy between law and institution. This finding is consistent with Šarčević's (1997) description of legal translation as receiver-oriented activity instituted into the operation of the law whereby the decisive factor in selecting a term for translation is not linguistic similarity but how a term will be interpreted and applied by legal institutions, a factor that automated translation systems are structurally incapable of satisfying without legal reasoning aware of authority.

The quantitative results reported in Table 3 show an obvious hierarchy of terminological reliability for the translation of Malaysian laws. While DBP resources provide some support and reasonable alignment with judicial usage, the DBP resources are still insufficient where legal meaning is determined by judicial convention and functional operation. Google Translate by contrast, does not understand most categories of juristic terms and cannot be used as either an authoritative or auxiliary source. These results empirically prove the model based on the hierarchy emphasised in Table 3 that legal authority, especially judicial use, rather than linguistic or technological efficiency, must guide terminological choice in legal translation.

Analytical Framework and Theoretical Positioning

In the Malaysian legal texts in particular, paying special attention to the interplay of hierarchical source of authority, judicial practises and functions of law. Rather than examining the quality of the translation on stylistic or linguistic contentions, the deliberate selection of translation decisions is embedded in institutional conditions of production of authoritative legal meaning. Consistent with term-oriented approaches to legal translation, legal terms are conceptualised as system-specific units of legal doctrine and practise, rather than ordinary lexical items transferable in terms of semantic equivalence only (Šarčević, 1997; Bajčić, 2014; Engberg, 2020).

The main analytical focus is on the hierarchical source authority. Each legal term was scrutinised based on a graduated scale of references, including texts of statutes, judicial references, lexicographical references and secondary reference material or explanatory material. In accordance with the institutional translation theory, statutory provisions are the top level of terminological authority because of their binding legal force and normative status (Šarčević, 1997; Cao, 2010; Prieto Ramos, 2020). Where Malay formulations in Acts of Parliament or subsidiary legislation are authorised, then they are terminological and determinative and are not subject to stylistic modification. Lexicographical resources such as DBP dictionaries do have a secondary role and need to give way where statute or judicial usage results in a divergent legal meaning. This hierarchy - sensitive assessment, as a result, reflects the institutional constraints of legal translation and the primacy of the authority of law over that of general linguistic convention (Bidin, 1995; Prieto Ramos, 2020; Engberg 2020).

Judicial language is considered to be the space where legal meaning is interpreted, crystallised, and reproduced through judge-making (Termorshuizen-Arts, 2008; Engberg, 2020). Where consistent judicial usage is established that usage is regarded to be authoritative notwithstanding other renderings proposed by dictionaries. This approach is consistent with Bajčić's (2014) position that legal meaning is institutional interpretation rather than literal meaning.

Drawing on legal linguistics and translation theory of functionalism, such expressions are considered as indivisible terminological units, in which legal meaning cannot be broken down without the possibility to break it into doctrine units (Cao, 2010; Kocbek, 2012; Cosmulescu, 2021). Partial translation or semantic reduction are therefore graded as not legally optimal in so far as they create ambiguity or change procedural implications and reinforce the observation that legal meaning is more often found in structured multi word units than in individual words.

Another analytical level involves trans-systems of legal ideas and common laws doctrines such as Latin maxims and English legal terms inherited in Malaysian judicial thought. In line with the methodology of comparative law, these terms are analysed not with reference to seeming linguistic form, but with reference to their doctrinal function and systemic role (Zweigert & Kötz, 1983; Graziadei, 2024, 2025): Where the benefits of translation are not to provide conceptual imprecision or reduce the coherence between the different legal cases, the priority is rather to aim at the retention of the conceptual terminology and doctrinal terminology of the original text, in accordance with the findings of research in EU and comparative legal translation (Bajčić, 2014; Kocbek, 2015).

Terms referring to legal functions, constants of institutional action or procedures are evaluated by their operative legal effect in the Malaysian legal order and not due to their semantic close affinity to the source language (Šarčević, 1997; Kocbek, 2012; Kusik, 2024).

Translation decisions are assessed by reference to legal competency, institutional awareness and ethical responsibility. In line with the research on professionalisation, an accuracy in legal translation requires legal knowledge and interpretive judgement along with being bilingual (Bajčić and Basaneže, 2016; Sulaiman et al., 2024). Insights from the research in machine translation also help put the results in context as automated systems lack the interpretive capacity necessary to resolve legal polysemy, doctrinal ambiguity, and understanding of context-dependent meaning (Orozco & Sanchez-Gijon, 2011; Meenal & Govindarajan, 2023; Nan, 2026).

DISCUSSION

It is evident throughout that the authorised statutory language is at the top of the hierarchy. Where Malay formulation is legislated in Acts of Parliament or subsidiary legislation, the texts of such formulation are given binding legal force and shall be reproduced word for word in translation. Any deviation, in the form of paraphrase, synonym replacement, or change of form, presents a risk of changing the normative content of the provision, and may change its legal interpretation or enforceability. Lexicographical resources, even DBP dictionaries, therefore only serve as supplementary tools and cannot prevail against the statutory wordage without affecting the legality of the law.

Where statutory authority is absent or silent, the judiciary's usage is the second and equally important level of authority. The analysis confirms that terminology used repeatedly by courts, in written judgments and grounds of decision, and reported cases, especially in the form of MLJ - BM, constitutes an independent source of legally authoritative meaning. Expressions like “melampaui keraguan munasabah”, “dipanggil membela diri”, “pengakuan salah and dilepaskan dan dibebaskan” had as a procedural and doctrinal function - signalling evidentiary thresholds, stages of proceedings as well as legal outcomes. In cases where there is divergence between dictionary definitions and court established usage, judicial practise always prevails and this reflects the manner in which legal meaning is interpreted, stabilised and operationalised within the Malaysian legal systemThe case for a more complex scenario is made by differing statutory authority and judicial developments — i.e., the legislative wording does not reflect changes to either doctrine or methodology. Therefore, as part of the TODCM process, the translator would have to use principled discretion in terms of what the "operative" terminology standards are — namely, where a court has repeatedly abandoned the exact wording of a statute in favor of a more contextual definition, then the stabilized judicial definition should be considered the operative terminological standard regardless of whether it modifies or adds to the language of the statute. This approach aligns with Malaysia's judicial tradition of giving effect to the purpose and function of a statutory provision (i.e., purposive statutory interpretation) over merely its bare words. Mechanical adherence to outdated statutory definitions can result in terminological rigidity which impairs understanding of the current law and therefore undermines one of the major purposes of developing an institutional hierarchical structure which is promoting institutional coherence.

A further interest is that legal meaning is often expressed by means of fixed collocations and binomial expressions that are preserved by the courts to allow which to express cumulative legal effects. These findings challenge translating anything that emphasizes brevity or stylistic elegance at the expense of including completeness or making sure that something is legally recognisable.

With regard to common-law and trans-systemic legal doctrines, the data demonstrates a great judicial preference for taking Latin or English terms as it were, with only minimal localisation wherever necessary. This practice takes its toll from judicial concern for conceptual precision, inter-case coherence, and continuity in a mixed legal system. Descriptive Malay paraphrases, though linguistically transparent, are unsatisfactory substitutes on which a term is a doctrinal anchor across the cases. The results are therefore a confirmation that legal concepts cannot be fully localised without losing too much of their doctrinal integrity.

Crucially, the results emphasize the importance of translating legal texts, by pointing out that good legal translation requires a professional competence beyond being a simple bilingual. In line with Bajčić and Basaneže (2016), the analysis shows that the legal translators must possess substantive legal knowledge, be acquainted with the institutional structure, procedural functions and judicial reasoning patterns. Translators need to be able to recognise authoritative sources, recognise stabilised judicial terminology and be able to predict how courts are likely to interpret a term being translated. Translation decisions in the data set cannot be accounted for like decisions made based on linguistic knowledge, but they are based on an understanding of how the legal meaning is produced, validated, and get constrained in institutional settings.

The results also highlight the dangers and effects of faulty legal translation. Where translators draw on sources not recognised in the primary language or even invent terms, or where they focus on semantic similarity rather than legal function, there is a chance that such translations can result in ambiguity, that they wrongly represent the procedural stages, or that they misrepresent the substantive rights and obligations. Such mistakes can result in the misinterpretation of courts, lack of consistency in legal documents, difficulty in accordance with procedural fairness, or even of an invalidation of legal acts. In cases of high stakes such as criminal and in enforcement of contract terminological inaccuracy can affect the due process, prejudice parties or put institutions at risk of legal action. The latter have consequences for the sense of ethical and professional responsibility of the practitioners of this profession to follow the authoritative sources and conformity conventions, which are institutional.

The findings determine an explicit order of categories ordering terminological priority in the process of legal translation in Malaysia. At the top of such a hierarchy are Acts of Parliament and subsidiary legislation, then judicial usage in the form of judgments, legal documents and case law. Lexicographical resources, such as DBP dictionaries and legal glossaries also hold a supporting and subordinate role and can only be referred to where there is a match with statutory or judicial usage. Online translation, pop sources and linguistic neologisms comprise the worst levels of the hierarchy and hold no legal force; their use as determinative sources is incompatible with the practice of translating professionally as lawyers.

The results of the research support an approach of term-oriented, hierarchy aware and institutionally anchored legal translation in Malaysia. They confirm the belief that legal translation and legal interpretation have mutual and common hermeneutic background (Bajčić 2014; Termorshuizen-Arts 2008). Like judges, translators therefore have to engage in purposive and context - sensitive reasoning, anticipating the construction, stabilisation and formulation of legal meaning through judicial practise. This is consistent with the teleological approaches found in EU and comparative jurisprudence and is no less applicable to the Malaysian bilingual legal context.

Scott's (2017) examination of information asymmetry and Hsieh's (2018) way of conceptualising legal translation as an economic activity bring issues concerning accountability, risk management and professional responsibility to the forefront. The intersection of such points of view reveals a demand for organized translational procedures that can bring together legal function, institutional hierarchy and communicative efficiency. Within this scheme of reflection, terminological accuracy does not constitute a matter of linguistic convenience; rather, it is a condition for legal validity, institutional trust and the rule of law.

CONCLUSION

Translators speak in an environment defined in its competence by competing sources of authority - the statutory text, the dictionaries, the judicial usages, the general lexicography, authorised legal instruments and informal or technologically mediated products. These tensions are amplified by legal polysemy, conceptual incongruity between legal systems, rigid judicial formulae, and the coexistence of three legal concepts, that is, statutory law, common law, and Islamic legal concepts. Such complexity cannot be resolved through surface level semantic equivalence only and requires an understanding of how the legal meaning is produced and stabilised institutionally (Bidin, 1995; Šarčević, 1997; Bajčić, 2014; Engberg, 2020).

The results suggest that the most effective way of dealing with these challenges is using a hierarchy-sensitive and function-oriented approach to terminological choice. Where legislative authority is found, authorised statutory formulations take precedence. Where statutes are silent or indeterminate, established judicial formulations with the benefit of stabilisation that results from repeated adjudicative invocation takes rule of termination. Fixed collocations and binomial expressions continue to keep composite doctrinal effects, whereas "role" and "mechanism"-based terms need to have functional equivalence that shows operative legal machinery and not theatrical literal meaning. By operationalising these priorities in the context of a rationale of scenario-based decision-making, the research helps to convert abstruse concepts of "accuracy" into a method of analysis that can be replicated to resolve real-world terminological conflicts in professional practise (Cao, 2010; Prieto Ramos, 2020; Kocbek, 2012). Legal translation is limited above all by legal hierarchy and communicative norms, rather than by general linguistic preference (Prieto Ramos, 2020; Biel & Kockaert, 2023).

TODCM offers a coherent link between fields such as between comparative law and legal translation studies. Thus, by conceptualising legal terms as system bound legal units with the meanings inscribed in authoritative sources, TODCM allows translators and researcher-translators to analyse the meaning in a procedural way, to evaluate functional equivalence between legal system, and to test choices of translation by the expected lens of judicial reception and legal effect (Zweigert & Kötz, 1983; Graziadei,2024, 2025; Bajčić and Basaneže 2016).

Legal terminology doesn't always call for a one and only equivalent to be found. Certain terms permit controlled flexibility within a legally capable degree that can be followed as long as functional and contextual parameters are honoured. For instance, aggravating factors can be translated as "rayuan pemberatan" or "hujahan pemberatan" depending on whether there is focus on the argumentation procedure or the evaluation of the sentencing. Similarly, terms like mitigation and conviction allow some grammatical and morphological variation (e.g. sabit, disabitkan, menyabitkan) in accordance with the position in the sentence and function in the discourse. This flexibility, however, is not arbitrary as it occurs within bounds, within boundaries created by judicial usage and legal convention. By comparison, other terms have a high terminological stability and allow only one-to-one translation, for example, *prima facie*, which is consistently translated as "kes prima facie". An appreciation of this difference between terms used in a stable fashion and variants degrees that are sensitive to a specific context is critical for both legal precision and linguistic coherence.

Legal translation in Malaysia as one which is best described as norm-governed, institutionally-embedded interpretive activity-both in its context as a linguistic activity. Part of ensuring legal certainty and coherence in a multilingual legal system is to recognise translation as an integral part of legal interpretation and institutional communication (Engberg, 2020; Termorshuizen-Arts, 2008; Bajčić, 2014). The study is a contribution that brings to the foreground source hierarchy, judicial stabilisation of meaning, and functional equivalence, based on legal doctrine. By taking terminological choice as a legal act having possible doctrinal and procedural implications, the proposed approach will provide, at once, a powerful analytical tool for study and a practical tool for professional legal translators working in schemes of a plurality of legal systems.

Future Research Directions

The future studies should explore cases where there exists divergence in statutory authority and evolutionary development in the judiciary; e.g., when obsolete legislative terms conflict with contemporary interpretative standards created by judicial precedents. Establishing a coherent framework for resolution of such hierarchy conflicts will significantly enhance the practical utility of the TODCM methodology in actual world translation projects.

Secondly, the future research may refine the simple binary accuracy measures used in this study (i.e. correct/incorrect) using multi-dimensional assessment criteria including degree of functional equivalence, contextuality of appropriateness, and terminological stability. In addition, incorporating inter-coder reliability assessments will increase the methodological quality of evaluations made by comparison.

Finally, given the increasing use of AI assisted translation technology in Malaysia's legal community, it is recommended that researchers investigate systematically the potential of fine tuning large language models with authoritative legal corpora to better align them with usage in court and with statutory authorities. Longitudinal studies examining changes in judicial terminology over time will demonstrate the dynamic character of stabilization of terminology in Malaysia's developing bilingual legal system.

AI Declaration

No AI-based Text Generation Tool was applied to create this chapter. The e-Hakim Database was searched independently for data extraction purposes by the Author. If an AI-based tool was employed at all during either the creation process or editing process, it was only for checking grammar as no contribution existed with regard to the intellectual content, analysis or conclusion within this Chapter.

REFERENCES

Alwazna, R. Y. (2018). Translation and legal terminology: Techniques for coping with the untranslatability of legal terms between Arabic and English. International Journal for the Semiotics of Law - Revue internationale de Sémiotique juridique, 32(1), 75-94. DOI: 10.1007/s11196-018-9580-y

Azizah binti Harun & Ors. v. Pentadbir Tanah Kerian & Anor. (2025). *Alasan penghakiman* [Grounds of judgment]. Mahkamah Tinggi Malaya di Taiping, Perak. Saman Pemula No. AB-24NCVC-294-10/2024.

Bajčić, M. (2014). Towards a terminological approach to translating European Contract Law. In Pasa, B., & Morra, L. (Eds.), *Translating the DCFR and drafting the CESL: a pragmatic perspective* (pp. 125–145). Seller European Law Publishers., DOI: 10.1515/9783866536067.125

Bajčić, M., & Basaneže, K. D. (2016). Towards the professionalization of legal translators and court interpreters in the EU: Introduction and overview. In Bajčić, M., & Basaneže, K. D. (Eds.), *Towards the professionalization of legal translators and court interpreters in the EU* (pp. 1–11). Cambridge Scholars Publishing.

Bidin, A. (1995). Issues in translation of legal texts in Malaysia. *Perspectives - Gerontological Nursing Association, 3*(2), 205–213. DOI: 10.1080/0907676X.1995.9961261

Biel, L., & Kockaert, H. J. (2023). Introduction: Legal terminology. In Resi, R., & Steurs, F. (Eds.), *Handbook of Terminology* (pp. 1–14). John Benjamins Publishing Company., DOI: 10.1075/hot.3.int3

Cao, D. (2010). Legal Translation. In Y. Gambier & L. Van Doorslaer (Eds.), Handbook of Translation Studies, Volume 1 (pp. 191-195). John Benjamins Publishing Company. DOI: 10.1075/hts.1.leg1

Che Mohd Faiz bin Che Zulkifle v. Pendakwa Raya. (2026). *Alasan penghakiman* [Grounds of judgment]. Mahkamah Tinggi Kuala Terengganu. Rayuan Jenayah No. TC-83D-42-01/2022.

Cheng, L., & Sin, K. K. (2008). Terminological equivalence in legal translation: A semiotic approach. *Semiotica, 2008*(172), 33–45. DOI: 10.1515/SEMI.2008.088

Cosmulescu, A. M. (2021). A terminological perspective on legal translation. *Professional Communication and Translation Studies, 14*, 151–157. DOI: 10.59168/EPBG9565

DBP. (2026, February 5). Carian umum. Pusat Rujukan Persuratan Melayu @PRPM. https://prpm.dbp.gov.my/Cari1?keyword=conviction&d=382696&#LIHATSINI

Engberg, J. (2020). Comparative law for legal translation: Through multiple perspectives to multidimensional knowledge. International Journal for the Semiotics of Law - Revue internationale de Sémiotique juridique, 33, 263-282. DOI: 10.1007/s11196-020-09706-9

Goh, S. S., & Harjit Singh, D. S. (Eds.). (2015). Glosari Undang-undang jenayah Bahasa Inggeris-Bahasa Melayu. UTHM Publisher. https://publisher.uthm.edu.my/omp/index.php/penerbituthm/catalog/download/156/176/767?inline=1

Graziadei, M. (2024). Rodolfo Sacco's theoretical contribution to comparative law: A personal account. International Journal for the Semiotics of Law - Revue internationale de Sémiotique juridique, 37, 1471-1484. DOI: 10.1007/s11196-024-10128-0

Graziadei, M. (2025). Legal translation and the quest for authenticity. International Journal for the Semiotics of Law - Revue internationale de Sémiotique juridique, 38, 2565-2593. DOI: 10.1007/s11196-025-10283-y

Heylen, K., & Steurs, F. (2014). Translating legal and administrative language: How to deal with legal terms and their flexiblemeaning potential. *Turjuman Numero spécial octobre*, 96-146. https://revues.imist.ma/index.php/Turjuman/article/view/52714/27347

Hsieh, H. P. (2018). Crossing Language Lines and Legal Tradition Lines—Legal Translation as an Economic Phenomenon. University College Cork. https://www.academia.edu/40008818/Crossing_Language_Lines_and_Legal_Tradition_Lines_Legal_Translation_as_an_Economic_Phenomenon

Huong, N. T., & Anh, V. T. (2024). The Application of ChatGPT in Translation Learning: A Case Study in Vietnam. *Journal of Institutional Research South East Asia, 23*(2), 224–245. https://www.seaairweb.info/journal/articles/JIRSEA_v23_n02/JIRSEA_v23_n02_Article12.pdf

Kocbek, A. (2012). An integrated model for translating legal texts. Vertimo studijos, 5(5), 64-75. DOI: 10.15388/VertStud.2012.5.10560

Kocbek, A. (2015). The Decalogue of Legal Translation – Contracts in Intercultural Legal Communication. *CLINA*, *1*(1), 71–86.

Kusik, P. (2024). Legal communication as a point of contact between legal translation and comparative law. *Journal of International Legal Communication*, *14*(3), 92–109. DOI: 10.32612/uw.27201643.2024.14.3.pp.92-109

Malayan Law Journal (MLJ) Articles and Cases

Meenal, T. S., & Govindarajan, P. (2023). The challenges of using machine translation while translating Polysemous words. *Studies in Media and Communication, 11*(2), 63–67. DOI: 10.11114/smc.v11i2.5944

Mokhtar, H. S. (1983). Undang-undang Malaysia Akta 32 Akta Bahasa 1963/67. Percetakan Negara, Kuala Lumpur. https://eseminar.dbp.gov.my

Mustafa 'Afifi Ab Halim, Mohd Mahyeddin Mohd Salleh, Rezki Perdani Sawai, Nurhafizah Muhd Shukor, Dini Farhana Baharuddin, Joki Perdani Sawai, & Abd Halim Mohd Hussin. (2013). Bayi yang dibuang: Hak dan kedudukan bayi di sisi undang-undang. Malayan Law Journal, 5, i–xii.

Hisyamudin bin Ahmad v. Pendakwa Raya. (2020). [2020] 7 Malayan Law Journal 187 (High Court of Malaya, Johor Bahru). Ketua Pengarah Laut, Jabatan Laut Malaysia & Ors v. Straits Bunker & Trading Sdn Bhd & Anor. (2020). [2020] 7 Malayan Law Journal 71 (High Court of Malaya, Johor Bahru).

Nan, Y. (2026). Current English–Chinese legal language mutual translation based on the comparison of the three theoretical levels of words, sentences, and articles. *International Journal of Data Science and Analytics*, *22*(1), 1–13. DOI: 10.1007/s41060-025-01007-3

Orozco, M., & Sánchez-Gijón, P. (2011). New resources for legal translators. *Perspectives, 19*(1), 25–44. DOI: 10.1080/0907676I003784979

Pendakwa Raya lwn Mohd Jairulnizam bin Mohd Nordin dan satu lagi. (2020). [2020] 7 *Malayan Law Journal* 103 (Mahkamah Tinggi Malaya, Taiping).

Pendakwa Raya v. Akhil Mursyid bin Nor Hisham & Anor. (2026). *Alasan penghakiman* [Grounds of judgment]. Mahkamah Majistret Kota Bharu, Kelantan. Kes Tangkap No. DA-83RS-135-08/2023.

Pendakwa Raya v. Aliff Syukri bin Kamarzaman. (2026). *Alasan penghakiman* [Unpublished grounds of judgment]. Mahkamah Sesyen Sepang, Selangor. Kes No. BK-63-(11,12,13,14)-10/2022.

Pendakwa Raya v. Aminuddin bin Jusoh @ Yusof. (2026). *Alasan penghakiman* [Grounds of judgment]. Mahkamah Majistret Kuala Berang, Terengganu. Kes Tangkap No. TE-82JS-1-07/2021.

Pendakwa Raya v. Firdaus Rizal bin Abdul Manan. (2026). *Alasan penghakiman* [Grounds of judgment]. Mahkamah Sesyen Teluk Intan, Perak. Kes Jenayah No. AC-62K-1-02/2023 & Ors.

Pendakwa Raya v. Hazmi Ruzaini bin Azlihudin. (2026). *Alasan penghakiman* [Grounds of judgment]. Mahkamah Sesyen Sepang, Selangor. Kes Jenayah No. BK-62D-100-10/2025.

Pendakwa Raya v. Ibrahim bin Harun. (2026). *Alasan penghakiman* [Grounds of judgment]. Mahkamah Tinggi Malaya di Temerloh, Pahang. Perbicaraan Jenayah No. CB-45A-07-02/2022.

Pendakwa Raya v. Ku Mahamad Isa bin Jaafar. (2026). *Alasan penghakiman* [Grounds of judgment]. Mahkamah Majistret Kuala Kangsar, Perak. Kes Jenayah No. AG-83RS-6-01/2026.

Pendakwa Raya v. Ku Mahamad Isa bin Jaafar. (2026). *Alasan penghakiman* [Grounds of judgment]. Mahkamah Majistret Lenggong, Perak. Kes Jenayah No. AR-83RS-2-01/2026.

Pendakwa Raya v. Mohamad Sukry bin Wahab & Muhammad Hafiszan bin Naser. (2026). *Alasan penghakiman* [Grounds of judgment]. Mahkamah Sesyen Sepang, Selangor. Perbicaraan Jenayah No. BK-63ES-1-07/2022.

Pendakwa Raya v. Mohamad Zakir Husim bin Mohd Alwi. (2026). *Alasan penghakiman.* Mahkamah Sesyen Kuala Pilah, Negeri Sembilan. Kes Tangkap No. NB-62D-222-10/2023.

Pendakwa Raya v. Mohd Nazuli bin Mohd Nazari. (2026). *Alasan penghakiman* [Grounds of judgment]. Mahkamah Sesyen Jenayah (2) Alor Setar, Kedah. Kes Jenayah No. KA-61R-2-01/2022.

Pendakwa Raya v. Mustapha bin Ibrahim. (2026). *Alasan penghakiman* [Grounds of judgment]. Mahkamah Tinggi Malaya di Kota Bharu, Kelantan. Rayuan Jenayah No. DA-41S-1-01/2025.

Pendakwa Raya v. Sarimah binti Abdul Rahman. (2026). *Alasan penghakiman* [Grounds of judgment]. Mahkamah Majistret Melaka. Kes Saman No. MA-85-138-05/2024.

Pendakwa Raya v. Syed Akmar bin Syed Othman. (2026). *Alasan penghakiman* [Grounds of judgment]. Mahkamah Majistret Kangar, Perlis. Kes Jenayah No. RA-83D-408-02/2023.

Pendakwa Raya v. Tee Wei Xuan. (2026, January 30). *Alasan penghakiman* [Unpublished grounds of judgment]. Mahkamah Sesyen Jenayah 10, Wilayah Persekutuan Kuala Lumpur. Kes Tangkap No. WA-62K-269-12/2025.

Pendakwa Raya v. Viknshpran a/l Batu Malai. (2026). *Alasan penghakiman* [Grounds of judgment]. Mahkamah Majistret Teluk Intan, Perak. Kes Tangkap No. AC-83D-1448-11/2025.

Phillvin Guachin v. Pendakwa Raya. (2026). *Grounds of judgment.* Mahkamah Tinggi Johor Bahru, Johor. Usul No. JA-44-39-10/2025.

Powell, R., & Saw, T. G. (2021). Multilingual legal practice and law student internships in Malaysia. *World Englishes*, *42*(3), 579–592. DOI: 10.1111/weng.12570

Prieto Ramos, F. (2020). Translation at International Organizations: The Legal and Linguistic Hierarchies of Multilingualism. In Ji, M., & Laviosa, S. (Eds.), *The Oxford Handbook of Translation and Social Practices* (pp. 455–477). Oxford University Press., DOI: 10.1093/oxfordhb/9780190067205.013.13

Prieto Ramos, F., & Cerutti, G. (2021). Terminology as a source of difficulty in translating international legal discourses: An empirical cross-genre study. *International Journal of Legal Discourse*, *6*(2), 155–179. DOI: 10.1515/ijld-2021-2052

Public Prosecutor v. Mohd Idham bin Mokhtar. (2026). *Grounds of judgment.* Sessions Court Johor Bahru. Criminal Case Nos. JA-61R-24-12/2021 & JA-61R-9-06/2022.

Ramalingam, S., Sabaruddin, J. S., & Dhanapal, S. (2022). The language of justice in Malaysian courts: The law and the reality. *IIUM Law Journal*, *30*(2), 23–48. DOI: 10.31436/iiumlj.v30i2.758

Sacco, R. (1991). Legal formants: A dynamic approach to comparative law (Installment II of II). *The American Journal of Comparative Law*, *39*(2), 343–401. DOI: 10.2307/840784

Šarčević, S. (1997). *New approach to legal translation.* Kluwer Law International B.V.

Scott, J. (2017). Legal translation – a multidimensional endeavour. *Comparative Legilinguistics*, *32*, 37–66. DOI: 10.14746/cl.2017.32.2

Sopjani, V., & Hamiti, V. (2022). Challenges in the translation of legal texts: The case in Kosovo. *Comparative Legilinguistics*, *52*, 351–380. DOI: 10.14746/cl.52.2022.15

Sulaiman, M. Z., Zainudin, I. S., & Haroon, H. (2024). Pemprofesionalan Amalan Terjemahan Dan Kejurubahasaan Di Malaysia: Satu Tinjauan Awal (The professionalisation of translation and interpreting practice in Malaysia: A preliminary study). *GEMA Online Journal of Language Studies*, *24*(4), 387–409. DOI: 10.17576/gema-2024-2404-21

Sun, X., & Chen, X. (2024). Review of legal terminology translation research. *International Journal of Education and Humanities, 17*(3), 343–348. DOI: 10.54097/1zy4e144

Syameel, D. (2025a, April 28). 1.HONORIFICS TEST 1 [Ms Word]. Malaysian Institute of Translation and Books.

Syameel, D. (2025b, April 28). 2. Hierarchy of Sources [Ms Word]. Malaysian Institute of Translation and Books.

Syameel, D. (2025c, April 28). 3. LEGAL TERMS/PHRASES [Ms Word]. Malaysian Institute of Translation and Books.

Termorshuizen-Arts, M. (2008). Legal Semantics: A contribution to the methodology of legal comparison, jurisprudence and legal translation (S. Kahn, Trans.). Willem-Jan and René van der Wolf. https://www.researchgate.net/publication/275462781_Legal_semantics_A_contribution_to_the_methodology_of_legal_comparison_jurisprudence_and_legal_translation#fullTextFileContent

Turaeva, U. (2020). Characteristics, Methods, and Challenges Of Translating Law Terminology. JournalNX—A Multidisciplinary Peer-Reviewed Journal, 6(11), 312-316.

Wan Mahmud, W. A. (2026, Jan 7). Asas penterjemahan teks Undang-undang [PPT].

Zweigert, K., & Kötz, H. (1983). An Introduction to Comparative Law (3rd ed.). Oxford University Press. Malaysian Court Judgments (Alasan Penghakiman / Grounds of Judgment)

ADDITIONAL READING

Altuwairesh, N. S., & AlGhamedi, N. A. (2025). Challenges & Solutions in legal translation training: Translator trainees' perspectives. *Theory and Practice in Language Studies, 15*(4), 1188–1195. DOI: 10.17507/tpls.1504.17

Baaij, C. J. (2012). Fifty Years of Multilingual Interpretation in the European Union. In Tiersma, P. M., & Solan, L. M. (Eds.), *The Oxford handbook of language and law* (pp. 217–232). Oxford University Press., DOI: 10.1093/oxfordhb/9780199572120.013.0016

Biel, Ł. (2014). *Lost in the Eurofog: The textual fit of translated law.* Peter Lang Edition., DOI: 10.3726/978-3-653-03986-3

Campos, M. F. (2025). Comment on Patricia Jeronimo's 'Legal translation and the challenges of overcoming language barriers in court practice: Evidence from Portuguese courts'. *International Journal for the Semiotics of Law - Revue internationale de Sémiotique juridique, 38*, 2651-2655. https://doi.org/DOI: 10.1007/s11196-025-10319-3

Cao, D. (2007). *Translating law*. Multilingual Matters.

Farghal, T., Shraideh, K., & Al-Omari, A. M. (2025). Evaluating free legal translation tools between Arabic and English: A comparative study of Google translate, ChatGPT, and Gemini. *International Journal for the Semiotics of Law - Revue internationale de Sémiotique juridique, 38*(6), 2083-2110. https://doi.org/DOI: 10.1007/s11196-025-10282-z

Giczela-Pastwa, J. (2025). How can a learner translation corpus assist L2 translator trainers in fostering trainees' cross-linguistic competence in the context of legal translation? *The Interpreter and Translator Trainer, 20*(1), 1–20. DOI: 10.1080/1750399X.2025.2554464

Jovanović, V. (2026). Translation errors in Serbian legal regulations and eir impact on text interpretation and law application. *Nauka bezbednost policija, 31*(1), 81-94. https://doi.org/DOI: 10.5937/nabepo31-53008

Mau, B. R., Wu, Y. P., & Feng, H. H. (2026). Mind the cognitive load gap: Student translators' cognitive demands and translation behaviors in genai-assisted legal translation. *System, 139*, 104033. DOI: 10.1016/j.system.2026.104033

Yaqin, A. (2008). *Legal research and writing methods*. LexisNexis Butterworths Wadhwa Nagpur.

KEY TERMS AND DEFINITIONS

Bilingual Legal System: A legal framework in which two languages carry official legal force, as in Malaysia where both Malay and English are used in legislation, adjudication, and legal administration, requiring systematic approaches to terminological equivalence.

Doctrinal Legal Research: A methodology that examines the meaning of legal provisions through analysis of primary authoritative sources such as statutes, judicial decisions, and scholarly commentary, with the aim of identifying legal rules and principles.

Functional Equivalence: In legal translation, a correspondence between source and target terms based on their legal effect and institutional function rather than surface linguistic similarity. A functionally equivalent term performs the same doctrinal and procedural role in the target legal system as the original term in the source system.

Judicial Usage: The consistent deployment of specific legal terminology by judges in written judgments, grounds of judgment, and appellate reasoning. In the context of this chapter, judicial usage constitutes an authoritative source of legal meaning that may override dictionary definitions where courts have established stabilised terminological conventions.

Legal Formant: A concept developed by Rodolfo Sacco referring to the distinct layers that constitute legal meaning within any legal system, including enacted rules, judicial reasoning, professional doctrine, and tacit institutional knowledge. These layers may diverge, meaning that what the law says on paper may differ from how it operates in practice.

Legal Polysemy: The phenomenon where a single legal term carries multiple distinct meanings depending on context, jurisdiction, or area of law. Legal polysemy poses particular challenges for translators as selecting the wrong meaning can alter the normative content of a legal provision.

Source Hierarchy: An ordered framework ranking sources of legal terminology according to their institutional authority. In the Malaysian bilingual legal context, this hierarchy places statutory authority at the apex, followed by judicial usage, lexicographical references, and informal sources, with each level taking precedence over those below it in terminological decision-making.

Terminological Priority: The principled preference for one terminological option over another in legal translation, based on institutional authority rather than linguistic preference. Terminological priority ensures that legal certainty, doctrinal stability, and institutional coherence are maintained across bilingual legal documents.

Terminological Stability: The consistent and repeated use of a particular legal term across judicial decisions, statutory instruments, and professional practice to the point where it acquires a settled institutional meaning. High terminological stability indicates that a term has been validated by authoritative legal sources and should be preserved in translation.

Term-Oriented Doctrinal Comparative Method (TODCM): A hybrid methodology proposed in this chapter for the analysis of English-Malay legal translation. TODCM combines doctrinal legal research with term-oriented translation analysis to evaluate legal terminology based on its authoritative meaning, institutional function, and interpretive alignment with judicial practice rather than on surface linguistic equivalence alone.

Chapter 4

Exploring False Friend Risk in Hong Kong English-Chinese Bilingual Legal Texts: A Corpus-Assisted Study on Legal Terminology

Chen Yang
http://orcid.org/0009-0004-5939-5331
Universiti Sains Malaysia, Malaysia

Mansour Amini
http://orcid.org/0000-0003-2149-4604
Universiti Sains Malaysia, Malaysia

Malini N. G. Ganapathy
Universiti Sains Malaysia, Malaysia

ABSTRACT

This chapter examines false friend risk in Hong Kong English-Chinese bilingual legal texts, analyzing conceptual equivalence between English legal terms and their official Chinese equivalents. The study selects four marriage and family laws from Hong Kong e-Legislation (HKeL) to construct a small-scale English-Chinese parallel legal corpus. Adopting a research methodology that involves corpus retrieval using AntConc, candidate term selection, assessment of equivalence levels, and slot-based framework analysis, the study conducts a qualitative analysis of representative terms. The research indicates that the risks do not manifest as overt mistranslations, but

DOI: 10.4018/979-8-3373-9179-3.ch004

rather as implicit conceptual risks under standardized translations. This chapter conceptualizes the false friend risks as incomplete conceptual equivalence in the cross-linguistic reconstruction of legal, thereby deepening our understanding of conceptual asymmetry in the translation of legal terminology.

INTRODUCTION

Legal translation differs from general translation as it involves not only cross-linguistic lexical and syntactic correspondence but also the transmission of legal concepts, institutions, and systems (Graziadei, 2025). Unlike common vocabulary, legal terminology is tied to specific legal systems and contexts, encoding system-specific concepts rather than general meanings (Doczekalska, 2023). Its scope, procedural role, and normative function often can't be fully conveyed through surface-level lexical translation (Šarčević, 1997). With corpus-assisted translation studies, legal translation research now relies on authentic corpora rather than intuition or isolated examples. Baker (1995) pioneered this empirical approach, observing translation patterns. Biel (2008) notes that corpus methods are especially useful for examining terminology and set phrases. In Hong Kong's bilingual legal system, English-Chinese texts offer ideal material for studying conceptual shifts and equivalence in legal terminology (Chan & Cham, 2023). Thus, terminology in legal translation is crucial for reconstructing legal knowledge across languages (Biel & Kockaert, 2023; Prieto Ramos & Cerutti, 2023).

Consequently, numerous English legal terms have been assigned standardized official Chinese translations. However, the stability of these translations does not necessarily guarantee the effective conveyance of conceptual meaning, particularly within the realms of marriage and family law. Some English terms may be superficially recognizable in everyday usage, yet they possess markedly different institutional implications and procedural functions within a legal context (Wu et al., 2026). The inherent risks are often more challenging to identify as translators may presume that a concept has been thoroughly communicated when, in fact, they have only achieved a partial understanding. This phenomenon generally manifests not as clear translation errors but as the risk posed by false friends, surface-level equivalents that do not represent true conceptual equivalents. This risk is intrinsic, concealed, and difficult to detect; it warrants greater scholarly attention than is given to conventional mistranslations (Šarčević, 1997; Engberg, 2023).

Existing research has addressed issues related to legal terminology from various perspectives, including false friends, legal equivalence, comparative law, and legal knowledge frameworks. However, no systematic, corpus-based study has examined the operation of false friend risk in Hong Kong's officially standardized bilingual legal terminology. Although legal concepts possess distinct system-bound characteristics and emphasize that the equivalence of legal terminology should not be understood as mere lexical substitution but rather analyzed at the levels of legal concepts, institutional functions, and knowledge representation, discussions concerning the tension between stable official correspondence and adequate conceptual conveyance in authoritative bilingual legal texts remain insufficient (Jopek-Bosiacka, 2023; Peruzzo, 2023). In particular, regarding Hong Kong bilingual legal texts, existing scholarship has concentrated more on bilingual legislation, translation norms, or general features of legal language, with few studies specifically analyzing, at the terminological level, how false friend risks manifest in various forms, such as interference from general meanings, legal semantic shifts, partial equivalence, and conceptual compression (Zhou & Hu, 2024).

To address this research gap, this paper examines English-Chinese bilingual legal texts in the field of Hong Kong marriage and family law to explore the false friend risk associated with legal terminology in cross-linguistic conversion and its manifestations. The research corpus is drawn from relevant bilingual legal texts in the HKeL. Based on this, the paper constructs a small-scale English-Chinese parallel legal corpus and employs a corpus-assisted qualitative research design for analysis (Hamed, 2025). Specifically, this study uses AntConc to retrieve candidate terms from the English legal corpus (Anthony, 2024). Building on this, manual screening and qualitative analysis are conducted in conjunction with the corresponding official Chinese provisions to compare the relationships between these terms in general English, within the Hong Kong legal context, and in their official Chinese equivalents, and to further examine the preservation and compression of concepts during cross-linguistic translation. To advance this research, the following research questions are proposed.

RQ1: What are the primary manifestations of the false friend risk in bilingual family law terminology in Hong Kong?

RQ2: How do these risks manifest as general meaning interference, legal semantic shift, partial equivalence, or conceptual compression?

RQ3: How does slot analysis elucidate the mechanisms of conceptual retention and compression in the official Chinese equivalents?

Positioned at the intersection of translation studies, legal linguistics, and terminology studies, this chapter aims to make the following three contributions. First, it advances the concept of false friend risk from a general lexical misguidance issue to a conceptual risk within Hong Kong bilingual legal terminology, emphasizing that its essence lies not in overt mistranslation but in the insufficiency of equivalence arising from cross-linguistic reconstruction of legal knowledge. Second, this chapter presents a replicable research pathway of corpus retrieval, terminology screening, equivalence assessment, and framework analysis, organically integrating corpus-assisted translation studies with legal terminology analysis to strengthen the empirical foundation and interpretive power of related research (Biel & Kockaert, 2023; Prieto Ramos & Cerutti, 2023). Furthermore, this study offers insights for research on bilingual legal terminology in Hong Kong, legal translation pedagogy, and the interpretation of bilingual legal texts, and further demonstrates that in authoritative bilingual legal texts, stable official correspondences do not necessarily imply that the legal framework of the source language has been fully preserved or reconstructed (Chan & Cham, 2023).

LITERATURE REVIEW

Legal Terminology, Equivalence, and Conceptual Reconstruction

Hong Kong's bilingual legal system influences its terminology. Starting in 1986, the Attorney General's Chambers translated all English legislation into Chinese, which was declared equally authentic under the Basic Law (Department of Justice, 2012). Completed before 1997, this process required the creation of Chinese terms for common law concepts lacking Chinese legal equivalents (Chan, 2020). The official terminology reflects constraints such as institutional pressure, time limits, and the challenge of adapting common-law concepts into civil-law language. This chapter explores the tension between terminological stability and conceptual adequacy (Chan & Cham, 2023).

Research in legal translation has long emphasized that the cross-linguistic conversion of legal texts is not merely a matter of linguistic substitution in the general sense, but rather the re-articulation of legal concepts, institutional logic, and normative functions across different languages and legal systems (Clay, 2026). Consequently, the centrality of legal terminology in legal translation stems not only from the fact that terms constitute high-frequency linguistic units in legal texts, but also because terms themselves embody legal classifications, institutional positioning, and normative effects (Graziadei, 2025).

Within this theoretical tradition, Šarčević's (1997) discussion of the hierarchy of legal equivalence is foundational. She distinguishes relationships among legal terms into approximate equivalence, partial equivalence, and non-equivalence, thereby advancing the issue of equivalence in legal translation from general linguistic equivalence to the level of comparative legal concepts and institutional functions. The significance of this theory lies in the fact that it provides legal terminology research with a more nuanced analytical framework than the "correct/incorrect" dichotomy, enabling researchers to explain terminological correspondences that, while not superficially mistranslations, exhibit shifts in conceptual scope, institutional positioning, or legal effects (Graziadei, 2025; Šarčević, 1997).

Subsequent research has further demonstrated that the core difficulty of legal translation lies not merely in cross-linguistic conversion, but in the repositioning of concepts from one legal system to another within the target language. Formal terminological stability does not automatically guarantee conceptual adequacy or functional equivalence, especially for terms whose meaning is inseparable from the institutional structures of a particular legal system (Koteva, 2023). Therefore, in institutionalized bilingual legal texts, what truly warrants vigilance may not be overt mistranslations, but rather those terminological pairs that are already accepted, formally stable, and possess official and conventional status (Pavliuk, 2023).

This theoretical starting point also implies that the false friend risk examined here cannot be reduced to surface-level confusion between words that look alike but mean different things, the classic concern of foreign language pedagogy. At the level of legal terminology, the issue is even more complex, as the meaning of a term is not a single lexical definition but is closely linked to institutional relationships, legal consequences, and knowledge structures (Wu et al., 2025). For this reason, this paper understands the false friend risk as a false sense of equivalence induced by superficial transparency, partial semantic overlap, or the stability of official correspondences. The essence of this risk is not that the target-language expression is entirely incorrect, but rather that it is sufficient to trigger a judgment of seeming to have understood, yet insufficient to fully convey the legal knowledge structure attached to the source-language term (Engberg, 2023; Graziadei, 2025; Šarčević, 1997).

The institutional dynamics in this chapter are not unique to Hong Kong. Comparative legal linguistics shows similar tensions in other multilingual jurisdictions. In the EU, legislation must be drafted in 24 languages, often leading to formal stability but conceptual divergence, a pattern Šarčević (2012) calls "deceptive equivalence". In Canada, bilingual legislation in English and French can have different legal effects depending on whether it is interpreted under common-law or civil-law systems (Baaij, 2012). These cases suggest that the false friend issue in Hong Kong reflects a broader tension in bilingual legal governance: the push for stable, normative equivalents conflicts with the conceptual differences of legal terms.

False Friends, Partial Equivalence, and Risk in Legal Terminology

Traditional research on false friends typically begins with terms that are formally similar but semantically distinct, discussing their disruptive effects on language comprehension, vocabulary acquisition, and translation judgment. However, recent studies increasingly show that what is truly misleading is not always terms with separate meanings, but rather expressions that share partial semantic overlap and are thus immediately understandable at the surface level (Marín & Fernández Toledo, 2015). Legrand (1996) argues that legal concepts are so rooted in their original culture that true equivalence is impossible; translations instead create new target-system concepts. The false friend risk isn't just a translation error but a feature of cross-system legal communication; the critique highlights that gaps in equivalence are structural limits of the translation principle.

The equivalence framework in legal translation has drawn criticism, with some scholars questioning its coherence when the source and target legal systems are incommensurable. Legrand (1996) argues that true equivalence is impossible because legal concepts are deeply embedded in their original cultures, making translation produce new target-system concepts rather than reproducing the source. The false friend risk isn't just a translation flaw but an inherent challenge in cross-system legal communication. However, this chapter adopts a more moderate view, considering the practical viability of functional equivalence.

This is particularly important in legal contexts. The meaning of legal terms is influenced not only by general lexical semantics but is also constrained by categorical relationships, institutional positioning, and legal consequences within the legal system. Marín and Fernández Toledo (2015) point out that cognates have a dual effect in legal terminology learning. On the one hand, they can help learners form an initial understanding. On the other hand, they may also lead to misjudgments due to surface familiarity, causing learners to mistakenly believe they have mastered the term's specialized meaning. The implication is that the risk does not necessarily stem from unfamiliar terms but may instead arise from those that seem understood. For legal translation, this is particularly critical, as surface familiarity with a term does not guarantee understanding of its legal connotations, scope of application, and institutional positioning (Kemp, 2022; Marín & Fernández Toledo, 2015).

From the perspective of legal translation theory, this phenomenon is best explained within the framework of partial equivalence. Many term pairs prone to false friend risk are not entirely incorrect translations, but rather align with the source-language term in certain semantic or functional dimensions while diverging in other critical dimensions. In other words, the risk of false friends in legal translation does not primarily manifest as obvious mistranslations, but rather as a form of misleading conceptual proximity; the target-language expression provides sufficient familiarity at the surface level, yet fails to convey the source-language term's complete legal framework. This also explains why, even in authoritative bilingual legal texts, certain institutionalized terms may still pose comprehension risks (Engberg, 2023; Graziadei, 2025).

Recent research has begun to treat legal false friends as a topic worthy of independent discussion, but overall, it has yet to delve deeply into the internal mechanisms of institutionalized bilingual legal texts. Existing discussions focus primarily on legal foreign language teaching, terminology identification, and learning interventions, indicating that researchers have recognized legal false friends and their pedagogical implications (Engberg, 2023). However, the literature still lacks a sufficient explanation for the question. Why certain terms continue to create conceptual risks in standardized, official bilingual legal contexts, even when they already have established translations. In other words, while existing research has identified the phenomenon of risk, it has not yet systematically explained how such risks are embedded within the bilingual legal terminology system.

Therefore, this study's understanding of false friend risk is not limited to the traditional definition of false friends; rather, it defines it as a false sense of equivalence arising in bilingual legal terminology due to formal similarity, partial semantic overlap, or the stability of official correspondences. This definition transforms false friend risk from a general lexical interference issue into a conceptual risk issue within legal terminology research (Graziadei, 2025). It also shifts the focus of this study's analysis from the question of whether terms are like the more explanatory question of why terms create misleading transparency within an institutional context (Marín & Fernández Toledo, 2015).

Corpus Assisted Legal Translation Research and Frame-Based Terminology Analysis

If the theory of legal equivalence and research on false friends provide the theoretical framework for this paper, then corpus-assisted translation studies and frame-based analysis offer empirical research pathways and interpretive tools for addressing this issue. Baker (1995) argued that the significance of the corpus-assisted approach lies not merely in conducting frequency statistics, but in observing translation phenomena through authentic corpora, thereby shifting translation studies from isolated examples and intuitive judgments toward testable empirical analysis. This methodological shift is particularly important for legal translation studies, as the meaning of legal terminology is not a static definition detached from context, but is constantly activated and constrained within the structure of legal provisions, fixed collocations, co-occurrence patterns, and institutional discourse (Pontrandolfo, 2023).

In the field of legal translation, Biel (2008) systematically demonstrated the applicability of the corpus-assisted approach to the study of legal language and translation, noting that both parallel and contrastive corpora can serve as important tools for identifying terminological asymmetry, usage differences, and translation issues. It was emphasized that research on legal terminology must not remain at the level of dictionary definitions but should return to authentic legal discourse to observe typical collocations, register features, and institutionalized usage patterns of terms. Subsequently, Biel and Engberg (2013) further demonstrated that corpus research has become one of the key approaches within the methodology of legal translation, driving the field from purely qualitative descriptions toward more evidence-based analytical frameworks (Biel, 2008; Biel & Engberg, 2013).

This paper emphasizes the importance of the corpus-assisted approach in identifying correctly translated legal terminology in Hong Kong's bilingual texts, where authority and standardization reduce overt errors. Instead, it highlights issues with collocation, semantic extension, or institutional ties that may not align despite surface stability, especially in legal translation, where hybridity and challenges of conceptual transfer coexist (Prieto Ramos, 2014). By retrieving terms from legal English and examining their Chinese counterparts in context, the method provides an empirical basis to detect false friends. The approach is not statistical but serves as a tool for problem identification and evidence gathering for further analysis (Baker, 1995; Biel & Engberg, 2013).

However, corpus evidence alone cannot automatically clarify the level at which the terminological risk occurs. This limitation highlights a methodological tension in the field. Corpus-based approaches reveal what translators do but struggle to explain why certain patterns recur or to account for the institutional knowledge involved. Frame-based terminology offers conceptual depth but relies on analyst intuition for frame slots. This integrated approach combines empirical corpus analysis with frame analysis to leverage their strengths while acknowledging each method's limitations. While it can inform researchers about how a term appears in authentic discourse, it cannot, on its own, explain which dimensions of legal knowledge the target-language expression retains or which conceptual relationships it omits (Wu et al., 2026) Consequently, if research remains confined to the corpus retrieval and term listing stage, it is easy to reduce false friend risk to a mere issue of general usage differences, failing to further elucidate the knowledge-structural basis of the risk. For this very reason, the corpus-assisted approach must be combined with more explanatory frameworks for terminological analysis, thereby forming a continuous chain linking empirical observations to conceptual explanations (Baker, 1993; Engberg, 2023).

Unlike terminology research centered on term-definition correspondence, frame-based terminology understands terms as linguistic manifestations of knowledge rather than context-free labels. Drawing on Fillmore's (1976) foundational account of frame semantics, which holds that word meaning cannot be understood without access to the conceptual frames and background knowledge they invoke. Engberg (2023) extends this insight to legal terminology, noting that the meaning of legal terms is not a single lexical definition but rather a frame composed of related knowledge dimensions; these dimensions can be described in terms of slots and fillers. Its key contribution lies in advancing terminology research from the term-definition level to the knowledge-structure-conceptual-organization level, enabling researchers to analyze more precisely what is retained, compressed, or shifted in terminology translation (Engberg, 2023; Faber, 2022).

This theory is particularly important for this paper because the false friend risk discussed here does not primarily manifest as errors in the dictionary sense, but rather as the target-language expression failing to fully reproduce the legal knowledge framework to which the source-language term is attached. In other words, an official Chinese equivalent may appear natural in everyday usage and acceptable in institutional practice, but it does not necessarily preserve the key slots of the English term for legal subjects, procedural relationships, rights and obligations, institutional functions, or categorical affiliations. It is precisely at this point that frame-based analysis can concretize conceptual non-equivalence, moving the discussion of false friend risk away from abstract judgment and into an analyzable, demonstrable knowledge dimension (Engberg, 2023; Faber, 2022).

Furthermore, frame-based terminology provides this paper with a bridge connecting theoretical underpinnings to analytical operations. This paper does not intend merely to list differences between legal terms, but rather to integrate corpus retrieval, candidate term screening, equivalence-level assessment, and slot analysis into a continuous analytical pathway. First, using corpus data to observe the contextual behavior of candidate terms in Hong Kong legal English. Second, using Šarčević's (1997) equivalence framework to determine whether the relationship between the candidate terms and their official Chinese counterparts is approximate equivalence, partial equivalence, or non-equivalence; finally, using Engberg's (2023) frame approach to further elucidate the specific knowledge dimensions where such shifts occur. In this way, the analytical framework of this paper retains the conceptual sensitivity of legal translation theory while incorporating the empirical foundation of corpus research and the interpretive depth of frame analysis (Biel, 2008; Engberg, 2023; Šarčević, 1997).

In this sense, the contribution of this paper is not a new method but a new integration: it brings together legal equivalence theory, corpus-assisted translation studies, and frame-based terminology analysis. Three approaches that have rarely been combined to examine false friend risk in Hong Kong bilingual legal texts. Unlike glossary comparisons, which can only tell us whether a correspondence is standard, this integrated framework can explain why a standard correspondence may still mislead and, at the lexical, procedural, or institutional level, why a conceptual gap occurs (Engberg, 2023; Graziadei, 2025).

These studies demonstrate that research on legal terminology cannot be limited to superficial correspondences; it must also examine conceptual equivalence, institutional contexts, and knowledge frameworks. This is particularly important for this paper, as the false friend risk does not primarily manifest as explicit translation errors but rather as conceptual shifts and comprehension risks that underlie seemingly stable correspondences. In this study, corpus-assisted terminology identification forms the foundation of the analysis, enabling the screening of candidate terms to be grounded in authentic legal texts; simultaneously, the combination of legal equivalence assessment and frame-based analysis allows this paper to further examine the preservation and deviation of key knowledge dimensions between English terms and their official Chinese counterparts. Therefore, this study aims to provide new empirical evidence on the risk of false friends in Hong Kong's bilingual legal texts and to propose a practical analytical framework integrating corpus retrieval, equivalence-level assessment, and slot analysis. Unlike existing research, which primarily focuses on identifying legal false friends and their pedagogical applications, this study extends this issue to the context of institutionalized bilingual legal practice.

METHODOLOGY

This study employs a corpus-assisted qualitative analysis to examine the risk of false friends in legal terminology and their manifestations within bilingual marriage and family law texts in Hong Kong. The study focuses on specific terminology cases within authentic legal contexts, identifying terms that appear straightforward in general English but carry a distinct legal meaning in Hong Kong law, and whose official Chinese equivalents look adequate on the surface while leaving key institutional dimensions unencoded. It further reveals semantic misalignment and conceptual gaps among terms across general linguistic knowledge, legal institutional contexts, and standardized bilingual expressions.

The study is divided into two interconnected phases. The first phase is the corpus retrieval phase, using AntConc to systematically search English legal texts, examine the degree of terminalization of candidate terms through index-line distribution, fixed collocations, and co-occurrence relationships, and preliminarily assess their potential false friend risk. The second phase is the qualitative analysis phase: building on the corpus retrieval, it conducts case studies of representative terms alongside corresponding official Chinese legal provisions. It examines the relationships between the terms' general English meanings, their meanings within the Hong Kong legal context, and their Chinese expressions. Furthermore, it employs Šarčević's theory of equivalence in legal translation and Engberg's frame-based analysis to explain conceptual shifts and the mechanisms underlying their risks (Engberg, 2023; Šarčević, 1997). The case analysis process is detailed for Figure 1.

Figure 1. The overall framework of the study

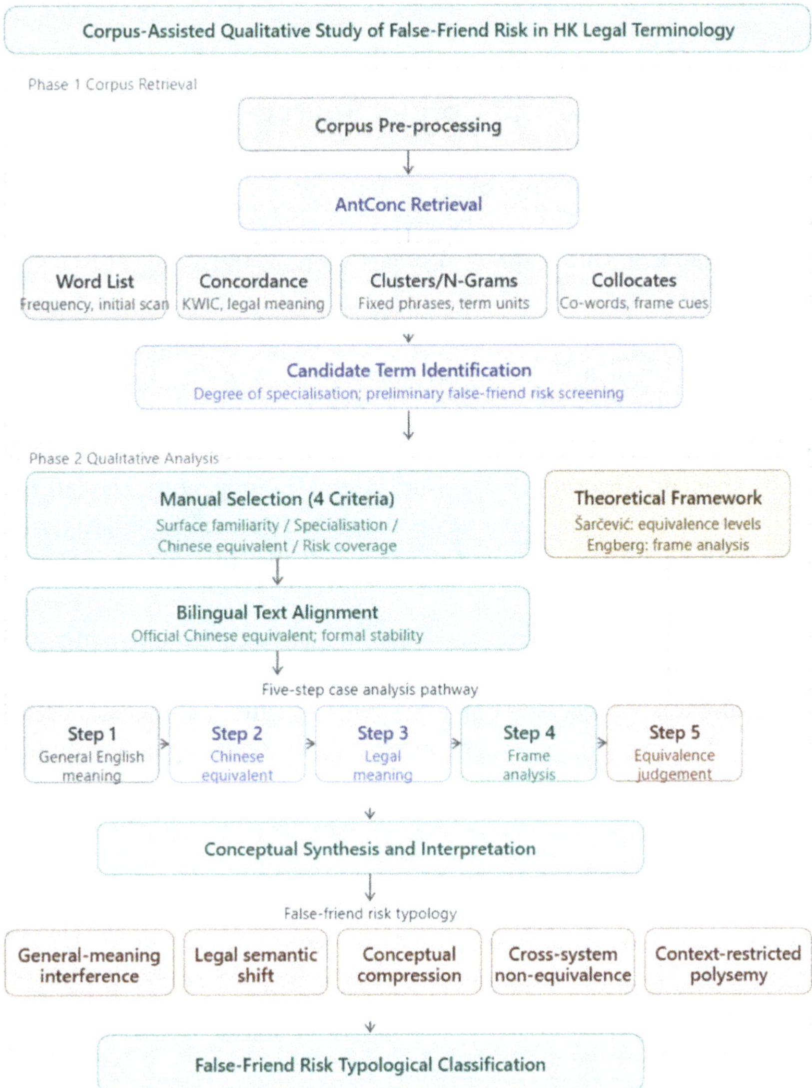

Specifically, the case analysis follows a five-step process. First, I start with the general English meaning of the candidate term, describing its everyday meaning and the everyday knowledge frameworks it may activate. Second, drawing on AntConc search results to reconstruct its specialized legal meaning within the context of Hong Kong marriage and family law. Third, examining its official Chinese equivalent, analyzing the formal stability and terminological nature of the translation. Fourth, through a comparative analysis of frame slots, the study examines whether each slot is retained, weakened, compressed, or omitted in the Chinese expression. Fifth, by applying Šarčević's equivalence hierarchy to the term pairs, we classify them by false friend risk type.

Terminological Scope and Corpus Source

This study examines the terminology of marriage and family law in Hong Kong's official bilingual legal texts. The selection of legal texts is based on two considerations. First, Hong Kong is a common-law jurisdiction, and its legal English reflects the conceptual structures, procedures, and legal relationships of the common-law system. Second, Hong Kong bilingual legislation possesses a high degree of authority and stability in English-Chinese correspondence, providing a normative corpus foundation for parallel comparison at the terminological level.

The study focuses on marriage and family law, primarily based on two considerations. First, specialized corpora help ensure internal homogeneity. Second, marriage and family law texts contain many terms that blend general familiarity with legal specificity, making them well suited to observing the different manifestations of the false friend risk.

The corpus consists of four interrelated bilingual marriage and family law legislation from the Hong Kong Electronic Legislation System. These four Legislations are thematically interconnected yet have distinct institutional focuses, collectively forming a small yet comprehensive thematic parallel legal corpus. The composition of the corpus is shown in Table 1.

Table 1. Corpus composition of the study

Text	Abbreviation	Legal focus	Corpus function
Separation and Maintenance Orders Ordinance (Cap.16)	SMOO	Separation and maintenance orders	Support and maintenance terminology
Matrimonial Causes Ordinance (Cap.179)	MCO	divorce, nullity, judicial separation	procedural matrimonial terminology
Matrimonial Proceedings and Property Ordinance (Cap.192)	MPPO	financial relief and property arrangements	property- and remedy-related terminology
Matrimonial Causes Rules (Cap. 179 sub. Leg. A)	MCR	procedural implementation	procedural phraseology and collocational patterns

Term Selection Criteria

The key terms analyzed in this paper were identified through a process of gradual screening based on corpus retrieval combined with human judgment. The selection criteria are as follows. First, surface familiarity. Referring to the number of definitions in *The Oxford English Dictionary* and the frequency of use in everyday contexts, this paper defines terms with two or more common everyday definitions that general English speakers can recognize in non-legal contexts as having high surface familiarity. This surface familiarity is a key prerequisite for the emergence of the false friend risk.

Second, candidate terms should exhibit distinct features of specialization within the Hong Kong legal context. This study applies three corpus-assisted criteria as the basis for judgment, with all thresholds operationally defined for the purposes of this study, following standard practice in corpus-based terminology research (Biel, 2016): (a) The specialised legal sense constitutes the dominant sense across concordance lines, with general-language readings confined to peripheral or clearly context-marked instances, consistent with criteria for identifying specialised terms in corpus-based terminology studies (Biel, 2016). (b) The presence of at least two fixed legal collocations with a frequency of ≥3 in Clusters/N-Grams. (c) The presence of legal relationships or procedural co-occurring terms with an effect value of ≥3 in Collocates, indicating statistically meaningful association with the institutional vocabulary of Hong Kong matrimonial law beyond chance co-occurrence (Stubbs, 2001).

Third, the stability of official Chinese equivalents. Candidate terms should have relatively stable official Chinese equivalents. That is, the Chinese translation of the term should remain consistent across the four laws' Chinese versions or exhibit only expected variations. Surface equivalence is observable only when a standardized correspondence has been established between English and Chinese.

Fourth, coverage of risk types. The term pairs ultimately included in the analysis must collectively cover the following five false friends risk types. That is general-meaning interference, legal semantic shift and incomplete manifestation, conceptual compression and pseudo-transparency, institutional asymmetry across legal systems, and context-restricted polysemy, to enhance the depth and explanatory power of the research conclusions.

It should be noted that candidate term screening and frame slot analysis in this study were conducted by a single researcher. The slot identification and equivalence judgments reported in the case studies should therefore be understood as analytically motivated interpretations. Future research could address this by involving a second coder and reporting Cohen's kappa or percentage agreement for both the screening and slot-coding stages.

Data Collection and Corpus Construction

Before formal retrieval, the original legal texts are preprocessed and formatted into UTF-8 plain text suitable for import into AntConc. Preprocessing involves removing non-substantive content such as page numbers, headers, footers, and duplicate headings, standardizing spacing, line breaks, and punctuation to reduce formatting noise. And retaining structurally significant information such as article numbers, paragraph numbers, and chapter titles to ensure that search results are interpretable and traceable.

During the AntConc processing phase, only English text files are imported. The Chinese portions are introduced during the qualitative analysis phase through English-Chinese text alignment. Frequency data is reported as raw counts across the entire corpus without PMW normalization, as the purpose of using frequency data in this study is to confirm the terminological distribution of candidate terms within the specialized corpus, rather than to conduct cross-text frequency comparisons (Biel, 2008; Engberg, 2020). This study employs the following standardized operational parameters:

Word List: Stopword filtering was used to exclude function words, including articles, prepositions, auxiliary verbs, and high-frequency legal terms such as shall, any, such, and where. The minimum frequency threshold was set to 5 to filter out occasional low-frequency terms, generating a list of high-frequency substantive content words as the starting point for candidate term discovery.

Concordance: The context window was set to 5 words to the left and 5 words to the right. Exact matching was used for retrieval, with wildcards employed to search for word variants when necessary.

Clusters/N-Grams: The cluster size was set to 2-4 words, and the minimum frequency threshold was set to 3. The target word position was set to run once at the left end and once at the right end.

Collocates: Window span set to 5 words on each side, statistical metric set to effect, minimum co-occurrence frequency threshold set to 2, and co-occurring words with an effect ≥ 3 reported as valid collocations.

RESULTS

Corpus Retrieval Results

After conducting a preliminary search of the English corpus on Hong Kong marriage and family law, the Word List results showed that the corpus contained 58,122 tokens and 1,913 distinct word types. After filtering out stop words, the high-frequency substantive terms included court, order, maintenance, spouse, property, decree, petition, relief, custody, and proceeding. The corpus topics were highly concentrated on core issues such as matrimonial litigation, maintenance obligations, divorce proceedings, and property arrangements, and the terminology network exhibited strong internal coherence. The AntConc retrieval results are shown in Figure 2 below.

Figure 2. AntConc word list output

Judging by the text, English terms in family law corpora often do not appear in isolation but rather enter specific legal frameworks through fixed procedural expressions and institutional collocations. Concordance search results further confirm that terms such as petition, decree, and maintenance are highly concentrated in procedural and institutional contexts, with their general English meanings rarely appearing in the corpus. This provides a preliminary corpus-assisted foundation for identifying false friend risk. The core value of AntConc at this stage lies in grounding the identification of candidate terms in evidence from the actual corpus, rather than relying solely on subjective judgment.

Candidate Term Identification Results

The first round of screening using the word list and concordance yielded 42 candidate terms. 37 were excluded following stepwise application of the four selection criteria. The principal grounds for exclusion were: insufficient surface familiarity in general English (n=14), failure to meet the legal specialization threshold in concordance distribution (n=11), inconsistent Chinese equivalents across the four ordinances (n=8), and inadequate coverage of distinct risk types (n=4). After applying four selection criteria in a stepwise process, five core analytical terms were ultimately identified. The five terms collectively instantiate all five risk types identified in the preliminary typology: general-meaning interference (maintenance), legal semantic shift (decree), conceptual compression and pseudo-transparency (relief), institutional asymmetry across legal systems (petition), and context-restricted polysemy (custody), ensuring that the analysis does not over-represent any single mechanism. Besides, each term occupies a structurally central role in Hong Kong matrimonial proceedings, appearing in core statutory provisions rather than marginal or transitional clauses, and each has a stable, normative Chinese equivalent that has persisted across all four ordinances without variation. Terms that met the screening criteria but overlapped in risk type with an already-selected term. The results of the main candidate terms are summarize in the following Table 2.

Table 2. Candidate terms and selection results

Term	**Surface familiarity in general English**	**Degree of legal specialization in corpus**	**Stability of official Chinese equivalent**	**Main risk type**
maintenance	High	High	High	general-meaning interference; partial compression
decree	Medium	High	High	semantic shift; procedural under-explicitness
relief	High	High	High	conceptual compression; pseudo-transparency
petition	Medium	High	High	procedural specialization from general meaning
custody	High	High	High	legal specialization from everyday meaning

Based on the corpus retrieval results, the five terms exhibit strong terminological characteristics in their distribution across index entries, fixed collocations, and co-occurrence networks. The corpus features are summarized in Table 3.

Table 3. Corpus-assisted profiles of five terms

Term	Typical clusters (frequency)	Salient collocates (effect≥ 3)	legal frame
maintenance	maintenance order (82) maintenance payer (22) maintenance agreement (10)	enforcing (4.854) comes (4.854) total (4.738)	support obligation and enforcement frame
decree	decree nisi (44) decree absolute (11) final decree (4)	rescind (5.483) draw (5.389) nisi (4.930)	adjudicative and procedural-stage frame
relief	ancillary relief (44) financial relief (41) relief claimed (2)	ancillary (5.818) reducing (5.818) prayer (5.818)	financial provision and judicial discretion frame
petition	amended petition (6) supplemental petition (5) petition replaced (4)	presentation (4.616) supplemental (4.436) preceding (4.294)	adversarial matrimonial proceedings frame
custody	custody care (3) legal custody (2) custody maintenance (1)	control (6.961) education (6.505) care (5.698)	Child welfare and parental responsibility frame

In Table 3, only the top three results are shown for typical clusters and salient collocates. The original frequency refers to the total number of occurrences across the entire corpus. The cluster size is set to 2, the search term position is set to search both before and after the search term, and the minimum occurrence frequency is 1. The effect values in parentheses will be automatically populated when co-occurring terms are retrieved using AntConc, with a window span of 5 on either side of the search term and a minimum co-occurrence frequency of 2.

The following five case studies use the analytical framework from the methodology on selected terms. Each case has five parts: corpus retrieval, comparison of general and legal meanings, Chinese equivalent, frame slot comparison, and an equivalence judgment with risk type. The cases are ordered by increasing institutional complexity: from interference (maintenance), semantic shift (decree), conceptual compression (relief), asymmetry (petition), to polysemy (custody).

Representative Terminology Cases

The following five case studies follow a consistent analytical framework, each including: corpus retrieval characteristics; a comparison of general English meanings and legal meanings; official Chinese equivalents; a comparative analysis of frame slots; and an assessment of equivalence and a classification of risk types.

Maintenance: General Interference

Corpus Retrieval Characteristics

A search in AntConc reveals that maintenance appears 201 times in the corpus, with examples highly concentrated in legal contexts. The Clusters/N-Grams results show that the most frequent collocations for this term are, in order: maintenance order (82 times), maintenance payer (22 times), maintenance agreement (10 times), maintenance pending (8 times), and maintenance payments (7 times). In the Collocates results, the substantive co-occurring terms with the highest effect values are, in order: enforcing (4.854), comes (4.854), total (4.738), accrue (4.631), and salary (4.439). The results are shown in Figure 3.

Figure 3. AntConc Concordance lines for maintenance (n = 201)

General Versus Legal Meanings

In general English, the term "maintenance" refers to keeping something in good working order, such as a building or a car. And it is unrelated to concepts such as legal obligations or court orders. In the context of Hong Kong law, however, maintenance specifically refers to the obligation to provide support, care, or financial assistance arising from marital or family relationships. It is closely associated with court orders and payment arrangements and constitutes a distinct legal concept.

Official Chinese Equivalent

The Chinese equivalents generally take the form of "赡养" (maintenance), "赡养费" (maintenance payments), or "赡养令" (maintenance order). Their usage is consistent across the four pieces of legislation, demonstrating a high degree of translation consistency. This terminology effectively eliminates interference from the general English meaning and, to a significant extent, preserves core dimensions such as the parties involved and the obligation of financial support.

Frame Slot Analysis

Table 4 presents a slot-by-slot comparison of the legal knowledge frame activated by maintenance in the source text and the degree to which each slot is retained in the Chinese equivalent 赡养/赡养令.

Table 4. Frame slot comparison: maintenance vs. 赡养/赡养令

Frame slot	Content in English legal frame	Status in Chinese equivalent	Notes
Obligation party	Spouse / parent liable for support	Retained	"赡养" presupposes the existence of an obligated party and adequately conveys this dimension.
Beneficiary	Spouse / child entitled to support	Partially retained	"赡养" carries a semantic bias toward providing for elders, leaving the dual-beneficiary nature encompassing both the spouse and the children insufficiently activated.
Legal instrument	Court order (maintenance order)	Retained	"赡养令" adequately conveys the court-order nature through the character "令".
Financial nature	Periodic monetary payment obligation	Partially retained	"赡养费" conveys monetary payment, but the periodicity feature is weakened.
Procedural consequences	Arrears accrual / enforcement proceedings	Absent	"赡养" / "赡养令" entirely fail to activate the mechanisms for determining and enforcing arrears.
Variation mechanism	Court application to vary order	Absent	"赡养令" does not convey the institutional dimension whereby the order is subject to variation upon application.

As shown in the Table 4 above, the obligor and the legal instrument are fully retained in the Chinese equivalent. The obligee's role is adequately conveyed, as "赡养" inherently presupposes a party that bears the support obligation. The legal instrument slot is likewise well-preserved through the morpheme "令" in "赡养令", which signals the court-order nature of the arrangement. Two further slots, beneficiary and financial nature, are only partially retained. The term "赡养"carries a cultural connotation more closely associated with supporting elderly parents than with spousal or child maintenance, meaning that the dual-beneficiary scope of maintenance (spouse and child) is not fully activated. Similarly, while "赡养费"conveys a monetary payment sense, the periodic and recurrent nature of the obligation is not explicitly encoded. Most critically, the Chinese equivalent lacks two slots, procedural consequences, and a mechanism for variation. The collocates evidence of enforcement (4.854) and accrue (4.631) indicate that arrears accumulation and enforcement proceedings are structurally central to the English legal framework of maintenance.

Equivalence Judgment and Risk Type

While the obligation party and legal instrument slots are retained, the two slots of procedural consequences and variation mechanism are systematically absent, and two further slots of beneficiary and financial nature are only partially preserved. The false friend risk associated with maintenance operates through two reinforcing mechanisms: general-meaning interference and procedural conceptual compression. The Chinese equivalent, "赡养/赡养令", while formally stable and terminologically well-established, encodes only the core obligation-and-order structure of maintenance, leaving the procedural dimensions of arrears accumulation, enforcement proceedings, and order variation entirely inactivated. The Chinese equivalent partially preserves the conceptual structure of the source term, yet systematically omits the procedural consequences that, as the corpus evidence of enforcing (MI = 4.854) and accrue (MI = 4.631) confirms, are structurally central to the term's legal function. It is this combination of partial conceptual preservation and selective procedural omission that characterizes the false friend risk type associated with maintenance, and that renders near-equivalence, rather than partial equivalence, the more precise classification within Šarčević's (1997) framework.

Decree: Semantic Shifts and Incomplete Manifestation of Procedure

Corpus Retrieval Characteristics

The term decree appears 208 times in the corpus. The most frequent phrases are, in order: decree nisi (44 times), decree absolute (11 times), final decree (4 times), and decree should (3 times). The co-occurrence terms with the highest co-occurrence index are, in order: rescind (5.483), draw (5.389), and nisi (4.930). This distribution confirms that the decree has become highly proceduralized in Hong

Kong matrimonial litigation texts, with a significant shift in meaning between its general English meaning and its legal meaning.

Figure 4. AntConc concordance lines for decree (n = 208)

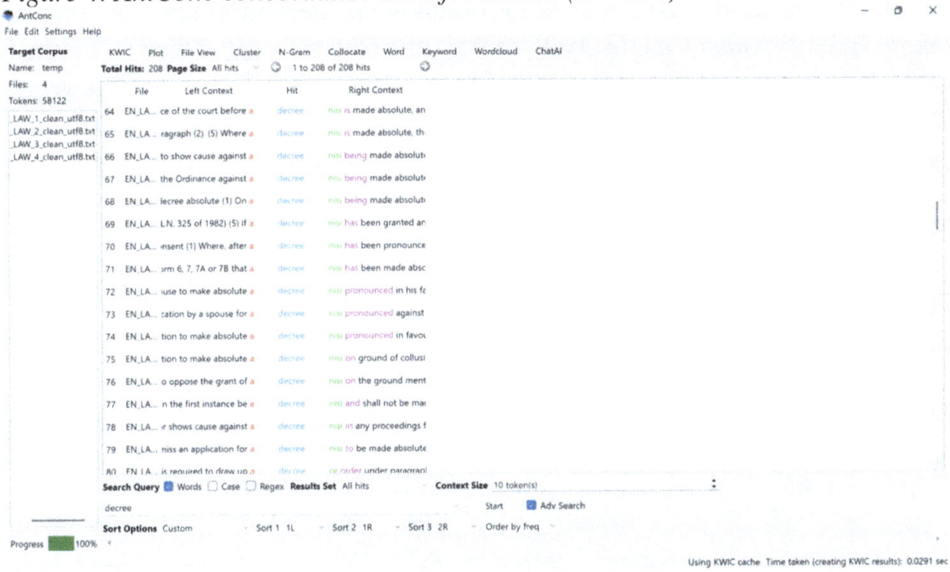

General Versus Legal Meanings

In general English, "decree" refers to a formal, authoritative order or ruling, often used in contexts such as "presidential decree" and "papal decree," which emphasize the authority of the issuing entity. However, its scope is relatively broad and does not presuppose any specific procedural structure. In the legal context of Hong Kong matrimonial litigation, a decree is imbued with a highly specific procedural meaning: it specifically refers to a formal judicial order issued by a court in divorce or annulment proceedings and operates critically within a two-stage procedural sequence. A decree nisi is a conditional order that must be converted into a decree absolute after the statutory waiting period expires. Only the latter produces the legal effect of definitively dissolving the marriage. This procedural dependency is absent from the general English meaning of decree, constituting the primary source of the term's false friend risk: readers familiar with the general English meaning may correctly identify the term as a formal court order, yet lack awareness of its specific stage within the procedural sequence and the legal consequences attached to each stage.

Official Chinese Equivalent

The term Decree is consistently rendered as "判令" across the four statutes, with stable usage and no apparent variations. "判令" has become a well-established legal term in bilingual legal texts in Hong Kong. Composed of the morphemes "判" (judicial ruling) and "令"(order), it effectively conveys the core meaning of a court's formal judicial act and possesses a high degree of naturalness and acceptability. However, this very formal stability and naturalness constitute a key prerequisite for avoiding the risk of incomplete conceptual activation; the fluency of the translation provides no linguistic prompt to question its conceptual completeness, thereby overlooking the procedural dimension underlying the translation.

Frame Slot Analysis

Table 5 provides a detailed comparison of the various slots contained in the term "decree" within the source language's legal framework and how these are preserved in the corresponding Chinese term "判令".

Table 5. Frame slot comparison: decree vs. 判令

Frame slot	Content in English legal frame	Status in Chinese equivalent	Notes
Adjudicative authority	Court's formal judicial pronouncement	Retained	"判令" conveys judicial adjudication through "判"; court authority fully activated
Legal consequence	Effect on marital status upon decree absolute	Partially retained	"判令" implies legal effect but does not specify conditionality or finality
Procedural stage 1	Decree nisi conditional, subject to waiting period	Absent	"判令" does not encode the conditional and interim nature of decree nisi
Procedural stage 2	Decree absolute final dissolution of marriage	Absent	"判令" does not distinguish the finality and irreversibility of decree absolute
Procedural progression	Sequential nisi absolute relationship with time lapse	Absent	The two-stage sequential structure is not activated by "判令"

As shown in the Table 5 above, among the five slots for "decree", only the "judicial" slot is fully preserved in the Chinese translation. The term "judgment" effectively captures the core meaning of a court's formal judicial act through the character "判", thereby fully conveying the judicial dimension. The "legal consequences" slot is only partially preserved. "Judgment" implies the basic notion that a court ruling has legal effect, but fails to distinguish the substantive difference between the conditional legal status created by a decree nisi and the final dissolution of marriage effect created by a decree absolute. Most critically, three slots, procedural stage one, procedural stage two, and the relationship between stages, are completely inactivated in the Chinese translation. The high frequency of "decree nisi" (44 times) and "decree absolute" (11 times) in the corpus directly confirms that this two-stage sequential structure occupies a central position within the English legal framework of "decree". However, "judgment" conveys no information regarding procedural stages. When readers relying solely on the Chinese text have no textual basis for inferring that the term specifically refers to a phased judicial order, one in which the first stage is conditional and subject to a statutory waiting period, and the second stage produces the final legal effect, or any of the associated institutional details.

Equivalence Judgment and Risk Type

Based on the above analysis, the core concept of judicial nature is retained, the procedural stage dimension, which is the most institutionally distinctive aspect of the English legal knowledge framework for decree, is systematically absent in the Chinese equivalent, particularly the distinction between "nisi" and "absolute" and their sequential progression. The false friend risk associated with "decree" arises primarily from two mechanisms: legal semantic shift and incomplete procedural positioning. In the context of matrimonial litigation, the term has undergone significant semantic narrowing, acquiring a procedural, stage-specific meaning that is absent from its general English usage. Meanwhile, its Chinese equivalent, while formally natural and highly terminological, fails to encode the procedural-stage structure that constitutes the term's core legal function. This combination of surface adequacy and conceptual inactivation is a classic manifestation of the risk types of legal semantic shift and incomplete explication identified in this paper.

Relief: Conceptual Compression and Pseudo-Transparency

Corpus Retrieval Characteristics

The term relief appears 103 times in the corpus. The most frequent phrases are, in order: ancillary relief (44 times), financial relief (41 times), and relief claimed (2 times). The co-occurrence terms with the highest co-occurrence index are, in order: ancillary (5.818), reducing (5.818), and prayer (5.818). This distribution confirms that "relief" has become highly proceduralized in Hong Kong matrimonial litigation texts, with a significant shift in meaning between its general English meaning and its legal meaning.

Figure 5. AntConc concordance lines for relief (n = 103)

General Versus Legal Meanings

In general English, the term "relief" conveys a broad sense of "alleviation or assistance" and is commonly used in contexts such as disaster relief, pain relief, and tax relief. Its core meaning is to alleviate a burden or help, without implying any court intervention, institutionalized form of relief, or judicial discretion. In the legal context of Hong Kong matrimonial proceedings, "relief" refers to the various forms of legal remedies a court may grant to parties, including property adjustment orders, lump-sum payment orders, periodic payment orders, and orders for the sale of property. Crucially, the granting of relief is not automatic but must be triggered through formal application procedures; it is subject to the court's broad judicial discretion and must be determined in accordance with statutory factors. The fundamental disparity between the general English framework (broad, non-institutional, and non-procedural) and the legal framework (institutionally complex, procedurally constrained, and reliant on judicial discretion) constitutes the primary source of the term's false friend risk. Readers familiar with the general English meaning may interpret relief as a generic term for aid or assistance, thereby overlooking the institutional specificity and procedural complexity inherent in its legal usage.

Official Chinese Equivalent

The term "Relief" is consistently rendered as "济助" across the four pieces of legislation. The usage is stable, with no apparent variations. "济助" has become a highly technical term in Hong Kong bilingual legal texts. Composed of the morphemes "济" (relief/assistance) and"助" (help), it effectively conveys the core meaning of providing assistance or relief to parties, exhibiting a high degree of surface naturalness and standardization. However, it is precisely this apparent adequacy that constitutes the core characteristic of the pseudo-transparency risk type. That is the very fluency and stability of "济助" as a translation that obscures the institutional complexity of the English legal framework, making it extremely easy to form the mistaken impression that the concept has been fully conveyed.

Frame Slot Analysis

Table 6 provides a detailed comparison of the various slots contained in the source-language legal framework for "relief" and their preservation in the corresponding Chinese term "济助".

Table 6. Frame slot comparison: relief vs. 济助

Frame slot	Content in English legal frame	Status in Chinese equivalent	Notes
General remedial direction	Provision of a legal remedy to a party in need	Retained	"济助" conveys the core sense of providing aid; remedial direction adequately activated
Specific relief types	Property adjustment / lump sum / periodical payments / order for sale	Absent	"济助" does not distinguish among structurally distinct remedy types; all collapsed into a single undifferentiated term
Judicial discretion	Court exercises broad statutory discretion in granting relief	Absent	"济助" does not activate the discretionary and evaluative dimension of the court's role
Procedural triggering	Relief must be formally applied for; subject to procedural rules and time limits	Absent	"济助" does not encode the requirement of formal application or procedural preconditions
Statutory assessment framework	Court must consider specified statutory factors in determining relief	Absent	"济助" provides no signal of the statutory criteria governing the court's determination
Ancillary procedural dependency	Relief is ancillary to and dependent on main matrimonial proceedings	Absent	"济助" does not encode the procedurally subordinate and dependent status of relief

As shown in the Table 6 above, among the slots of relief, only the direction of the relief slot is retained in the Chinese translation, while the other slots remain completely inactive. This is the case with the most pronounced degree of conceptual compression among the five cases in this study. The direction of the relief slot is retained, the morpheme "济助" successfully conveys the core direction of providing assistance to the parties involved, and the surface meaning of relief is essentially activated. However, the specific type of relief slot is entirely absent: the structurally distinct types of relief covered by "relief" in the English legal framework, such as orders for property adjustment, lump-sum payments, periodic payments, and the sale of property, are all collapsed into a single, undifferentiated expression in "济助", leaving unable to infer the institutional independence and structural specificity of each type of relief. The judicial discretion slot is similarly absent: the high co-occurrence of financial and ancillary confirms that relief in the corpus is consistently associated with the court's evaluative and discretionary role, whereas "济助" fails to activate this dimension at all. The procedural initiation requirements slot is missing: in the context of Hong Kong matrimonial law, relief must be triggered through formal application procedures and is subject to procedural rules and statutes of limitations; neither party can obtain relief without initiating the appropriate proceedings, yet these prerequisites are entirely absent from the term "relief". Absence of the statutory framework slot: Under the MPPO, the court must consider a series of statutory factors when determining relief, including the parties' financial resources, earning capacity, financial needs, and the welfare of children; the term "relief" does not indicate this statutory framework. Finally, the procedural dependency slot is missing: in Hong Kong matrimonial law, relief is procedurally subordinate to and dependent upon the main matrimonial proceedings. This structural relationship is likewise not reflected in the term "relief".

Equivalence Judgment and Risk Type

Based on the above analysis, the surface-level slot corresponding to "救济方向" is retained. However, five of the six slots that constitute the English legal knowledge framework for "relief" are systematically absent in the Chinese equivalent, making this the most striking case of conceptual compression in this study. The false friend risk associated with "relief" operates through mechanisms of conceptual compression and pseudo-transparency: the Chinese equivalent "济助" is stable in form, highly terminological, and morpheme-transparent, yet it encodes only the most superficial dimension of a legally complex concept. It is precisely the fluency and naturalness of "济助" as a translation that constitute the risk: readers encountering this translation in bilingual legal texts are highly unlikely to question whether it adequately conveys the source-language concept, and may instead directly assume that "relief" generally refers to some form of assistance provided by the court, completely unaware of the specific types of relief presupposed by the term, the procedural requirements, the framework of judicial discretion, and the statutory criteria for consideration. This combination of "superficial adequacy coexisting with incomplete conceptual activation" is precisely the defining characteristic of the pseudo-transparency risk type identified in this paper, and the translation of "relief" as "济助" represents the most concentrated manifestation of this risk mechanism among the five case studies.

Petition: Institutional Inequality across Legal Systems

Corpus Retrieval Characteristics

The term petition appears 237 times in the corpus. The most frequent phrases, in order, are: amended petition (6 times), supplemental petition (5 times), and petition replaced (4 times). The co-occurrence terms with the highest co-occurrence index are, in order: presentation (4.616), supplemental (4.436), preceding (4.294). This distribution confirms that the petition has become highly proceduralized in Hong Kong matrimonial litigation texts, with a significant shift in meaning between its general English meaning and its legal meaning.

Figure 6. AntConc concordance lines for petition (n = 237)

General Versus Legal Meanings

In general English, "petition" refers to a formal request or application submitted to an authoritative body, typically filed by a single party and not presupposing an opposing party or an adversarial structure. In the legal context of matrimonial proceedings in Hong Kong, however, "petition" specifically refers to the statutory document used to initiate matrimonial proceedings under the common law adversarial system: the party filing the petition becomes the petitioner, the named opposing party becomes the respondent, and the proceedings proceed within this adversarial framework. Furthermore, a petition must be filed on statutory grounds, comply with prescribed formal requirements, be formally served on the respondent in accordance with the law, and trigger a series of subsequent procedural steps. This adversarial framework has no direct counterpart in the civil law system, where divorce proceedings are typically initiated through non-adversarial administrative or judicial application procedures. The fundamental discrepancy between the general English meaning of "petition" (a unilateral formal request) and its legal meaning (the document initiating adversarial litigation under common law) constitutes the primary source of the term's false friend risk.

Official Chinese Equivalent

"Petition" is uniformly rendered as "呈请" in four pieces of legislation, with consistent usage. While "呈请" conveys the basic meaning of submitting a formal application to a court or authoritative body, its linguistic context and connotation are closer to a unilateral administrative application rather than the act of initiating an adversarial legal proceeding. This structural disparity between the institutional framework presupposed by "petition" and the administrative connotation of "呈请" is precisely the core characteristic of the cross-legal-system institutional asymmetry risk identified in this case.

Frame Slot Analysis

Table 7 provides a detailed comparison of the various slots contained in the term "petition" within the source language's legal framework and how they are preserved in the corresponding Chinese term "呈请".

Table 7. Frame slot comparison: petition vs. 呈请

Frame slot	Content in English legal frame	Status in Chinese equivalent	Notes
Initiating act	Formal act of commencing matrimonial proceedings	Retained	It conveys the sense of a formal submission; initiating function adequately activated
Adversarial structure	Presupposes petitioner vs. respondent opposition	Absent	It carries an administrative register incompatible with adversarial proceedings; opposing party structure not activated
Statutory grounds	Must be grounded in specified statutory grounds	Absent	It does not encode the requirement of statutory grounding
Formal service requirement	Must be formally served on the respondent	Absent	It does not signal the procedural obligation of formal service
Subsequent procedural chain	Triggers acknowledgment, directions, hearing, decree	Absent	It does not encode the chain of procedural consequences triggered by filing
Cross-system institutional basis	Rooted in common law adversarial civil procedure	Absent	It does not activate the common law institutional framework; no equivalent institutional structure exists in civil law systems

Of the slots associated with "petition", only the litigation initiation slot is retained in "呈请"; the other five slots are absent. The "litigation initiation" slot is retained: "呈请" conveys the basic meaning of filing a formal application with the court, thereby essentially activating the litigation initiation function. However, the adversarial procedural structure slot is absent: the distribution of petitioner and respondent as co-occurring terms with the highest MI values in the corpus directly confirms that a petition always presupposes a structure of opposing parties, whereas the administrative application connotation of "呈请" is structurally incompatible with this adversarial framework and cannot activate the existence of opposing parties. The statutory grounds slot is missing. A petition must be filed based on the statutory grounds specified in the Matrimonial Proceedings Ordinance; this procedural prerequisite is absent from "呈请". The formal service requirement slot is missing. After a petition is filed, formal service must be completed on the respondent in accordance with procedural rules; this legally binding procedural obligation is not conveyed by "呈请". The subsequent procedural chain slot was missing. The filing of a petition triggers a series of procedural steps, including acknowledgment of service, procedural directions, a hearing, and the final issuance of an order. "Petition" does not indicate these procedural consequences. Most fundamentally, the cross-legal system institutional foundation slot is entirely missing. The petition is rooted in the common-law adversarial civil litigation system, which has no structural counterpart in the civil-law system. Not only does the petition fail to activate this framework, but its administrative application connotation instead suggests an institutional model that is structurally incompatible with it.

Equivalence Judgment and Risk Type

While the initiation-of-litigation slot is preserved, five other slots, including the adversarial procedural structure and cross-legal-system institutional foundations, are systematically absent. The risk of this term becoming a false friend arises from the combined effects of systemic asymmetry across legal systems and the compression of procedural initiation functions: the common law adversarial litigation framework presupposed by "petition" lacks a structural counterpart in the civil law system, while the administrative application connotation of "呈请" not only fails to activate this framework but actively implies an application model that is fundamentally incompatible with it in institutional terms. This creates a fundamental distinction in nature between the connection and the other four case studies in this research: the risks associated with "maintenance", "decree", and "relief" involve conceptual compression within the same legal tradition, whereas "petition" involves cross-legal-system institutional incommensurability, a gap that cannot be bridged through mere terminological adjustments.

Custody: Context-Dependent Polysemy

Corpus Retrieval Characteristics

The term custody appears 28 times in the corpus. The most frequent phrases, in order, are custody care (3 times), legal custody (2 times), and child custody (1 time). The co-occurrence terms with the highest co-occurrence index are, in order: control (6.961), education (6.505), care (5.698), and children (4.890). This distribution confirms that custody has become highly proceduralized in Hong Kong matrimonial litigation texts, with a significant shift in meaning between its general English meaning and its legal meaning.

Figure 7. AntConc Concordance lines for custody (n = 28)

General Versus Legal Meanings

In general English, the term "custody" has two high-frequency meanings with distinctly different connotations: "guardianship" (in the custody of) and "detention" (police custody). The meanings are highly recognizable to non-specialist readers, which poses a risk of context-dependent ambiguity. In the context of Hong Kong family law, "custody" is limited to the child's welfare, specifically referring to one parent's authority to determine the child's living arrangements and the responsibility for the child's upbringing. It establishes a tripartite structural relationship among "care" (day-to-day substantive care), "access" (the non-custodial parent's visitation rights), and "contact" (the non-custodial parent's right to contact the child). Furthermore, institutional evolution has introduced additional conceptual instability: following the enactment of the Children Act 1989 in England and Wales, "custody" has been replaced by "residence orders" and "contact orders", whereas Hong Kong has retained the term, leading to cross-jurisdictional conceptual divergences with similar common law jurisdictions.

Official Chinese Equivalent

The term "custody" is consistently rendered as "管养权" across the four pieces of legislation, demonstrating consistent usage. The term "管养权" effectively neutralizes the connotation of detention by using the morpheme "养" (meaning child care), and its function of contextual restriction is well realized. However, "管养权" fails to encode the structural relationships among custody, care, and visitation as independent legal concepts, nor does it reflect the conceptual discrepancies across judicial jurisdictions that arise from institutional evolution.

Frame Slot Analysis

Table 8 provides a detailed comparison of the retention status of each custody slot in terms of "custody rights".

Table 8. Frame slot comparison: custody vs. 管养权

Frame slot	Content in English legal frame	Status in Chinese equivalent	Notes
Custodial party	Parent awarded right to have child reside with them	Retained	Core entitlement dimension adequately conveyed
Care content	Day-to-day physical care and upbringing	Partially retained	General caregiving sense present; day-to-day specificity absent
Access arrangement	Non-custodial parent's right of contact with child	Absent	Tripartite structure collapsed into single undifferentiated term
Child welfare principle	Paramount consideration of child's best interests	Absent	Statutory welfare principle not encoded
Court supervisory jurisdiction	Court retains jurisdiction to vary or discharge orders	Absent	Continuing supervisory role not signalled
Legislative evolution background	Shift away from custody terminology in comparable jurisdictions	Absent	Cross-jurisdictional conceptual divergence not reflected
Polysemy risk detention sense	Risk of confusion with detention/police custody	Neutralized	Morpheme effectively suppresses detention sense

As shown in Table 8 above, the custodial entity slot is fully preserved, and interference with custody is effectively neutralized. These two elements constitute the primary strengths of custodial rights. The custodial content slot is partially preserved: while "custody" conveys a general sense of care, the specific dimensions of daily, substantive care are not encoded. Four slots are completely missing. The visitation arrangements slot is missing. The high effect value of access confirms that custody is embedded in a tripartite structure, but "custody rights" collapses this into a single expression. The absence of the best interests of the child and court oversight slots reflects that "custody rights" fail to encode the statutory principles governing custody determinations and the court's ongoing supervisory role. Most notably, the Institutional Evolutionary Context slot is missing: the legislative divergence between Hong Kong and England and Wales regarding the use of the term "custody" introduces a cross-jurisdictional conceptual gap that "管养权" fails to encode.

Equivalence judgment and risk type. Custody and custody rights can be defined as near equivalents within the framework of Šarčević (1997). The false friend risk associated with this term arises from the combined effect of two mechanisms: context-restricted polysemy, where the meaning of "detention" poses a potential source of confusion for non-specialist readers; and conceptual instability resulting from institutional evolution, where legislative divergences between Hong Kong and similar common law jurisdictions introduce cross-jurisdictional conceptual gaps not encoded by "custody". This dual risk mechanism distinguishes "custody" from the other four case studies in this research and demonstrates that the false friend risk of legal terminology stems not only from synchronic semantic misalignment but can also arise from diachronic divergences in institutional evolution.

DISCUSSION

This study examines manifestations of false friend risk in bilingual marriage and family law terminology in Hong Kong by integrating a qualitative approach that combines AntConc corpus retrieval with frame-slot analysis. The following discussion addresses the three research questions in turn and further elucidates the study's theoretical and methodological significance.

Regarding RQ1, stable official equivalents can leave key institutional dimensions of source-language terms unexpressed. This finding extends the conceptual boundaries of false friend risk from the traditional lexical-level definition to the institutional level: in the context of legal translation, the risk is not limited to semantic confusion caused by formal similarity, but extends to the systematic suppression of procedural, institutional, and jurisdictional knowledge dimensions in the target-language expression (Marín & Fernández, 2015). The five risk types identified in this study, general-meaning interference, semantic shift, and incomplete manifestation, conceptual compression and pseudo-transparency, institutional asymmetry across legal systems, and context-restricted polysemy, collectively constitute a typological way that surpasses existing research frameworks on legal false friends in both typological diversity and institutional grounding.

Regarding RQ2, the five case studies reveal a consistent pattern: a systemic dissociation between terminological stability and conceptual adequacy. The Chinese equivalents "赡养令", "判令", "济助", "呈请", and "管养权", which have all established normative, stable bilingual correspondences. However, frame slot analysis reveals systemic slot deficiencies in each case. This dissociation has significant theoretical implications: within Šarčević's (1997) equivalence framework, the examined cases focus on the levels of approximate and partial equivalence, not because of inaccurate translation, but because the institutional complexity of the source-language terms exceeds the scope of any single lexical correspondence. In this sense, terminological standardization itself may become a source of pseudo-transparency. Prieto Ramos (2014) observes that in institutionalized translation contexts, terminological regularity may create an illusion of equivalence that discourages re-examination of underlying conceptual relationships.

Regarding RQ3, the integrated approach combining AntConc retrieval with frame slot analysis has proven effective in meeting the methodological demands of specialized legal terminology research. Corpus retrieval operationalizes terminology selection through traceable empirical criteria, frequency, chunking patterns, and co-occurrence networks based on effect values, ensuring that analysis is grounded in distributional evidence rather than the researcher's subjective judgment. Frame slot analysis, in turn, transforms this evidence into structured conceptual comparisons, providing a principled basis for equivalence judgments that transcends impressionistic evaluation (Farhan, 2022). This combination also demonstrates that when the research objective is conceptual depth rather than statistical generalization, small, specialized corpora are sufficient for analytical purposes in terminology research (Biel, 2008; Engberg, 2023), effectively addressing the methodological critique that qualitative legal terminology research must trade rigor for interpretability.

This study contributes to existing research in three ways. First, it extends the conceptual boundaries of the false friend risk from the lexical level to the institutional level. Previous studies have primarily treated false friends as lexical phenomena where formal similarity masks semantic differences (Marín & Fernández, 2015). This study demonstrates that false friend risk can occur even in the absence of formal similarity: while "relief" and "济助" share no morphological resemblance, "济助" encodes only the most superficial dimension of a legally complex concept, thereby creating a pseudo-transparency effect. Consequently, the defining characteristic of false friend risk in the context of legal translation is not formal similarity, but rather the ability of the target-language term to suppress awareness of conceptual incompleteness, a distinction with direct practical implications for the evaluation and selection of legal equivalents in bilingual legal texts.

Second, the study reveals the diachronic dimension of false friend risk, which is largely absent from existing research. The "custody" case study demonstrates that conceptual instability may not stem from current semantic misalignment, but rather from diachronic legislative divergences across jurisdictions. "Custody" was superseded, whereas Hong Kong law retained the term, introducing a cross-jurisdictional conceptual gap not encoded by the term "管养权". This finding suggests that terminology research in bilingual legal contexts must focus on the legislative history of source-language terms rather than merely their current institutional functions, and that the risk of false friends can also arise from divergent diachronic institutional evolution.

Third, integrating Engberg's (2021) frame approach with Šarčević's (1997) equivalence framework yields an analytical tool more refined than any single theory. Equivalence judgments based on slot-level analysis, which explicitly identify which institutional dimensions are retained, partially retained, or missing, are more operational than holistic labels of approximate or partial equivalence and provide a basis for targeted interventions in legal translation practice and teaching. Unlike existing corpus-assisted legal translation studies that primarily focus on text-level translation patterns (Biel, 2008). This study uses corpus distribution data as an entry point into conceptual analysis and treats the co-occurrence network of effect value as evidence of institutional framework activation rather than the endpoint of analysis.

The semantic gaps identified in the "maintenance order" case, specifically the complete absence of provisions regarding the accumulation of arrears and enforcement procedures in "maintenance order," indicate that practitioners and students using this term face a potential conceptual gap concerning the procedural consequences of maintenance orders. They tend to interpret these orders as static obligations rather than as dynamic, legally enforceable, and modifiable institutional tools. The incomplete articulation of procedural stages in the "decree" case suggests that readers relying solely on the Chinese text may fail to distinguish between the conditional nature of a decree nisi and the finality of a decree absolute. This distinction directly impacts the substantive legal rights of the parties involved. The five identified gaps in the "relief" case expose a significant disparity between the meaning conveyed by the term "relief" and the complexity of the court's property relief system. Practitioners lacking a background in common law may struggle to recognize the scope of available remedies or understand the broad discretion exercised by the court in granting relief. The absence of an adversarial procedural structure in petition cases suggests that Chinese text readers might perceive matrimonial proceedings as unilateral administrative applications rather than adversarial legal processes. Such perception could lead to systematic misunderstandings regarding the parties' rights and obligations. Furthermore, the lack of codification concerning the institutional development of custody cases suggests that, when comparing Hong Kong's custody provisions with those of England and Wales, the Chinese text does not signal jurisdictional divergence despite institutional differences. Overall, the documented "slot gaps" are not only of academic interest but also pose risks of specific conceptual misunderstandings in legal practice. This analysis underscores the importance of providing supplementary annotations or definitional clarifications in bilingual legal texts to ensure the full and accurate conveyance of legal concepts across languages and jurisdictions.

In summary, by systematically identifying and analyzing the false friend risk in bilingual marriage and family law terminology in Hong Kong, this study demonstrates that the gap between terminological normativity and conceptual equivalence is not an accident of translation, but a structural consequence of transposing common law concepts into a target-language context where those institutional frameworks have no direct equivalent. The conceptual risks comprising these five risk types, ranging from interference by general meanings to systemic disparities across legal systems, and from conceptual compression to diachronic institutional evolution, collectively point to a single core conclusion: in Hong Kong bilingual legal texts, stable official correspondences do not necessarily equate to full conceptual transmission. The corpus-assisted frame slot analysis approach proposed in this study provides traceable empirical evidence and a replicable analytical framework for this conclusion, and offers concrete operational guidelines for targeted conceptual verification in legal translation practice, the drafting of bilingual legal texts, and legal terminology instruction.

Limitation and Future Research Directions

This study has several limitations in its scope and methodological design, warranting further exploration and refinement in future research. First, regarding corpus coverage, this study focuses on Hong Kong marriage and family law, and the parallel corpus constructed is of limited size. While a thematic design helps ensure homogeneity within the corpus and a focused analysis, it also, to some extent, limits the generalizability of the study's conclusions to other areas of law. Future research could expand the scope of analysis to other legal fields in Hong Kong, such as commercial law, corporate law, or criminal procedure law, to test whether the false friend risk mechanism identified in this study is applicable across different fields and to further enrich the description of risk types.

Second, regarding the retrieval process, this study primarily relies on English corpora, with the Chinese portion introduced through manual article comparison; true bilingual automated retrieval has not yet been achieved. While this approach ensures feasibility, it may also overlook certain instances of conceptual shifts observable only in Chinese legal provisions. Future research could explore more comprehensive bidirectional bilingual retrieval pathways, such as incorporating Chinese corpus tools or constructing aligned bilingual corpora, to enhance the analysis's systematic nature and bidirectional coverage.

This study focuses solely on Hong Kong's English-Chinese legal corpus, limiting its broader applicability. Initial analysis suggests the false friend risk varies across jurisdictions. For example, Singapore, with a monolingual common law system and Chinese as a community language, shows an impact on lay understanding rather than official texts. Macao's trilingual system presents another form of systemic asymmetry within a civil law tradition. Canada's bi-jural model, which requires equivalence across legal traditions, may closely parallel Hong Kong's challenge of encoding common-law concepts in a civil-law-associated language. Future research on cognate terms across these jurisdictions can reveal if the typology is specific to Hong Kong or a broader phenomenon.

Finally, regarding the potential to extend the theoretical framework, the AntConc retrieval, manual screening, and frame slot analysis approach proposed in this paper can, in principle, be applied to other areas of legal translation research. With the continued penetration of artificial intelligence and automated tools in legal translation, integrating mechanisms to identify false friend risk into computer-assisted translation tools or legal terminology databases is also a promising direction for applied research.

CONCLUSION

Drawing on Šarčević's (1997) equivalence framework and Engberg's (2021) frame-based analysis as theoretical foundations, this study systematically examines the risk of false friends in bilingual marriage and family law terminology in Hong Kong through a qualitative research approach that integrates AntConc corpus retrieval with frame slot comparison analysis. The findings indicate that the risk of false friends in bilingual legal texts does not primarily arise from overt mistranslations but rather manifests as the systematic under-activation of source-language legal knowledge frameworks in their target-language equivalents. In the five case studies examined, the Chinese equivalents, maintenance order, judgment, relief, petition, and custody, have all established normative and stable bilingual correspondences. However, analysis at the slot level reveals that core institutional dimensions, such as procedural stages, distinctions in types of relief, adversarial procedural structures, and the framework of parental responsibility, are systematically missing in each case.

Specifically, the core obligations and command structure of "maintenance" are largely preserved, but the procedural consequences dimension is significantly compressed. "Decree" conveys the adjudicative nature but fails to encode the two-stage progression of nisi that lies at the core of its legal function. "Relief" retains only the most superficial direction of relief, while the full institutional complexity of court-ordered property relief is significantly compressed. "Petition" successfully conveys the act of initiating litigation but fails to activate the adversarial party structure and cross-jurisdictional institutional foundations presupposed by the term. "custody" effectively neutralizes the polysemous interference of the "detention" meaning, yet slots such as visitation arrangements, the principle of the child's welfare, and the institutional evolutionary context remain unmanifested. These findings collectively indicate that the false friend risk is not a singular phenomenon but rather a typological mechanism that operates in overlapping ways across the lexical, procedural, and institutional levels (Badah et al., 2025).

In summary, by combining distributional corpus evidence from AntConc with structured conceptual comparisons of five representative cases, this study bridges the under-explored intersection between corpus-assisted legal terminology research and frame-based equivalence analysis. The study further demonstrates that formally stable official correspondences cannot be assumed to guarantee full conceptual equivalence. For terms embedded in the structure of the common law system that lack direct counterparts in the civil law system, supplementary annotations or definitional clarifications may be necessary. The findings of this study contribute to legal translation research and provide a replicable analytical framework for terminology studies in other bilingual legal jurisdictions.

REFERENCES

Baaij, C. J. (Ed.). (2012). *The role of legal translation in legal harmonization*. Kluwer Law International BV.

Badah, A. M., Khalaf, C. N., Dwaikat, F. J., & AlQbailat, N. (2025). The usage of artificial intelligence in legal translation: Bridging the gap between law and language. *Ampersand (Oxford, UK), 100248*. Advance online publication. DOI: 10.1016/j.amper.2025.100248

Baker, M. (1993). Corpus linguistics and translation studies: Implications and applications. In Baker, M., Francis, G., & Tognini-Bonelli, E. (Eds.), *Text and technology: In honour of John Sinclair* (pp. 233–250). John Benjamins. DOI: 10.1075/z.64.15bak

Baker, M. (1995). Corpora in translation studies: An overview and some suggestions for future research. *International Journal of Translation Studies*, *7*(2), 223–243. DOI: 10.1075/target.7.2.03bak

Biel, Ł. (2008). Corpus assisted studies of legal language for translation purposes: Methodological and practical potential. In Kredens, K., & Goźdź-Roszkowski, S. (Eds.), *Language and the law: International outlooks* (pp. 21–38). Peter Lang.

Biel, Ł. (2016). Phraseology in legal translation: A corpus-based analysis of textual mapping in EU law. In *The Ashgate handbook of legal translation* (pp. 177–192). Routledge., DOI: 10.4324/9781315612706-13

Biel, Ł., & Engberg, J. (2013). Research models and methods in legal translation. *Linguistica Antverpiensia. New Series: Themes in Translation Studies*, *12*. Advance online publication. DOI: 10.52034/lanstts.v12i.316

Biel, Ł., & Kockaert, H. J. (Eds.). (2023). Handbook of terminology: Vol. 3. *Legal terminology*. John Benjamins., DOI: 10.1075/hot.3

Chan, C. H., & Cham, C. (2023). *Legal terminology* (Vol. 3). Past, present and future: Bilingual legal terminology in Hong Kong. *Handbook of terminology*. John Benjamins.

Chan, C. H. Y. (2020). *Legal translation and bilingual law drafting in Hong Kong: Challenges and interactions in Chinese regions*. Routledge., DOI: 10.4324/9780429443466

Clay, E. (2026). Measuring divergence in migration-related terminology between EU legal discourse and press articles in English and French. *International Journal of Corpus Linguistics*, *31*(1), 13–35. DOI: 10.1075/ijcl.25082.cla

Department of Justice. (2012). *A guide to styles and practices.* https://www.doj.gov.hk/en/publications/pub20030011.html

Department of Justice. (2023). *Law Drafting Division: Chinese and English.* https://www.doj.gov.hk/en/about/orgchart_ldd_drafting_chi_eng.html

Doczekalska, A. (2023). *Legal terms, concepts and definitions in the transposition of EU law. Handbook of Terminology.* John Benjamins., DOI: 10.1075/hot.3.leg3

Engberg, J. (2023). *Legal terminology* (Vol. 3). Frame approach to legal terminology: What may be gained from seeing terminology as manifestation of legal knowledge? *Handbook of terminology.* John Benjamins., DOI: 10.1075/hot.3.fra2

Faber, P. (2022). *Frame-based terminology. Theoretical linguistics research perspectives.* John Benjamins. DOI: 10.1075/tlrp.23

Farhan, A. K. (2022). Divergence in the translation of criminal law: A corpus assisted study of prohibition in Iraqi penal code and its English translation. *Ampersand (Oxford, UK), 10,* 100104. DOI: 10.1016/j.amper.2022.100104

Fillmore, C. J. (1976). Frame semantics and the nature of language. *Annals of the New York Academy of Sciences, 280*(1), 20–32. DOI: 10.1111/j.1749-6632.1976.tb25467.x

Graziadei, M. (2025). Legal translation and the quest for authenticity. *International Journal for the Semiotics of Law, 38*(8), 2565–2593. DOI: 10.1007/s11196-025-10283-y

Hamed, D. M., & Alqurashi, N. (2025). A corpus-driven study on legal translation challenges among Arab law students: Examining gender and academic level in applied legal linguistics. *Humanities & Social Sciences Communications, 12*(1), 1–17. DOI: 10.1057/s41599-025-05451-1

Jopek-Bosiacka, A. (2023). *Definitions in law across legal cultures and jurisdictions. Handbook of terminology.* John Benjamins., https://www.jbe-platform.com/content/books/9789027249388-hot.3.def1

Kemp, J. (2022). *An investigation of the vocabulary representative of postgraduate International Law texts* (Doctoral dissertation, University of Leicester). DOI: 10.25392/Leicester.data.20317362

Koteva, G. (2023). Dealing with legal terminology in the translation of business documents. *Научни трудове на УНСС, 2*(2), 137-154. DOI: 10.37075/RP.2023.2.10

Legrand, P. (1996). How to compare now. *Legal Studies, 16*(2), 232–242. DOI: 10.1111/j.1748-121X.1996.tb00005.x

Marín, M. J., & Fernández Toledo, P. (2015). The influence of cognates on the acquisition of legal terminology: Help or hindrance? A corpus assisted study. *Procedia: Social and Behavioral Sciences, 198*, 320–329. DOI: 10.1016/j.sbspro.2015.07.450

Oxford University Press. (n.d.). *Oxford English dictionary*. In *OED Online*. Retrieved April 20, 2026, from https://www.oed.com

Pavliuk, N. (2023). A potential of legal terminology to be translated: The case of "regulation" translated into Ukrainian. *International Journal for the Semiotics of Law-Revue internationale de Sémiotique juridique, 36*(6), 2429-2454. DOI: 10.1007/s11196-023-10034-x

Peruzzo, K. (2023). *Legal terms that travel: Constraints to presenting national legal terminology to international audiences. Handbook of terminology*. John Benjamins., DOI: 10.1075/hot.3.leg1

Pontrandolfo, G. (2023). The importance of being patterned: Old and new perspectives on legal phraseology. In *Handbook of terminology* (pp. 124–150). John Benjamins. DOI: 10.1075/hot.3.imp1

Prieto Ramos, F. (2014). Legal translation studies as interdiscipline: Scope and evolution. *Meta, 59*(2), 260–277. DOI: 10.7202/1027475ar

Prieto Ramos, F., & Cerutti, G. (2023). Terminological hybridity in institutional legal translation: A corpus-driven analysis of key genres of EU and international law. *Terminology, 29*(1), 45–77. DOI: 10.1075/term.21047.pri

Šarčević, S. (1997). *New approach to legal translation*. Kluwer Law International.

Šarčević, S. (2012). *Challenges to the legal translator. The Oxford handbook of language and law*. Oxford University Press., DOI: 10.1093/oxfordhb/9780199572120.013.0014

Stubbs, M. (2001). *Words and phrases: Corpus studies of lexical semantics*. John Wiley & Sons.

Wu, S., Amini, M., & Mahfoodh, O. H. A. (2025). A corpus assisted analysis of modality shifts in English-to-Chinese courtroom translation. *Eurasian Journal of Applied Linguistics, 11*(1), 152–166. https://files.eric.ed.gov/fulltext/EJ1474997.pdf

Wu, S., Amini, M., & Mahfoodh, O. H. A. (2026). Exploring translators' perceptions of translation decisions in courtroom translation. *International Journal for the Semiotics of Law-Revue internationale de Sémiotique juridique, 39*(1), 319-339. DOI: 10.1007/s11196-025-10274-z

Zhou, X., & Hu, C. (2024). A review of research on correspondence and processing of legal terminology in legal translation. *International Journal of Education and Humanities, 16*(2), 290–295. DOI: 10.54097/t5cbrj67

ADDITIONAL READINGS

Alghamdi, F. A., & Alotaibi, H. (2025). Using AI in translation quality assessment: A case study of ChatGPT and legal translation texts. *Electronics (Basel), 14*(19), 3893. Advance online publication. DOI: 10.3390/electronics14193893

Duběda, T. (2026). Risk perception and risk management in legal translation: A questionnaire survey. *Perspectives, 34*(1), 152–168. DOI: 10.1080/0907676X.2024.2386447

Farghal, T., Shraideh, K., & Al-Omari, A. M. (2025). Evaluating free legal translation tools between Arabic and English: A comparative study of Google Translate, ChatGPT, and Gemini. *International Journal for the Semiotics of Law-Revue internationale de Sémiotique juridique, 38*(6), 2083-2110. DOI: 10.1007/s11196-025-10282-z

Giczela-Pastwa, J. (2026). How can a learner translation corpus assist L2 translator trainers in fostering trainees' cross-linguistic competence in the context of legal translation? *The Interpreter and Translator Trainer, 20*(1), 1–20. DOI: 10.1080/1750399X.2025.2554464

Moneus, A. M., & Sahari, Y. (2024). Artificial intelligence and human translation: A contrastive study based on legal texts. *Heliyon, 10*(6), e28106. Advance online publication. DOI: 10.1016/j.heliyon.2024.e28106 PMID: 38524597

Wang, Q., Amini, M., Yang, C., & He, Q. (2026). Translating culture-specific items in The True Story of Ah Q: A comparative evaluation of GPT-4o, KIMI, and Google Translate under multimodal prompts. *SAGE Open, 16*(1), 21582440251412225. Advance online publication. DOI: 10.1177/21582440251412225

KEY TERMS AND DEFINITIONS

Corpus-Assisted Analysis: A research approach that employs corpus retrieval tools to provide empirical, distributional evidence for qualitative analysis. In this study, AntConc is used to identify frequency patterns, fixed collocations, and co-occurrence networks as the basis for subsequent frame-based interpretation.

False Friend Risk: In legal translation, the risk that a target-language term appears formally adequate or terminologically stable while failing to activate the institutional knowledge frame presupposed by the source-language term, thereby generating conceptual under-activation in the reader. The risk operates not only through formal similarity but also through surface terminological regularity that suppresses awareness of conceptual incompleteness.

Hong Kong e-Legislation (HKeL): The official electronic database of Hong Kong legislation maintained by the Department of Justice of the Hong Kong SAR Government. Established under section 3 of the Legislation Publication Ordinance (Cap. 614), it provides public access to Hong Kong's consolidated legislation in electronic form and serves as the authoritative online source for current and past legislative texts.

Legal Semantic Shift: A type of false friend risk in which a legal term acquires a highly specific institutional or procedural meaning within a particular legal domain that diverges significantly from both its general English sense and its target-language equivalent, resulting in incomplete conceptual transfer.

Pseudo-Transparency: A characteristic of target-language legal equivalents that are formally stable, morphologically transparent, and terminologically well-established, yet encode only the surface-level dimension of a legally complex concept. The very fluency and regularity of such equivalents may suppress readers' awareness of the conceptual incompleteness they entail.

Chapter 5
Legal Translation: The Case of Personal Data Translations From Greek Into English

Marina Pappa
http://orcid.org/0000-0002-1372-1013
National and Kapodistrian University of Athens, Greece

ABSTRACT

The translation of legal texts constitutes one of the most demanding areas of professional translation due to the high degree of conceptual density, terminological precision, and normative force embedded in legal discourse. When the legal domain intersects with the regulation of personal data, an area characterized by rapid technological evolution, supranational governance, and complex rights based framework, the challenges multiply. This paper examines the linguistic, conceptual, and pragmatic difficulties inherent in translating legal texts, with a particular focus on personal data legislation such as the EU General Data Protection Regulation (GDPR) and related national implementations. This paper examines the linguistic, conceptual, and pragmatic difficulties inherent in translating legal texts, with a particular focus on personal data legislation such as the EU General Data Protection Regulation (GDPR), and related national implementations from Greek into English.

INTRODUCTION

Legal translation occupies a unique position within translation studies due to its dual anchoring in language and law, two systems that are simultaneously autonomous and interdependent. Unlike literary or technical translation, legal translation

DOI: 10.4018/979-8-3373-9179-3.ch005

operates within a framework of institutional authority and jurisdictional specificity. As scholars have repeatedly emphasized, legal translation is not merely a linguistic transfer but a juridical act that participates in the construction, interpretation, and application of law (Cao, 2007; Šarčević 1997). The translator must navigate the conceptual asymmetries between legal systems, the pragmatic constraints of legal genres, and the communicative expectations of legal institutions and end-users. This is very demanding and studies focus on legal translation issues the past years (Altuwairesh & AlGhamedi, 2025; Pontrandolfo & Peruzzo, 2017; Pisulińska, 2021).

This chapter presents approaches on legal translation, integrates recent research, and contextualizes these insights within the specific challenges of Greek into English legal translation, with a particular focus on personal data protection law. The latter constitutes a highly dynamic field shaped by the General Data Protection Regulation (GDPR), Greek Law 4624/2019 and the preceding law 2472/1997, and the interpretative practice of the Hellenic Data Protection Authority (HDPA). The translation of personal data law provisions raises acute issues of terminological harmonization, conceptual equivalence, and institutional multilingualism, making it an ideal case study for illustrating the theoretical principles of legal translation.

Legal texts are semiotic artefacts and as Engberg (2021) argues, legal meaning is not inherent in linguistic signs but emerges from the interaction between text, legal system, and interpretative community. Translation therefore requires the reconstruction of meaning within a different semiotic and legal environment in the target language. The translator must interpret the illocutionary force of legal utterances namely commands, permissions, prohibitions, and reproduce them in a target language that may encode legal authority differently.

A central theoretical issue is the authenticity of legal translations. In multilingual legal orders such as the European Union, multiple language versions are equally authentic, yet they may diverge linguistically or conceptually. Thus, the translator's role positions him/her both as mediator and co-author of legal meaning.

LITERATURE REVIEW

Legal translation is inseparable from comparative law. As de Groot and van Laer (2006) note, translation requires an understanding of the functional equivalence between legal concepts across jurisdictions. However, equivalence is rarely perfect. Šarčević (1997) distinguishes between near-equivalence (similar concepts with minor differences), partial equivalence, and non-equivalence (unique concepts with no counterpart). In this framework Greek law, rooted in the continental law tradition, often lacks direct equivalents in English-speaking common-law systems.

This structural asymmetry is particularly visible in areas such as administrative law, property law, and personal-data provisions especially in the United States.

Jean-Claude Gémar (2014) offers a comprehensive reflection on the evolution of legal translation, the persistent challenge of equivalence, and the emergence of co-drafting as an alternative method for producing bilingual legislation. He begins by revisiting the long-standing suspicion toward translation, depicted in the proverb *traduttore traditore,* and the central dilemma between literal and free translation. In legal contexts, this dilemma becomes acute because the translator must reproduce both the letter and the spirit of the law.

He traces Canada's unique trajectory from literal translations of statutes to the development of jurilinguistique, a field born from the interaction of legal translation and linguistics. Following the 1969 Official Languages Act, Canadian institutions experimented with functional equivalence, inspired by Nida. In this model, bilingual teams draft legislation simultaneously in English and French, avoiding translation altogether. This shift reflects Canada's bilingual and bijural reality, where translators must navigate both common law and civil law traditions. Gémar emphasizes that legal translation is not a mechanical transfer of words but a complex interpretive act shaped by culture, legal tradition, and drafting style.

Gémar examines the elusive notion of equivalence since perfect equivalence is unattainable because legal concepts are culturally embedded and often system-specific. Terms like contract, property, fairness, or equity resist direct translation since at best, translators achieve functional equivalence.Gémar proposes a four-part approach to equivalence, distinguishing between semantic equivalents, partial equivalents, untranslatable terms, and culturally bound concepts requiring comparative legal analysis. This framework indicates that equivalence is always relative and context-dependent.

Co-drafting produces separate but equal legislative texts, each written in the natural idiom of its legal culture. Gémar illustrates this with side-by-side provisions from Canada's *Interpretation Act*, showing how French can express the same legal content more concisely than English. While co-drafting enhances readability and cultural authenticity, it also raises interpretive challenges, since courts must reconcile two equally authoritative versions. Ultimately, Gémar argues that translation and co-drafting both seek the same goal, namely capturing the spirit of the law. Translation remains indispensable, but co-drafting offers a promising model for multilingual legal systems.

In the European framework Baaij (2012) examines the internal contradictions of the European Union's policy on institutional multilingualism, arguing that the EU's public narrative, grounded in principles of democracy, equality, linguistic diversity, and transparent governance, sits uneasily alongside the pragmatic and budgetary constraints that shape actual language practice. Although EU institutions repeatedly affirm that linguistic diversity is a core value and that all languages possess equal dignity, the operational reality is far more limited: only 23 of the more than 80 languages spoken in Europe are official EU languages, leaving many regional and minority language speakers without access to EU legislation in their mother tongue.

In this framework Baaij further highlights the gap between principle and practice in the internal functioning of EU institutions. Despite formal commitments to equal representation, approximately 95% of legislative drafting occurs in English, which has become the de facto working language of the Commission, Parliament, and Council. Cost-cutting measures in translation and interpretation reinforce this trend, effectively privileging English and undermining the proclaimed ideal of linguistic equality.

In this research a pragmatic approach is proposed, namely integrating language learning into the policy narrative and encouraging all European citizens to master at least one of the languages used by EU institutions, particularly English. This would acknowledge the existing linguistic reality while preserving the EU's commitment to democratic inclusion. The article concludes that further research is needed on whether the EU should accept or even encourage the spontaneous development of English as a de facto pan-European lingua franca.

In a similar approach Prieto-Ramos (2017) argues that global law is fundamentally a network of translated texts, because international and supranational institutions rely structurally on multilingual drafting, negotiation, and adjudication. He maps the legal genres produced and translated in three major institutional settings, the United Nations, the World Trade Organization, and the European Union. The study shows that although these institutions differ in their language regimes (24 official languages in the EU, 6 in the UN, 3 in the WTO), they share structural similarities in how legal texts are produced, translated, and interpreted. Translation is not a peripheral activity but a constitutive element of legal validity, since multilingual versions often have equal authenticity. The role of institutional translators in giving shape to texts that become sources of law is highlighted. Through extensive mapping of genres, treaties, resolutions, reports, judicial decisions, press releases, it is demonstrated how multilingualism shapes legal meaning, uniform interpretation, and the functioning of global governance.

It is imperative to mention that functionalist approaches, especially Skopos theory, have been influential in legal translation. Duan in *Legal Text Translation under the Guidance of Skopos Theory* (2023) demonstrates how translation strategies must align with the purpose of the target text and the translator must therefore adapt terminology, syntax, and discourse conventions to the intended function of the translation.

Though the lens of Skopos theory Duan (2023) examines English into Chinese legal translation arguing that the purpose (*skopos*) of a translation should guide all translational decisions. As globalization accelerates and China's legal and economic interactions with other countries deepen, the demand for accurate legal translation has grown significantly. Legal texts now regulate foreign trade, comparative law, and international dispute resolution, making translation quality a matter of both practical and legal importance. Yet, linguistic and cultural differences between English and Chinese create substantial challenges, and many translators lack legal training, leading to literal, renderings that depict only the surface.

The Skopos Theory as developed by Reiss and Vermeer, emphasizes its three core principles, purpose, coherence, and fidelity. Under this framework, translation strategies must be selected according to the intended function of the target text and the needs of its readers. As Duan cites, Skopos theory rejects one-size-fits-all approaches as translators may adopt foreignization or domestication depending on the legal context, communicative intent, and cultural expectations. This teleological orientation allows translators to prioritize functional adequacy over rigid linguistic correspondence.

Duan then analyzes the linguistic features of English legal texts that complicate translation. At the lexical level, legal English is characterized by extensive use of Latin and French loanwords (e.g., *ultra vires*, *force majeure*), common words with specialized legal meanings (*brief*, *construction*), fixed legal jargon (*cause of action*, *due process of law*), and archaic forms from Old and Middle English (*thereof*, *pursuant to*). These features require translators to possess not only linguistic competence but also legal literacy, since mistranslation of technical terms can lead to serious consequences.

At the syntactic level, English legal texts frequently employ long, tightly structured sentences, heavy nominalization, and passive constructions to achieve precision and objectivity. Chinese legal writing, by contrast, favors active voice, clearer logical sequencing, and shorter, more direct structures. Duan illustrates how translators must adjust voice, reorder clauses, and sometimes split long sentences to produce coherent and readable Chinese legal texts. For example, the article shows how transforming passive constructions into active ones and reorganizing complex modifiers improves clarity for Chinese readers.

The conclusion emphasizes that even under Skopos Theory, translators must respect linguistic and cultural differences while balancing fidelity and accuracy. Mastery of legal terminology, familiarity with legal systems, and extensive practical experience are essential. Duan argues that legal translators must cultivate interdisciplinary knowledge, treat uncertainties with caution, and continually expand their expertise to ensure that translations remain both functionally appropriate and legally reliable.

Legal genres, statutes, judgments, contracts, administrative decisions often impose specific constraints. Tiersma (1999) notes that legal language is characterized by archaism, nominalization, and syntactic complexity. Greek legal texts, particularly administrative decisions, often employ long hypotactic structures and dense nominal phrases. Translating these into English requires balancing fidelity to legal meaning with readability and genre conventions of English language legal drafting.

Michele Graziadei (2025) examines legal translation as a historically essential yet often misunderstood practice, arguing that its importance has been underestimated despite its centrality to the development of modern legal systems. He opens with the paradox that the translator is legally the "author" of a translation, yet only if the work is openly presented as such, otherwise it risks being treated as plagiarism. This paradox, he notes, contributed to the long-standing perception of translation as a derivative, secondary activity. However, contemporary translation studies have reframed translation as a complex, interpretive, and creative process, and legal translation has followed this evolution. As he writes, legal translation requires reconciling concepts "that often lack direct equivalents across languages," making authenticity and functional equivalence difficult but indispensable goals.

Graziadei traces the historical role of translation in shaping national legal cultures, particularly during the era of nineteenth century codifications. Italy serves as a paradigmatic example since thousands of legal works, French, German, Belgian, and others, were translated into Italian, profoundly influencing legal scholarship, terminology, and the interpretation of the new civil codes. Similar patterns occurred in Spain, Latin America, France, Germany, England, and beyond.

Courts in multilingual jurisdictions and international courts routinely publish judgments in multiple languages, while national supreme courts increasingly provide informative translations to foster transparency and cross-jurisdictional dialogue. Non-governmental organizations and academic projects also use translation to coordinate legal strategies and enable comparative analysis.

The quest for authenticity in legal translation remains challenging, especially when multiple linguistic versions must share equal authority, but Graziadei concludes that while no solution is perfect, certain frameworks allow these difficulties to be managed with clarity and rigor.

Legal Translation Approaches Across Languages

Research across the EU consistently highlights several recurring issues like conceptual non-equivalence between legal systems, syntactic and stylistic divergence, terminological instability, and the structural constraints of multilingual drafting. Studies examining translation practices in countries such as France, Spain, Italy, Poland, and Germany demonstrate that legal translators must navigate both linguistic complexity and the institutional requirements of the EU acquis, where co authenticity of language versions and harmonized terminology impose additional constraints (Baaij, 2012; Prieto-Ramos, 2017).

General types of legal translation like statutes, regulations, judgments, administrative acts, and contracts, pose distinct challenges. Statutes and regulations require strict terminological consistency and alignment with EU terminology while judgments demand sensitivity to judicial reasoning and genre conventions; administrative acts often contain dense bureaucratic phrasing; and contracts require precision and awareness of private-law concepts. Specialized legal translation, particularly of EU directives and regulations, introduces further complexity due to the need to reconcile national legal traditions with supranational drafting norms. Comparative studies across EU languages show that translators frequently struggle with long hypotactic structures (common in Romance and Slavic languages), culturally embedded legal concepts, and the tension between literal fidelity and functional clarity (Gémar, 2014; Engberg, 2021).For example, Romance languages such as French, Italian, and Spanish face similar issues with nominalization, long sentences, and dense legal phrasing. Solutions proposed in the literature, such as restructuring sentences for clarity, adopting functional equivalence, and relying on harmonized EU terminology, are directly applicable to Greek–English translation.

Other EU languages, such as Polish, Czech, and Slovak, share challenges related to minority-language status, the need to align with English-dominant EU terminology, and the risk of calques. These studies emphasize the importance of terminological consolidation, genre-specific templates, and adherence to EU drafting guidelines such as the *Joint Practical Guide* and the *Interinstitutional Style Guide*. Applying these insights to Greek–English translation would strengthen the chapter's practical contribution by showing how established solutions can be adapted to the Greek context.

Languages with structural similarities are Italian, Spanish, French (Romance languages). These languages share features such as extensive use of nominalization, hypotactic sentence structures, and dense legal phrasing. Their civil-law drafting traditions also resemble Greek administrative and legislative style.

Bulgarian and Romanian (South-East European languages) These languages exhibit similar bureaucratic genres, long administrative sentences, and legal terminology influenced by EU harmonization.

Languages with legal-cultural similarities are French and Italian. French legal culture has historically influenced Greek administrative law, especially in public law and bureaucratic style. Both systems rely heavily on civil-law conceptual frameworks. Italian legal drafting shares rhetorical patterns with Greek, including multi-clause sentences and formalized administrative phrasing.

Languages with similar EU translation challenges are Polish, Czech, Slovak These minority-status EU languages face similar pressures to align with English-dominant

EU terminology and often struggle with calques, terminological inconsistency, and syntactic transfer.

Greek Language and Translation From Greek Into English

Greek, despite its millennia long literary and cultural legacy, functions today as a minority language in global communication. With a few million speakers worldwide, Greek occupies a marginal position compared to dominant global languages such as English, Spanish, or Mandarin. This demographic reality shapes the dynamics of translation since most translation flows outward from Greek into English, and this work is overwhelmingly carried out by Greek translators who possess the cultural, historical, and linguistic competence required to mediate meaning across systems that differ profoundly.

It is not the lingua franca of the past in diplomacy, science, technology, or international trade and therefore most academic, legal, administrative, and cultural communication addressed to global audiences must therefore be translated into English. The minority status of Greek means that translation is not optional but a structural necessity for visibility, participation, and representation in global discourse.

Due to the cultural, legal, historical and administrative background of the Hellenic civilization, texts in Greek are deeply embedded in historical references, culturally specific institutions, idiomatic expressions, intertextual layers extending from antiquity to the present. Therefore, only translators with intimate knowledge of Greek society can reliably decode these layers.

Genres in Greek language, in legal, administrative, and political sector often lack direct equivalents in English. Examples include administrative acts framework and pragmatic issues that are inherent in the Greek way of life and legal provisions. Consciously or implicitly Greek language translators perform conceptual mapping, not word substitution.

Greek genres, especially legal decisions, ministerial circulars, and public sector documents, follow rhetorical patterns unfamiliar to English-speaking audiences. Greek translators understand the underlying hierarchical structure of Greek administrative reasoning, the implicit logic of judicial argumentation and the stylistic conventions of Greek bureaucratic discourse.

In terms of accuracy, since Greek is a minority language, mistranslation can erase or distort Greek institutional reality. Greek translators ensure effective terminological consistency, fidelity to Greek legal concepts and preservation of cultural nuances.

In terms of morpho syntactical issues and source language features, in Greek there are four cases, extensive verb conjugation and aspect distinctions (perfective and imperfective). Thus, translators have to take these encoded features when interpreting and rendering the passages into English. In addition, Greek aspect carries semantic weight that English tenses cannot replicate directly obliging translators to reconstruct meaning through periphrasis. As in most languages, there is lexical density and polysemy that is clarified through context.

A key feature in Greek language is flexible word order for emphasis. In English there is on the contrary fixed subject, verb, object structure. In the rendering process, translators must interpret pragmatic intention and not merely reorder words.

It is obvious that Greek as a minority language makes translation into English a strategic necessity for international communication. Because Greek linguistic structures, cultural references, and conceptual frameworks differ substantially from English, Greek into English translation must be carried out by translators with deep knowledge of Greek language and culture. This ensures accuracy, preserves meaning, and safeguards the visibility of Greek discourse in the global arena.

The European Union is the most developed multilingual legal order and Prieto-Ramos (2017) argues that European Union law is fundamentally translation based as legal norms are co-constructed across languages. This has direct implications for Greek into English translation, as many Greek legal concepts derive from European Union directives and regulations whose English versions serve as terminological anchors.

Data bases such as IATE, EUR-Lex, and other institutional resources provide harmonized terminology. However, harmonization does not eliminate conceptual divergence. For example, the Greek term δεδομένα προσωπικού χαρακτήρα corresponds to personal data, but the Greek legal tradition often embeds the concept within constitutional rights (Article 9A), whereas the English term is rooted in European Union regulatory language.

Greek law belongs to the continental law family, while English is predominantly a common-law language. This creates challenges such as different legal taxonomies, different sources of law, different drafting conventions.

Greek administrative decisions (e.g., Hellenic Data Protection decisions) develop long, multi-layered reasoning sections, frequent references to European Union law, embedded quotations from legislation, formulaic openings and closings. As a consequence, translating these into English requires genre awareness and careful handling of intertextuality.

METHODOLOGY

We examine the rendering of the summaries of the Hellenic Data Protection Authority (HDPA) into English. The analysis is based on the recurring translation patterns identified in these summaries, focusing on lexical and terminological issues, syntactic structures, register and style, micro-level issues, and micro-structural cohesion. The examples cited in the article are drawn directly from the English versions of the HDPA Annual Reports, which constitute a hybrid institutional genre combining legal terminology, administrative reporting, public-facing communication, and political-institutional discourse. The methodology consists of qualitative examination of these summaries, identification of literal calques, syntactic transfers from Greek, register inconsistencies, and terminological variation, and comparison with expected English language institutional and legal drafting conventions.

FINDINGS

The Case of Personal-Data Law

Personal data legislation is conceptually dense and highly harmonized at the EU level. Key terms such as controller, processor, data subject, profiling, and special categories of data have precise definitions in the General Data Protection Legislation. The initial Greek law 2472/1997 and Greek Law 4624/2019 supplements these definitions with national provisions, creating a layered normative structure. There are Greek terms have no perfect English equivalents like Αρχή Προστασίας Δεδομένων Προσωπικού Χαρακτήρα → Hellenic Data Protection Authority

The translator must rely on European Union harmonized terminology while ensuring consistency with Greek legal context. The Hellenic Data Protection Authority Decisions are rich sources of terminological and conceptual complexity. They require accurate rendering of legal reasoning, consistent use of terminology and careful rendering of the Greek constitutional and administrative law concepts.

Personal data protection decisions frequently cite European legislation, European Court of Justice case law, Greek constitutional provisions as well as prior decisions. The translator is obliged to maintain citation integrity and ensure that quoted European Union provisions match the official English version.

Legal translation is a complex interdisciplinary activity requiring mastery of language, law, comparative methodology, and institutional practice. Greek into English legal translation presents additional challenges due to structural differences between legal systems and the need to align Greek terminology with EU harmonized English. Personal data law exemplifies these challenges, offering a rich case study in conceptual equivalence, terminological precision, and intertextual coherence.

It is worth examining the rendering of the summaries of the Hellenic Data Protection Authority into English. The information presented reflects the official presentation of the legal framework and decisions issued in the framework of the European data protection framework. As the Decisions issued depict the actual challenges Greek authorities have to handle in the sensitive sector of personal data, they also present the outcome of the application of the legal framework in Greece. This presentation is essential for the harmonization and the diffusion of legal information.

The English "Summary of the Annual Report" of the Hellenic Data Protection Authority (HDPA) is a hybrid institutional genre combining legal terminology (General Data Protection Regulation, national laws, decisions, sanctions), administrative reporting (statistics, budgets, staffing), public-facing communication (awareness-raising, events, outreach) and of course the political institutional discourse (independence, constitutional role) of an independent authority functioning according to the provisions of the Greek constitution.

This hybridity creates high translation complexity, especially when the target language is English, demanding terminological precision, idiomatic institutional phrasing and collocations, clarity and conciseness and provisions to avoid Greek influenced syntactic structures in translation.

The summaries presented exhibit recurring translation patterns that reveal both strengths like generally accurate terminology but also in some cases systemic weaknesses like calques, unnatural phrasing, cohesion issues, register inconsistencies that are probably inherent to the nature of the Greek legal framework, the particular feature of data protection discourse and the fact that the translation process is highly demanding in complexity. This analysis identifies the main categories of translation problems and illustrates them with examples concerning lexical and terminological issues, syntactic and issues, register and style, microlevel issues, and micro-structural issues.

In terms of lexical and terminological issues, there are calques from Greek administrative language that is often use nominal, heavy, abstract phrasing, which the translation reproduces too literally. Some examples are:

"the Authority responded well to the challenges raised by the pandemic, adjusting almost immediately and switching to telework"

→ The phrase "responded well" is a literal rendering of ανταποκρίθηκε επαρκώς/antapokrithike eparkos, but in English institutional reports, one expects phrasing like:

"the Authority ensured operational continuity despite pandemic-related disruptions."

"the Authority was burdened by the pandemic"

→ Literal translation of επιβαρύνθηκε/epivarinthike, but in English this sounds physical or emotional.

Better: "the pandemic placed additional operational pressure on the Authority."

Across the years, the same concepts appear with different English renderings, which undermines terminological coherence like examples:

"Complaints were handled" vs. "complaints were resolved" vs. "cases of complaints were resolved"

"Data breach incidents notified" vs. "notifications of data breach incident

"Electronic communications service providers" vs. "providers of electronic communications services"

Taking into consideration that the target language reader has the English language translation as source of information, inconsistent terminology weakens the legal reliability of the translation and complicates citation in academic or professional contexts.

Some English legal collocations are mistranslated or used inappropriately, as

"The Authority imposed the sanction of reprimand – warning"

→ English administrative law does not use "sanction of reprimand–warning."

it might be rendered: "the Authority issued a reprimand" or "the Authority issued a warning."

"The Authority judged that the appointment of a DPO... cannot guarantee the effective performance of the DPO's duties"

→ "judged" is too judicial; however, the HDPA is not a court.

it might be rendered: "the Authority found/considered that..."

It is obvious that incorrect collocations may distort the legal meaning or imply powers the Authority does not possess. In terms of syntactic and structural issues the usage of long sentences that are the result of the transfer of the Greek syntactic patterns. Greek legal and administrative style favors extended multi-clause sentences, the English translations often preserve this structure, resulting in reduced readability. One may observe the following example:

"The Authority is competent for the performance of its tasks (Article 57 of the GDPR and Article 13 of Law 4624/2019) and the exercise of the powers conferred on it (Article 58 of the GDPR and Article 15 of Law 4624/2019) on its territory (Article 55(1), Recitals 122, 129 of the GDPR; Article 9 of Law 4624/2019) acting with complete independence..." 2020 Annual Report

One may observe the underlying single syntax of 70+ words that has a Greek syntactical pattern. The native English speaker or the international audience may observe the reduced clarity, the burden in understanding and active reading and the obscurity in the hierarchy of information. Greek institutional writing often repeats information for emphasis or legal completeness. The English translation retains this repetition even when unnecessary. There are actually cases of redundancy, that render the English version stylistically heavy and less natural "*the Authority responded to its European and international obligations and was actively present in the working groups and committees operating under European data protection legislation*"

→ "responded to its obligations" + "actively present" is redundant

" the Authority continued to enrich its website... the Authority continuously makes systematic efforts... the Authority took initiatives... the Authority responded..."
→ Excessive repetition of "the Authority" without pronoun substitution.

The need to include information leads to the syntax of paragraphs that often combine heterogeneous topics, reflecting Greek rhetorical structure rather than English expectations for thematic unity. The work of rendering effectively in English language the annual report is extremely demanding and leads sometimes to the coexistence of formal and semi-formal register. In the framework of institutional output, one might expect meticulously stable institutional voice, a task that is highly demanding. Some passages are highly formal ("*in accordance with Article 52(4) GDPR*"), while others use conversational or vague language ("*the Authority was burdened*", "*it is noteworthy that...*").

The translation presents the essence and in general accurately the meaning but there are cases where there are literal translations Greek idiomatic expressions. One may note examples such:

Examples

"*It is noted that...*"

→ literal translation of *σημειώνεται ότι*, but overused in English.

"*It should be clarified that...*"

→ literal *πρέπει να διευκρινιστεί*, but English prefers:

"It should be noted that..." or "Importantly..."

The fact that Greek administrative style favors passive constructions leads to the reproduction of such structures in the English translation and renders the text less dynamic and easy to follow:

"*43 decisions were issued and 8 opinions*"

It would be advisable to use: "The Authority issued 43 decisions and 8 opinions."

Considering a different cultural and institutional framework, there is a Greek institutional framework with no direct English equivalent. Some Greek administrative/legal concepts require functional rather than literal translation, but the summaries often choose literal forms.

"*Plenary or Chamber*"

→ These are internal HDPA bodies; therefore, English language readers may not understand their function.

"*Personal Number*" (Προσωπικός Αριθμός/prossopikos arithmos)

The introduction of personal number in the framework of Hellenic publication administration procedures needs contextual explanation, since one may not understand the framework of introducing personal number in the everyday transactions of the Greek citizens in administrative procedures. In addition, Greek legal citations are often translated mechanically, without adapting to English citation norms:

"Law 4624/2019 ('Hellenic Data Protection Authority, measures for implementing Regulation…')"

Traditionally English legal writing norms would shorten this drastically as noted in administrative documents in English speaking countries.

In terms of micro level structure, it is known that Greek language often omits articles and while English structures require such syntactic forms

"Authority issued guidelines" → should be "the Authority issued guidelines."

"in context of telework" → should be "in the context of telework."

Likewise, some structures are influenced by the Greek syntax, while in an English-speaking framework that verb would be placed earlier in order to avoid awkward syntactic form:

"the Authority examined a complaint filed by an unemployed person against the Hellenic Manpower Employment Organisation regarding the leak of his personal data"

→ too long before the verb; English prefers earlier placement of the verb.

The task of producing natural output is really demanding. Sometimes the English headings often reflect Greek structure and will not be used in an English-speaking environment.

"Selection of decisions on complaints"

The native English structure would be "Selected Decisions on Complaints."

"Advisory – Consultative Work".

There is redundancy the semantic meaning of "advisory" already implies consultation. It is advisable to translate meaning and not merely form by avoiding Greek syntactic and rhetorical patterns. There is the need to standardize data protection terminology in European context, in the Hellenic Data Protection Authority internal administrative procedures and sanctions. The usage of shorter sentences, clearer paragraph structure and consisted of register would improve readability along with brief explanations of the Greek specific structures and procedures. Key sources of standardized structures in the sector are European Commission reports and European Union Agency reports. English translations of the Hellenic Data Protection Annual Report Summaries are accurate in content but exhibit systemic translation issues root due to the Greek administrative style, literal translation choices, syntactic transfer and sporadically minor register and terminology inconsistency. Addressing these issues would significantly enhance the clarity, and international usability of the reports.

Linguistic Challenges

Linguistic and conceptual challenges that arise when translating Greek legal texts into English, with particular emphasis on the structural features of Greek legal language, the influence of EU multilingualism, and the genre-specific constraints of regulatory summaries. Building on the case studies presented earlier a systematic analysis of the linguistic phenomena is provided that complicate translation and demonstrate how these phenomena manifest in the English summaries of the HD-PA's annual reports. Dual translation versions, commentary versions, and summary versions previously introduced are integrated, using them as analytical anchors for discussing broader translation issues. The aim is to show how micro-level linguistic choices (lexis, syntax, phraseology) interact with macro-level legal and institutional structures. Greek legal language is characterized by extensive nominalization, often resulting in dense, multi-layered sentences. For example, *η μη ικανοποίηση του δικαιώματος πρόσβασης, η παράλειψη γνωστοποίησης του περιστατικού, η εξέταση της υπόθεσης ολοκληρώθηκε με την έκδοση απόφασης*

These structures compress complex legal actions into noun phrases. English legal drafting, however, prefers verbal constructions like *failure to satisfy the right of access, failure to notify the incident, the case was concluded with the issuance of a decision.* The literal translation of Greek nominalizations often produces heavy, unnatural English. This is evident in the HDPA summaries, where phrases such as "breach of the principle of lawfulness of processing" reflect Greek syntactic patterns rather than English legal style.

Literal translation preserves legal form but risks syntactic awkwardness, reduced readability, and conceptual opacity. Functional translation improves readability but risks by altering legal nuance, introducing interpretative elements and shifting institutional tone.

Greek legal texts frequently employ participial constructions like *λαμβάνοντας υπόψη, εξετάζοντας τα στοιχεία, διαπιστώνοντας ότι, εντοπίζοντας παραβάσεις*/ lamvantas ypopsi, exetazontas ta stixia, diapistonontas oti entopizontas paravasis

These constructions allow Greek legal texts to accumulate information without segmenting sentences. English, however, prefers explicit clause boundaries. For example, the Greek structure: *Εξετάζοντας τα στοιχεία της υπόθεσης, η Αρχή διαπίστωσε ότι/ Exetazontas ta stoicheia tis ypothesis, i Archi diapistose oti... ...* is often translated literally as: "Examining the elements of the case, the Authority found that..."

While grammatically correct, this structure is stylistically marked in English legal writing. A more natural rendering would be: "After examining the evidence, the Authority found that..." This shift from participial to prepositional structure is a common functional adaptation.

Greek legal language retains archaic elements, such as: *εφεξής, εντεύθεν, ως εκ τούτου, προδήλως, συναφώς*/ efexis, enteuthen, os ek toutou, prodilos, sinafos. These terms have no direct English equivalents and require contextual adaptation. Literal translations often sound overly formal or unnatural.

For example: *αβάσιμος/avasimos* → "manifestly unfounded" (EU-standardized), *ως εκ τούτου*/os ek toutou→ "therefore", *συναφώς*/synafos→ "accordingly" or "in this regard"

The Hellenic Data Protection Authority summaries generally avoid archaic vocabulary in English, but traces of Greek formality remain in phrases such as "the examination of the case was completed with the adoption of a decision." Greek legal terminology often encodes civil-law concepts that lack direct English equivalents. Examples include, *έννομο συμφέρον, διοικητική πράξη, καταχρηστική άσκηση δικαιώματος, προδικαστικό ερώτημα./ enomo symferon, diikitiki prazi, kataxristiki askisi, dikaiomatos, prodikastiko erotima.* These terms require careful comparative-law analysis. For instance, *έννομο συμφέρον* is not identical to "legitimate interest" (GDPR), *διοικητική πράξη* varies depending on context (administrative act, decision, measure), *καταχρηστική άσκηση δικαιώματος* has no direct common-law equivalent. The Hellenic Data Protection Authority (HDPA) summaries often use approximations that flatten conceptual distinctions.

EU Multilingualism and Hybrid Terminology

EU law imposes standardized terminology across all official languages. Terms such as *controller, processor, data subject, personal data breach, supervisory authority* must be used consistently.

Greek regulatory texts often incorporate these terms directly, but hybrid forms emerge like *υπεύθυνος επεξεργασίας/ektelon epexergasia (controller), εκτελών την επεξεργασία (processor).*

The English summaries sometimes reflect this hybridization, resulting in inconsistent terminology. Greek translations of EU texts often produce calques that reappear in Greek regulatory writing. For example, *αρχή της λογοδοσίας/arxi logodosias* → "principle of accountability", *μέτρα ασφάλειας/* metra asfalias→ "security measures", *δικαίωμα πρόσβασης/dikaioma prosvasis* → "right of access". The terms are correct but may carry slightly different connotations in English.

Tension Between National and EU Legal Concepts

Greek administrative law and EU data-protection law sometimes use similar terms with different meanings. Translators must distinguish between Greek administrative concepts, EU data-protection concepts, English common-law concepts.

Genre-Specific Challenges in Translating Regulatory Summaries

Annual report summaries combine, legal analysis, administrative reporting, financial disclosure, institutional communication. This hybridity complicates translation because each genre has distinct stylistic norms. Regulatory summaries must be legally accurate, institutionally authoritative, internationally intelligible. Literal translations often preserve legal accuracy but reduce clarity. Functional translations improve clarity but risk altering legal nuance. In Greek regulatory writing tends to be formal, impersonal, nominalized, syntactically dense. English regulatory writing tends to be concise, segmented, action-oriented. The HDPA summaries often fall between these two styles, producing hybrid English that is neither fully natural nor fully literal.

Greek-to-English legal translation is shaped by deep linguistic, conceptual, and genre-specific challenges. These challenges are not merely technical since they reflect broader tensions between legal systems, institutional practices, and communicative norms. The HDPA summaries provide a rich corpus for analyzing these issues, revealing patterns of nominalization, syntactic density, terminological asymmetry, and hybrid EU-Greek phrasing.

Towards a Framework for Improving Legal Translation in Greece: Methodological, Institutional, and Pedagogical Proposals

Legal translation in Greece is shaped by a constellation of linguistic, conceptual, institutional, and genre-specific challenges. These challenges are not isolated phenomena as they reflect deeper structural tensions between Greek legal culture, EU multilingualism, and the communicative demands of international audiences. The translation of regulatory summaries, such as those produced by the Hellenic Data Protection Authority (HDPA), provides a particularly revealing case study, as these texts must simultaneously satisfy legal precision, institutional authority, and cross-linguistic intelligibility.

One of the most effective ways to improve legal translation quality is through the use of corpus-based methods, which allow translators to identify recurring phraseological patterns, compare Greek and English legal genres, detect terminological inconsistencies, align translations with international drafting norms. This would allow increased terminological consistency, improved syntactic naturalness, better alignment with EU terminology, enhanced institutional coherence. The Greek legal translation may present inconsistent terminology patterns, particularly in areas such as administrative law, data protection, financial regulation, corporate governance.

A standardized terminology database, similar to IATE data base of the European Union but tailored to Greek national law, would significantly improve translation quality. While literal translation preserves legal form, functional equivalence ensures communicative clarity. A balanced approach is necessary that is the use of literal translation for doctrinally loaded terms, the use of functional translation for procedural or administrative language, avoidance of calques that distort English legal style and efforts to maintain institutional tone without replicating Greek syntactic density. Greek regulatory authorities often rely on ad hoc translation practices. Establishing bilingual drafting teams would ensure consistency across documents, alignment with EU terminology, improved quality control, reduced reliance on literal translation. These teams should include legal experts, linguists, translators, subject-matter specialists. Regulatory translations should undergo terminological review, legal review, linguistic editing, cross-linguistic consistency checks. A standardized quality assurance protocol would prevent errors such as inconsistent terminology, syntactic calques, conceptual flattening, mistranslation of procedural steps. It would be advisable that Regulatory authorities should publish translation guidelines, terminology lists, drafting conventions, style guides. This approach would enhance transparency and improve public trust in bilingual regulatory communication.

Legal translation requires more than linguistic competence since it requires comparative-law literacy. Translator training programs should include, introduction to Greek legal system, introduction to common-law systems, EU law and multilingualism, comparative administrative law, legal drafting conventions. Students should be trained to recognize the specific features of statutes, judgments, administrative decisions, regulatory summaries, financial reports. Genre awareness improves translation accuracy and stylistic appropriateness. The Hellenic Data Protection Authority annual summaries in English would allow translation and law students to learn to identify calques, detect syntactic interference, evaluate terminological choices, propose functional equivalents. Through this approach the gap between theory and practice in bridged.

The findings suggest that improving legal translation in Greece requires a multi-layered approach in order to reduce nominalization, avoid syntactic calques, adopt functional equivalents where appropriate, standardize key terms, align with EU terminology, clarify conceptual distinctions, to establish bilingual drafting teams, implement quality protocols, publish translation guidelines, integrate comparative law, teach genre-specific translation, use real regulatory texts in training. These reforms would significantly enhance the clarity, accuracy, and international credibility of Greek legal translations.

Legal translation in Greece is a complex, multi-dimensional activity shaped by linguistic, conceptual, institutional, and pedagogical factors. The translation of regulatory summaries, such as those produced by the Hellenic Data Protection

Authority, reveals the structural challenges inherent in Greek legal language and the need for a more systematic, interdisciplinary approach to translation practice. Different translational strategies produce different legal and communicative effects. The proposed framework offers a path toward improving legal translation in Greece through methodological rigor, institutional reform, and pedagogical innovation.

Rendering of HDPA Decisions: Examples drawn from the Annual Report Summaries (2019–2023)

Greek administrative decisions, especially those of the HDPA, use long hypotactic sentences, dense nominalizations, and embedded subordinate clauses. English legal drafting prefers shorter, clearer and more modular structures.

"Taking into account that the management of school spaces when they are not closed and the responsibility for maintenance, cleaning and guarding of school buildings belong to the municipalities…" (Decision 21/2019)

Greek originals typically contain even longer chains of participles and subordinate clauses while English requires syntactic unpacking to avoid ambiguity. Literal translation risks producing unreadable or legally unclear English. It would be advisable to break meaning into shorter units while preserving legal logic and to use explicit connectors ("since", "because", "therefore") rather than Greek style implicit cohesion. Many Greek legal terms derive from civil law and administrative law, lacking direct English equivalents, especially in personal data law as "η αρχή της αναλογικότητας" → "the principle of proportionality". In Greek administrative law, proportionality has constitutional status and a specific doctrinal meaning while in English, "proportionality" exists but varies across jurisdictions (UK, EU, US). It would be advisable to anchor terminology in EU law English, not UK/US common law and when necessary, add clarifying modifiers like "proportionality principle under EU data protection law".

Some Greek terms must be translated using EU-harmonized English, not literal English like "Αρχή Προστασίας Δεδομένων Προσωπικού Χαρακτήρα" that is "Hellenic Data Protection Authority. So, one may always cross-check with EUR-Lex, institutional framework and official HDPA English versions.

Greek decisions often refer to legal constructs that have no English counterpart like "η αρχή της λογοδοσίας" → "the principle of accountability". "Accountability" in GDPR English is a technical term, not the broader Greek administrative concept of λογοδοσία. Greek usage may include moral, political, or administrative responsibility. In such a case one may use GDPR terminology when the context is data protection. A standard feature in Greek legal phraseology is the use of participles to compress legal reasoning like "having taken into account the provisions set out in the Authority's Directive 1/2011. Thus, Greek originals often contain multiple participles in a row, which English cannot sustain without losing clarity. One solution might be to convert participles into finite clauses or to use explicit logical connectors.

Greek legal vocabulary often uses polysemous terms whose meaning depends on context, like: "επεξεργασία"/epexergassia for "processing" (in the GDPR sense), "φορέας"/foreas for "entity", "body", "institution", depending on context, "υπεύθυνος"/ypefthinosfor "controller" (GDPR), but also "responsible person" in other contexts. In these cases, misinterpretation leads to terminological inconsistency while English requires contextual disambiguation.

Greek Legal Reasoning Structure

Greek decisions follow a narrative in the legal structure consisting in factual background, legal framework, reasoning into a conclusion while English decisions often follow a more segmented, analytical structure: "The Authority considered that the processing of personal data when entering the hospital is lawful." In this fragment Greek original often embeds the legal reasoning inside long narrative paragraphs while English readers expect clearer segmentation. One may also use headings ("Facts", "Legal Assessment", "Conclusion") by preserving content while reorganizing for clarity.

Greek decisions use standardized expressions for sanctions: "the Authority imposed a fine of EUR 772,000", that is there is use of passive voice or nominalizations, while English legal drafting prefers active voice. One may suggest the use of active voice consistently: "The Authority imposed…". In the framework of cultural bound references Greek decisions sometimes refer to Greek constitutional principles or administrative doctrines like: "the need to address serious risks may lead to a shift in the balance point, but without exceeding the limits laid down by the principle of proportionality." In such cases English speaking readers may not English readers may not understand the constitutional context and literal translation may obscure the underlying legal meaning. A brief clarifying phrase may help: "the constitutionally established principle of proportionality".

Terminology Handling Issues

Chioccheti (2017) examines how terminological databases (TDBs) function as essential tools for translation quality assurance, especially multilingual legal contexts. Because legal translation depends heavily on conceptual precision, TDBs provide structured, metadata rich repositories that help translators maintain consistency, accuracy, and conceptual clarity. As the authors note, TDBs ensure uniform, consistent terminology throughout a translation, making them indispensable for legal drafting, multilingual lawmaking, and institutional translation workflows.

There is identification of the specific challenges of legal terminology, abstraction, vagueness, polysemy, synonymy, and the coexistence of multiple legal systems. These characteristics require TDBs to include definitions, comparative notes, conceptual relations, usage contexts, and clear indications of the legal system to which each term belongs. The proposed comprehensive framework includes three dimensions: workflow quality assessment (process documentation, revision cycles, standards such as ISO 17100, and workflow management tools), product level quality assurance (quality of terminological entries, metadata, conceptual accuracy, domain attribution, equivalence strategies) and staff level quality assurance (competence profiles, training, and role allocation). Quality assurance must be embedded throughout the entire terminology lifecycle, not only at the final revision stage. High-quality multilingual legal TDBs require coordinated attention to processes, products, and people, and that such databases significantly enhance the reliability and efficiency of legal translation in institutional settings.

Legal translation approaches

Legal translation emerges as a profoundly interdisciplinary, norm-governed, and culturally embedded activity, that cannot be reduced to linguistic substitution or mechanical transfer. Legal translation is anchored simultaneously in language and law, two autonomous yet interdependent systems whose interaction produces a unique semiotic and normative environment. Legal translation is not merely a linguistic transfer but a juridical act that participates in the construction, interpretation, and application of law. This insight provides the conceptual foundation for understanding why legal translation requires not only linguistic competence but also legal literacy, comparative methodology, and sensitivity to institutional practice. The theoretical, methodological, and empirical strands draw together the contributions of major scholars, the structural features of Greek legal language, the challenges of Greek→English translation, and the specific complexities of personal data law and HDPA report summaries.

We have shown that legal translation operates within a semiotic universe in which meaning is not inherent in linguistic signs but emerges from the interaction between text, legal system, and interpretative community. Engberg's argument that legal meaning is coconstructed rather than fixed underscores the translator's role as an interpreter who must reconstruct meaning within a new legal and cultural environment. This semiotic dimension is inseparable from the normative dimension that legal texts do not merely describe reality but create rights, obligations, permissions, and prohibitions. Translating such texts therefore requires reproducing their illocutionary force in a target language that may encode legal authority differently.

The comparative dimension is equally indispensable since de Groot and van Laer emphasize, translation presupposes an understanding of functional equivalence between legal concepts across jurisdictions. Yet, as Šarčević's typology of equivalence demonstrates, perfect equivalence is rarely attainable. Concepts may be near-equivalent, partially equivalent, or entirely non-equivalent, depending on the degree of structural and cultural divergence between legal systems. Greek law that is rooted in the continental civil law tradition, often lacks direct equivalents in English-speaking common law systems. This asymmetry is particularly visible in administrative law, property law, and personal data regulation, where Greek concepts are embedded in constitutional and administrative traditions that have no direct counterpart in English legal culture.

Gémar further reinforces the idea that legal translation is an interpretive act shaped by legal tradition, drafting style, and cultural expectations. The analysis of Canada's evolution from literal translation to co-drafting illustrates how multilingual legal systems can move beyond translation to produce parallel, equally authentic texts that reflect the idiomatic and conceptual structures of each legal culture. Yet even co-drafting does not eliminate interpretive challenges, since courts must reconcile divergences between equally authoritative versions. The broader implication is that legal translation, whether through translation or co-drafting, must always negotiate between fidelity to the source legal system and functional adequacy in the target system.

Legal translation is placed within the broader context of institutional multilingualism, particularly in the European Union. Baaij's analysis of the EU's multilingualism policy reveals the tension between the EU's normative commitment to linguistic equality and the pragmatic dominance of English in legislative drafting. Although the EU proclaims that all languages possess equal dignity, the operational reality is that English functions as the de facto working language of most institutions. This tension has direct implications for translation, as translators must navigate between official multilingualism and the practical constraints of institutional workflows.

Prieto-Ramos's mapping of global law as a network of translated texts further underscores the centrality of translation to legal validity in multilingual legal orders. In the EU, UN, and WTO, multilingual versions of legal texts often share equal authenticity, making translation a constitutive element of law rather than a secondary activity. This insight is particularly relevant for Greek→English translation, since many Greek legal concepts derive from EU directives and regulations whose English versions serve as terminological anchors. Yet harmonization does not eliminate conceptual divergence. The uploaded text illustrates this with the example of "δεδομένα προσωπικού χαρακτήρα", which corresponds to "personal data" but carries additional constitutional connotations in Greek law.

Institutional multilingualism thus creates both opportunities and constraints. On the one hand, resources such as IATE and EUR-Lex provide harmonized terminology that supports consistency and legal certainty. On the other hand, the coexistence of multiple authentic versions introduces interpretive complexity, requiring translators to balance fidelity to EU terminology with sensitivity to national legal traditions.

Greek to English Legal Translation: Structural, Linguistic, and Genre-Specific Challenges

The chapter's detailed analysis of Greek to English translation reveals the depth of the linguistic and conceptual challenges involved. Greek legal language is characterized by long hypotactic structures, dense nominal phrases, heavy use of participles, and a preference for passive constructions. These features reflect the rhetorical traditions of Greek administrative and legal writing, which prioritize completeness, precision, and hierarchical structuring of information. When transferred into English, however, these structures often result in reduced readability, syntactic heaviness, and obscured information hierarchy.

The uploaded text provides numerous examples of such syntactic transfer, including a 70-word sentence from the HDPA's 2020 Annual Report that illustrates how Greek syntactic patterns can overwhelm English readers. The text notes that "the underlying single syntax of 70+ words has a Greek syntactical pattern," leading to reduced clarity and increased cognitive load for international audiences. This example encapsulates the broader challenge: Greek legal syntax is not inherently incompatible with English, but it requires restructuring to meet English-language expectations for clarity, conciseness, and thematic coherence.

Lexical and terminological issues further complicate translation. Greek administrative language often employs abstract, nominalized expressions that do not map neatly onto English institutional phrasing. Calques such as "the Authority was burdened by the pandemic" or "responded well to the challenges" reproduce Greek idiomatic structures but sound unnatural in English. Terminological inconsistency across years—e.g., "complaints were handled" vs. "complaints were resolved"—undermines coherence and legal reliability. Incorrect collocations, such as "sanction of reprimand–warning," distort legal meaning and may imply powers the HDPA does not possess.

Register and style also pose challenges. Greek institutional writing often oscillates between highly formal legal phrasing and more conversational expressions, a pattern that is sometimes reproduced in English translations. The uploaded text notes that translations may contain both "in accordance with Article 52(4) GDPR" and "it is noteworthy that...," creating stylistic inconsistency. English institutional writing typically requires a stable, formal register, making such oscillation problematic.

Micro structural issues, such as omission of articles, unnatural word order, and literal translation of Greek idioms, further contribute to the perception of translatedness, given the impression that it is a word for word translation. For example, "Authority issued guidelines" lacks the definite article required in English, while "in context of telework" omits the necessary preposition. These issues may seem minor individually, but collectively they affect the fluency, professionalism, and credibility of the translation.

Personal Data Law as a Translation-Intensive Domain

Personal data law represents an ideal case study for examining the complexities of Greek to English legal translation. The field is conceptually dense, highly harmonized at the EU level, and deeply embedded in both constitutional and administrative traditions. Key terms such as controller, processor, data subject, and profiling have precise definitions in the GDPR, and Greek Law 4624/2019 supplements these definitions with national provisions. Translators must therefore navigate a layered normative structure in which EU terminology coexists with Greek legal concepts that may have no perfect English equivalents.

The HDPA's decisions and annual report summaries exemplify the challenges of translating personal data law. These documents combine legal reasoning, administrative reporting, public communication, and institutional discourse, creating a hybrid genre that demands terminological precision, idiomatic phrasing, and genre-appropriate structure. Texts such as the English "Summary of the Annual Report" of the Hellenic Data Protection Authority is a hybrid institutional genre that includes legal terminology, administrative reporting, public-facing communication, and political-institutional discourse. This hybridity increases translation complexity, requiring translators to balance legal accuracy with readability and institutional tone.

The analysis of translation issues in HDPA summaries reveals systemic patterns: calques, unnatural phrasing, terminological inconsistency, incorrect collocations, syntactic transfer, redundancy, and register fluctuation. These issues are not merely linguistic; they reflect deeper structural differences between Greek and English legal-administrative discourse. Addressing them requires not only linguistic adjustments but also a rethinking of how Greek institutional content is presented to international audiences.

The Role of Skopos Theory in the Corpus

The discussion of Duan (2023) highlights the relevance of functionalist approaches, particularly Skopos Theory, for legal translation. Skopos Theory emphasizes that translation strategies must be guided by the purpose of the target text and the needs of its readers. This teleological orientation is particularly useful for legal translation, where the function of the target text may differ from that of the source text. For example, an HDPA annual report summary translated into English may serve informational, comparative, or transparency-related purposes rather than legal enforcement purposes.

Duan's analysis of English to Chinese translation illustrates how translators must adapt terminology, syntax, and discourse conventions to the target language's expectations. Although the linguistic direction differs, the underlying principles apply equally to Greek to English translation. Translators must adjust voice, reorder clauses, split long sentences, and avoid literal reproduction of source-language structures. They must also balance fidelity to legal meaning with readability and genre conventions in the target language.

Skopos Theory thus provides a conceptual framework for addressing many of the issues identified in annual summaries that are issued to inform and contribute towards handling modern legal issues. It encourages translators to prioritize functional adequacy over rigid linguistic correspondence, to adapt institutional phrasing to English norms, and to restructure information to enhance clarity and coherence.

The Historical and Cultural Interactions of Legal Translation

Graziadei's contribution situates legal translation within a broader historical and cultural context. His analysis of nineteenth-century codifications demonstrates how translation has shaped national legal cultures by introducing foreign concepts, terminology, and interpretive frameworks. This historical perspective reinforces the idea that legal translation is not a peripheral activity but a foundational practice that influences legal development, comparative law, and cross-jurisdictional dialogue.

Graziadei's observation that legal translation requires reconciling concepts that often lack direct equivalents across languages is highlighting the enduring challenge of authenticity and functional equivalence. This challenge is particularly acute in multilingual legal orders, where multiple linguistic versions must share equal authority.

CONCLUSION

Drawing together the theoretical, linguistic, and empirical insights, a coherent model of Greek to English legal translation emerges, one that integrates semiotic, normative, comparative, institutional, and functionalist dimensions. Translators must reconstruct legal meaning within a new semiotic and legal environment, preserving illocutionary force and normative effect. Functional equivalence must guide the selection of terminology and conceptual mapping, particularly in areas where Greek and English legal systems diverge. In European Union, terminology provides a harmonized framework, but translators must remain attentive to national legal traditions and conceptual nuances. Greek syntactic patterns, nominalizations, and rhetorical structures must be reconfigured to meet English expectations for clarity, conciseness, and coherence. Hybrid institutional genres such as HDPA summaries require careful balancing of legal accuracy, administrative reporting, and public communication. In an overall approach Skopos Theory provides a practical framework for aligning translation strategies with the purpose and audience of the target text.

Legal translation, particularly Greek to English translation in the domain of personal data law, is a demanding, intellectually rigorous activity that requires mastery of multiple disciplines. It is not sufficient to know the languages involved; translators must understand legal systems, institutional practices, genre conventions, and the socio-political context of multilingual law. They must navigate conceptual asymmetries, terminological challenges, syntactic differences, and register expectations, all while ensuring fidelity to legal meaning and functional adequacy in the target language.

The analysis of HDPA annual report summaries illustrates both the strengths and weaknesses of current translation practices. While the translations accurately convey content, they exhibit systemic issues rooted in Greek administrative style, literal translation choices, syntactic transfer, and register inconsistency. Addressing these issues requires a combination of linguistic adaptation, terminological standardization, genre awareness, and functionalist orientation.

Ultimately, legal translation is a semiotic, normative, comparative, institutional, and functional activity, one that participates in the construction of legal meaning and the functioning of multilingual legal orders. Greek to English translation, particularly in the field of personal data law, exemplifies the complexity and importance of this activity. By integrating theoretical insights, linguistic analysis, and empirical case studies, the chapter provides a comprehensive framework for understanding and improving legal translation in this domain.

REFERENCES

Altuwairesh, N. S., & AlGhamedi, N. A. (2025). Challenges & Solutions in Legal Translation Training: Translator Trainees' Perspectives. *Theory and Practice in Language Studies*, *15*(4), 1188–1195. DOI: 10.17507/tpls.1504.17

Baaij, C. J. W. (2012). The EU policy on institutional multilingualism: Between principles and practicality. *International Journal of Language & Law*, *1*, 14–32. DOI: 10.14762/jll.2012.014

Cao, D. (2007). *Translating law*. Multilingual Matters.

de Groot, G.-R., & van Laer, C. J. P. (2006). The quality of legal dictionaries: An assessment. In Kredens, H., & Goźdź Roszkowski, S. (Eds.), *Language and the law: International outlooks* (pp. 159–178). Peter Lang.

Duan, Y. J. (2023). Legal text translation (E to C) under the guidance of Skopos Theory. *Open Journal of Modern Linguistics*, *13*(5), 581–586. DOI: 10.4236/ojml.2023.135035

Engberg, J. (2021). Legal translation as communication of knowledge: On the creation of bridges. *Parallèles*, *33*(1), 9–26.

European Union. (2015). *Joint Practical Guide for persons involved in the drafting of EU legislation*. https://eur-lex.europa.eu/content/techleg/EN-legislative-drafting-guide.pdf

European Union. (2023). *Interinstitutional Style Guide*. Home - Interinstitutional Style Guide - Publications Office of the EU

Gémar, J.-C. (2013). *Langage du droit et traduction*. Presses de l'Université de Montréal.

Gémar, J.-C. (2014). Catching the spirit of the law: From translation to co-drafting. In Glanert, S. (Ed.), *Comparative law: Engaging translation* (pp. 85–104). Routledge.

Hellenic Data Protection Authority. (n.d.). *Annual reports*. https://www.dpa.gr/en/advanced-search/all?field_keywords=annual+reports

Pisulińska, J. (2021). Wincenty Zakrzewski o roli Kościoła w dziejach Polski. *Klio Polska*, (13), 103–122.

Pontrandolfo, G., & Peruzzo, K. (2017). Legal translation and interpreting: between old and new theoretical, discursive and professional perspectives. *International journal of legal discourse, 2*(2), 171-176.

Prieto-Ramos, F. (2017). Global law as translated text: Mapping institutional legal translation. *Tilburg Law Review, 22*(1–2), 185–214. DOI: 10.1163/22112596-02201009

Šarčević, S. (1997). *New approach to legal translation.* Kluwer Law International.

Tiersma, P. M. (1999). *Legal language.* University of Chicago Press. DOI: 10.7208/chicago/9780226854809.001.0001

ADDITIONAL READING

Baker, M. (2018). *In other words: A coursebook on translation* (3rd ed.). Routledge. DOI: 10.4324/9781315619187

de Groot, G.-R., & van Laer, C. J. P. (2006). The quality of legal dictionaries: An assessment. In *Translation and the law* (pp. 215–227). American Translators Association.

Mazzarese, T. (2020). *Legal translation: A survey of traditional problems and new challenges.* Rivista di Filosofia del Diritto. (60) 2020 – T. Mazzarese, Legal Translation. A Survey of Traditional Problems and New Challenges

Munday, J. (2016). *Introducing translation studies: Theories and applications* (4th ed.). Routledge. DOI: 10.4324/9781315691862

Newmark, P. (1988). *A textbook of translation.* Prentice Hall.

Nida, E. A., & Taber, C. R. (2003). *The theory and practice of translation.* Brill. DOI: 10.1163/9789004496330

Reiss, K., & Vermeer, H. J. (2014). *Towards a general theory of translational action: Skopos theory explained.* Routledge. DOI: 10.4324/9781315759715

Soriano Barabino, G. (2020). Cultural, textual and linguistic aspects of legal translation: A model of text analysis for training legal translators. *International Journal of Legal Discourse, 5*(2), 285–300. https://www.researchgate.net/publication/347847370_Cultural_textual_and_linguistic_aspects_of_legal_translation_A_model_of_text_analysis_for_training_legal_translators. DOI: 10.1515/ijld-2020-2037

Venuti, L. (2018). *The translator's invisibility: A history of translation* (3rd ed.). Routledge.

KEY TERMS AND DEFINITIONS

Calque: A literal translation that reproduces source-language structure or phrasing unnaturally in the target language, often causing register or clarity issues.

Co-Drafting: A bilingual legislative drafting method where two language versions are produced simultaneously, avoiding translation and ensuring cultural authenticity.

Functional Equivalence: A translation principle aiming to reproduce the legal function of a concept in the target system rather than its literal form.

Institutional Multilingualism: The policy of producing legal texts in multiple official languages within supranational institutions, shaping drafting and translation practices.

Legal Translation: Translation of texts that create, interpret, or apply legal norms, requiring both linguistic and legal expertise.

Skopos Theory: A functionalist translation theory stating that the purpose (*skopos*) of the translation determines strategy, structure, and linguistic choices.

Terminological Harmonization: The alignment of legal terminology across languages and jurisdictions to ensure consistency, clarity, and legal certainty.

Section 2
Technology, AI, and Future Directions

Chapter 6
Artificial Intelligence, Legal Translation, and Linguistic Complexity:
A Critical Study of Technology, Meaning, and Power in Multilingual Legal Systems

Kranti Devidas Deshmukh
http://orcid.org/0009-0006-5287-4983
MMM's Shankarao Chavan Law College, Pune, India

Sanjana Bharadwaj
http://orcid.org/0000-0003-1371-7572
NALSAR University of Law, India

Rahul Dattu Gangurde
http://orcid.org/0009-0005-9599-0063
Government Law College, Mumbai, India

ABSTRACT

This chapter examines the growing role of Artificial Intelligence (AI) in legal translation and multilingual legal governance, with particular focus on the relationship between technology, language, constitutionalism, and institutional power. The chapter argues that legal translation is not merely a technical process of linguistic conversion but an interpretive exercise shaped by legal culture, procedural context, and constitutional values. Through an interdisciplinary socio-legal and doctrinal analysis, the chapter explores how AI-driven translation systems influence access to justice, linguistic equality, democratic participation, and legal interpretation in

DOI: 10.4018/979-8-3373-9179-3.ch006

multilingual constitutional democracies such as India. It further analyses challenges relating to algorithmic bias, low-resource languages, data colonialism, and technological centralization, demonstrating how AI systems often reproduce existing linguistic hierarchies.

INTRODUCTION

In recent years, the evolution of modern legal frameworks has been marked by the progressive advancement and adoption of Artificial Intelligence (AI), which has profoundly impacted the creation, understanding, dissemination, and retrieval of legal knowledge across different jurisdictions. The fusion of digital governance systems, automated legal analysis, natural language processing (NLP), and large language models (LLMs) is becoming increasingly apparent across judicial administration, legal research, contractual analysis, and multilingual communication processes (Thapa et al., 2025). The implications of these developments lie not only in their technical development but also in their impact on every dimension of language as a site of power and identity, of legality, and of democratic process in the context of multilingual constitutional democracies. The law is a language system of basic nature. The law, in every form – statued, constitutional, precedential, regulatory and procedural – is about language. It can also be a rather complex phenomenon in a multilingual society because the meaning of the law is communicated in complex ways through interaction among a variety of linguistic practices, orientations, and social-political structures. This is clearly visible in postcolonial societies such as India, where constitutional multilingualism is juxtaposed with the continuing institutional dominance of English in superior courts, legal pedagogy and legal legislation and writing (Fisher & Ayres-Bennett, 2022). Linguistic asymmetry can influence access to justice, knowledge of the Law, and engagement in democratic governance.

In the field of legal translation, AI-powered tools and technologies are increasingly tackling these systemic challenges. Public officials, legal bodies, and tech firms are increasingly investing in the creation of multilingual AI systems to efficiently and even accurately translate legal texts, judicial opinions, procedural documents, and administrative records from one language to another, or vice versa (Lai et al., 2024). Since the emergence of amazing transformer-based language models and domain-specific legal natural language processing (LNLP) architectures, the status of machine translation (MT) has significantly improved. Most such innovations have been related to the general ideas of accessibility, efficacy, and the "democratization" of information about the Law.

Despite the great technological progress achieved in recent years, legal translation remains a challenging field for AI-powered translation systems. Professional translation is not merely the act of conveying meaning; it also entails the conversion of meaning across norms and institutions in the context of legal translation. In a legal context, language is often very precise; the text exhibits a high level of ambiguity; and it includes practical aspects and procedures as well as historical profundity. One translation error can have a significant impact on the evidence, constitutional safeguards, and the content of rights or duties. Therefore, legal translation is not simply the translation of language, but requires interpretation based on the Law's background and is supported by legal culture, legal doctrines, and legal operational procedures.

Multilingual legal systems, where language can be heterogeneous and where there is diversity in how languages are represented in technology, have been a particular area where the limitations of AI frameworks become apparent. Most existing AI translation models are trained on a feature set that unfairly reflects the dominance of high-resource languages. Minimal legal corpora and the absence of digitization pose significant challenges for languages, often resulting in semantic inaccuracies, contextual distortions, and variations in translation quality in machine learning models. AI tools in multi-language democracies have the potential to reproduce existing language hierarchies rather than break them. The potential for technology-based inclusion may coincide with emerging modes of algorithmic exclusion.

Such concerns are all the more relevant in the Indian context. India is an example of a large, linguistically diverse country where several languages and dialects coexist within a complex legal and administrative framework within a constitutional democracy. Thus, the system of institutional legal communication, notwithstanding the incorporation of language diversity into the Constitution through the Eighth Schedule, remains essentially centralized and English-dominated. These recent governmental and judicial efforts on AI-driven translations, multilingual e-courts, and digital legal governance offer a clear sign of the growing institutional commitment to promoting technological multilingualism. However, many more questions remain regarding the accuracy, legality, linguistic justice, and the preservation of the legal semantics of the automated translator. The issue of artificial intelligence and legal translation should not be addressed just technically, but also in constitutional and socio-legal contexts. AI is situated within a complex network of political orders, resource access inequities, and language dominance. Training datasets, institutional priorities, and assumptions about what language is will impact the computational models created. However, multilingual legal frameworks, with the help of AI, introduce several meaningful issues regarding epistemic bias, the accessibility of the legal system to democracy, procedural justice, and equality in the constitution.

This chapter proposes that implementing AI in legal translation is both an opportunity and a challenge for today's multilingual legal system. AI's significant role in the legal landscape could enhance access to legal resources and reduce language barriers. How it does that: it fails to take into account algorithmic bias, fails to simplify legal jargon, and makes technology centralized in the legal sector. The chapter contends that three points of interpretive fidelity, linguistic pluralism, and values of constitutionalism of AI-based legal communications can form the basis of the third position in which AI-based oral interpretation tools can be established in different legal systems.

LITERATURE REVIEW

The relationship between language and the law has been an important issue in legal theory, sociolinguistics, and constitutional studies. Despite the promises of their times, past conceptualizations still inform current debates on mediation technology and natural language processing (NLP) in legal translation and continue to provoke questions around algorithmic governance, linguistic inequality, and mediation. Institutional and political aspects of power, interpretative frameworks, and the accessibility of justice shape legal translation, according to the latest literature (Serttaş et al., 2025). When understood within the context of the current research, it is not surprising that while intelligent machine translation may be claimed to be impartial and effective, it may also and does reinforce the privileges that multilingual legal systems put into play.

Solan and Tiersma argue that the language of the law is part of a language system other than and inaccessible to common use (P. Tiersma et al., 2015). It might become legally significant in many ways as a result of the use of different vocabulary, institutional interpretation, precedent, liturgical context, and changes in doctrine. Tiersma's emphasis is on the continuity of history and stability of interpretation as the foundation of the authority of the legal language. This creates difficulties since the legal and legal-cultural elements overlap. This is particularly true in multilingual legal systems, where there may not be a linguistically equivalent counterpart to some concepts in constitutional and/or procedural law across all languages (P. M. Tiersma, 1999).

Sociolinguistic concepts that give theoretical support and aid in comprehending the language/power relationship are included in the analysis. Pierre Bourdieu's notion of 'linguistic capital' has remained relevant to the analysis of how languages are being institutionalized and others marginalized (Bourdieu, 1977). Bourdieu believes language is not just a tool for communication, but also a source of power that needs to be regarded in the light of the social and political situation in which it is used. In the legal system, dominant languages are accepted as capable of articulating law and thus gaining authority within the system. English has remained a "main" language of the institutions in postcolonial countries like India, and it is the language of access to legal education, legal argument, and constitutional interpretation. It is clear right now on the academic circuit that there is significant interest in Indian law institutions. This hierarchy of language becomes significant for structuring interactions in the justice system during these discussions.

Postcolonial scholars have also studied the relationship between language and institutional power. Beyond formal colonialism and the colonial power system are the colonial language machines that affect knowledge, administration, and governance (Wa Thiong'o, 1998). This, therefore, led to the presentation of a proposed plan to understand better how language can continue to perpetuate power dynamics in a postcolonial context. Taking this description to the law area, one can argue that colonial language exists in various legal systems, potentially marginalizing language minority communities and hampering their meaningful involvement in constitutional decision-making. The relationship between the constitutional multilingualism norm and the predominance of English in the higher judiciary has been recognized in several studies on Indian constitutionalism.

Linguistic justice themes are further explored in the existing literature, which examines the effects of language inequalities on democratic participation and the legitimacy of institutions. Philippe Van Parijs argues that such differences in linguistic apparatus translate into differences in distribution, as individuals' access to economic, political, and institutional opportunities greatly depends on whether they can speak the dominant language (Van Parijs, 2011). De Schutter (2007) proposes that, beyond the formal notion of equality, linguistic justice will always involve the institutional recognition of language diversity. The effects of such theories are magnified in the context of digital legal governance, as AI systems tend to favor high-resource languages, communities, and the people who use them, while diminishing low-resource languages, communities, and the people who use them.

In legal pluralist scholarship and constitutional theory, the significance of language to the constitution's legitimacy has been noted. In general, modern laws are developed with existing epistemologies in mind, alienating indigenous and Old World forms of knowing and expression, as Boaventura de Sousa Santos has pointed out (Santos, 2009). This kind of critique of the idea of 'epistemic injustice' is critical in multilingual legal systems where dominant languages of the law can obstruct the recognition of other-language readings of the law and rights. Ensuring that AI-based legal translation systems do not exacerbate this problem requires legal language standardization where relevant, which can be executed using the most representative institutional datasets.

The development of AI in law has generated considerable academic work on the topic. The first research focused primarily on the development of rule-based expert systems and computational legal reasoning. The use of machine learning, predictive analytics, and natural language processing in judicial and administrative systems has attracted increasing attention in academia. Mireille Hildebrandt's contributions to the field of algorithmic governance are particularly significant in this context (Hildebrandt, 2015). Hildebrandt argues that AI systems by making legal interpretation more predictive, expressed in probability affect the normativity of the law. Algorithmic systems are not only used to support legal institutions but also have a substantial influence on how law is reasoned about, categorized, and decision-making in legal institutions (Hildebrandt, 2015).

Sociotechnical systems theory offers a powerful analytical tool for understanding AI within the legal institution. Theorists such as Langdon Winner and Bruno Latour cast doubt on the idea of technology as a disengaged "tool" without a social context (Latour, 2012; Winner, 1980). Winner suggests that the very nature of technologies is political; that technologies result from different institutional priorities and power distributions. Similarly, Latour's construction of actor-network theory postulates a role for technological systems as dynamic agents within networks defined by institutions of authority. Their take on AI-driven translation tools suggests that they are not just tools for communication but institutions that shape the accessibility and interpretive authority of law.

Critical algorithm studies focus on a systematic inquiry into the supposed neutrality of AI systems. Safiya Noble's work in algorithmic oppression demonstrates how computational systems can establish socially inequitable structures through biased datasets and institutional defaults (Noble, 2018). One such intervention, argues Ruha Benjamin, has been to reproduce racial, class, and linguistic gradients through automated systems while maintaining the illusion of technological neutrality (Benjamin, 2024). What is described here may be of great importance in the field of multilingual legal translation, since machine learning systems have been known to prefer languages with large digitally available corpora and institutional representation. Low-resource languages, therefore, achieve lower translation accuracy and less context in AI systems.

The current literature on MT is generally technical and aware of the limitations of using artificial intelligence in the legal field. Academics researching neural machine translation systems note that legal language is particularly ambiguous, highly procedural, and doctrinally complex. Legal translation requires a certain level of context understanding that goes beyond the grammatical or semantic level. Numerous scientific projects have encountered significant difficulties in dealing with culturally bound legal terms and concepts, constitutional terminology, and context-dependent procedural language (Piszcz & Sierocka, 2020). This can be especially stark in multilingual democracies, where legal concepts can be grounded in a mix of hybrid colonial, constitutional, and customary concepts.

The discussion around AI for multilingual governance has become increasingly focused on issues of low-resource languages and implications of digital inequality in the context of AI. Those who have studied artificial intelligence in the context of natural language processing have noticed that most advances in AI are for languages that are dominant worldwide, such as English, Mandarin, and French. This phenomenon occurs because vast quantities of digitized datasets are required for machine learning processes. Languages with limited digital representation often end up out of the picture in technological development. In the legal environment, the consequences of this exclusion can be profound, as the precision and accuracy of translation can directly affect constitutional rights, procedural safeguards, and the outcomes of legal proceedings.

While the field of AI-assisted legal translation in the Indian context is still in its early stages, it is undergoing a gradual evolution and growth. The majority of the literature concerns multilingual justice websites, computer-assisted translation tools, and efforts to make the law more accessible electronically. Studies on such projects are often situated within the broader conversation on access to justice and digital constitutionalism. For some, AI translation is seen as a potentially revolutionary technique that may make legal knowledge far more accessible to non-English-speaking populations. Institutional language hierarchies are put in place to serve some scholars' belief that simply translations into and out of technology is not enough to solve the more complex systemic inequalities.

Despite the major works contained in this literature, there are still signs of fragmentation. The study of AI translation technologies tends to focus on how efficient the processing is or on the factors affecting the model's performance, while neglecting the constitutional, political, and socio-legal issues that are implicitly tied to them. By contrast, research on multilingualism in the legal field more often failed to account for the institutional consequences of algorithmic systems. This is where the interdisciplinary research on the relationship between legal translation and AI technology, and law-related concepts such as linguistic justice, constitutional equality, and postcolonial power dynamics in multilingual democracies, consists of a relatively small corpus.

This research proposes a synthesis of perspectives from legal linguistics, socio-technical systems theory, linguistic justice scholarship, and critical algorithm studies to address gaps in the existing literature. In this paper, we suggest a way of thinking about AI-enabled legal translation not simply as technological progress, but as a form of institutional control that reconfigures access to legal systems, interpretive power, and the idea of linguistic citizenship. This paper situates AI translation within broader debates on language, authority, and constitutional democracy, thereby extending a growing literature on the political facets of multilingual AI governance in contemporary legal frameworks.

The literature on this topic, as it relates to artificial intelligence, legal translation, and multilingual governance, is found to be fragmented across technical, legal, and sociolinguistic aspects. Many studies in the field of artificial intelligence and natural language processing primarily focus on translation speed, computational accuracy, and improvements to neural language architectures. Notably, however, is the lack of any real consideration of the constitutional, political, and socio-legal consequences of AI-assisted legal communication. Similarly, multilingualism and linguistic justice in legal academia are frequently examined in relation to language rights, access to justice, and constitutional pluralism. It, however, fails to consider the institutional consequences of algorithmic systems and automated translation technologies. There is a clear dearth of interdisciplinary research that has so far examined how AI-assisted legal translation reproduces and/or disrupts linguistic power dynamics in multilingual post-colonial democracies such as India. Existing scholarship is limited on the relationship between low-resource languages, algorithmic bias, and the availability of legal structures in technology-enabled legal systems. Consequently, there has been a lack of attention to the intersection of these aspects of artificial intelligence, legal translation, linguistic plurality, and constitutional governance, especially in multilingual legal systems where language functions as a legal, political, and epistemic tool of power.

METHODOLOGY

The study is multi-layered, using both doctrinal and socio-legal approaches to discuss AI and legal translation, as well as the complexity of language in multilingual legal systems. The research employs a multi-faceted methodological framework that integrates doctrinal and socio-legal methods. The doctrinal approach analyses constitutional provisions, legislation, court rulings, policy papers, and international instruments related to language rights, legal translation, digital governance, and artificial intelligence (Hutchinson, 2015; Van Hoecke, 2011). Doctrinal legal research focuses on finding, assessing, and systematising legal rules, principles, and normative frameworks by interpreting authoritative legal sources. The socio-legal approach contextualises law within its extensive social, cultural, technical, and institutional framework (Banakar & Travers, 2005; Cotterrell, 1995; Tamanaha, 2001). Instead of seeing law as an isolated system, socio-legal studies examines the interplay between legal norms and social practices, power dynamics, language variety, technical frameworks, and institutional contexts. This research integrates these methodologies to assess both the formal legal regulation of AI-assisted translation and its practical ramifications for linguistic justice, access to justice, and the management of multilingual legal systems (McConville & Chui, 2017).

This work adopts a research perspective primarily of a qualitative nature, drawing on theories of constitution, law, language, and computer governance documents;

sociotechnical system theory; and critical algorithm studies. It is about comprehending the effects on access to law, legal interpretation, and democratic participation stemming from AI-based translation technologies. It presents a doctrinal analysis of the study's purposes, namely the constitutional principles of equality, due process, informational autonomy, linguistic plurality, and the right to access to justice. It is built upon the analysis of constitutional documents, case law, and other constitutional developments in other countries. This paper melds a qualitative, case-based analysis of AI translation platforms with multilingual governance platforms and judicial translation debates to discern the practical and constitutional implications of machine translation in judicial contexts. This approach thoroughly examines AI Legal translation in the constitutional, postcolonial institutional, technological, and digital context, discussing the ambivalent possibilities of AI-facilitated law in translation for greater access to the law, as well as for new linguistic marginalization and algorithmic hierarchization in multilingual constitutions and democracies.

RESULTS AND FINDINGS

The analysis carried out in this chapter shows that Artificial Intelligence in legal translation should not be seen as a technological development that aims solely to improve communication effectiveness across multilingual legal systems. Instead, AI-based translation is an institutional power that shapes the dissemination of legal knowledge, interprets interpretive rights, and influences access to justice in different linguistic circles. The findings show that the legal governance system and AI translation are deeply intertwined with existing linguistic hierarchies, constitutional discourses, and technological disparities.

A major finding is the relation between the technological performance and language representation. The project leads develop a linear relationship between the quantity and quality of the input that machine learning systems receive and the quality and reliability of legal AI translations. Languages with extensive numbers of legal documents digitized, a legal database of court cases, and legal institutional documentation produce more accurate and sophisticated translations (Badah et al., 2026). Conversely, languages not well represented in the digital world remain under-resourced in AI systems. This pattern suggests that AI systems are not autonomous from the social realities in which they operate, but often serve predispositions and reinforce existing inequalities. In the Indian context, AI translation systems might further entrench English's current dominance in legal education, judicial reasoning, and record-keeping.

This discovery corroborates Bourdieu's theory of linguistic capital. The results indicate that, through the use of technological infrastructures, the institutionalization of authority tied to dominant languages is being reproduced (Bourdieu, 1977). As well as being a language of legal authority, English is also part of the architecture of AI systems. Technological advancement, then, can be a reinforcing force, promoting symbolically and practically the status of those who speak strong legal languages. Instead of a level playing field in which multilingualism prevails in the legal field, AI-powered legal translation could foster what the authors call "algorithmic linguistic hierarchies" that mandate that the legality of a language must be linked to its technological visibility (Leung, 2026).

The study further reveals that legal translation is fundamentally different from ordinary language translation in many respects. Definitions of legal terms with their doctrinal connotations, historical evolution, cognitive background, and constitutional implications and consequences are not always semantically identical. The results show that state-of-the-art NMT systems still fail to detect the context or jurisprudential implication from a piece of legal text. Words such as constitutional, morality, reasonable, restrictions, natural justice, due process, public order, etc. have a meaning, not in the general language but in what is interpreted as the words in court and the history of the Constitution (Demertzis et al., 2023). This means that even translation work that appears linguistically correct could be legally irrelevant!

This is a key disadvantage of the current wave of AI platforms. Large Language Models can provide answers based on probability rather than an actual understanding of the law. The challenge is demonstrated by highlighting the aspects of legal interpretation grounded in norms, history, and constitutional culture, an area where machine learning systems are always limited. Legal translation, therefore, cannot be considered a purely technical task. The law abhors a vacuum because the only way to give it meaning is to interpret it, and that is not easy to automate completely. Then there is another noteworthy discovery relating to the constitutional consequences of mistranslation. The study focuses on the effects of using AI-generated translations, not only to understand gaps. The quality of translation in multilingual courts can impact the right to active participation in the court process, access to the law, and procedural fairness. Access to rights, in particular within criminal justice, constitutional litigation, and immigration, but also in welfare administration, is of critical importance, and the clear expression and translation of legal rules and obligations are crucial. The implications of this are especially significant.

Results indicate that translation errors can contribute to procedural implementation errors, which can be detrimental for speakers of low-resource and minority languages. This is thus quite worrying for the constitutional requirements of access to justice, dignity, due process, and equality. In this view, translation is not merely a technical issue; it is also a constitutional issue. So, the investigation concludes that there is a direct connection between constitutional legitimacy and linguistic precision. The lawfulness of courts and the legal system in general partially resides in citizens' ability to understand and actively engage with the legal process. AI translations, which are less apt to carry legal significance, hinder the constitutional principle of equal access to justice.

The results also indicate that the use of AI translation systems is increasingly becoming an institutional actor rather than a neutral technology. Based on sociotechnical systems theory and actor-network theory, the analysis shows that AI systems do not merely act as silent actors in the production of legal texts. The analysis reveals that AI systems do not simply copycat legal texts, but also actively shape them in terms of linguistic accessibility/openness and thereby influence the spread of legal knowledge. Translation technologies currently play a role in indirect governance as they become increasingly involved in the communication interactions citizens have with legal actors.

This finding represents a significant paradigm shift in the legal landscape regarding technology. From the traditional point of view, the Software Translation (OT) acts as a passive communication instrument. Current research proposes that AI systems are involved in the construction of legal realities and that they determine who and what can be made meaningful whose language needs technological help and who gets access to what is possible and usable with respect to legal information (Novelli et al., 2022). Later, the question of technological design is felt to be necessarily intertwined with institutional responsibility and democratic forms of governance. An analytical point on algorithmic bias is separate. The study reaffirms concerns voiced by critical algorithmic studies concerning the (re)production of social inequalities in computational systems. AI translation tools could also be based on past information, institutional records, and language corpora, perpetuating centuries-old patterns of exclusion. Technological systems can then be systemically biased and, as such, embedded in these legal systems. Thus, this apparent neutrality of AI translation masks somewhat larger structural differences.

As Safiya Noble and Ruha Benjamin have argued, technological systems often enact the same social power that preceded them and, at the same time, actively bill themselves as fair and unwavering (Benjamin, 2024; Noble, 2018). These dynamics can lead to differing degrees of legal access across language communities in multilingual settings. Dominant languages are more likely to have high-quality translation and high institutional visibility, whereas marginalized languages are more likely to face misunderstanding, exclusion, and procedural disadvantage. In addition, this analysis highlights the strong relationship between AI legal translation and related areas such as data colonialism and digital constitutionalism. The location of technological know-how, computational infrastructure, and linguistic datasets in a few global tech companies creates new forms of dependency for legal institutions. Proprietary platforms that operate outside the normal democratic accountability system are increasingly gaining ground in the realm of legal communication.

This is an important find for postcolonised democracies like India. The use of external AI systems could reinforce the knowledge-production and institutional-control disparities characteristic of the past, the study assumes (McEwan, 2008). Globally salient languages are likely to dominate the training data of AI systems, potentially marginalizing local/regional languages and alternative legal practices. This means that technological centralization can be not just a governance problem but also a constitutional one, affecting democratic participation and linguistic pluralism.

Overall, these findings suggest that AI legal translation serves an interdisciplinary role across constitutional governance, law, technology, and language. The findings of this analysis indicate that AI could greatly improve access to legal information and reduce barriers to communication in multilingual societies. However, benefits from technological innovation can only be derived if structural inequalities inherent in linguistic data are recognized, there is meaningful human oversight, constitutional values are maintained, and governance frameworks are built to promote transparency, accountability, and linguistic inclusion. The findings support the main thesis of this chapter, namely that the use of AI for legal translation must not be judged solely by technological measures and efficiency. Instead, it should be assessed against broader constitutional principles, such as equal access to law and to the court, interpretive fidelity, and democratic participation and linguistic justice. One of the most important challenges for multilingual legal AI systems will be their ability to uphold not only constitutional values as the bedrock of democratic legal orders, but also linguistic diversity, alongside technological progress.

DISCUSSION

AI and Legal Translation Technologies

The utilization of artificial intelligence as an integral part of law has profoundly impacted how different jurisdictions, legal practices, methods, and workflows create, translate, share, and understand legal information. Judicially, the use of AI-driven translation tools by court systems, administrative institutions, and lawtech companies has significantly accelerated, making it easier than ever to translate judgements, legislation, contracts, and other procedural documents into multiple languages. In multilingual constitutional democracies, these technologies in particular are promoted as tools to improve access to justice and reduce linguistic exclusion. Integrating AI into the legal translation process raises several issues, including interpretive accuracy, algorithmic bias, and institutional power. Legal translation is not simply translating words between languages and systems, but a combination of both, with the meanings of words or entities in one system and its legally binding concepts being interconnected with concepts in the other and culturally and constitutionally bound (Monzó-Nebot & Mellinger, 2022).

Key to understanding this transformation is sociotechnical systems theory. Technologies are as much a set of institutional preferences and power as they are a means of serving political ends, says Langdon Winner. Similarly, the concept of technological systems as dynamic institutional, or 'actor-network-like,' actors with the capacity to shape and reconfigure social and legal relationships is expressed through Bruno Latour's actor-network theory. AI translation technologies, as well as being a communication tool, are reshaping perceptions of legal language, the preservation of legal meaning, and the meaningful possibilities for community access to the law.

Evolution of AI-Based Legal Translation

The development of AI-powered legal translation has coincided with significant advances in natural language processing (NLP) and machine learning. The first real translation technologies were based on rule-based systems that attempted to translate texts using well-defined grammars and bilingual dictionaries (Moneus & Sahari, 2024). Their effect in the legal context has been seriously constrained by the context-sensitive nature of legal language, by legal contexts (institutional interpretation), and by the accuracy of doctrinal systems. A challenge in translating into many regional languages is the English legal term 'consideration', a specialized common law doctrine that does not correspond to a conventional contract law concept.

The development of statistical machine translation marks an important milestone in the evolution of computational linguistics. These systems learned probabilistic relationships among languages without relying solely on manually encoded rules and were built on comprehensive bilingual datasets. Though statistical/computerized systems have improved legal terminology and procedures, difficulties arise in accurately translating certain legal terms and procedures. The meaning of legal terms is often more closely derived from the practices in the courts and the understanding thereof than from the extent to which they are used in ordinary language. Therefore, the statistical translation was typically accompanied by a message that was formally correct but not legally accurate.

Recent advancements in neural machine translation and large language models (LLMs) have markedly enhanced AI's translation capabilities. Transformer (GPT, BERT, and multilingual Legal NLP) models demonstrate the ability to process large volumes of legal information and generate contextually appropriate translations that are more fluent than those produced by previous models (Nie et al., 2025). More and more, judicial bodies and governmental institutions are using such systems to enhance the dependable access to judicial information that transcends language barriers. To facilitate the translation of judicial decisions into various regional languages, the Supreme Court of India has launched the SUVAS (Supreme Court Vidhik Anuvaad Software) initiative, which uses AI-powered translation tools. Similarly, the government-backed Bhashini program is to build multilingual infrastructure in digital media to improve within-language communication (*Bhashini*, n.d.).

This issue's complexity is further compounded by the mechanisms of these large language models, which are based on predicting the most likely word sequence rather than comprehending the meaning of a text. Even the highest-grammatically-capable LLM can generate translations that show grammatical complexity, but its understanding of constitutional history, doctrine, and context will remain inherently out of range. An artificially intelligent system that translates a legal judgment into multiple languages will be able to recover from a surface text the underlying jurisprudential content and accurately translate its meaning into the target languages. However, it may also mask the original content and significance of the judgment. This limitation becomes especially relevant in a constitutional context, where the interpretation of both the Constitution's history and its norms will frequently have to be used, rather than just the literal text.

The results of this study are further strengthened by exploring the current status of initiatives in India. One of the most prominent institutional initiatives in AI-assisted legal translation is the Supreme Court Vidhik Anuvaad Software (SUVAS), introduced in 2019. The platform was initially created to translate Supreme Court judgments into nine Indian languages, but its scope has since been extended. Currently, SUVAS supports the rendering of judicial documents into various Indian languages, even though it was built to provide English translation support to judges, and has helped translate thousands of Supreme Court judgements found on the e-SCR platform in India, say government sources. According to recent reports, over 31,184 judgments have been translated into the regional language, providing significant access to judicial information.

However, the available evidence reveals significant limitations. Institutional reports focus on accessibility and volume of translation. However, little publicly available information exists on the accuracy of the translations, the percentage of errors, the judicial measures for validation, and comparative evaluations across the different languages. Several High Courts have put in place monitoring mechanisms for translated judgments, indicating a continuous need for human intervention in monitoring and quality control. This corroborates the chapter's main concept: the role of legal translation should not be regarded as purely automated. A lack of clarity around performance measures would not enable one to measure the extent to which doctrinal clarity and meaning within the context are maintained through linguistic versions.

The same can be seen in the BHASHINI mission of the National Language Translation mission. BHASHINI seeks to support translation and language processing across the 22 scheduled Indian languages and is an essential enabler for multilingual digital governance. Now the platform has been integrated into public-service delivery systems, and it continues to expand with the help of crowdsourced language datasets and the development of AI models. The platform, however, acknowledges the need for ongoing improvement, expanding the dataset, and further enhancing the model, especially for less-represented languages. Recent government discussions have focused on continued work on reliability, inclusiveness, and translation quality.

Thus, the practical experiences of SUVAS and BHASHINI paint a conflicting picture. These services, on the other hand, illustrate the potential of AI in enhancing the multilingual accessibility of legal and governmental data. However, these do demonstrate the ongoing reliance of AI systems on language resources, institutional oversight, and human verification. What once seemed like debating whether AI can enable legal translation has now shifted to the question of whether AI can do so without compromising constitutional ideals such as accuracy, equality, transparency, and linguistic justice among different language communities.

Challenges of Translating Legal Language

Moreover, legal language itself is complex, and the role of law depends on the specific use of the language system, which, in a way, has an impact on legal translation. Precedents, doctrines, and applications of law in particular cases shape legal language that, as others have noted, such as Lawrence Solan and Peter Tiersma, differs from other languages. Translation in the legal area is not a translation by word substitution, but a translation by reconstruction with interpretation . A key challenge is interpreting information in context. Different constitutional and institutional narratives imbue legal notions with meaning. For example, the idea of constitutional morality is not self-translatable into regional languages, as it arose in judicial interpretations of privacy, dignity, and the rights of minorities. A translation obtained through an AI-based system trained primarily on general-language corpora can be very literal, preserving the sense of the contexts in which the doctrine appears.

One problem with machine translation systems is ambiguity. In many cases, this semantic flexibility is inherited from the language of the law and facilitates judges in making sound judgements in different circumstances. Certain terms, such as 'reasonable restriction', 'public order', and 'natural justice', can be given a fixed interpretation only by a judicial official. Semantic continuity and prediction reliability form the essence of artificial intelligence systems. This raises a tension between the uniformity of algorithmic workings and the flair and subjectivity of legal interpretation (Edwards, 1993). For instance, "reasonable restriction" is translated into local tongues, which gives rise to hard-and-fast ideas that do not capture the liberal reading it carries in Indian free speech jurisprudence.

The jargon and complexity of the procedure also contribute to AI translation. Some legal systems have peculiar procedural lexica. Other words, such as "writ petition," "certiorari," and "injunction," do not have counterparts in many languages. Machine translation systems can produce false or simplified translations of the TBs and alter the meanings of the procedures they belong to. The errors also influence the interpretation of criminal law and the basic concepts of justice in criminal proceedings. Even a misinformed understanding of the conditions placed upon bail, the bail process, or constitutional guarantees may have a huge impact on the person's understanding of their legal obligations and constitutional protections.

It becomes much more complicated if the constitutional principles come into play. The vocabulary in the Constitution mirrors the institutions, compromises, and political and normative philosophies of its history. The constitutional context (background) and the democratic meaning of the constitutional provisions must be interpreted sensitively in translation. Recognizing this, comparative constitutional studies have found that the interpretation of the Constitution may vary widely depending on its language or the meanings of its terms. Canada is a bilingual constitutional system, where both the languages of law (English and French) are equally effective, and where the role of the courts is to resolve disputes over differing interpretations between the English and French versions. The cases presented demonstrate that legal translation, which is, by nature, a technical process, is also a constitutional process.

The challenges are even greater in postcolonial jurisdictions, where legal systems are multilingual and legal terminology may be hybrid, dependent on complex historical development. The Indian vocabulary in the law is an amalgamation of common law, the colonial administrative system, the constitutional governmental system, and local linguistics. Many Indian languages lack Indianized legal terminology that corresponds to English-language legal terminology in the processes. AI can therefore be left with very conceptually empty gaps that statistical prediction tools (usually) cannot fill.

The challenges is based on Bourdieu's theory of lingual capital, which led to an understanding of the institutional meaning. Institutions that regard such legal languages as authoritative modes of discourse confer legitimacy on the former. English is a form of symbolic power within the Indian legal system. Most AI-based translation systems are trained on an English legal corpus, which could inadvertently perpetuate a hierarchy, with English legal terms becoming the "target" language when used with a regional language.

Algorithmic Bias and Low-Resource Languages

As the AI legal translation industry expands, there are also concerns regarding algorithmic bias and language disparities. This is due to the fact that large digitised datasets are essential for the training and optimisation of contemporary machine learning frameworks. Technologically advanced languages are benefited by more precise translations, while less advanced languages do not experience any technological advancements. This leads to structural disparities in multilingual legislation.

This encompasses a wide range of topics, such as computational studies, legal databases, and English digitisations, all of which are part of the AI infrastructure. This suggests that English remains the primary language of interest in multilingual Artificial Intelligence Systems. In this context, Safiya Noble's concept of algorithmic oppression is particularly pertinent, as institutional oppression is a recurring phenomenon in "data and digital technologies" (Noble, 2018). AI translation platforms can also perpetuate the dissemination of the dominant language in the legal arena, while simultaneously underprivilege minority communities of regional languages, despite their apparent neutrality. These extant asymmetries are underscored by the discrepancies in the data set. The term "languages with rich resources" denotes languages that possess readily accessible and beneficial corpora, court case archives, and legal databases, which are indispensable for the development of machine learning methods.

Numerous local and native languages lack digitized laws and a legal translation system for native terminology. Compared with many tribal and minority languages, Hindi and Tamil have a relatively high level of digital presence in India. There is, of course, a high degree of variation across language communities in the quality of AI translation (Debbarma, 2025).

This has implications in the legal setting, as inaccurate translations can directly impact constitutional protections and rights. In the field of asylum, reported applications of automated translation technologies in asylum procedures across various jurisdictions have proven to have shortcomings that undermine the fairness of adjudication, as errors in the translation of procedural information and witnesses' testimony compromise the fairness and acceptance of asylum procedures. Multilingual criminal justice settings can also present issues of a similar nature, as MHT can affect the presentation of procedural rights or evidentiary statements, with a negative impact on due process protections.

Ruha Benjamin's writing on the 'New Jim Code' provides examples of how automated systems may remain structurally unequal and, nonetheless, seem technologically neutral: AI-based legal translation systems might exacerbate that language gap by valuing and translating the languages of institutional and economic centers (Benjamin, 2024). In multilingual democracies, a hierarchy of legal accessibility forms exists at the expense of marginalized people whose language is not yet legally accessible. On the other hand, those who speak dominant languages have more institutionalized and precise modes of communication.

The idea now in dispute is not a technical one; it is constitutional and political. Language is an important element in accessing legal regimes, participating in democracy, and engaging in governance. The role of closely engaged legal translation practice with AI portrays major anti-effects on the notions of linguistic citizenship or institutional belonging. Despite the potential benefits AI systems might bring, there is still a possibility of reinforcing current linguistic inequalities, especially in the absence of AI systems that account for linguistic bias, participatory data collection, and context-specific training for legal staff. The challenge for multilingual legal systems is not just the ability of AI to translate legal texts, but also its capacity to do so without perpetuating the institutional hierarchy that is entrenched in constitutional governance, language, and technology.

Constitutional and Ethical Implications

AI, Due Process, and Legal Accuracy

Ensuring constitutional fairness and protecting the integrity and equality of language are intertwined with the potential of AI-powered legal translation. The law is not only the text itself, but also layers of interpretive, historical, and doctrinal communities. AI translation inaccuracies have implications that extend beyond the technicalities, reaching the realm of constitutional harm. In a multilingual setting such as India, the procedural aspects of both Articles 14 and 21 of the Constitution could be significantly undermined by such errors in their applicability to laws, witness testimony, administrative acts, or even judgments.

Legal hermeneutical frameworks show that context greatly shapes the legal interpretation process. However, a new way of reflecting on the form of legal words, the 'open texture' theory developed by H.L.A. Hart, can help clarify the meaning of those words within a legal context. AI-based translation systems, which are primarily developed from large bodies of language data, are likewise unable to convey context (Hart, 2012). The terms “custody”, “possession,” “consent,” and “intention” are easily misunderstood and can trigger a 180-degree difference in accountability. Such risks can be even more dangerous in criminal cases, as the protections of the system depend on what the accused knows.

The Constitution has clear implications for procedural fairness. In Hussainara Khatoon v. State of Bihar, the Supreme Court once again emphasized the significance of the right to fair procedure in Article 21. Clarity around language is needed to be effective in court proceedings. This can create an intersection of misunderstandings and confusion, and complicate legal intent when they are subjected to AI's influence in translation, resulting in litigants from nondominant language communities being faced with “digital procedural exclusion,” in the words of scholars. Firstly, the issue related to technology is not per se an issue, but rather arises from poor institutional choices to rely on automated interpretation systems in judicial systems.

Of algorithmic governance, there are some common concerns raised internationally. In the United States, the controversy over the COMPAS algorithm has highlighted one of the many potential implications of opacity in legal results, particularly in the absence of sufficient accountability mechanisms (Wang et al., 2026). Elements of the constitutionality concerns recur in COMPAS. However, the issue of translation to and from languages is not central to it: A common theme is a lack of transparency, explainability, and review codes for technology systems, which affect legal rights. One example that seemed most relevant to this viewpoint was the "black box society" case that was argued by Frank Pasquale in his thesis at Carleton University's School of Computer Science (Pasquale, 2019) . As AI translation tools become increasingly integrated into the judiciary process, issues of accessibility and transparency with these tools surface. If the tools shape the type of judges they produce, there is a real danger that constitutional due process will be technologized in a nondemocratic fashion.

As multilingual legal systems gain greater traction in court, immigration, law enforcement, and administration, significant constitutional and procedural questions have emerged with the advent of AI-powered translation tools for these legal processes. Although machine translation products such as Google Translate may be seen as unbiased technologies used to facilitate communication with multilingual individuals, mistakes in conveying sentence context, idiomatic expressions, and omitting special meanings embedded in laws may severely affect the integrity of testimony, procedural documents, and judicial interpretation (Abas et al., 2026). These risks are particularly relevant in the context of asylum procedures, criminal proceedings, and multilingual litigation, where correct legal conclusions are intertwined with linguistic accuracy and understanding. The probabilistic nature of machine-learning systems limits their ability to accurately translate concepts such as consent, coercion, custody, procedural fairness, and constitutional rights. This trend relies much more heavily on automated translation technologies and raises concerns about "automation bias" within institutions (Rivas Ginel & Moorkens, 2025). This is because translations generated by technology are perceived as objective despite their limitations and mismatches in the linguistic dataset. Indeed, the hardships of a low-resource and minority language are amplified by inadequate digital representation, thereby providing a mathematical underpinning to algorithmic linguistic inequalities in laws (Heimgärtner, 2026). Within the realm of the Indian constitutional framework, these incidents pose serious constitutional issues concerning the equality before law (under Article 14), dignity (under Article 21) and informational privacy, protection of linguistic and cultural identity (under Article 29) and the linguistic minority protections (under Article 350A). AI translation frameworks make it difficult to hold institutions liable for mistranslations and procedural harm due to a lack of transparency and accountability. This scenario highlights the urgent need for human oversight and constitutional principles to be applied in AI-powered legal communication systems, and for effective rights-based governance to be established (van Kolfschooten et al., 2025).

Thus, it becomes clear how judicial reliability and linguistic reliability are connected. The legitimacy of courts is not just a function of their power to judge: much depends on the public's perception that the processes of legal reasoning are understandable, open, and fair. Over-dependencies on AI translation systems without human verification may erode their legitimacy, particularly in multilingual constitutional democracies where language is a key factor in the right to access justice.

Linguistic Equality and Democratic Participation

The use of artificial intelligence in legal translation raises a crucial constitutional question: whose language is the "standard" in AI-enabled legal translation within digital governance? Multimedia technologies developed largely using common languages reflect certain language constructs, lexicons, and socio-political norms. It creates a hierarchy, under which certain languages gain access to the digital sphere while others remain technologized. This phenomenon can contribute to an understanding of Pierre Bourdieu's theory of linguistic capital (Bourdieu, 1977). Institutional languages become more legitimate for administrative and technological purposes. AI systems can also reinforce inequalities if they are trained on test data that is predominantly English and/or dominant regional languages at the expense of minority or Indigenous linguistic traditions. The constitutional pluralism in the Indian context recognizes linguistic diversity through the Eighth Schedule and the protection of federal languages. Consequently, such exclusion bears significant democratic ramifications.

The connection between language and being part of a democratic society is important. Constitutional citizenship requires a full knowledge of the law and its contestation, as well as meaningful engagement with legal institutions. AI translation systems may normalize the predominant linguistic forms, thereby limiting the interaction of users of lesser-spoken languages in legal, administrative, and other contexts. The issue goes beyond the basic question of whether translation can be done more efficiently; it involves the most basic concepts of equality in a constitution.

Digital constitutionalism, as an analytical framework, is useful for fully appreciating these changes. Digital constitutionalism scholars argue that technological infrastructures are important in shaping how constitutional rights are put into practice. In this context, AI language systems become active, impacting access to justice, state communication, and the dynamics of democratic engagement (De

Gregorio & Radu, 2022). Their functioning has profound consequences for the right to informational autonomy, the right of equality before the law, and the mode of participatory government.

This is emphasized by the Indian Supreme Court's recognition of privacy and dignity in Justice K.S. Puttaswamy v. Union of India. Informational autonomy includes the right to substantive involvement in government structures. The structural equality of democratic participation can be undermined when citizens are unable to make meaningful sense of the functioning of legal procedures because AI systems are unable to adequately represent their linguistic realities. The constitutional predicament lies in the growing nature of a phenomenon known as "digital linguistic majoritarianism": the technological norms institutionalize dominant languages. At the same time, exclusion is understood not as a political choice but as an inevitable by-product of technology.

Data Colonialism and Technological Centralization

Many of these factors—including comprehensive linguistic databases, robust technological systems, and distinctive algorithmic models—are firmly within the grasp of leading technology companies, giving them a significant advantage in the effectiveness of their AI legal translation capabilities. The notion of "data colonialism," as coined by Nick Couldry and Ulises Mejias, is raised by this centralization of technological power. This is a recently coined term used to describe the exploitation and monetization of human experiences through digital infrastructures (Couldry & Mejias, 2020). The most sophisticated language AI systems are trained primarily using the world's most common languages, with English having a particular impact. Like any multilingual country, such as India, the legal translation system is often unable to grasp the nuances and local legal terminology of regional words and phrases, or the bedrock concepts of law embedded in regional culture. This leads to incongruence and the need to establish external infrastructure, which may not be in harmony with the local constitutional status quo. Governance issues stem from the centralization of language action on dominant techno-platforms. The private sector's role as a gatekeeper to the judiciary, government, and law is increasing. These developments involve a shift of technical system competence from the public sector to technically managed services without democratic accountability as a priority, set up to make a profit.

Surveillance capitalism (as articulated by Shoshana Zuboff) can help us understand how digital infrastructures become visible, giving shape to linguistic expression by turning it into measurable behavioral data (Zuboff, 2020). Over the life of the centralized AI-powered translation system, they have the potential to access legal data of all kinds, perform detailed analyses, and consider possible avenues for capitalization. This situation poses a dual risk not only to the privacy of the individual but also to the constitutional governance of information regulation within lawful frameworks. A constitutional tension arises in two ways regarding the centralization of linguistic infrastructure. First, it could perpetuate linguistic inequality if the issue of widely used data sets is given priority. However, more than that, it cedes decision-making power from democratic institutions to corporations that exercise technological control. It is not only about the use of AI to assist in legal translation, but also about the implications of such developments for constitutional democracies in general, their commitment to linguistic justice, models of responsibility, and the involvement of citizens in gradually more centralized techno-societies.

Policy Recommendations and Implications

The findings of this chapter highlight the pressing need for rights-based and constitutional principles to provide foundations for governance regimes addressing the growing use of AI in legal translation and multilingual legal digital governance systems. AI legal translation holds substantial ramifications that policymakers, judicial officials, and regulatory agencies need to take note of. This progress goes beyond mere technical uses, transforming legal practice as a whole. The representation of democratic ideals and the integrity of the constitution are fundamental principles. Partly, this is because of the concepts of access to justice, language equality, procedural justice, and democratic participation. In the legal domain, for example, transparency, accountability, inclusivity, precision of understanding, and multilingualism are fundamental aspects of the governance of AI-based communication tools.

The results highlight the importance of holistic approaches for AI-supported legal translation with efficient human oversight. An automated translation system, by itself, is too limited to solve the problems of legal translation in judicial/administrative departments. Legal translators (along with language professionals and legal professionals in the courtroom) must take an active role in monitoring the use of such tools and in maximizing safeguards to ensure the integrity of the constitutional, infrastructural, and doctrinal elements of their documents in their generated outputs and products. However, the risk of exposure to mistranslation and other procedural inclusion and constitutional harms can be reduced by incorporating governance mechanisms that balance the technical effectiveness of the tools with interpretive protections for human involvement. This practice has a profound significance in the context of criminal trials, adjudication of refugee status, welfare, and constitutional law conflicts. This chapter emphasizes the crucial role of institutions in law and law enforcement, and the importance of ensuring their strength, transparency, understanding, and high level of accountability in the implementation of AI systems.

There is a desperate need for a unified, binding auditing system for an artificial intelligence system that may aid governmental and judicial institutions. These audits are important for uncovering algorithmic bias and linguistic inaccuracies, as well as the differential impacts on communities that speak low-resource languages. The challenge for organizations using AI translation technologies is to accept the consequences of faulty translations and the weaknesses in procedures that could arise from automated translation. To mitigate the negative consequences of existing gaps in algorithmic communication of law, a set of explicit guidelines and standards should be established, including liability, institutional accountability, and mechanisms to address grievances wherever applicable.

The implications of this research are significant for safeguarding and integrating low-resource and marginalized languages into the digital legal framework. Continuous public-sector funding is a prerequisite for developing large multilingual legal corpora, digitalizing legal databases, and creating multilingual legal data spanning the languages of Indigenous, tribal, and minority peoples across extensive, region-specific collections. Leveraging AI models trained in widely adopted language(s) could animate and deepen linguistic divisions and institutional hierarchies. In this regard, language inclusion policies must be developed to ensure equitable representation in the social-technological space: beyond federally recognized languages, these policies must also provide equitable representation for underrepresented languages in the context of legal artificial intelligence. The creation, in collaboration with the public institutions that contributed to the constitutional framework, of AI-based translation systems favorably oriented towards local contexts and that include regional language specialists and local communities, is also possible through the use of participatory methods.

This chapter offers important new insights into the concepts of digital constitutionalism and data governance. For policymakers, a key element in the field of Artificial Intelligence systems used for communication within the legal sector is strengthening privacy safeguards, protecting informational autonomy, reinforcing cybersecurity, and adopting robust data protection approaches. Now, confidential judicial, personal, and administrative information is routinely translated for legal purposes by legal translation platforms as a whole, underscoring the urgent need for robust data governance strategies. In addition, the harmful tendency to concentrate linguistic and technological power in the hands of a few large corporate businesses is growing stronger, and an increase in regulatory power is imperative. Given the current dominance of proprietary AI systems, they could have a profound impact on reducing democratic control over legal communication infrastructures, resulting in a significant loss of control over such systems from state institutions to the private sector. It is imperative that multilingual legal AI infrastructures be developed that put the public in charge, aiming to reduce the risks of data colonialism and the centralization of technology.

In addition, emerging issues include multilingual constitutions and access to justice in India. The need of the hour is to "make the law" more "language-friendly" through constitution-responsive AI in institutions such as courts, legal aid organizations, and the administration. The focus of this project should be on ensuring doctrinal purity and procedural justice. With government initiatives such as the new judicial translation program incorporating AI technologies and the digital governance platform, which requires translation into multiple languages, there is an urgent need for constitutional protections to ensure linguistic equality and enable citizens to participate in government. The implementation of AI Governance, Legal Linguistics, and Digital Rights Training Programs for Judges, Lawyers, Translators, and Public Officials is crucial to improving institutional preparedness for the responsible management of AI-driven legal systems.

CONCLUSION

It is with these that we should understand the new role of language, which is no longer merely a means of communication in today's constitutional democracies, but can be used alongside artificial intelligence. The technology platform has become a common mode of law engagement and negotiation of issues of law, welfare, citizenship, and democratic participation. In this chapter, the authors explore in depth the complex role of AI-powered information technology translation systems intended to create inclusive spaces and overcome linguistic barriers. However, this study found that, as a result, those technologies produce new exclusions, inequalities, and institutional injustices. Translation in the context of the law is not simply a technical process; it has cultural connotations, history, procedure, and constitutional implications. In addition, the language used in legal contexts is often more complex than what computational analysis can process.

The findings suggest that translation errors have significant implications for due process, judicial reliability, and equitable legal procedures, particularly in multilingual societies where access to justice depends on the accuracy of language translation. Language use is often highly socio-cultural, dialectal, and legal, and training in language models on well-known linguistic resources may not adequately capture these properties. These shortcomings constitute a real danger to the development of 'algorithmic linguistic homogenization', the increasing technological standardization of language and, consequently, of the basic principles of linguistic pluralism. As a consequence, marginalized language communities are exposed to the risk of becoming visible through digital means, while at the same time missing the opportunity to tackle key substantive concerns.

In this chapter, it is argued that the governance of AI translation is connected and reflective of broader questions about digital constitutionalism and the overall power dynamics in the technosphere. With respect to linguistic accessibility, data infrastructures, and algorithmic transparency, proprietary systems with limited democratic governance are increasingly impacting big tech companies. Power centralization raises serious concerns about data colonialism, platform governance, and the commercialization of the constitutional space of communication. Language can be seen, in this context, as a site of technological extraction and a means of institutional power repositioning.

AI-designed legal translation goes beyond the technological gauntlet of perfect calculation; it is also about a commitment to constitutional values in a world driven by technology that shapes governance. In democratic societies, it is essential to challenge the idea that tackling the problem of linguistic diversity reduction is merely a matter of convenience or the efficiency of language algorithms. Language is an important element of citizenship, civic engagement, and constitutional identity, and therefore should be recognized in governance structures. If not adequately safeguarded, this AI-driven multilingualism can deepen entrenched inequalities and foster a false sense of "democratic inclusion" through technology.

Recommendations for Further Research

Ongoing research could examine the potential constitutional and democratic impacts of AI-based translation tools in multilingual or cross-linguistic settings. The research interests should focus on the following themes: Procedural Justice, linguistic parity, judicial trust, and equitable access to justice. This comparative study is designed to analyze the regulatory landscape of AI-powered legal translation workflows and the regulatory frameworks for digital governance in multilingual contexts such as India, the European Union, Canada, and other applicable jurisdictions. In addition to its relevance in sectors such as welfare administration, immigration policies, and law enforcement, further empirical investigation is warranted regarding the application of MT across various judicial types. This research examines the effects of translation shortcomings on marginalized language users and communities in general, and on low-resource language communities in particular. Future research lines should investigate the convergence of artificial intelligence and legal structures and systems, especially from the perspectives of legal interpretation, data colonialism, and the centralization and platform governance of language infrastructures. Further research can explore regional disparities related to access to AI tools, regional differences in digital literacy, and the impact of language diversity on the acceptance of AI tools for translation in public institutions in India. Moreover, it will examine the effectiveness of rights protection in the context of governance and constitutional thinking, and highlight the inherent values of dignity, transparency, plurality, and participatory democracy.

REFERENCES

Abas, I. H., Rasli, A., Alipour, M., & Mustafa, F. (2026). AI and the Future of Translation: Trends and Challenges. In *Bridging Theory and Practice in Translation: Perspectives, Challenges, and Innovations* (pp. 243–284). IGI Global Scientific Publishing. DOI: 10.4018/979-8-3373-3705-0.ch008

Badah, A. M., Khalaf, C. N., Dwaikat, F. J., & AlQbailat, N. (2026). The usage of artificial intelligence in legal translation: Bridging the gap between law and language. *Ampersand (Oxford, UK)*, *16*, 100248. DOI: 10.1016/j.amper.2025.100248

Banakar, R., & Travers, M. (Eds.). (2005). *Theory and method in socio-legal research*. Hart Publishing.

Benjamin, R. (2024). *Viral Justice: How We Grow the World We Want*. Princeton University Press.

Bhashini. (n.d.). Retrieved May 17, 2026, from https://bhashini.gov.in/about-bhashini

Bourdieu, P. (1977). *Outline of a Theory of Practice* (R. Nice, Trans.). Cambridge University Press. DOI: 10.1017/CBO9780511812507

Cotterrell, R. (1995). *Law's community: Legal theory in sociological perspective*. Clarendon Press.

Couldry, N., & Mejias, U. A. (2020). *The Costs of Connection: How Data Is Colonizing Human Life and Appropriating It for Capitalism*. Stanford University Press., DOI: 10.1515/9781503609754

De Gregorio, G., & Radu, R. (2022). Digital constitutionalism in the new era of Internet governance. *International Journal of Law and Information Technology*, *30*(1), 68–87. DOI: 10.1093/ijlit/eaac004

De Schutter, H. (2007). Language policy and political philosophy: On the emerging linguistic justice debate. *Language Problems and Language Planning*, *31*(1), 1–23. DOI: 10.1075/lplp.31.1.02des

Debbarma, M. (2025). Linguistic Diversity and National Integration in India: Challenges, Policies and Pathways to Inclusivity. *Journal of Asian and African Studies*, *00219096251400655*, 00219096251400655. Advance online publication. DOI: 10.1177/00219096251400655

Demertzis, K., Rantos, K., Magafas, L., Skianis, C., & Iliadis, L. (2023). A Secure and Privacy-Preserving Blockchain-Based XAI-Justice System. *Information (Basel)*, *14*(9), 477. Advance online publication. DOI: 10.3390/info14090477

Edwards, R. C. (1993). The legal fact as a work of art: Artificial intelligence and the pragmatics of legal interpretation [University of British Columbia]. DOI: 10.14288/1.0086106

Hart, H. L. A. (2012). *The Concept of Law*. OUP Oxford. DOI: 10.1093/he/9780199644704.001.0001

Heimgärtner, R. (2026). Intercultural Design for Human-Centered AI Solutions. In *Handbook of Human-Centered Artificial Intelligence* (pp. 1–65). Springer., DOI: 10.1007/978-981-97-8440-0_77-2

Hildebrandt, M. (2015). *Smart Technologies and the End(s) of Law*. https://www.elgaronline.com/monobook/9781849808767.xml

Hutchinson, T. (2015). Doctrinal research: Researching the jury. In Watkins, D., & Burton, M. (Eds.), *Research methods in law* (2nd ed., pp. 7–31). Routledge.

Lai, J., Gan, W., Wu, J., Qi, Z., & Yu, P. S. (2024). Large language models in law: A survey. *AI Open*, *5*, 181–196. DOI: 10.1016/j.aiopen.2024.09.002

Latour, B. (2012). *We Have Never Been Modern*. Harvard University Press.

Leung, J. H. C. (2026). *Digital Multilingualism and Platform Governance*. Elements in Forensic Linguistics., DOI: 10.1017/9781009263177

McConville, M., & Chui, W. H. (Eds.). (2017). *Research methods for law*. Edinburgh University Press. DOI: 10.1515/9781474404259

McEwan, C. (2008). Postcolonialism and Development. *Postcolonialism and Development*, 1–354. DOI: 10.4324/9780203887387

Moneus, A. M., & Sahari, Y. (2024). Artificial intelligence and human translation: A contrastive study based on legal texts. *Heliyon*, *10*(6), e28106. DOI: 10.1016/j.heliyon.2024.e28106 PMID: 38524597

Monzó-Nebot, E., & Mellinger, C. D. (2022). Language policies for social justice—Translation, interpreting, and access. *Just. Journal of Language Rights & Minorities. Revista de Drets Lingüístics i Minories*, *1*(1–2), 15–35.

Nie, T., Sun, J., & Ma, W. (2025). Exploring the roles of large language models in reshaping transportation systems: A survey, framework, and roadmap. *Artificial Intelligence for Transportation*, *1*, 100003. DOI: 10.1016/j.ait.2025.100003

Noble, S. U. (2018). *Algorithms of oppression: How search engines reinforce racism* (pp. xv, 229). New York University Press.

Novelli, C., Bongiovanni, G., & Sartor, G. (2022). A conceptual framework for legal personality and its application to AI. *Jurisprudence*, *13*(2), 194–219. DOI: 10.1080/20403313.2021.2010936

Pasquale, F. (2019). A Rule of Persons, Not Machines: The Limits of Legal Automation. *The George Washington Law Review*, *87*(1), 1–55.

Piszcz, A., & Sierocka, H. (2020). The Role of Culture in Legal Languages, Legal Interpretation and Legal Translation. *International Journal for the Semiotics of Law*, *33*(3), 533–542. DOI: 10.1007/s11196-020-09760-3 PMID: 33214737

Rivas Ginel, M. I., & Moorkens, J. (2025). Translators' trust and distrust in the times of GenAI. *Translation Studies*, *18*(2), 283–299. DOI: 10.1080/14781700.2025.2507594

Santos, B. D. S. (2009). Democratizar a democracia: os caminhos da democracia participativa. In *Democratizar a democracia: os caminhos da democracia participativa* (pp. 678-678).

Serttaş, A., Gürkan, H., & Dere, G. (2025). Synthetic Social Alienation: The Role of Algorithm-Driven Content in Shaping Digital Discourse and User Perspectives. *Journalism and Media*, *6*(3), 149. Advance online publication. DOI: 10.3390/journalmedia6030149

(2022). Situated Multilingualism and Identity. InFisher, L., & Ayres-Bennett, W. (Eds.), *Multilingualism and Identity: Interdisciplinary Perspectives* (pp. 19–152). Cambridge University Press., https://www.cambridge.org/core/books/multilingualism-and-identity/situated-multilingualism-and-identity/D0A2C715AD8EF38F036C6336B0E9D581

Tamanaha, B. Z. (2001). *A general jurisprudence of law and society*. Oxford University Press. DOI: 10.1093/acprof:oso/9780199244676.001.0001

Thapa, S., Shiwakoti, S., Shah, S. B., Adhikari, S., Veeramani, H., Nasim, M., & Naseem, U. (2025). Large language models (LLM) in computational social science: Prospects, current state, and challenges. *Social Network Analysis and Mining*, *15*(1), 4. DOI: 10.1007/s13278-025-01428-9

Tiersma, P., Solan, L., Ainsworth, J., Shuy, R. W., Tiersma, P., Solan, L., Ainsworth, J., & Shuy, R. W. (Eds.). (2015). *Speaking of Language and Law: Conversations on the Work of Peter Tiersma*. Oxford University Press.

Tiersma, P. M. (1999). *Legal Language*. University of Chicago Press. DOI: 10.7208/chicago/9780226854809.001.0001

Van Hoecke, M. (Ed.). (2011). *Methodologies of legal research: Which kind of method for what kind of discipline?* Hart Publishing.

van Kolfschooten, H., Goosen, S., van Oirschot, J., Schouten, B., Vajda, I., & Willems, L. (2025). Legal, ethical, and policy challenges of artificial intelligence translation tools in healthcare. *Discover Public Health*, *22*(1), 904. DOI: 10.1186/s12982-025-01277-z PMID: 41487681

Van Parijs, P. (2011). *Linguistic Justice for Europe and for the World*. Oxford University Press. DOI: 10.1093/acprof:osobl/9780199208876.001.0001

Wa Thiong'o, N. (1998). Decolonising the mind. *Diogenes*, *46*(184), 101–104. DOI: 10.1177/039219219804618409

Wang, C., Yin, Y., & Hu, H. (2026). The rise of algorithmic governance and the dual revolution: Applications, challenges, and governance of artificial intelligence in public administration. *Technology in Society*, *86*, 103264. DOI: 10.1016/j.techsoc.2026.103264

Winner, L. (1980). Do Artifacts Have Politics? *Daedalus*, *109*(1), 121–136.

Zuboff, S. (2020). L'âge du capitalisme de surveillance. *Le combat pour un avenir humain face aux nouvelles frontières du pouvoir*.

ADDITIONAL READING

Lai, J., Gan, W., Wu, J., Qi, Z., & Yu, P. S. (2024). Large Language Models in Law: A Survey. *AI Open*, *5*, 181–196. DOI: 10.1016/j.aiopen.2024.09.002

Noble, S. U. (2018). *Algorithms of Oppression: How Search Engines Reinforce Racism. New York University Press. Benjamin, R. (2024). Viral Justice: How We Grow the World We Want*. Princeton University Press.

Qi, Y. (2025). Challenges and Opportunities of Legal Translation in the Context of Artificial Intelligence. *Journal of Innovation and Development.*, *11*(3), 220–233. DOI: 10.54097/5q0pz449

Saldanha, G., & O'Brien, S. (2013). *Research Methodologies in Translation Studies*. Routledge.

Šarčević, S. (1997). *New Approach to Legal Translation*. Kluwer Law International.

KEY TERMS AND DEFINITIONS

Algorithmic Bias: Algorithmic bias refers to systematic errors or biases that AI systems may generate due to data imbalance, the institutions' underlying assumptions, or certain design choices in the technology. Algorithmic bias can discriminate against minority groups and against minority or low-resource languages in the context of multilingual artificial intelligence systems.

Artificial Intelligence (AI): Artificial Intelligence is a collection of technologies that enable computing systems to perform tasks that typically require human intelligence. These tasks include, but are not limited to, language processing, decision-making, pattern recognition, prediction, and automated communication. In legal translation, AI tools can use machine learning algorithms and natural language processing techniques to assist with translating legal documents across different language contexts.

Legal Translation: Legal translation is the task of translating legal documents, such as judgments, laws, contracts, and procedural information, from one language to another and back again. This process is important for legal meaning, doctrinal precision, procedural implications, and constitutional context embedded in the original text. Unlike common translation tasks, legal translation requires a highly nuanced approach performed within a specific legal or institutional context.

Linguistic Justice: Linguistic justice involves the equitable and fair distribution of speech, the legitimate access of individuals and communities to the legal system, governance structures, education, and participatory democracy without discrimination based on their spoken language. The emphasis is on the recognition and protection of linguistic diversity from both constitutional and digital infrastructures.

Multilingual Constitutional Democracy: A multilingual constitutional democracy is a constitutional system in which multiple languages are enjoyed in legal, political, and administrative structures, a formal recognition of language diversity and an effort to enable equitable democratic engagement of language communities. One significant example of this system in India is the country itself.

Chapter 7
The Illusion of Accuracy: How AI Reshapes Discourse and Authority in Legal Translation

Gehan Khaled Ali
http://orcid.org/0009-0000-6887-3375
Universiti Sains Malaysia, Malaysia

Shatha Amer Jarrah
http://orcid.org/0009-0002-0269-1186
Universiti Sains Malaysia, Malaysia

ABSTRACT

The integration of artificial intelligence (AI) in legal translation has created a critical analytical blind spot: the "illusion of accuracy," where linguistic fluency masks the erosion of legal fidelity. This chapter argues that AI systems do not merely transfer meaning but reconstruct discourse, often sacrificing specialized legal nuance for statistical probability. Utilizing Systemic Functional Linguistics (SFL) and Critical Discourse Analysis (CDA), the study examines how algorithmic mediation weakens modal obligations and flattens syntactic complexity, thereby threatening institutional authority. To address this, the chapter proposes the AI–Legal Discourse Transformation Model (ALDTM), a three-layer diagnostic framework that maps transformations across input, processing, and output stages. By shifting the focus from surface-level correspondence to functional-discursive integrity, this research provides essential insights for AI governance and multilingual legal communication, ensuring that automated systems responsibly uphold the performative force of law.

DOI: 10.4018/979-8-3373-9179-3.ch007

INTRODUCTION

Accuracy, in the context of legal translation, is not a self-evident property; it is a claim, and one that depends entirely on what is being measured. Neural machine translation systems and large language models now produce legal translations of unprecedented fluency, prompting their adoption across international arbitration, contract drafting, and multilingual legislation. Most traditional evaluation methods still focus mainly on statistical similarity and do not directly assess legal equivalence (Koehn, 2020). According to Šarňvić (1997), the goal of legal translation is to maintain legal impact inside a target legal system rather than linguistic similarity. The inquiry that this chapter undertakes is consequently not centered on the accuracy of AI systems as assessed by traditional metrics, but instead on the sufficiency of these conventional metrics for effectively evaluating legal accuracy in any capacity.

The main argument here is that artificial intelligence systems do more than translate legal terminology; they may also reshape legal meaning within the target legal context. They simultaneously modify the normative structure of the source text, weakening modal obligations, resolving strategic ambiguities, and normalizing syntactic complexity to produce outputs that are both linguistically fluent and formally consistent. Surden (2014) argues that the features that make legal language legally operative, namely modal force, definitional precision, and institutional register, remain largely outside the scope of AI training and evaluation. This leads to a class of errors that appear to be equivalent but actually produce something quite different. Briva-Iglesias et al. (2024) found that legal translations generated by large language models could score well on automated evaluation metrics while still being judged problematic by professional legal translators, highlighting a gap between apparent equivalence and legal adequacy. This effect is referred to as the illusion of accuracy in this chapter.

This illusion is structurally specific to legal language.The density of legal discourse, the precision of modal expressions, and the intentional use of strategic ambiguity serve as mechanisms through which legal meaning is constructed and maintained; it is not intrinsically convoluted. As Austin (1962) argues, legal terminology does not simply describe rights and responsibilities; it also helps create them.A statutory provision does not merely recount an action; it enacts one. Bhatia (1983) further shows that syntactic complexity in legal texts is a genre-constrained professional strategy for managing interpretive possibilities, not stylistic excess. When this complexity is altered, however subtly, its legal effect may be altered with it. Any method that seems to maintain meaning while changing linguistic form runs the danger of creating the appearance of equivalency rather than actual equivalency. Giampieri (2024) shows that AI-generated legal translations may appear acceptable while still containing legally significant inaccuracies that become visible only upon closer examination. This gap between surface form and legal substance is not accidental; it is structural.

AI systems operate on a fundamentally different principle. As probabilistic systems, these engines prioritize fluency and coherence over normative intentionality, which encompasses the intentional selection of a modal verb, the calculated maintenance of ambiguity, or the authoritative nature of a formal register. Dworkin (1986) argues that legal meaning is not based only on repeated language patterns. It depends on reasoned interpretation within an institutional setting. This can be seen in the distinction between "shall" and "may," where the first typically indicates obligation and the second allows discretion (von Wright, 1951; Garzone, 2001). Substituting one for the other produces fluent text with altered legal force. AI systems optimize for the likely; legal discourse encodes the intentional. This difference is of kind rather than degree.

As AI-mediated legal translation becomes more common in institutional settings, these less visible shifts risk weakening legal precision in ways that are not always easy to identify or contest, particularly within opaque algorithmic systems (Pasquale, 2015). This chapter approaches that problem in stages. It first examines the functional complexity of legal discourse before turning to the probabilistic logic through which AI systems process legal language and the tensions this creates for legal equivalence. On that basis, the chapter develops the AI–Legal Discourse Transformation Model (ALDTM) as a framework for examining how AI-mediated translation may reshape legal meaning and institutional authority.

THE FUNCTIONAL COMPLEXITY OF LEGAL DISCOURSE

Legal language is often complex for institutional and interpretive reasons, not by accident. Its form does legal work: it defines relations, distributes obligations and permissions, and helps sustain authority within a legal system. This is why legal meaning cannot be separated easily from wording or structure. Small changes may matter. A translation or automated process that appears to preserve meaning while reshaping legal form may therefore produce not equivalence, but only the appearance of it.

Legal Discourse as Institutional and Performative Language

Legal discourse is an institutional, formal, performative, and authority-laden linguistic register. Legal language does more than communicate information. It helps define rights and responsibilities and also gives legal institutions authority to act. As Austin (1962) observed, certain utterances do not describe reality but constitute it; in legal contexts, a judicial ruling or statutory provision does not merely report an act; it performs it. Building upon this premise, Searle (1969) articulates the notion of speech acts as institutional actions, specifically encompassing declarations and directives, which are systematically employed within legal discourse to forge normative relations. Legal meaning remains closely bound to the language used to express it.

Framing language as a social semiotic system, Halliday (1994) highlights how meaning is shaped by ideational, interpersonal, and textual functions. This framework becomes especially relevant when examining modality in legal texts, where linguistic choices are designed not just for communication, but to mandate obligations, clear the way for permissions, and cement authority. The hierarchical nature of legal interactions is further accentuated by institutional discourse analysis, which elucidates how role asymmetry and task orientation inform legal communication. Empirical research on courtroom translation has shown that power asymmetries are actively negotiated through linguistic choices, including modality, politeness strategies, and framing decisions, in ways that directly shape meaning construction across languages (Wu et al., 2026b). These perspectives show that legal language is complex for functional reasons rather than by chance. Because it serves institutional purposes, even minor linguistic changes may influence legal meaning

Linguistic Density and Strategic Ambiguity

A central feature of this system is linguistic density. A defining trait of legal writing is its heavy reliance on winding, long-form sentences and deeply embedded clauses, all packed with highly specialized terminology. Many legal texts also rely heavily on nominalization. This density is not stylistic excess but a functional requirement: it constrains interpretation and minimizes unintended meanings in contexts where every lexical choice may carry legal consequences. Nominalization, specifically, assumes a pivotal function. As elucidated by Halliday and Matthiessen (2004), it functions as a variant of grammatical metaphor that encapsulates intricate processes into abstract constructs. Terms like "breach," "consideration," and "indemnification" hold precise meanings within the legal lexicon, shaped entirely by judicial precedent. From a genre perspective, Bhatia (1993) illustrates how this complexity is systematically structured through qualifications and post-modification, while Schauer (1991) maintains that a degree of linguistic determinacy is essential for rules to function predictably. Importantly, this density also increases the fragility of legal meaning: simplifying structure may preserve readability, but alter interpretive boundaries.

Beyond structural density, legal discourse relies on strategic ambiguity. Legal ambiguity frequently serves as a purposeful and essential tool, despite the widespread belief that it indicates poor writing. It allows courts to gradually build legal concepts, permits political compromise during legislative drafting, and permits statutes to apply to unforeseen instances The concept of open texture, developed by Hart (1961/1994), clarifies that indeterminacy is not a flaw but a structural condition of rule-based systems. Extending this argument, Endicott (2000) argues that vagueness is functionally indispensable, as it delegates context-sensitive interpretation to judicial authorities. It is imperative to recognize that hastily resolving such ambiguity, even if it yields a more coherent or fluent discourse, jeopardizes the expansive interpretive framework upon which legal systems are fundamentally dependent.

Modality, Legal Force, and Institutional Authority

In legal language, modality is often linked to ambiguity. Modal expressions help define obligations and permissions and may also restrict or prohibit particular actions. Shall, must, and may are examples of modal verbs that are not interchangeable since they each convey a unique deontic force with particular legal ramifications. Within Halliday's framework, modality forms part of the interpersonal metafunction, but in legal contexts it acquires heightened significance: even minor modal variation may distinguish between binding obligation and discretionary authority. Building on this, recent SFL-based research on courtroom discourse has shown how epistemic modal choices contribute to the construction of certainty, doubt, credibility, and institutional authority in legal settings (Wu et al., 2026c). Comparative legal-linguistic research (e.g., Šarčević, 1997; Garzone, 2001) indicates that modal systems vary across languages, complicating equivalence in multilingual legal contexts. From a jurisprudence standpoint,the analysis of the encoding of legal relations, such as rights, duties, powers, and immunities is provided by Hohfeld (1919), while their formalization in deontic logic is performed by von Wright (1951).In this sense, modality does not merely express meaning; it determines legal effect, and is therefore highly vulnerable to distortion under processes that prioritize fluency over force.

More broadly, legal discourse functions as an engine of institutional power. Generating, interpreting, and applying legal language is a mechanism that builds and enforces legal meaning. Following the views of Foucault (1972), discourse and power are intertwined, shaping the possibilities for speaking, knowing, and legitimizing things in institutions. In legal contexts, this authority is largely concentrated within specialized institutions that control access to legal language and its interpretation. Building on this, Fairclough (1989) illustrates how legal discourse naturalizes power relations, while Bourdieu (1987) explains that legal authority depends on the distribution of "juridical capital," enabling certain actors to monopolize legitimate interpretation. Far from merely reflecting power, legal language actively helps shape it. Shifts in linguistic form can alter both legal meaning and how authority is understood.

Beyond mere communication, legal complexity inherently drives how legal meaning evolves. While simplification might bolster accessibility, it risks altering institutional functions, restricting interpretive flexibility, and eroding precision. As Mattila (2006) notes, this complexity is not limited to one language, and can be found across different legal systems. Because legal meaning is embedded in linguistic form, even seemingly minor transformations, such as simplification, clarification, or normalization, may alter legal force and interpretive scope while still appearing accurate. This discrepancy between perceived equivalency and actual transformation ultimately drives the illusion of accuracy. The following section examines how contemporary AI systems, operating on probabilistic principles, systematically produce such transformations while appearing to preserve meaning.

AI in Legal Translation: Beyond Accuracy

The increasing use of artificial intelligence in legal translation raises a fundamental question: what happens when probabilistic language systems process a discourse that is structurally complex by design? Density, modality, and strategic ambiguity, features that are operationally necessary rather than incidental, are what give legal discourse its meaning, as stated in Section 2. Progress in neural machine translation and large language models has driven wider adoption of legal translation tools, often yielding more accessible and linguistically fluent legal content. Yet fluency does not necessarily preserve legal effect. This section explores how AI systems parse legal language, uncovering the deep tensions surrounding legal equivalence. It further examines how this friction actively shapes legal discourse and, occasionally, institutional authority.

Legal Equivalence in AI Translation

Over the last decade, artificial intelligence has become increasingly visible in legal translation. Neural machine translation (NMT) has largely displaced earlier rule-based and statistical approaches by producing translations of considerably greater fluency (Bahdanau et al., 2015). More recently, large language models (LLMs), including systems used in legal language processing and domain-adapted models such as LEGAL-BERT (Chalkidis et al., 2020), have expanded AI applications into legal drafting, contract review, document summarization, and multilingual legal communication. Their growing presence has been difficult to ignore. Yet a more important question tends to receive less attention: what, exactly, is being preserved when legal texts are translated through AI systems, and what may be quietly altered in the process? In many cases, AI performance continues to be evaluated in terms of fluency and surface similarity rather than legal adequacy. According to Koehn

(2020), standard metrics like BLEU fall short because they measure statistical overlap rather than true semantic or legal alignment. Cross-system comparisons of NMT engines and LLMs have further confirmed that automated metrics alone cannot capture qualitatively distinct failure modes in AI-generated translations, as different metrics yield divergent rankings that reflect evaluative priorities rather than actual translation adequacy (Wang et al., 2026a). Yet, in legal translation, this distinction is everything. As Šarčević (1997) argues, the objective is not linguistic resemblance alone but the preservation of equivalent legal effect within the target legal system.

This distinction points to a deeper structural tension. Surden (2014) observes that AI systems applied to legal materials are typically assessed through general linguistic benchmarks, while the features that make legal discourse legally operative, modal force, definitional precision, and institutional register, often remain outside the scope of evaluation. Consequently, a translated legal clause can easily look polished and fluent on the surface while completely stripping away the legal conditions of the original text. This means the problem goes far beyond mere technicalities. It reflects a difference between how AI systems process language and how legal meaning is constituted within institutional settings. A closer look at how AI systems process language helps explain this tension.

Probabilistic Processing in Legal Contexts

To understand why legal equivalence becomes difficult under AI systems, some attention must first be given to what these systems actually do. Neural machine translation and large language models operate probabilistically. Instead of genuinely interpreting language within a legal or institutional framework, these models simply spot patterns in massive datasets to guess the next likely word. Such dynamics reflect statistical natural language processing, shifting focus from true comprehension toward a probabilistic matrix governed by distributional regularities (Manning & Schütze, 1999). Neural approaches extended this logic by improving how systems generalize across related linguistic patterns, yet the underlying mechanism remains probabilistic rather than semantic (Bengio et al., 2003). On the ground, this usually yields text that reads well and looks ready for immediate use. Sometimes impressively so. Yet, fluency should not be mistaken for actual legal comprehension. Though AI excels at mapping linguistic patterns, models lack insight into the core intent behind specific legal phrasing, the institutional contexts driving meaning, and the actual functions those formulations must perform.

Legal meaning operates differently. Dworkin (1986) explicitly counters viewing legal interpretation through statistical regularities, arguing instead that it flows from foundational principles, institutional purposes, and genuine statutory intent. A legal provision means what it means not simply because certain words appear together with frequency, but because those words were selected to produce a particular legal effect within a defined institutional setting. Some legal formulations are intentionally open-ended. Endicott (2000) explains that legal standards such as *reasonable* or *undue* are often intentionally open-ended rather than imprecise, leaving room for interpretation within institutional and judicial contexts. In these scenarios, meaning and context are effectively locked together. This echoes Searle's (1969) view on institutional language, where he argues that linguistic form alone is never enough; meaning is inherently tied to the conditions that make an utterance valid and authoritative in the first place.This creates a mismatch that is easy to overlook: AI systems work through probabilistic patterns, whereas legal discourse depends on interpretation, institutional authority, and deliberate legal choices. As a result, legal translations that appear linguistically successful may still struggle to preserve legal meaning in ways that are not immediately visible.

The Illusion of Accuracy

The gap between statistical processing and true legal interpretation creates an unforeseen risk. On the surface, an AI-generated legal translation might look perfectly credible, yet underneath, it can quietly warp the intended legal meaning. This chapter refers to this problem as the *illusion of accuracy*. Fluency and legal accuracy are not the same thing. Neural systems prioritize smooth, natural-sounding outputs, whereas legal translation uniquely requires preserving statutory authority, interpretive parameters, and institutional functions. This gap highlights a known blind spot in machine translation evaluation: as Martindale and Carpuat (2018) point out, highly fluent outputs frequently trick readers into looking past underlying inaccuracies. Evidence from legal translation points in the same direction: Quinci and Pontrandolfo (2023) found that NMT outputs could achieve acceptable fluency while their main errors remained concentrated in legal terminology and semantic accuracy. More recent evaluations of large language models confirm a similar pattern: even when systems such as GPT-4o are applied to semantically dense, culturally specific texts, outputs may appear fluent and contextually appropriate while still exhibiting forms of semantic reduction and cultural simplification (Wang et al., 2026). This is why fluency alone serves as a deceptive gauge for legal accuracy, since a text can sound flawlessly professional while remaining deeply flawed under the surface.

This problem becomes especially visible in modality. Legal meaning often depends on precise wording and carefully calibrated lexical distinctions rather than general semantic approximation (Coulthard & Johnson, 2007). In legal drafting, selecting "shall" over "may" constitutes a normative directive rather than a stylistic preference, as the former enforces strict obligation whereas the latter confers discretionary authority. Replacing one with the other may produce fluent and readable text, but its legal implications are no longer equivalent. Courts routinely interpret legal language through precisely such distinctions (Solan, 1993). The problem is not always obvious mistranslation; more often, it appears as small shifts in legal effect that become visible only when interpretation, dispute, or enforcement is required. Dahl et al. (2024) make a related point in their work on legal hallucinations, showing that fluent legal outputs may remain inconsistent with legal facts or fail to correct legally incorrect assumptions. The appearance of accuracy is therefore not the same as legal adequacy.

Transforming Legal Discourse

Once legal language passes through AI-mediated translation, the concern is no longer limited to whether particular words have been translated correctly. The broader issue is what happens to the structure of legal discourse itself. Features discussed earlier, including density, ambiguity, and modality, may be reshaped through processes of simplification and normalization, tendencies increasingly observed in machine-translated texts (Niu & Jiang, 2024). Linguistic complexity that supports legal precision may be reduced, while formulations that leave room for interpretation may become narrower or more determinate. Such shifts can make translated texts appear clearer and easier to process. They may also alter the interpretive safeguards embedded in the source text. Contextually, stylistic alterations designed to enhance linguistic readability often directly compromise the necessary legal precision within translated texts.

A related issue concerns modality and the organization of legal relations. Legal discourse often depends on distinctions that structure obligation, permission, restriction, and discretion, and even subtle linguistic adjustments may affect how these relations are understood. Similar tendencies toward normalization have long been observed in translated texts, where translated language may become less marked or more conventional than the source (Bhatia, 1983; Volansky et al., 2015). In legal translation, however, such normalization carries different implications. AI-mediated systems may do more than transfer legal discourse across languages; they may also reshape some of the linguistic conditions through which legal meaning is organized.

Legal Authority and Institutional Risk

Ultimately, these transformations reshape more than just translation quality, striking at the very heart of legal authority and institutional trust. An AI-generated text can easily mask its flaws behind a polished, highly professional exterior, even as it quietly alters the underlying legal meaning. This becomes dangerous in a field where institutions rely less on rigid rule-following and far more on absolute confidence in the stability of their texts. When legal professionals, translators, or institutions begin to rely on AI-assisted outputs that appear reliable but remain difficult to verify, the risk is not simply error but misplaced confidence (Wachter et al., 2024). A text may look legally sound and still carry distortions that are difficult to notice without careful scrutiny. Conversely, actual legal reasoning remains deeply anchored in interpretative practices, precedent, and institutional understanding. These human elements go far beyond the mere pattern-matching logic that AI models use to produce text, as Ashley (2017) points out. This view is further supported by recent research in courtroom translation, where professional legal translators themselves report that translation decisions involve complex interpretive judgements shaped by institutional expectations, stakeholder interactions, and contextual considerations that extend beyond lexical substitution (Wu et al., 2026a).

A further concern lies in opacity. As Pasquale (2015) observes, algorithmic systems essentially operate as "black boxes." They turn out results while keeping the underlying logic, assumptions, and decision-making processes completely hidden from view. In legal translation, this creates a practical difficulty: it may be unclear not only how a translation was produced, but whether legally consequential distinctions have been preserved at all. The cumulative effect is subtle rather than dramatic. Small shifts in wording, modality, or interpretive scope may gradually shape legal understanding in ways that are not immediately visible yet still matter in practice. Broadly, these interconnected issues drive home the core argument of this chapter. Rather than performing static cross-linguistic transfers, AI applications in legal translation inherently reconstruct the foundational architecture of the surrounding legal discourse. The following section turns to a framework designed to identify and assess such transformations.

Theoretical Framework: Bridging the Micro–Macro Gap in Legal Translation

The current trajectory of legal translation is increasingly defined by pervasive technological mediation, underscoring the need for a revised theoretical approach. As Koehn (2020) observed regarding the shift toward neural machine translation (NMT), the rapid evolution of generative architectures fundamentally challenges traditional concepts of translator competency and drafting precision.

While these automated tools have accelerated production speeds, they have simultaneously created a competence gap: surface-level linguistic fluency frequently masks a loss of specialized legal accuracy (Wagner & Marusek, 2025) . This tension reflects a broader systemic issue within the discipline. As Bhatia (1983) suggests regarding the struggle between textual reduction and the preservation of functional integrity, the field is experiencing a technological turn that lacks a corresponding discursive turn. Consequently, despite the growing integration of machine learning applications in law (Surden, 2014), practitioners continue to face persistent difficulties in maintaining the integrity of culturally embedded legal concepts (Šarčević, 1997) alongside a lack of robust frameworks to evaluate these automated outputs.

In order to overcome these analytical constraints, artificial intelligence must be viewed as an active discursive actor that radically rewrites legal content rather than as a passive medium for language transfer. Because they disregard the complex reality of institutional power dynamics and the strict, formulaic restrictions of legal wording, traditional equivalency-based models are simply unable to follow this algorithmic reconstruction (Biel, 2014; Giampieri, 2025). By combining Systemic Functional Linguistics (SFL) with Critical Discourse Analysis (CDA), this work purposefully transcends static ideas of textual symmetry. By combining these two viewpoints, the exact theoretical framework required to bridge van Dijk's (2015) macro–micro split is established, drawing a clear connection between the macroscopic decline of institutional authority and tiny machine-learning decisions.

The Micro-Level: SFL, Modality, and the Mechanics of Choice

Systemic Functional Linguistics (SFL) offers a comprehensive framework for perceiving language not as a static collection of rules, but as a dynamic resource for making meaning (Halliday & Matthiessen, 2014). This framework is particularly well-suited for analyzing AI-mediated translation because it rejects the assumption of neutral lexical substitution; instead, it treats every clause as a series of functional choices within a complex system network (Fontaine, 2013). In legal discourse, the interpersonal metafunction is paramount, as it governs how a text establishes authority, actualizes social connections, and allocates obligations through conscious linguistic positioning (Bhatia, 1993; Hyland, 2005).

Modality is the main force behind this interpersonal metafunction. Within the rigorous constraints of legal drafting, the specific calibration of modal markers the distinct boundary between deontic obligation (e.g., "is required to") and epistemic possibility (e.g., "is entitled to") effectively dictates the legal force of a given clause (Tiersma, 1999). This systematic precision is frequently destabilized under algorithmic mediation. As Garzone (2001) demonstrates in her analysis of deontic modality, the performative force of legal discourse relies on precise modal anchors that are easily compromised during automated processing. These algorithms' opaque, "black box" characteristics frequently result in linguistic attrition, when the subtle differences necessary in high-stakes situations are lost (Pasquale, 2015). This failure typically manifests as a simplification of the text (Bhatia, 1983), characterized by a partial loss of the functional redundancy that human drafters rely on to ensure absolute interpretive stability (Šarčević, 1997).

Within the SFL framework, what an algorithm might interpret as redundancy is actually a deliberate structural safeguard engineered to forestall interpretive instability (Šarčević, 1997). Because modern neural architectures rely on probabilistic token prediction a process that inherently favors high-frequency linguistic patterns over the specialized, low-frequency precision needed in legal drafting these systems often strip the discourse of its vital functional layers (Koehn, 2020). This phenomenon extends beyond mere stylistic oversight; as Pasquale (2015) contends, such micro-level erosion of precision introduces a structural risk within the black box of algorithmic mediation. These failures can escalate into profound judicial challenges, potentially compromising the clarity and fairness required within international legal frameworks a concern that echoes Surden's (2014) warnings about the limitations of applying machine learning to the open texture of law.

The utilization of SFL in AI-mediated translation is fundamentally anchored in the framework's capacity for interdisciplinary application. By conceptualizing SFL principles as a diagnostic instrument, researchers can move beyond traditional error analysis to evaluate how automated outputs function as performative acts within the legal field (Austin, 1962). This approach facilitates the assessment of machine learning outputs as active participants within a specialized community of practice, where the validity of a translation is determined not by literal word-for-word accuracy, but by its functional fit within a specific institutional setting (Bhatia, 1983; Šarčević, 1997). In this context, the machine's output must be scrutinized for its ability to maintain the deontic logic and normative force required for professional legal communication (von Wright, 1951).

Recent academic discourse argues that although artificial intelligence may attain high degrees of statistical accuracy, it fundamentally lacks the discursive competence essential for navigating high-stakes legal environments. By rendering the systemic functional model visible within the analysis of machine-generated outputs, this study demonstrates that the perceived impermeable nature of legal discourse is a complex web of lexicogrammatical selections. The machine's recurrent inability to traverse these networks—frequently sacrificing the strategic ambiguity necessary for judicial flexibility (Šarčević, 1997) in favor of the probabilistic simplification identified by Bhatia (1983) underscores a profound deficiency in systemic awareness. Thus, as legal discourse transitions from human-centric drafting to AI-assisted reconstruction, it becomes imperative to examine these micro-level choices through the lens of deontic modality (Garzone, 2001) to ensure they do not undermine the institutional authority and interpretive integrity they are designed to uphold (Dworkin, 1986).

The Macro-Level: CDA, Power, and Algorithmic Authority

While SFL offers the tools necessary to evaluate micro-linguistic shifts, Critical Discourse Analysis (CDA) provides the framework to assess their broader institutional and societal implications. At this macro-level, translation is understood as a context-dependent act of cultural and ideological negotiation (Tabrizi & House, 2025). Within the juridical field, language operates as a primary medium of symbolic authority (Bourdieu, 1987); consequently, any systematic alteration of linguistic choices signifies a fundamental shift in institutional power dynamics.

As legal drafting increasingly intersects with algorithmic frameworks, the discourses that underpin societal governance are no longer exclusively the product of legislative deliberation. Instead, legal meaning is shaped by the technical architecture of artificial intelligence platforms, showing how digital structures now function as sites of institutional discourse (Breeze, 2021; Foucault, 1972). This shift introduces a technocratic prioritization of market efficiency and speed over the preservation of procedural rights and liberties (Svitych, 2026). From a Faircloughian (1989) perspective, this linguistic simplification is not a neutral technical byproduct but a form of ideological work. It obscures the technocratic redirection of legal power by presenting computational efficiency as a legitimate replacement for democratic responsibility.

By extension, when a machine misinterprets a legal modal, it alters the performative force of the law itself (Austin, 1962). The broader consequences of such discursive framing are well-documented in recent CDA scholarship, which demonstrates how structural inequalities are reinforced through the strategic exclusion of marginalized narratives in public sectors. By utilizing Fairclough's (1989) three-dimensional framework—moving from microstructural word choices to macrostructural institutional relationships—it becomes clear that AI-mediated legal translation operates as a powerful mechanism with the capacity to either preserve or suppress public rights. If algorithmic engines continue to prioritize market-driven fluency over the normative sensitivity required for social justice (Šarčević, 1997), the resulting legal discourse risks reflecting the geographical and economic marginalization found in other public domains. Ultimately, bridging the micro–macro gap reveals that legal translation in the digital age is an active struggle for symbolic capital (Bourdieu, 1987). It represents a critical site for defending institutional legitimacy, ensuring that technology does not produce a thinner, less accessible version of justice

Discursive Synthesis: Mapping Micro-Level Selections to Macro-Level Authority

The micro-level linguistic selections observed through Systemic Functional Linguistics (SFL) align directly with Prieto Ramos's (2011) taxonomy of legal translation competence. Prieto Ramos establishes that professional translation expertise requires more than semantic decoding; it demands a comprehensive understanding of how minor lexicogrammatical changes influence the overarching legal objective within a specific institutional framework. This integrated competence operates as a bridge between textual mechanics and systemic application. It requires the translator to maintain a specialized cognizance of how micro-level modal choices function within the macro-level constraints of a given legal system. When automated translation platforms process these texts, they regularly overlook this required "textual fit," thereby jeopardizing the institutional legitimacy of the target text (Šarčević, 1997). Because large language models are engineered to map statistical frequencies rather than comprehend legal intent, their processing mechanics frequently disrupt the delicate linguistic balance used to establish statutory mandates, particularly when handling the complex distribution of permissions and prohibitions (Garzone, 2001; von Wright, 1951).

By synthesizing SFL and CDA within the AI–Legal Discourse Transformation Model (ALDTM), this study demonstrates that these automated linguistic transformations are never ideologically neutral. As Fairclough (1989) emphasizes, textual characteristics serve as the directly observable markers of broader social, political, and institutional practices. Within the domain of algorithmic mediation, the systematic "flattening" of intricate syntactical structures or the forced resolution of strategic ambiguities constitutes an inadvertent exercise of discursive authority. Strategic ambiguity and linguistic indeterminacy are not structural flaws; rather, as Silk (2019) observes, they are essential characteristics that reflect the dual nature of law, balancing rigid rules with situational fairness.

Automated systems often perform an unprompted "correction" of this necessary vagueness because algorithmic logic lacks the pragmatic intuition required to distinguish between a drafting error and an intentional choice designed for judicial discretion. By prioritizing high-probability statistical meanings over these open-textured nuances, the machine risks stripping the legal text of the flexibility required for equitable application, directly compromising what Dworkin (1986) terms the "interpretive integrity" of the legal order. Dworkin contends that law must speak with a single, coherent moral voice; when an algorithm randomly alters modal values based on data frequency, it fractures this coherence.

Consequently, explicitly correlating these micro-level choices to macro-level governance structures is crucial for unpacking the opaque reasoning inherent in modern artificial intelligence architectures (Pasquale, 2015). Without this deliberate discursive synthesis, the "illusion of accuracy" identified by Bhatia (1983) and Tiersma (1999) continues to prevail. This illusion presents a highly fluent, grammatically flawless surface text that effectively conceals the significant ways in which automated reconstruction modifies the performative efficacy, legal validity, and systemic accessibility of legal discourse.

Proposed Theoretical Framework: The AI–Legal Discourse Transformation Model (ALDTM)

This section transitions from a theoretical critique of automated processes to the formal presentation of an analytical model. While Section 4 outlined the conceptual conflicts between linguistic selection and institutional authority, the AI–Legal Discourse Transformation Model (ALDTM) offers a structured operational framework to monitor and evaluate the alteration of legal meaning as it undergoes algorithmic mediation. This model does not operate merely as an error analysis tool for spotting typos or translation mistakes; instead, it serves as a functional-discursive framework aimed at describing how legal authority is actively reconstructed during the deployment of Large Language Models (LLMs). The development of the ALDTM is necessitated by the deep-seated limitations of existing evaluation metrics like BLEU or METEOR, which prioritize surface-level linguistic fluency and n-gram overlap over functional accuracy and contextual fit. As Šarčević (1997) observes, the communicative competence required in professional legal settings involves significantly more than generating grammatically flawless sentences; it requires an acute awareness of the legal effects triggered by specific lexical choices. By centering the model on three distinct layers of transformation—Input, Processing, and Output—the ALDTM seeks to expose the underlying calculations within the computational "black box" (Pasquale, 2015), revealing how mathematical probability often clashes with the rigorous demands of deontic logic (von Wright, 1951) and the open texture of statutory rules (Surden, 2014).

Furthermore, this model responds directly to the macro–micro gap identified by van Dijk (2015). It assumes that micro-level drifts in modality and structural ambiguity are not isolated technical glitches or minor code errors, but are, in fact, the precise mechanisms through which the broader institutional legitimacy of law is reshaped and challenged (Svitych, 2026). By providing a granular analysis of these shifting layers, this framework offers a practical diagnostic instrument for legal practitioners, translators, and scholars to evaluate whether automated outputs are fit for purpose within their specific institutional contexts (Bhatia, 1993). Ultimately, the ALDTM serves as a methodological roadmap to ensure that integrating artificial intelligence into legal workflows does not lead to a silent thinning of substantive justice, but rather encourages a more transparent, predictable, and discursively responsible drafting process.

An accurate apprehending of grammatical structure is essential to understand the structural changes that take place all through algorithmic processing. As Biber et al. (2025) elucidate in their assessment of structural evaluation frameworks, the quantification of syntactic density and grammatical complexity necessitates methodologies that extend beyond superficial sentence structures. Within the ALDTM framework, this understanding underscores a significant vulnerability in AI translation systems: when algorithms prioritize superficial fluency, they undermine the intricate syntactic dependencies and dense clausal relationships that encode legal authority within a text. By neglecting to replicate the complex grammatical frameworks delineated by contemporary corpus linguistics (Biber et al., 2025), generative outputs inevitably condense the intricate syntactic layer requisite for accurate jurisprudential interpretation.

Layer 1: The Input – Linguistic Archetypes and Legal Force

In the ALDTM framework, the initial layer involves identifying and cataloging the human-authored source text's specific linguistic archetypes. As established by Halliday and Matthiessen (2014), legal discourse is characterized by an exceptionally high density of interpersonal structural features. These choices function as performative utterances that do not simply describe the world, but actively create, alter, or terminate legal realities and social relationships (Austin, 1962). Within this foundational input layer, two primary variables must be isolated and evaluated: modality calibration and strategic ambiguity.

Modality calibration serves as the central structural component of the input phase. The use of deontic markers such as shall, must, may, or should in statutory and contractual prose is never a matter of stylistic variation or accidental selection; rather, it is a precise exercise in the distribution of rights, permissions, and obligations across legal subjects (Tiersma, 1999). Within the ALDTM, these markers are split following von Wright's (1951) structural logic:

1 **Deontic Necessity:** High-value modal anchors (e.g., shall, is required to) establish rigid, non-negotiable obligations that leave no room for administrative or judicial discretion (Garzone, 2001).

2 **Deontic Possibility:** Low-value modal markers (e.g., may, is entitled to) explicitly grant a discretionary power, a privilege, or a conditional permission (Garzone, 2001).

We refer to these specialized configurations in the ALDTM as stability anchors. The entire legal validity and binding force of the subsequent translation is jeopardized if these anchors are not identified as high-priority tokens during the initial input phase.

Concurrently, the second core pillar in Layer 1 is strategic ambiguity. In direct opposition to the common assumption that legal language must always be absolute and unambiguous, human drafters frequently utilize what Hart and Surden (2014) refer to as the "open texture of law" to preserve room for future judicial flexibility and contextual interpretation (Šarčević, 1997). In practice, this drafting strategy intentionally embeds elastic terms like *reasonable*, *due diligence*, *satisfactory*, or *adequate* directly into the text. Rather than projecting fixed definitions, these open-ended qualifiers are hardcoded into the legal document specifically to allow for narrow, highly contextualized interpretation based on real-time situational developments.

The ALDTM framework treats such structural ambiguity not as an instance of poor drafting, but as a deliberate and necessary legal instrument. A clause mandating that property remediation occur within a "reasonable time" provides a perfect illustration. This language establishes a flexible boundary, allowing tribunals or courts to evaluate compliance dynamically when unpredictable events such as material shortages, labor disruptions, or unseasonable weather alter performance conditions.

The primary challenge for artificial intelligence architectures, as noted by (Lam et al., 2025) is that these intricate, calculated textual gaps are often the first elements modified or erased during automated translation. Because large language models rely on mathematical probability rather than pragmatic situational awareness, they naturally favor literal or high-frequency linguistic patterns. This bias often causes the machine to "correct" or simplify a strategic ambiguity into a fixed, rigid value—such as arbitrarily defining a "reasonable time" as a static window of thirty days. Therefore, Layer 1 serves as the essential baseline for the audit process: it documents the original intertextual and pragmatic complexity, capturing the deliberate gaps designed by human drafters so that the underlying legal strategy can be monitored before it faces algorithmic flattening (Lam et al., 2025).

Layer 2: The Processing – Algorithmic Intervention and the Computational Box

The transition from Layer 1 to Layer 2 marks the critical phase where human-authored normative intent meets the mathematical logic of algorithmic intervention. In this processing layer of the ALDTM, legal discourse ceases to function as an active system of purposeful social meaning; instead, it is disassembled and converted into numerical vectors within a multi-dimensional semantic space.

The core conflict within Layer 2 stems from the fundamental divergence between human legal reasoning and the probabilistic token prediction inherent in the Transformer architecture that powers modern Large Language Models (LLMs). While a professional legal drafter carefully selects a specific lexical marker to secure a long-term legal obligation, the algorithm operates on a purely statistical plane (Ameen et al., 2026). It calculates the likelihood of a specific token appearing based on distributional patterns found across massive, highly generalized training datasets. This structural shift from meaning-based drafting to probability-based generation frequently causes a distinct phenomenon that this model defines as algorithmic flattening.

This flattening process becomes highly problematic when the machine encounters low-frequency legal precision. In professional drafting, the most legally significant terms are often rare, archaic, or highly specific formulaic strings, chosen deliberately because their historical interpretations remain exceptionally stable within the courts. As Lam et al.(2025) noted, neural networks naturally accord greater mathematical weight to high-frequency tokens to maximize the statistical fluency and general "smoothness" of the output. Consequently, during the processing phase, the algorithm may inadvertently replace a highly specific Latinate term or a specialized boilerplate expression with a common conversational synonym. While this adjustments makes the target text much easier for a general audience to read, it simultaneously dilutes its illocutionary force, directly compromising the performative capacity of the language (Austin, 1962).

Furthermore, the processing layer introduces a systemic bias toward normative standardization, where the specialized, dense structures of legal prose are optimized to align with general linguistic averages. Within the SFL framework, what a human practitioner utilizes as functional redundancy—the deliberate repetition of specific terms or structural patterns to prevent any potential misinterpretation (Šarčević, 1997)—is misinterpreted by the algorithm as a stylistic inefficiency or a redundant error. By cleaning the text of these perceived redundancies to prioritize conversational clarity, the machine unintentionally dismantles the structural safeguards engineered to withstand high-stakes courtroom scrutiny.

This processing mechanism creates a dangerous veneer of accuracy. The resulting text may appear professional, highly fluent, and completely coherent to an untrained reader, yet it lacks the underlying normative sensitivity and precise textual fit required to maintain statutory certainty. This hidden loss of precise deontic modality means that while the output functions perfectly as a piece of general writing, it no longer carries the specific binding force needed to uphold the original legal intent (Garzone, 2001). Ultimately, by converting situational legal strategy into mathematical weights, the processing layer acts as a de-contextualizing filter that erases the pragmatic history of the document, leading directly to the semantic simplification that characterizes many contemporary AI-mediated legal outputs (Lam et al., 2025).

Layer 3: The Output – Transformed Discourse and the Displacement of Authority

The final layer of the ALDTM evaluates the transformed discourse that emerges from the processing phase, tracking its specific socio-legal consequences within the target environment. Even when an algorithmic system produces a target text that achieves exceptional scores on standard linguistic fluency metrics, Layer 3 shifts the analytical focus to a more critical structural issue: the systematic displacement of authority. This phenomenon occurs when interpretive and regulatory power is subtly transferred away from the human legislator, drafter, or practitioner and reallocated to the technical architecture and training biases of the AI platform.

This displacement manifests primarily as modality drift. When the precise, low-frequency deontic calibrations identified in Layer 1 are altered by the probabilistic calculations of Layer 2, the performative capacity of the law is compromised. As Austin (1962) notes regarding the mechanics of illocutionary force, a performative utterance relies entirely on its conventional structure to enact a legal reality. When an algorithm accidentally downgrades a mandatory duty to a descriptive or discretionary statement, it affects the binding force of the text. This is not a minor translation error; it is a structural reconfiguration that introduces what can be described as a thinner version of justice, characterized by a lack of the discursive competence and interpretive integrity required to sustain statutory authority (Dworkin, 1986).

The resulting output may appear flawless to a non-specialist reviewer, but it frequently lacks the normative sensitivity required to navigate high-stakes legal environments. As Lam et al.(2025) highlight, the regular misinterpretation of intricate terminology in machine-generated documentation creates a systemic risk where the broader "regime of truth" (Foucault, 1972) is dictated by statistical token frequency rather than democratic deliberation or legislative intent. This trend signifies a shift toward a technocratic jurisprudence, where the operational efficiency and speed of the automated process take precedence over the careful protection of substantive legal rights.

Finally, Layer 3 presupposes that AI-mediated legal translation acts as a indirect site for the redistribution of symbolic capital (Bourdieu, 1987). By favoring market-driven fluency and standardized accessibility over specialized precision, the transformed discourse risks creating an illusion of accuracy that conceals a genuine loss of regulatory power. If the algorithmic engine continues to prioritize statistical probability over the situational precision required for social justice, the legal output risks becoming a tool for automated policy legitimation rather than a medium for judicial protection. Thus, the ALDTM concludes that the validity of an AI-mediated translation cannot be measured by surface-level clarity; it must instead be assessed by its capacity to maintain the functional integrity and institutional authority of the law within its specific socio-political context.

To operationalize these theoretical shifts across all three dimensions, the AI–Legal Discourse Transformation Model (ALDTM) is synthesized into a formal analytical matrix. As illustrated in Table 1, the framework maps the mechanical transition from human normative intent to algorithmic reconstruction, highlighting the specific discursive risks associated with each phase of the transformation.

Table 1. Cross-layer alignment matrix of algorithmic discourse transformation

Analysis Level	Layer 1: Micro-Linguistic Variables	Layer 2: Mathematical Intervention Elements	Layer 3: Macro-Societal Implications
Operational Focus	Deontic Modality, Lexical Precision, Syntactic Structures	Tokenization Bias, Temperature Settings, Prediction Probability Vectors	Jurisdictional Validity, Institutional Trust, Structural Accountability
Systemic Risk Factor	Semantic Flattening (e.g., converting “shall” to “is” or “may”)	Elimination of Strategic Ambiguity via Fluidity Optimization	Erosion of Enforceability in International Commercial Arbitration
Theoretical Anchor	Halliday and Matthiessen (2014)	(Lam et al., 2025).	Fairclough (1989); Biber (2024)

This conceptual matrix maps the trajectory from fine-grained linguistic modifications to automated processing filters, concluding with the broader erosion of institutional validity. The underlying structural taxonomy scales from the systemic functional linguistic models of Halliday and Matthiessen (2014) to the contemporary algorithmic failure points identified by Lam et al. (2025).

Operationalizing the ALDTM: A Discursive Audit of Algorithmic Translation

In this section, the AI–Legal Discourse Transformation Model (ALDTM) is implemented through a case study that examines a conventional contractual clause. While standard evaluation metrics often prioritize surface-level fluency, this audit demonstrates how algorithmic mediation can lead to a “discursive drift” that alters the legal force of a text. By scrutinizing a translation from English to Arabic, we can discern how the model finds transformations of intent, processing, and the final output.

Layer 1: The Input (Normative Intent)

Source Text (English): *The Licensee shall not disclose any Confidential Information to third parties.*

Explanation: The input layer signifies the original legal objective articulated by the human drafter. In this context, the employment of "is prohibited from" is a judicious choice of a high-value modal. As mentioned by Garzone (2001), this choice establishes a stringent deontic necessity, thereby instituting a compulsory prohibition that is integral to the performative essence of a confidentiality agreement. The normative intent is to create a binding legal constraint, not a factual description.

Layer 2: The Processing (Algorithmic Mediation)

The Transformation: The AI system identifies "shall not" as a high-frequency token but optimizes for statistical "smoothness."

Explanation: During the processing stage, the "Black Box" mechanism (Pasquale, 2015) prioritizes distributional frequency over the specialized logic of legal linguistics. Instead of treating the modal as a command, the algorithm may interpret it as a factual statement. It substitutes the mandatory "shall" with a descriptive present tense in Arabic, reflecting what Koehn (2020) describes as the probabilistic nature of neural architectures (see Figure 1).

Figure 1. Targeted prompting for fluency optimization in AI legal translation

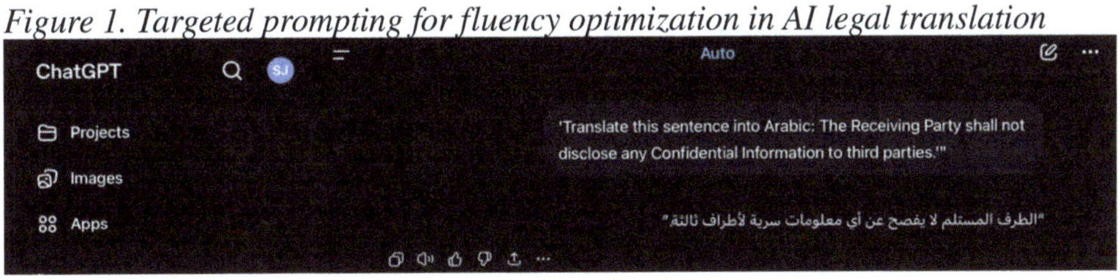

This figure captures the transformation of the English mandatory "shall not" into a descriptive Arabic indicative form (la yafsah). This demonstrates the "flattening" effect where algorithmic mediation prioritizes general readability over legal normative intent.

Layer 3: The Output (Discursive Result)

The final layer represents the actual text produced by the algorithmic system, which, in this case study, reveals a distinct "discursive drift" from the original normative intent. As evidenced in the output captured in Figure 1, while the Arabic sentence is grammatically correct and highly fluent, it fails the test of functional fidelity (Šarčević, 1997). By utilizing the indicative mood (la yafsah), the output shifts the discourse from a mandatory legal prohibition to a mere description of behavior.

This flattening of the text creates what Bhatia (1983) and Tiersma (1999) describe as an "illusion of accuracy" a surface-level clarity that bury the loss of performative efficacy. Effectively, the AI has exercised an inadvertent discursive authority by granting the legal subject a degree of discretion that was never authorized in the source text. Consequently, this layer confirms that without the oversight of the ALDTM, the transformation of legal meaning remains invisible, potentially compromising the "interpretive integrity" (Dworkin, 1986) of the entire legal framework.

Case Study 1: Strategic Ambiguity in Commercial Risk Allocation

To verify the model's analytical breadth across different legal genres, a second audit is applied to a standard risk-mitigation clause within a commercial supplier agreement. This case study demonstrates how algorithmic processing addresses calculated contractual indeterminacy.

Layer 1: The Input (Normative Intent)

Source Text (English): "The Supplier shall use all reasonable endeavors to minimize operational delays."

Analysis: The human drafter balances a strict deontic command (shall) with an open-textured qualification (reasonable endeavors). In commercial practice, this phrase represents a calculated strategic ambiguity (Šarčević, 1997). It establishes a flexible standard of effort rather than an absolute guarantee of success, allowing future arbitrators to evaluate performance contextually based on market disruptions or supply chain constraints.

Layer 2: The Processing (Algorithmic Mediation)

The Transformation: The Transformer architecture projects these terms into vector spaces that prioritize high-frequency distributional averages over low-frequency contextual nuances (Koehn, 2020).

Analysis: Because large language models optimize for statistical smoothness, they struggle with phrases designed specifically for legal elasticity. The system attempts to resolve the open texture by substituting a high-frequency, literal synonym in Arabic meaning “to take all necessary measures” (اتخاذ كافة التدابير اللازمة / ittikhādh kāffat al-tadābīr al-lāzimah).

Layer 3: The Output (Discursive Result)

Analysis: While the Arabic target text is highly fluent, it introduces an unnegotiated shift in legal liability. By flattening “reasonable endeavors” into “necessary measures” (التدابير اللازمة), the AI converts a flexible obligation of effort into a strict obligation of result. This concrete drift strips the supplier of their contractual safety valve, proving that algorithmic flattening systematically targets open-textured language and reallocates commercial liability without human consent.

DISCUSSION

The synthesis provided in the ALDTM matrix (see Table 1) demonstrates that the transformation of legal discourse is more than a simple, linear loss of meaning. Instead, it represents a structural, multidimensional reconfiguration of institutional authority. Utilizing this three-layer diagnostic technique allows researchers and legal professionals to look past the surface-level fluency that typically misleads standard AI evaluation examinations. The analysis points out ongoing tension between the efficiency of algorithms and the effectiveness of legal systems, often leading to a decrease in statutory certainty for the sake of computational optimization. While Layer 2 (Processing) provides the technical explanation for linguistic flattening through probabilistic prediction and statistical smoothing, Layer 3 (Output) identifies the eventual dilution of legal force and symbolic capital.This matrix serves as a crucial diagnostic tool, allowing scholars to pinpoint exactly where the sequence of legal meaning is interrupted. Whether the failure occurs at the stage of input miscalibration where human intent is not properly codified for the machine—or through the systemic displacement of authority during algorithmic output, the final consequence remains identical: the performative power of the legal framework is compromised. This analysis demonstrates that automating the simplification of legal language is inherently a politically charged process. As the case study illustrates, the shift from the mandatory jussive or imperative moods to the descriptive indicative mood in Arabic represents more than a minor grammatical change; it represents a direct reallocation of power. When a strict prohibition is transformed into a factual description, the legal subject is inadvertently granted a degree of interpretive freedom that undermines the statutory certainty of the law. This finding reinforces the necessity of the ALDTM as a functional tool for discursive auditing, ensuring that the transition from human-led to machine-mediated legal practice does not result in the silent hollowing out of binding legal obligations. The structural necessity of this new model stems from a significant theoretical divide in current evaluation paradigms. Conventional frameworks for legal translation, like those developed by Šarčević (1997) and Prieto Ramos (2011), concentrate solely on human cognitive abilities. They assume translation is a conscious, meaning-driven act of cultural negotiation. Consequently, these human-centric models cannot anticipate or diagnose the automated patterns of algorithmic flattening because they lack a structural interface to track the mathematical mechanics behind probabilistic token prediction. Thus, solely quantitative computational metrics such as BLEU, METEOR, or COMET suffer from the opposite limitation. These metrics assess the quality of machine translation by comparing literal n-gram overlap or semantic vector distance with a human-generated reference text. While effective for general text types, they are entirely blind to deontic logic and normative institutional force. A target sentence where a strict legal command is reduced to a plain descriptive statement is still rewarded with a high accuracy score by a computational metric because the remaining vocabulary tokens match. The ALDTM is unique precisely because it functions as a hybrid, functional-discursive diagnostic framework. It fills the gap between technical token processing and macro-level institutional sociology, by integrating Systemic Functional Linguistics (SFL) and Critical Discourse Analysis (CDA). Rather than treating machine translation errors as random human-like slips, the ALDTM recognizes them as predictable outcomes of statistical data optimization, offering an actionable audit track to protect the interpretive integrity of international legal frameworks.

The implementation of the AI–Legal Discourse Transformation Model (ALDTM) highlights a critical need for a paradigm shift in how artificial intelligence is integrated into the legal profession. To alleviate the risks of "algorithmic flattening" and "modality drift," the following solutions and research trajectories are proposed. Furthermore, to maintain the "interpretive integrity" of legal frameworks, practitioners must progress toward a comprehensive "Human-in-the-loop" (HITL) framework. Operationally, the ALDTM serves as a practical diagnostic audit tool to trace these shifts. Legal translators and drafters should employ what Prieto Ramos (2011) refers to as "integrative competence" the capacity to understand how micro-linguistic changes affect macro-legal goals instead of serving as passive proofreaders of AI output. It is advised that legal practitioners use the ALDTM matrix to keep an eye on "high-stakes" language anchors such strategic ambiguity and deontic modals (shall, must, may). Practitioners can make sure that the machine's need for statistical fluency does not take precedence over the document's normative power by conducting a discursive audit prior to finalization. This human-centered intervention serves as an essential filter, identifying the "invisible" changes that are often missed by conventional automated measurements.

A viable solution involves the advancement of Prompt Engineering for legal contexts. Practitioners should integrate "deontic safeguards" into prompts to enhance specificity. This means instructing the AI to put practical accuracy ahead of aesthetic simplicity.

Prompts must be designed to maintain essential modal values and legal syntactical complexities. By conditioning the algorithm to honor the source text's institutional authority, the risk of unintended discursive power from the AI is notably mitigated.

Future Research Directions: Sub-Genres and Explainable AI (XAI)

Future research should empirically assess the ALDTM across various legal subgenres. While this chapter examines the overarching shifts in legal discourse, subsequent studies should explore algorithmic mediation's effects in specialized domains like Intellectual Property, Maritime Law, or International Arbitration, where textual fit and modality drift implications differ. Concurrently, the demand for transparent Explainable AI (XAI) frameworks has intensified. Ultimately, the ALDTM serves as a methodological roadmap to ensure that integrating artificial intelligence into legal workflows does not lead to a silent thinning of substantive justice, but rather encourages a more transparent, predictable, and discursively responsible drafting process. This imperative heavily mirrors the broader guidelines proposed by Amini et al. (2026) regarding the ethical use of generative AI in high-stakes writing. Their conceptual review highlights that preserving text integrity and preventing algorithmic misattribution are essential conditions for maintaining quality education, strict data accountability, and professional standards in automated settings.

CONCLUSION

This chapter has argued that AI systems used in legal translation do more than transfer meaning between languages. In many cases, they also reshape legal discourse, suggesting that the problem is not purely technical. Instead, it reflects a broader difference between the statistical approach used by AI systems and the interpretive character of legal discourse. Legal meaning is not incidental to linguistic form; it is embedded within the density, modal precision, strategic ambiguity, and institutional authority through which legal texts produce and enforce normative relations. Because AI systems rely on distributional patterns rather than normative principles, they often struggle to preserve the structure of legal meaning. In many cases, linguistic complexity is reduced and certain ambiguities disappear, making modal distinctions less clear. As a result, the output may appear fluent and reliable even when important aspects of legal effect have changed. This chapter conceptualized this dynamic as the illusion of accuracy: the production of texts that simulate equivalence while embedding legally consequential shifts that remain largely invisible to evaluation frameworks calibrated to measure surface-level correspondence rather than legal equivalence. In response to this problem, the chapter proposed the AI–Legal Discourse Transformation Model (ALDTM) as an integrated analytical framework capable of identifying and evaluating the transformations AI systems introduce into legal texts by bridging micro-level linguistic analysis with macro-level analysis of institutional authority. The significance of this analysis extends beyond translation quality itself. As AI systems become increasingly common in legal communication, they may gradually influence how legal language is interpreted within institutions. The field therefore requires not only more advanced AI systems, but more rigorous frameworks for understanding what AI systems do to legal discourse and why those transformations matter. Future research should seek to refine the ALDTM through empirical analysis of AI-translated legal corpora and through the development of legally calibrated evaluation standards capable of detecting the specific transformations identified in this chapter. The question is not whether AI will continue to transform legal translation practice it will. The question is whether legal institutions will develop the analytical capacity to recognize and govern that transformation responsibly.

ACKNOWLEDGMENT

In writing this chapter, Google Gemini and QuillBot were used for proofreading, grammar checking, and language editing of the final version of the manuscript.

REFERENCES

Ameen, K. S., Towfiq, T. A., Mousa, K. M., & Pooyanmehr, M. (2026). Judicial review of algorithmic administrative systems: Legality, evidence, and remedies in the smart city state. *Frontiers in Artificial Intelligence*, *9*, 1802986. Advance online publication. DOI: 10.3389/frai.2026.1802986 PMID: 42052213

Amini, M., Lee, K. F., Yiqiu, W., & Ravindran, L. (2026). Proposing a framework for ethical use of AI in academic writing based on a conceptual review: Implications for quality education. *Interactive Learning Environments*, *34*(3), 1394–1418. DOI: 10.1080/10494820.2025.2523382

Ashley, K. D. (2017). *Artificial intelligence and legal analytics: New tools for law practice in the digital age*. Cambridge University Press. DOI: 10.1017/9781316761380

Austin, J. L. (1962). *How to do things with words*. Clarendon Press.

Bahdanau, D., Cho, K., & Bengio, Y. (2015). Neural machine translation by jointly learning to align and translate. In *Proceedings of the 3rd International Conference on Learning Representations (ICLR 2015)*. https://arxiv.org/abs/1409.0473

Bengio, Y., Ducharme, R., Vincent, P., & Jauvin, C. (2003). A neural probabilistic language model. *Journal of Machine Learning Research*, *3*, 1137–1155. https://www.jmlr.org/papers/v3/bengio03a.html

Bhatia, V. K. (1983). Simplification vs. easification: The case of legal texts. *Applied Linguistics*, *4*(1), 42–54. DOI: 10.1093/applin/4.1.42

Bhatia, V. K. (1993). *Analysing genre: Language use in professional settings*. Longman.

Biber, D., Larsson, T., Hancock, G. R., Reppen, R., Staples, S., & Gray, B. (2025). Comparing theory-based models of grammatical complexity in student writing. *International Journal of Learner Corpus Research*, *11*(1), 145–177. DOI: 10.1075/ijlcr.23036.bib

Biel, Ł. (2014). The textual fit of translated EU law: A corpus-based study of deontic modality. *The Translator*, *20*(3), 332–355. DOI: 10.1080/13556509.2014.909675

Bourdieu, P. (1987). The force of law: Toward a sociology of the juridical field. *The Hastings Law Journal, 38*(5), 814–853. https://repository.uclawsf.edu/hastings_law_journal/vol38/iss5/3

Breeze, R. (2021). Translating the principles of good governance: In search of accountability in Spanish and German. *International Journal of Legal Discourse, 6*(1), 43–67. DOI: 10.1515/ijld-2021-2045

Briva-Iglesias, V., Doğru, G., & Cavalheiro Camargo, J. L. (2024). Large language models "ad referendum": How good are they at machine translation in the legal domain? *MonTI. Monografías de Traducción e Interpretación, 16*(16), 75–107. DOI: 10.6035/MonTI.2024.16.02

Chalkidis, I., Fergadiotis, M., Malakasiotis, P., Aletras, N., & Androutsopoulos, I. (2020). LEGAL-BERT: The muppets straight out of law school. In *Findings of the Association for Computational Linguistics: EMNLP 2020* (pp. 2898–2904). *Association for Computational Linguistics*. https://doi.org/DOI: 10.18653/v1/2020.findings-emnlp.261

Coulthard, M., & Johnson, A. (2007). *An introduction to forensic linguistics: Language in evidence*. Routledge. DOI: 10.4324/9780203969717

Dahl, M., Magesh, V., Suzgun, M., & Ho, D. E. (2024). Large legal fictions: Profiling legal hallucinations in large language models. *The Journal of Legal Analysis, 16*(1), 64–93. DOI: 10.1093/jla/laae003

Dworkin, R. (1986). *Law's empire*. Harvard University Press.

Endicott, T. A. O. (2000). *Vagueness in law*. Oxford University Press., DOI: 10.1093/acprof:oso/9780198268406.001.0001

Fairclough, N. (1989). *Language and power*. Longman.

Fontaine, L. (2013). *Analysing English grammar: A systemic functional introduction*. Cambridge University Press.

Foucault, M. (1972). *The archaeology of knowledge* (Sheridan Smith, A. M., Trans.). Pantheon Books. (Original work published 1969)

Garzone, G. (2001). Deontic modality and performativity in English legal texts. In Gotti, M., & Dossena, M. (Eds.), *Modality in specialized texts* (pp. 153–173). Peter Lang.

Giampieri, P. (2024). The use of AI in the translation of legal documents: A critical analysis. *trans-kom, 17*(2), 343–358. https://www.trans-kom.eu/bd17nr02/trans-kom_17_02_05_Giampieri_AI.20241128.pdf

Giampieri, P. (2025). Legal language and legal translation. In *Legal formulae: Exploring legal multi-words in English, Italian and French* (pp. 7–38). Springer Nature Switzerland.

Halliday, M. A. K. (1994). *An introduction to functional grammar* (2nd ed.). Arnold.

Halliday, M. A. K., & Matthiessen, C. M. I. M. (2004). *An introduction to functional grammar* (3rd ed.). Arnold.

Halliday, M. A. K., & Matthiessen, C. M. I. M. (2014). *Halliday's introduction to functional grammar* (4th ed.). Routledge. DOI: 10.4324/9780203783771

Hart, H. L. A. (1994). *The concept of law* (2nd ed.). Oxford University Press. (Original work published 1961)

Hohfeld, W. N. (1919). *Fundamental legal conceptions as applied in judicial reasoning and other legal essays* (Cook, W. W., Ed.). Yale University Press., https://archive.org/details/fundamentallegal00hohfuoft

Hyland, K. (2005). Metadiscourse: Exploring interaction in writing. *Continuum.*

Koehn, P. (2020). *Neural machine translation.* Cambridge University Press. DOI: 10.1017/9781108608480

Lam, J., Chen, Y., Zulkernine, F., & Dahan, S. (2025). Legal text analytics for reasonable notice period prediction. *Journal of Computational and Cognitive Engineering*, *4*(3), 319–331. DOI: 10.47852/bonviewJCCE52024104

Manning, C. D., & Schütze, H. (1999). *Foundations of statistical natural language processing*. MIT Press.

Martindale, M. J., & Carpuat, M. (2018). Fluency over adequacy: A pilot study in measuring MT quality for post-editing. In *Proceedings of the 13th Conference of the Association for Machine Translation in the Americas* (pp. 113–124). Association for Machine Translation in the Americas.

Mattila, H. E. S. (2006). *Comparative legal linguistics.* Ashgate.

Niu, J., & Jiang, Y. (2024). Does simplification hold true for machine translations? A corpus-based analysis of lexical diversity in text varieties across genres. *Humanities & Social Sciences Communications*, *11*(1), 480. Advance online publication. DOI: 10.1057/s41599-024-02986-7

Open, A. I. (2026). *ChatGPT (May 2026 version) [Large language model].* https://chat.openai.com

Pasquale, F. (2015). *The black box society: The secret algorithms that control money and information*. Harvard University Press. DOI: 10.4159/harvard.9780674736061

Prieto Ramos, F. (2011). Developing legal translation competence: An integrative process-oriented approach. *Comparative Legilinguistics*, *5*(1), 7–22. DOI: 10.14746/cl.2020.41.1

Prieto Ramos, F. (2015). Quality assurance in legal translation: Evaluating process, competence and product in the pursuit of adequacy. *International Journal for the Semiotics of Law*, *28*(1), 11–30. DOI: 10.1007/s11196-014-9390-9

Quinci, C., & Pontrandolfo, G. (2023). *Testing neural machine translation against different levels of specialisation: An exploratory investigation across legal genres and languages. trans-kom, 16*(1), 174–209. trans-kom article

Šarčević, S. (1997). *New approach to legal translation*. Kluwer Law International.

Schauer, F. (1991). *Playing by the rules: A philosophical examination of rule-based decision-making in law and in life*. Clarendon Press.

Searle, J. R. (1969). *Speech acts: An essay in the philosophy of language*. Cambridge University Press. DOI: 10.1017/CBO9781139173438

Silk, A. (2019). Theories of vagueness and theories of law. *Legal Theory*, *25*(2), 132–152. DOI: 10.1017/S1352325219000028

Solan, L. M. (1993). *The language of judges*. University of Chicago Press. DOI: 10.7208/chicago/9780226767895.001.0001

Surden, H. (2014). Machine learning and law. *Washington Law Review (Seattle, Wash.)*, *89*(1), 87–115.

Svitych, O. (2026). Blind transparency: A critical discourse analysis of the EU AI Act. *Critical Policy Studies*, *20*(1), 127–143. DOI: 10.1080/19460171.2025.2496193

Tabrizi, H. H., & House, J. (2025). Moving beyond conventional tests: Performance assessment as an alternative for evaluating students' academic translations. *Contrastive Pragmatics, 6*(3), 608–639. https://brill.com/view/journals/jocp/6/3/article-p608_5.xml

Tiersma, P. M. (1999). *Legal language*. University of Chicago Press. DOI: 10.7208/chicago/9780226854809.001.0001

Volansky, V., Ordan, N., & Wintner, S. (2015). On the features of translationese. *Digital Scholarship in the Humanities*, *30*(1), 98–118. DOI: 10.1093/llc/fqt031 von Wright, G. H. (1951). Deontic logic. *Mind; A Quarterly Review of Psychology and Philosophy*, *60*(237), 1–15. DOI: 10.1093/mind/LX.237.1

Wachter, S., Mittelstadt, B., & Russell, C. (2024). Do large language models have a legal duty to tell the truth? *Royal Society Open Science*, *11*(8), 240197. Advance online publication. DOI: 10.1098/rsos.240197 PMID: 39113763

Wagner, A., & Marusek, S. (2025). Law without roots: Mapping the rhizomatic turn in legal thought and practice. *Undecidabilities and Law*, *5*(5), 9–13. DOI: 10.14195/2184-9781_5_0

Wang, Q., Amini, M., Yang, C., & He, Q. (2026). Translating culture-specific items in *The True Story of Ah Q*: A comparative evaluation of GPT-4o, KIMI, and Google Translate under multimodal prompts. *SAGE Open*, *16*(1), 21582440251412225. Advance online publication. DOI: 10.1177/21582440251412225

Wang, Q., Wang, Y., Amini, M., Xian, M., & Fu, Z. (2026). Quality assessment of Tibetan–Chinese poetry translation: Integrating automated metrics and qualitative insights through a cross-system comparison of dedicated NMT engines and a prompted LLM. *Language Resources and Evaluation*, *60*(2), 42. Advance online publication. DOI: 10.1007/s10579-026-09918-8

Wu, S., Amini, M., & Mahfoodh, O. H. A. (2026). Exploring translators' perceptions of translation decisions in courtroom translation. *International Journal for the Semiotics of Law*, *39*(1), 319–339. DOI: 10.1007/s11196-025-10274-z

Wu, S., Amini, M., & Mahfoodh, O. H. A. (2026). Unveiling certainty and doubt: A systemic functional exploration of epistemic modality in courtroom discourse. *International Journal for the Semiotics of Law*, *39*(2), 501–522. DOI: 10.1007/s11196-025-10321-9

Wu, S., Amini, M., & Wang, Y. (2026). Negotiating institutional hierarchy: Power, politeness, and meaning construction in English-to-Chinese courtroom translation. *SAGE Open*, *16*(1), 1–14. DOI: 10.1177/21582440261421582

ADDITIONAL READINGS

Al-Romany, T. A. H., & Kadhim, M. J. (2024). Artificial intelligence impact on human translation: Legal texts as a case study. *International Journal of Linguistics. Literature and Translation*, *7*(5), 89–95. DOI: 10.32996/ijllt.2024.7.5.11

Bajčić, M., & Golenko, D. (2024). Applying large language models in legal translation: The state-of-the-art. *International Journal of Language & Law, 13*, 171–196. DOI: 10.14762/jll.2024.171

Biber, S. E. (2024). Between humans and machines: Judicial interpretation of the automated decision-making practices in the EU. In Hofmann, H. C. H., & Pflücke, F. (Eds.), *Governance of automated decision-making and EU Law*. Oxford University Press., DOI: 10.1093/9780198919575.003.0007

Cheng, L. (2010). Discourse and judicial thinking: A corpus-based study of court judgments in Hong Kong, Taiwan and Mainland China. *International Journal of Speech Language and the Law, 17*(2), 295–298. DOI: 10.1558/ijsll.v17i2.295

Clément-Wilz, L., de Laforcade, A., & Cennamo, I. (2025). Translation in the European Union: Navigating technical and legal issues in the light of artificial intelligence—Conclusions. *International Journal of Language & Law, 14*, 240–255. DOI: 10.14762/jll.2025.240

Matoesian, G. (1999). Intertextuality, affect, and ideology in legal discourse. *Text, 19*(1), 73–109. DOI: 10.1515/text.1.1999.19.1.73

Moneus, A. M., & Sahari, Y. (2024). Artificial intelligence and human translation: A contrastive study based on legal texts. *Heliyon, 10*(6), e28106. Advance online publication. DOI: 10.1016/j.heliyon.2024.e28106 PMID: 38524597

Monzó-Nebot, E., & Moreno-Rivero, J. (2020). Jurilinguistics: Ways forward beyond law, translation, and discourse. *International Journal for the Semiotics of Law - Revue Internationale de Sémiotique Juridique, 33*(2), 253–262. https://doi.org/DOI: 10.1007/s11196-020-09721-w

Poscher, R. (2012). Ambiguity and vagueness in legal interpretation. In Solan, L. M., & Tiersma, P. M. (Eds.), *The Oxford Handbook of Language and Law* (pp. 128–144). Oxford University Press., DOI: 10.1093/oxfordhb/9780199572120.013.0010

Zhang, Z., Abdullah, S. N., Abdullah, M. A., & Duan, W. (2025). Translation quality in an evolving paradigm: Neural machine translation and large language models in technical domains. *International Journal of English Language Education, 13*(2), 52–71. DOI: 10.5296/ijele.v13i2.23057

KEY TERMS AND DEFINITIONS

Algorithmic Black Box: A metaphor used to describe the lack of transparency in automated decision-making systems. It refers to the internal processes of neural architectures where the relationship between the data input and the final output is opaque, making it difficult for legal practitioners to audit the specific reasoning or "discursive choices" made by the machine .

Deontic Modality: refers to a branch of linguistic logic focused on permission, obligation, and prohibition. In legal discourse, these concepts are typically indicated by modal verbs that serve as performative anchors to assert legal authority.

Functional Fit: The degree to which a translated legal text achieves the same communicative and legal effect as the source text within the target legal system. Rather than literal equivalence, functional fit prioritizes the "textual fit" of the discourse to ensure it meets the institutional and normative requirements of the receiving jurisdiction.

Legal Discourse: A specialized institutional register through which legal systems produce and enforce normative relations. In contrast to commonplace vernacular, legal discourse transcends the mere transmission of information; it actualizes legal reality through the establishment of rights, the imposition of obligations, and the endorsement of institutional actions.

Legal Equivalence: The preservation of legal effect, normative force, and institutional function across source and target legal texts rather than mere linguistic similarity.

Probabilistic Language Modeling: The computational paradigm underlying neural machine translation and large language models, in which language generation is driven by statistical patterns learned from large corpora rather than by semantic understanding or normative intention. Such models privilege fluency and distributional probability over the deliberate, institutionally grounded choices that characterize legal discourse.

Simplification vs. Easification: A conceptual distinction in legal linguistics where simplification involves reducing the complexity of the language (often at the cost of legal precision), while easification refers to making the text more accessible without compromising its technical integrity or functional force.

The Illusion of Accuracy: The occurrence in which translations of legal texts produced by artificial intelligence exhibit a high degree of fluency and linguistic precision, while concurrently effecting nuanced alterations to the legal significance or normative implications of the original text. The concept describes the structural gap between surface-level fluency and legal equivalence arising from the probabilistic logic of AI language systems.

Chapter 8
Algorithmic Mediation in Legal Translation: Discourse, Ambiguity, and Authority

Mohammed H. Alaqad
http://orcid.org/0000-0002-9953-5763
Universiti Malaya, Malaysia

Gisele El Khoury
http://orcid.org/0009-0000-0673-7570
St. Lawrence University, USA

ABSTRACT

The growing use of neural machine translation and large language models has improved the speed and consistency of legal translation, but fluent output may conceal errors in legal meaning, ambiguity, and normative force. This chapter examines AI through algorithmic mediation, understood as the active shaping of meaning by computational systems between source and target texts. Drawing on critical discourse analysis, genre theory, and systemic functional linguistics, it argues that legal meaning depends on conventions, intertextuality, deontic modality, and jurisdiction-specific concepts rather than lexical equivalence alone. It develops a fourfold taxonomy of lexical, syntactic, pragmatic, and systemic ambiguity and shows how AI may silently resolve or erase such indeterminacy. The chapter also considers authority, accountability, minority-language risks, and the responsibilities of certified translators. It concludes that AI should support, not replace, professional judgement through disclosure, human review, ambiguity-aware design, and responsibility for legal outcomes.

DOI: 10.4018/979-8-3373-9179-3.ch008

INTRODUCTION

The integration of artificial intelligence into legal translation practice has accelerated sharply over the past half-decade, moving from a peripheral productivity aid to a central fixture of institutional workflows in law firms, corporate legal departments, and multilingual judicial bodies. Neural machine translation (NMT) systems and, more recently, large language models (LLMs) have been adopted with enthusiasm by practitioners confronting growing volumes of cross-border contractual, regulatory, and litigation material (Briva-Iglesias et al., 2024). A broader overview of these adoption patterns across institutional and commercial contexts is provided by Kenny (2022). Empirical assessments suggest that these tools now achieve impressive fluency and terminological consistency, particularly in high-resource language pairs, with outputs often indistinguishable at surface level from those produced by certified human translators (Giampieri, 2025). Khan (2025) observes that institutional translation services, including those attached to courts and international organizations, increasingly deploy AI-assisted pipelines as first-draft engines subject to human review. Yet this operational shift has outpaced scholarly reflection on what is actually being delegated when legal meaning is entrusted to algorithmic mediation. The result is a field in which adoption has become normalized well before its epistemological and professional implications have been adequately theorized, a gap this chapter seeks to address. This concern aligns with recent work highlighting the ethical, quality, and accountability challenges embedded in AI-powered translation systems (Alaqad et al., 2026).

The gap between surface-level fluency and discourse-level accuracy is consequential because the apparent competence of AI systems masks a deeper structural limitation. Legal meaning is not encoded primarily at the lexical or syntactic level, where current tools perform reliably, but at the discourse level, where institutional conventions, normative force, and cross-cultural legal reasoning interact (Šarčević, 1997). A translated clause may be lexically accurate and grammatically fluent while nonetheless altering the deontic force, evidentiary standing, or jurisdictional applicability of the provision it purports to render (e.g., Wu et al., 2025). Giampieri (2025) and Briva-Iglesias et al. (2024) document patterns in which AI outputs display surface competence but systematically mishandle the pragmatic and intertextual features that carry legal consequences. The risk, as Ibrahim et al. (2025) demonstrate in the context of Arabic-speaking litigants in United States courts, is that such errors are often invisible to non-specialist users precisely because the translation reads fluently. Fluency, in this sense, functions as a form of epistemic camouflage: it signals reliability where none may exist, and does so most persuasively in exactly those high-stakes contexts where misjudgment carries the gravest consequences (Ziwei, 2025). Recent comparative evidence reinforces this concern. Altakhaineh et al. (2025) found that professional human translators outperformed ChatGPT in legal terminology, clarity, and conformity with Arabic legal conventions. Badah et al. (2026) likewise showed that ChatGPT and DeepSeek could produce coherent and terminologically plausible legal translations while still relying on literal structures and culturally inappropriate renderings that require expert intervention.

Against this backdrop, the current chapter attempts to address two interrelated objectives. First, it probes the ability of AI-assisted translation systems to manage the discourse-level complexity that characterizes legal language across jurisdictions with a focus on the typology of legal ambiguity and on deontic modality as an investigative site. Second, it analyses the impact of algorithmic mediation on issues of authority, responsibility, and professional ethics in certified legal translation. The empirical demonstration of the aforementioned claims, through a corpus-based case study, and the development of a human-in-the-loop framework are addressed. The investigation is explicitly cross-jurisdictional: comparative data from the legal systems of English, Arabic, and Malay are presented, and the French civil-law perspective is occasionally consulted for theoretical clarification. Then the chapter contextualizes legal language within Critical Discourse Analysis, genre studies, and Systemic Functional Linguistics. It explains the working mechanism of machine translation, and defines and elaborates on a typology of legal ambiguity. The chapter analyses issues of authority and power that arise from algorithmic mediation, and offers solutions and practical suggestions to legal translators, legal practitioners, and institutions, while the latter sections sketch out areas for recommendations, further research and conclusion.

Algorithmic Mediation requires a preliminary definition because it carries argumentative weight throughout. *"Algorithmic mediation"* refers in this chapter to the interposition of a computational system between source and target legal texts, such that the system actively shapes meaning rather than merely transmitting it; the term is preferred to "machine translation" because it foregrounds the interpretive and authoritative work performed by the algorithm, consistent with Ziwei's (2025) characterization of the algorithmic era. Two further terms central to the chapter, *legal ambiguity* and *cross-jurisdictional discourse*, are developed are formally defined in the Key Terms and Definitions section (Stiefenhofer et al., 2025). The concept of algorithmic mediation advanced here differs from prior uses of "machine translation" in foregrounding the interpretive and authoritative work performed by the algorithm rather than treating it as a neutral linguistic relay. Earlier discussions of AI translation quality focus primarily on lexical and syntactic accuracy (Giampieri, 2025; Khan, 2025); the present analysis shifts attention to the structural displacement of human judgment and the constitutive role of accountability opacity. Similarly, the fourfold taxonomy of ambiguity developed refines existing classifications in legal linguistics (Cao, 2007; Šarčević, 1997) by linking each type of ambiguity directly to the structural failure modes of AI systems and to specific consequences for legal validity and professional responsibility.

LEGAL LANGUAGE AS A COMPLEX DISCURSIVE SYSTEM

Legal Language as Genre: Registers, Text Types, and Institutional Authority

Legal language is most productively understood not as a specialized vocabulary layered onto ordinary usage but as a distinct discursive system whose meaning is constituted through genre conventions, institutional authority, and normative function. Bhatia (1993, 2004) has argued that legal texts constitute a family of genres, including statutes, contracts, judgments, pleadings, and treaties, each governed by conventionalized rhetorical structures that encode the communicative purposes of specific legal communities. These genres are not stylistic preferences but constitutive features of legal validity: a contract that fails to conform to the generic conventions of its jurisdiction may be legally ineffective regardless of the clarity of its propositional content (Šarčević, 1997). Cao (2007) emphasizes that legal translation is therefore never a matter of rendering equivalent propositions across languages but of reconstructing the institutional voice and generic architecture of the source text within the target legal culture, an operation that presupposes discursive competence well beyond bilingual fluency.

Sources of Complexity: Technicality, Intertextuality, and Normative Ambiguity

The complexity of legal discourse derives from at least three interacting sources. Technicality refers to the dense network of terms of art *consideration*, *estoppel*, *force majeure*, *mens rea* whose meanings are stipulated by legal doctrine rather than recoverable from ordinary usage and may have no equivalent in another legal system (Cao, 2007). The historically accretive and formulaic character of legal language, analyzed in depth by Tiersma (1999), further compounds this difficulty by embedding legal meanings in archaic expressions and Latin maxims that resist direct substitution in translation. Intertextuality, in Fairclough's (1992, 2003) sense, captures the way legal texts incorporate, cite, and presuppose other texts: a contractual clause refers implicitly to statutory provisions, prior case law, and standard-form conventions, such that its meaning is distributed across a web of documents rather than contained within its own wording. Normative ambiguity, finally, is the condition in which a legal provision permits more than one plausible interpretation by function rather than accident, either because drafters have deliberately left scope for judicial discretion or because the provision must govern factual situations not yet foreseen. Each of these sources generates distinctive translation challenges that cannot be resolved through lexical substitution.

Discourse Analysis Frameworks Applicable to Legal Texts

Three discourse-analytic frameworks are drawn upon in this chapter. Critical discourse analysis (Fairclough, 1992, 2003) examines how legal texts encode and reproduce relations of power and how translation between dominant and minority legal systems may amplify or attenuate those relations. Genre theory, in Bhatia's (1993, 2004) application, supplies the tools for analyzing the conventionalized structures through which legal texts perform their institutional functions. Systemic functional linguistics (Halliday & Matthiessen, 2014) offers a metafunctional account of language as simultaneously representational, interpersonal, and textual, particularly suited to analyzing deontic modality, since modal choices operate at the intersection of representing legal states of affairs and enacting obligations between parties (e.g., Wu et al., 2026). The frameworks are complementary: CDA situates legal translation within relations of authority, genre theory identifies the conventions through which that authority is exercised, and SFL provides the descriptive apparatus for tracing how authority is realized at the level of grammatical choice. The application of SFL's interpersonal metafunction to legal modality is explained, where deontic choices such as shall, must, and may are analysed as carriers of legally constitutive obligational force that AI systems routinely collapse into a single probabilistic rendering. El-Farahaty (2025) further demonstrates how specialised Arabic-English legal corpora and AI tools can support the analysis and teaching of legal terminology, collocation, and discourse patterns, while stressing that expert guidance remains necessary because AI does not consistently ensure accuracy or stylistic precision in complex legal texts.

The Problem of Legal Indeterminacy: Vagueness, Ambiguity, and Open Texture

A final source of complexity, bearing directly on the limits of algorithmic mediation, is legal indeterminacy. Three forms must be distinguished. *Vagueness* arises when the application of a legal term to borderline cases is unclear, as with the reasonable person standard or the threshold of material breach. *Ambiguity* arises when a term or construction admits two or more distinct interpretations, each internally coherent. *Open texture*, following Hart (1961/2012), describes the deeper condition that legal rules cannot fully anticipate the range of situations to which they will be applied and thus carry an irreducible interpretive openness. Endicott (2000) demonstrates that vagueness operates as a structural feature of law rather than a correctable drafting deficiency, reinforcing the argument that legal indeterminacy is constitutive rather than contingent. These three forms are not defects of legal drafting but constitutive features of legal language, and their faithful translation requires judgment about whether a source-text indeterminacy should be preserved, resolved, or flagged in the target text. It is precisely this judgment, as later sections argue, that algorithmic systems are structurally unequipped to exercise.

ALGORITHMIC MEDIATION: HOW AI TRANSLATES LEGAL TEXTS

Overview of AI Translation Technologies

The technologies now mediating legal translation belong to two overlapping generations. Neural machine translation (NMT), which became dominant during the late 2010s, represents source and target sentences as high-dimensional vectors and learns to map between them through encoder-decoder architectures trained on large parallel corpora (Bahdanau et al., 2015; Koehn, 2020). Large language models (LLMs), which have reshaped the field since the early 2020s, extend this architecture through transformer-based self-attention and training on vastly larger and more heterogeneous corpora, performing translation as one among many generative tasks (Vaswani et al., 2017). The emergence of GPT-3 and its successors (Brown et al., 2020) marked a qualitative shift, as general-purpose language models began outperforming domain-adapted NMT systems on a range of benchmarks, accelerating their adoption in specialised domains including law. Contemporary systems such as DeepL, Google Translate, and GPT-4 share a common computational logic: meaning is modeled as statistical regularity across tokens within a bounded context window, and translation is produced by predicting the most probable target-language sequence given the source. Briva-Iglesias et al. (2024) document the rapid deployment of LLMs into legal translation workflows, noting that their fluency in specialized registers now approaches that of domain-adapted NMT systems.

What AI Does Well: Terminological Consistency, Speed, High-Volume Processing

AI systems demonstrate strong performance in terminological consistency, particularly when supported by translation memories or glossaries that constrain lexical choice across long documents (Giampieri, 2025). They process high-volume repetitive material such as standard-form contractual boilerplate with a speed and uniformity that human translators cannot match, and handle syntactic transformation between typologically similar languages with considerable fluency. Khan (2025) observes that institutional translation services rely on these capabilities for first-pass processing of regulatory, administrative, and procedural texts, reserving human intervention for review. For genres of legal text in which meaning is genuinely distributed at the terminological and sentential levels, algorithmic mediation can deliver outputs of adequate quality at a fraction of the cost of wholly human translation. The question this chapter pursues is not whether such capabilities exist, but where their limits lie and what is concealed when those limits are crossed.

Structural Limitations: Pragmatics, Cultural-Legal Concepts, and Discourse Coherence

Those limits become visible at three levels of linguistic organization beyond the reach of token-level statistical modeling. The first is pragmatic: AI systems struggle with illocutionary force, what a legal utterance *does* rather than what it *says*, because illocutionary force is carried by discourse-level conventions rather than by lexical features recoverable from training data. The second is conceptual: culture-bound legal notions such as common-law *estoppel*, civil-law *Treu und Glauben*, or Islamic-law *waqf* designate institutional arrangements whose conceptual architectures have no equivalents in other traditions and cannot be translated by substitution at any level of granularity (Šarčević, 1997). The third is coherential: legal texts derive meaning from intertextual and intratextual relations that often exceed the context windows of even the most capable models, such that a provision rendered correctly in isolation may be rendered incorrectly once its relationship to a defined term, cross-referenced clause, or incorporated statutory provision is considered (Cao, 2007). These are not engineering problems that additional training data will resolve; they are consequences of the mismatch between statistical prediction and the discursive construction of legal meaning.

The Accountability Opacity Problem

A fourth limitation, distinct in kind, concerns authority and accountability rather than linguistic capacity. The much-discussed "black box" character of contemporary AI is frequently framed in terms of technical opacity, but the more consequential opacity for legal translation is *accountability opacity*: the chain of responsibility for interpretive choices becomes diffuse, distributed across model developers, training data, post-editors, and commissioning institutions (Ziwei, 2025). The ethical implications of such opacity have been theorized more broadly across algorithmic systems (Mittelstadt et al., 2016), but legal translation represents a particularly acute case because its outputs carry direct legal effect. Unlike a certified human translator, whose professional signature attaches responsibility to identifiable expert judgment, an algorithmic output carries no such locus of accountability, yet may enter legal proceedings with equivalent practical authority. Ibrahim et al. (2025) show that this gap has already produced tangible harms in judicial contexts involving minority-language litigants. Accountability opacity does not merely accompany algorithmic mediation as an incidental feature but is constitutive of it, and that any adequate framework for AI-assisted legal translation must address the question of where interpretive authority resides. These institutional concerns are already visible in European legal translation. Wright (2025) shows that the Court of Justice of the European Union must balance faster multilingual access to justice against output quality, human-resource effects, and fit-for-purpose review. Monjean-Decaudin (2025) similarly warns that inaccurate AI-mediated transfer of legal meaning may affect the legal effects of translated texts and undermine legal certainty.

AMBIGUITY AS THE CORE PROBLEM

A Taxonomy of Ambiguity in LEGAL DOCUMENTS

Legal language is often described as precise. In reality, it is precise in some places and deliberately or unavoidably vague in others. Four major types of ambiguity recur across legal texts, each posing a distinct translation problem.

The first is *lexical ambiguity*: a single word with more than one meaning. Many legal systems use ordinary words in technical senses. The English word *consideration* has a narrow meaning in contract law the exchange of promises or obligations between contracting parties while in everyday speech it refers to thoughtfulness or care. A translation may read well but be contextually incorrect if the translator is unaware of the legal definition. *Party*, *instrument*, *title*, and *execution* are further examples.

The second is *syntactic ambiguity*, arising from sentence structure. A clause that reads "The contractor shall not commence the works without written consent from the client or the site manager" is grammatically open to two readings, each creating a different legal obligation, and once translated into another language the choice will be irreversible.

Third is *pragmatic ambiguity*, arising from the circumstances under which the document will function. A contract between two corporations in the same industry can be terse because the parties share background knowledge; once translated into a new legal sphere, what is unstated may become consequential, even where the linguistic content is preserved.

The fourth and most significant is *systemic ambiguity*: a concept well-defined in one legal system has no parallel in another. This is not a translator's error but a feature of the receiving system. It is the form of ambiguity least amenable to translation software, since it cannot be detected by lexical matching or statistical inference, and it requires the translator to understand both legal systems simultaneously.

Deontic Modality and the Translation of Obligation

One of the most consequential sites of ambiguity is the expression of obligation, permission, and prohibition. As established through the interpersonal metafunction of systemic functional linguistics (Halliday & Matthiessen, 2014), modal choices in legal texts simultaneously represent a state of affairs and enact the obligational relationship between parties: they are not stylistic options but constitutive elements of legal effect. What linguists' term deontic modality is, in legal texts, not merely grammatical; it is the source of legal power. The gap between *shall* and *may* in a contract clause is not stylistic; it is the difference between an obligation and a permission, between a binding promise and a choice.

In the common law drafting tradition, *shall* is the conventional means of imposing a contractual obligation: *The Buyer shall pay the invoice within thirty days. Must*, in some traditions, has a stronger sense; *may* indicates permission. Some drafters now recommend *must* instead of *shall* for clarity (Garner & Kimble, 2024), but in cross-jurisdictional translation the distinctions remain critical.

Different languages encode obligation differently. French civil law uses *être tenu de* or the legal present tense. German distinguishes *müssen* (must) from *sollen* (shall/should). Arabic distinguishes يجب (*yajib*, must) from ينبغي (*yanbaghi*, ought to). Malay has *hendaklah* and *mestilah* carrying different deontic weight. AI translation across these systems typically produces outputs that are linguistically intelligible but legally incorrect, as demonstrated empirically in the companion chapter. The point here is theoretical: this is not accidental but systematic. AI systems are trained on language distributions rather than legal meanings, and where a model has been trained on many examples of *yajib* rendered as *must*, it will not produce *shall* even where *shall* would be the operative formula.

The following illustrative comparison demonstrates this failure mode concretely. Table 1 presents a single contractual clause in three versions: the English source, a human legal translation into Arabic, and the output of a leading AI translation system applied to the same clause.

Table 1. Human vs. AI translation of a deontic modal clause (English to Arabic)

Version	Text	Notes
Source (English)	*"The Supplier shall deliver the goods within 14 days. The Buyer may inspect the goods upon delivery."*	Shall = binding obligation; may = discretionary right. Deontic contrast is legally constitutive.
Human legal translation (Arabic)	Uses yajib for shall (strong obligation) and yajuzu for may (discretionary permission). Deontic contrast faithfully preserved. .	Correct deontic rendering. Obligation and permission are legally distinguishable in the target text.
AI translation output (Arabic)	Renders both shall and may with yajib, collapsing the obligation/permission distinction. The output is fluent but legally incorrect.	Critical error. Buyer's discretionary inspection right becomes a binding obligation. The error is invisible in fluent output.

The AI error is consequential: by rendering may as yajib rather than yajuzu, the system transforms a discretionary buyer right into a binding obligation. Under the correct translation, a buyer who does not inspect is fully compliant; under the AI output, the same buyer is in breach. The output is fluent and entirely readable, with no surface signal of the error. This is false fluency in its most legally significant form.

Untranslatability and the Culture-Bound Legal Concept

Some legal notions simply do not exist in another system. This is not a translation failure but a feature of law as a social construct. In such cases, the translator's task shifts from finding an equivalent to alerting the reader that none exists.

The English common-law doctrine of *estoppel* prevents a party from taking a legal position that contradicts something they previously said or did, when another party has reasonably relied on that earlier conduct. French and German law contain concepts that resemble this prohibition but are conceived differently and offer different remedies; rendering *estoppel* as French *forclusion* or German *Verwirkung* is not wrong but is imprecise in ways that may matter.

Conversely, the German doctrine of *Treu und Glauben* imposes a general obligation on contracting parties to act in good faith. English common law has never recognized such a general duty; good faith is accepted only in limited contexts. To an English lawyer, *Treu und Glauben* looks like good faith but with weaker standards, missing the discretionary force inherent in the German conception. The words match; the legal content does not.

From Islamic law, the distinction between وقف (*waqf*) and زكاة (*zakat*) illustrates the limits of substitution. A *waqf* is an endowment dedicating property to a charitable or religious cause; structurally it resembles a common-law trust but differs in its religious dimension and the prohibition on diverting the dedicated property. Translating *waqf* as *trust* or *charitable foundation* omits this religious dimension.

Zakat, as one of the five pillars of Islam, is the religious obligation to give a fixed proportion of wealth; it shares features with a state-administered tax but is not a tax in Western legal terms, since its foundation is religious duty rather than secular authority.

AI translation systems are engineered to produce flowing output and will always render something, even where the appropriate response is that the term has no equivalent and requires clarification. The translator's traditional ethical responsibility to signal untranslatability, foregrounded in Venuti's (1995) account of domesticating versus foreignizing translation strategies, is here rendered architecturally impossible by systems designed always to return a confident output. The result is *false fluency*: a target text that appears complete and reads naturally yet has effectively erased the juridical concept it purported to translate.

How AI Systems Resolve or Conceal Ambiguity

Underlying all four types of ambiguity is a shared feature of contemporary AI translation systems: they consistently turn ambiguity into a statement, whether the ambiguity is deliberate or accidental. Language models are trained to be fluent and coherent, to produce definitive, readable sentences. They are not trained to register uncertainty, display alternative renderings, or indicate that a concept present in the source lacks equivalent realization in the target. The distinction between strategic ambiguity, where drafters of treaties and constitutional documents deliberately leave provisions open to permit agreement among parties with opposing positions (Hansen, 2023), and unintentional ambiguity, which arises from poor drafting or unforeseen factual situations, is one that AI systems cannot draw. In both cases the system selects the statistically most probable reading and presents it as the translation.

Where a human legal translator meets an ambiguous passage, ethical practice dictates flagging the ambiguity through a translator's note or by consulting the client. Where an AI system meets the same passage, it produces a smooth translation and moves on. Bender et al. (2021), in their critique of large language models, characterize this as a structural feature of systems trained to maximize fluency without grounding in meaning: the model lacks a mechanism to recognize the limits of its competence and therefore cannot flag them. The ambiguity has disappeared from the output not because it was resolved, but because the system cannot perceive or signal it. The client receives a clean document that purports to state something definite, when the original clearly states something ambiguous. In legal translation, a hidden ambiguity is in some respects worse than a plain one, since the latter at least signals to the user the possibility of further interpretive work.

This is not merely a problem of translation quality. It is a structural displacement of human judgment. The decision how to treat an ambiguous legal notion, whether to replicate the uncertainty, note it, ask the client for clarification, or make a defensible interpretive choice, is arguably the most significant action a legal translator takes. Where that decision is rendered silently by an algorithm and presented as a completed translation, it has not been eliminated but made invisible, and made invisible by a system that bears no professional responsibility for its consequences. What does this mean for the legal translator and the legal integrity of cross-jurisdictional documents?

AUTHORITY, POWER, AND THE TRANSLATOR'S ROLE

Legal Translation as an Act of Authority: Who is Responsible for Meaning?

When a legal document is translated, more than just the language is affected. The meaning of the document what it obliges, permits, and prohibits passes through another person's judgment before reaching its new audience. That interpretation is not value-neutral; it is an act of authority. In the conventional legal translation workflow, the question of where that authority resides has a straightforward answer: the certified or sworn translator held a credential indicating competence and could be legally liable for inaccuracies, and their signature on the translation was a guarantee by an individual holding the appropriate professional credentials that the document did not differ in any material respect from the original. Graziadei (2025) frames this responsibility in terms of authenticity, arguing that legal translation must preserve the source text's intent, function, and authority across languages and legal systems, particularly where direct conceptual equivalents are unavailable.

This structure is now under strain. There is nothing analogous to such a warranty when an AI application produces a legal translation. The tool has no professional standing, cannot be held liable, and is unaware that it is making consequential decisions. The results look like finished, expert translations and may at times appear better written than human work. However, the line of responsibility among source document, certified translator, and client has been broken; meaning has been determined, but no responsible person has done so. This reveals a structural failing rather than a regulatory oversight. The law depends on human accountability for its authority, and a translated legal document acquires its authority through human attestation. A signature is meaningful because the signatory can be held responsible for it. An algorithm has no one in the chair who can account for anything; relying on AI-produced translations without substituting a new form of human accountability requires the legal system to grant authority to a document on the basis of no one.

The Displacement of Human Judgment by Algorithmic Outputs

Perhaps what is most characteristic of the adoption of AI translation in legal practice is how quickly human judgment is being phased out, often without any deliberate decision being taken to that effect. The substitution proceeds on practical rather than principled grounds: AI translation is quicker and cheaper; the workflow is rebuilt around it; the human translator shifts from being the author of the translation to a corrector of the machine output. In many places, even this step is dropped under time and cost pressure.

This matters because legal translation is not fundamentally a linguistic process but a process of judgment. The translator does not merely produce equivalent words but makes a series of decisions: identifying possible renderings while preserving original legal effect; handling non-equivalences; and deciding whether the source text contains ambiguity, deliberate or accidental, and how to flag it. When a system replaces those decisions with statistical outputs, the decisions do not disappear. They are still being made, but without awareness of the stakes, without understanding of the specific legal relationship the document defines, and without the capacity to recognize when knowledge runs out. The recipient may not even know that decisions have been made: a polished translation will not announce its embedded choices but will present itself as the text rather than as one possible translation among many.

Power Asymmetries in Cross-Jurisdictional Translation

Legal translation does not happen on a level playing field. A few legal systems and their associated languages enjoy disproportionate privilege within the global legal order. English common law, French civil law, and the mix of the two in international commercial arbitration provide the scaffolding of most global legal practice. The languages associated with these systems, above all English, but also French, German, and Spanish, are also the ones on which most major AI translation tools have been trained (Joshi et al., 2020). Cronin (2003) situates this within a broader critique of translation and globalization, arguing that the dominance of particular languages in global translation flows both reflects and reinforces wider inequalities of political and cultural power, a dynamic now amplified by the training distributions of AI systems. This creates a structural inequality that operates in every cross-jurisdictional translation involving a minority legal system.

The asymmetry operates in both directions. When a dominant system's text is translated into a minority system's language, its conceptual categories tend to impose themselves on the target. Terms without an equivalent are rendered using the nearest concept, which may not be legally equivalent; the receiving audience reads a document that looks as if it belongs to their tradition but carries assumptions from another. In the reverse direction, the translator faces implicit pressure to make minority-system material comprehensible to a dominant-system audience, often by erasing distinctions, substituting pragmatic approximations for explanations of difference, and producing translations that sound natural to common-law or civil-law readers without adequately reflecting source content.

AI tools extend this dynamic. Models are only as knowledgeable as the texts on which they were trained, and they have learned the conceptual universe of dominant legal systems far better than that of minority ones. When asked to translate Islamic commercial law, customary law, or the legal system of a small jurisdiction, the model draws on a far less developed conceptual basis than when faced with English or French law, and reads the material through the dominant system it knows best, generally English common law. This is not solved by better data alone. A model trained on more Islamic commercial law texts still will not grasp *waqf* the way a trained *fiqh* scholar does, and that misunderstanding will be reflected in every choice the model makes.

Critical Discourse Analysis of AI-Produced Legal Translations: Whose Norms are Encoded?

Read through the lens of critical discourse analysis (Fairclough, 1992, 2003), the asymmetry described above reveals a deeper feature of algorithmic mediation: AI-produced legal translations are not norm-neutral artifacts but vehicles through which the conceptual categories of dominant legal systems are silently propagated. The model's training distribution functions as an unacknowledged interpretive horizon, against which all source texts are reconstructed. When the source belongs to that horizon, the operation is invisible; when it does not, the source is reshaped to fit.

Two consequences follow. First, the conceptual vocabulary of common-law commerce, dominant in the training data, becomes the de facto target idiom even when the nominal target language belongs to another tradition. A clause translated from Arabic into English carries common-law contractual assumptions about consideration, offer, and acceptance that may be foreign to the source's conceptual structure but that the model treats as default. Second, the categories through which legal concepts are organized (contract and tort, public and private law, right and remedy) are encoded in the model's representation of the target language and applied to source texts where those categories may not natively operate. The translation thus carries a normative grammar of which neither the user nor, in any meaningful sense, the model itself is aware. Algorithmic mediation is, in this sense, not merely a translation technology but a discursive technology that actively reproduces particular normative categories as the natural form of legal expression.

Ethical and Professional Implications for Certified and Sworn Translators

All of the trends discussed above the displacement of judgment, the concealment of uncertainty, the structural bias toward dominant legal systems, and the silent encoding of normative categories intersect in the certified or sworn translator, the professional whose work occupies the nexus between language proficiency and legal liability and is now in flux. Certified and sworn translators in virtually all jurisdictions work under codes of conduct that require accurate and faithful translations, disclosure of conflicts of interest, and acknowledgment of their own limitations. These rules were written for a world in which the translator was the originator of the translation; they seem much less adequate for one in which the translator is largely a post-editor of machine output.

Post-editing and translation are distinct operations with different cognitive mechanisms. Post-editing relies heavily on "machine-anchoring": studies show that post-editors consistently produce output closer to the machine-generated text than would result from translation from scratch, even when explicitly asked to edit freely (Guerberof-Arenas & Toral, 2020). Drugan (2013) situates post-editing within a wider professional ethics framework, arguing that quality in translation requires sustained human accountability for the full range of interpretive decisions embedded in a translated text, a standard that cursory post-editing of AI output systematically fails to meet. This raises an issue of informed consent. A client submitting a document for sworn translation likely believes that a qualified human made all the translation decisions; if those decisions were made by a machine and only cursorily corrected by a human attending to the most obvious errors, the client did not receive what they paid for. The sworn translator's signature implies a human action that may not have occurred, which in some jurisdictions may constitute a professional ethical violation, in others a misrepresentation, and in others an unregulated grey area.

Professional bodies should respond by defining standards realistic about these conditions (e.g., Amini et al., 2026) rather than pretending the technology does not exist. Forbidding AI tools is impractical and would harm translators in the aggregate. The more sustainable path is to mandate disclosure of tool use, require human review proportionate to the legal significance of the document, and maintain that the certified translator's signature continues to mean what it has always meant: that a named professional takes responsibility for the accuracy and legal sufficiency of the translation. The detailed framework through which this principle can be implemented in practice is developed in the companion chapter.

Ethical Risks: Bias, Fairness, and Minority-Language Litigants

These power imbalances translate to practical ethical harms. AI models for translation embed the distributional biases of their training corpora: minority languages/legal systems will fare worse, and minority-system discourse will be implicitly interpreted through the legal concepts of majority systems. This is not an unfortunate technical fact, but an ethical failing. Litigants whose cases proceed under a minority legal system (e.g., Islamic commercial law, customary law, or the law of small jurisdictions) will be offered systematically less accurate translation services, adding to the general disadvantage they already face within the international legal system.

More troubling are the practical effects on minority-language litigants in adjudication: Ibrahim et al. (2025) described the plight of Arabic-speaking defendants in United States criminal trials, who were offered by a government agency what appeared to be high-quality, linguistically sophisticated AI translations of judicial proceedings but that failed to translate procedural rights accurately, evidentiary rules correctly, or the duties required by plea agreements. The defendants and, sometimes, the reviewing lawyers failed to notice the misrepresentations of law in an AI output that seemed fluent. Legal outcomes were determined based on a false picture of the law. This pattern reflects the structural disjuncture, already examined here, between the fluency of statistical modeling and the correctness of translation in legal discourse.

Ensuring fairness in AI-assisted legal translation thus necessitates considerations on at least three fronts: linguistic fairness (equitable translation quality across language pairs), conceptual fairness (fidelity to a source system's legal categories rather than reinterpretation through a dominant legal system's lens), and procedural fairness (ability to make legally informed decisions despite the algorithmic mediation of content). Existing AI systems have deficiencies on all three fronts, necessitating not only better data but also human review, auditability mechanisms, quality flags, and transparency.

DISCUSSION

The problems of accountability identified in this chapter are systemic and do not appear inherently unmanageable. The appropriate response must simultaneously operate on three levels: professional practice, institutional policy, and technology design. In what follows, concrete proposals for each are set out, bringing together the analytical threads developed in this chapter.

Implications

Certified and sworn translators who use AI tools should be required to disclose in their attestation that they used an AI tool, specify which system they used, and indicate how much human review the result underwent. Disclosure requirements should be graduated: a full human review of all parts should be adequate for high-stakes documents such as court judgments, asylum dossiers, or treaty clauses; and a light-touch review would be sufficient for administrative correspondence with negligible legal effect. Translators should resist cognitive machine-anchoring and review the AI output against the source document instead of treating it as a rough draft to be fine-tuned. If systemic ambiguities are encountered, or concepts for which there is no target-system equivalent, translators should continue to have a professional obligation to mark the missing concept with a translator's note, as they would in the case of a wholly human translation. The sworn translator's signature will continue to mean exactly what it has meant up until this point: a named professional, making the epistemic and legal claim that they are the source of the translation.

Lawyers who have received a translated legal document are under a duty of due diligence to examine the method by which the translation was done. If an AI-assisted translation was received, the lawyer should investigate the extent of human review, the translation pair, and the subject area, as quality varies with these parameters. Courts and the judiciary should establish admissibility frameworks that keep AI-generated and human-attested translations distinct, with minimal quality requirements defined for each category. Law firms and legal departments that have adopted AI-driven translation should implement audit trails linking every translation project to the system used, the post-editor, and the adopted protocol. Such a trail will not serve an administrative purpose; it should provide a basis for professional and institutional accountability when a problem arises.

AI translation tools for legal purposes should be developed to surface, not conceal, uncertainty. If the system receives a concept that it cannot find a reliable equivalent for in its training data, a cross-jurisdictional gap of the type analysed, the tool should indicate this to the user instead of issuing a confident but faulty answer. Features such as uncertainty scoring, flagging missing terms, and generating alternative versions are technically feasible and should be standard. The EU, by enacting the AI Act, has already imposed new responsibilities on high-risk AI, and the regulatory bodies and developers of other jurisdictions adopting such frameworks should place AI-driven legal translation at high risk in all high-stakes contexts, which requires conformity assessments, transparent composition of the training data, and bias auditing with regard to minority languages and legal systems (Ziwei, 2025).

Future Research Directions

This chapter has pursued primarily theoretical aims. Multiple lines of empirical and applied inquiry derive from the arguments presented here and warrant exploration in their own right. First and foremost are the empirical studies comparing human translations with AI-produced translations of ambiguous legal clauses across a range of language pairs and legal systems. These provide the evidentiary basis that the present investigation calls for but cannot provide. Such studies should focus on each of the four varieties of ambiguity and, in particular, include the calculation of "false fluency" (a seemingly accurate but erroneous resolution of the ambiguity) across different language-pair types (high-resource and low-resource).

Second, the accountability opacity problem calls for legal and sociotechnical research examining how liability should be allocated when AI translation errors cause legal harm. Comparative jurisdictional analysis covering common-law, civil-law, and Islamic-law systems would clarify whether existing professional liability frameworks can be adapted or whether new regulatory instruments are required. Third, research on the cognitive dimensions of post-editing in legal contexts is needed. Current evidence on machine-anchoring (Guerberof-Arenas & Toral, 2020) derives largely from non-legal domains; it is not yet known whether legal expertise modulates or compounds the anchoring effect, a question with direct implications for training and certification standards.

Fourth, designing and assessing ambiguity-aware legal translation tools remains an underdeveloped area of technical exploration. If such tools could identify potential areas of ambiguity in source text, flag gaps in conceptual meaning between jurisdictions, and provide alternative translations along with a measure of the confidence level, then the harms outlined in this chapter would be significantly mitigated, and this should be pursued through a cooperative approach among computational linguists, legal scholars, and translation professionals. Fifth, ongoing longitudinal studies tracing the effect of AI translation on minority-language access to justice, building upon previous research from Ibrahim et al. (2025) and Joshi et al. (2020), are necessary to track whether the issues of equity that this section described are becoming more or less of a problem as the technology advances.

CONCLUSION

This chapter has argued that integrating artificial intelligence into legal translation raises a problem that cannot be resolved at the level of technology alone. The challenge does not lie in the idiomatic output that algorithms are now clearly capable of, but in the discourse level generation of legal meaning, which cannot be achieved via prediction: it has been established that legal discourse is a system whereby meaning is generated in accordance with genre conventions, intertextual connections and the authority of law, rather than by way of the equivalences of individual words and sentences; we have seen that artificial intelligence produces output on the basis of predicting probabilities across tokens within a closed window of context; we have identified a fourfold typology of legal meaning and examined how algorithmic systems systematically hide, rather than help translation practitioners solve, each type of ambiguity; we have shown how meaning generation within the legal system should be analysed not through the lens of the mechanics of translation but in terms of authority, where mediation through artificial intelligence decentralizes responsibility to levels with which existing professional frameworks are not equipped to deal; all these points have been brought together to produce a series of proposals for translation practitioners, lawyers and institutions; finally, a road map for the academic work to come has been put forward.

The chapter's contribution is theoretical: it articulates a discourse-analytic account of why algorithmic mediation fails in legal contexts, drawing together critical discourse analysis (Fairclough, 1992, 2003), genre theory (Bhatia, 1993, 2004), and systemic functional linguistics (Halliday & Matthiessen, 2014) to locate the failure not in technical shortcomings but in the structural mismatch between statistical prediction and the discursive construction of legal meaning. The empirical demonstration of these claims and the proposal of a human-in-the-loop framework are developed in the companion chapter in this volume.

A closing reflection returns to legal certainty. Legal systems function because they produce outcomes that parties can anticipate and rely upon, and that anticipation depends on the stability of meaning across the documents, judgments, and proceedings that constitute legal practice. Algorithmic mediation does not threaten legal certainty by producing poor translations; it threatens it by producing fluent translations whose interpretive choices are invisible, unattributable, and constitutively unaccountable (Ziwei, 2025). The risk is not that machines will translate badly but that their outputs will be trusted beyond the limits of what their architecture can responsibly sustain. Preserving legal certainty in the algorithmic era does not require rejecting the tools; it requires reconstituting the structures of human authority through which legal meaning has always been rendered reliable (Cao, 2007; Šarčević, 1997). That reconstitution, rather than the technology itself, is the defining task for legal translation as a profession, a pedagogy, and a guarantor of cross-jurisdictional legal communication.

REFERENCES

Alaqad, M. H., Amirdabbaghian, A., & Alhasani, H. (2026). Beyond the algorithm: Navigating ethics, quality, and accountability in AI-powered translation. In Larchen Costuchen, A., & Otaif, F. A. (Eds.), *AI bots in applied linguistics: Practice, policy, and creativity* (pp. 283–312). IGI Global Scientific Publishing., DOI: 10.4018/979-8-3373-6420-9.ch010

Altakhaineh, A. R. M., Alghathian, G. A., & Jarrah, M. M. (2025). A comparative study of accuracy in human vs. AI translation of legal documents into Arabic. *International Journal of Language & Law*, *14*, 63–80. DOI: 10.14762/jll.2025.063

Amini, M., Lee, K. F., Yiqiu, W., & Ravindran, L. (2026). Proposing a framework for ethical use of AI in academic writing based on a conceptual review: Implications for quality education. *Interactive Learning Environments*, *34*(3), 1394–1418. DOI: 10.1080/10494820.2025.2523382

Badah, A. M., Khalaf, C. N., Dwaikat, F. J., & AlQbailat, N. (2026). The usage of artificial intelligence in legal translation: Bridging the gap between law and language. *Ampersand (Oxford, UK)*, *16*, 100248. Advance online publication. DOI: 10.1016/j.amper.2025.100248

Bahdanau, D., Cho, K., & Bengio, Y. (2015, May 7–9). *Neural machine translation by jointly learning to align and translate*. *3rd International Conference on Learning Representations (ICLR 2015)*, San Diego, CA, United States. https://arxiv.org/abs/1409.0473

Bender, E. M., Gebru, T., McMillan-Major, A., & Shmitchell, S. (2021, March 3–10). *On the dangers of stochastic parrots: Can language models be too big?* 2021 ACM Conference on Fairness, Accountability, and Transparency (ACM FAccT 2021), Virtual conference. DOI: 10.1145/3442188.3445922

Bhatia, V. K. (1993). *Analysing genre: Language use in professional settings*. Longman.

Bhatia, V. K. (2004). Worlds of written discourse: A genre-based view. *Continuum*.

Briva-Iglesias, V., Camargo, J., & Dogru, G. (2024). Large language models "ad referendum": How good are they at machine translation in the legal domain? *MonTI: Monographs in Translation and Interpreting*. /arXiv.2402.07681DOI: 10.48550

Brown, T., Mann, B., Ryder, N., Subbiah, M., Kaplan, J., Dhariwal, P., Neelakantan, A., Shyam, P., Sastry, G., Askell, A., Agarwal, S., Herbert-Voss, A., Krueger, G., Henighan, T., Child, R., Ramesh, A., Ziegler, D. M., Wu, J., Winter, C., & Amodei, D. (2020). Language models are few-shot learners. *Advances in Neural Information Processing Systems*, *33*, 1877–1901. DOI: 10.48550/arXiv.2005.14165

Cao, D. (2007). *Translating law*. Multilingual Matters.

Drugan, J. (2013). *Quality in professional translation: Assessment and improvement*. Bloomsbury Academic. Cronin, M. (2003). *Translation and globalization*. Routledge.

El-Farahaty, H. (2025). Integrating corpora and AI tools in the teaching, learning, and assessing of Arabic/English legal translation. *International Journal for the Semiotics of Law – Revue internationale de Sémiotique juridique, 38*, 2031–2060. DOI: 10.1007/s11196-025-10281-0

Endicott, T. A. O. (2000). *Vagueness in law*. Oxford University Press. DOI: 10.1093/acprof:oso/9780198268406.001.0001

Fairclough, N. (1992). *Discourse and social change*. Polity Press.

Fairclough, N. (2003). *Analysing discourse: Textual analysis for social research*. Routledge. DOI: 10.4324/9780203697078

Garner, B. A., & Kimble, J. (2024). *Essentials for drafting clear legal rules*. Administrative Office of the United States Courts.

Giampieri, P. (2025). *Assessing the quality of AI and MT in legal translation*. Altre Modernità., DOI: 10.54103/2035-7680/28886

Graziadei, M. (2025). Legal translation and the quest for authenticity. *International Journal for the Semiotics of Law – Revue internationale de Sémiotique juridique, 38*, 2565–2593. DOI: 10.1007/s11196-025-10283-y

Guerberof-Arenas, A., & Toral, A. (2020). The impact of post-editing and machine translation on creativity and reading experience. *Translation Spaces*, *9*(2), 255–282. DOI: 10.1075/ts.20035.gue

Halliday, M. A. K., & Matthiessen, C. M. I. M. (2014). *Halliday's introduction to functional grammar* (4th ed.). Routledge. DOI: 10.4324/9780203783771

Hansen, S. T. (2023). Exploiting and constructing legal ambiguity: UK arms exports to Saudi Arabia during the war in Yemen. *European Security*, *32*(4), 607–627. Advance online publication. DOI: 10.1080/09662839.2022.2144728

Hart, H. L. A. (2012). *The concept of law* (3rd ed.). Oxford University Press. (Original work published 1961) DOI: 10.1093/he/9780199644704.001.0001

Ibrahim, M. A. S., Abdalla, H. O. H., Idris, M. El. M., Eldouma, S., Abdallah, N. M. M., Taha, E. A. M., & Rushwan, I. M. H. (2025). The role of legal translation in ensuring fair trial rights for Arabic-speaking immigrants in U.S. courts. *Journal of Cultural Analysis and Social Change*. DOI: 10.64753/jcasc.v10i2.2215

Joshi, P., Santy, S., Budhiraja, A., Bali, K., & Choudhury, M. (2020). The state and fate of linguistic diversity and inclusion in the NLP world. *Proceedings of the 58th Annual Meeting of the Association for Computational Linguistics*, 6282–6293. https://aclanthology.org/2020.acl-main.560

Kenny, D. (Ed.). (2022). *Machine translation for everyone: Empowering users in the age of artificial intelligence*. Language Science Press. DOI:DOI: 10.26034/cm.jostrans.2023.537

Khan, M. I.Mohammad Imran Khan. (2025). Impact of AI on legal and institutional translation: Issues and strategies. *International Journal of Translation and Interpretation Studies*, *5*(6), 1–15. DOI: 10.32996/ijtis.2025.5.6.1

Koehn, P. (2020). *Neural machine translation*. Cambridge University Press. DOI: 10.1017/9781108608480

Mittelstadt, B. D., Allo, P., Taddeo, M., Wachter, S., & Floridi, L. (2016). The ethics of algorithms: Mapping the debate. *Big Data & Society*, *3*(2), 1–21. DOI: 10.1177/2053951716679679

Monjean-Decaudin, S. (2025). Les enjeux de l'intelligence artificielle pour la traduction juridique au sein de l'Union européenne: Observations générales du point de vue de la juritraductologie. *International Journal of Language & Law*, *14*, 194–203. DOI: 10.14762/jll.2025.194

Šarčević, S. (1997). *New approach to legal translation*. Kluwer Law International.

Stiefenhofer, P., Gergerlioğlu, U., & Deniz, C. (2025). *Delegating authority to algorithms: Legitimacy and public values in European tax administrations*. Philosophy and Realistic Reflection., DOI: 10.55121/prr.v3i1.757

Tiersma, P. M. (1999). *Legal language*. University of Chicago Press. DOI: 10.7208/chicago/9780226854809.001.0001

Vaswani, A., Shazeer, N., Parmar, N., Uszkoreit, J., Jones, L., Gomez, A. N., Kaiser, Ł., & Polosukhin, I. (2017, December 4–9). *Attention is all you need* [Paper presentation]. *31st Conference on Neural Information Processing Systems (NIPS 2017)*, Long Beach, CA, United States. DOI: 10.48550/arXiv.1706.03762

Venuti, L. (1995). *The translator's invisibility: A history of translation*. Routledge.

Wright, S. (2025). Artificial intelligence in legal translation at the Court of Justice of the European Union. *International Journal of Language & Law*, *14*, 120–142. DOI: 10.14762/jll.2025.120

Wu, S., Amini, M., & Mahfoodh, O. H. A. (2025). A corpus-based analysis of modality shifts in English-to-Chinese courtroom translation. *Eurasian Journal of Applied Linguistics*, *11*(1), 152–166. https://ejal.info/menuscript/index.php/ejal/article/view/995/364

Wu, S., Amini, M., & Mahfoodh, O. H. A. (2026). Unveiling certainty and doubt: A systemic functional exploration of epistemic modality in courtroom discourse. *International Journal for the Semiotics of Law*, *39*(2), 501–522. DOI: 10.1007/s11196-025-10321-9

Ziwei, C. (2025). *AI translation and data ownership: Ethical conflicts, legal risks, and translator agency in the algorithmic era. The Frontiers of Society*. Science and Technology., DOI: 10.25236/FSST.2025.070702

ADDITIONAL READING

Alwazna, R. Y., Hurley, Z., & Elyas, T. (2025). Integrating technology in translating laws from and into Arabic: Benefits, implications and limitations. *International Journal for the Semiotics of Law – Revue internationale de Sémiotique juridique, 38*, 1851–1862. DOI: 10.1007/s11196-025-10295-8

Brashi, A. (2025). AI adoption in legal translation: A study of intrinsic motivation among Saudi students. *International Journal for the Semiotics of Law – Revue internationale de Sémiotique juridique, 38*, 2061–2081. DOI: 10.1007/s11196-025-10273-0

Campos, M. F. (2025). Comment on Patrícia Jerónimo's "Legal translation and the challenges of overcoming language barriers in court practice: Evidence from Portuguese courts." *International Journal for the Semiotics of Law – Revue internationale de Sémiotique juridique, 38*, 2651–2655. DOI: 10.1007/s11196-025-10319-3

Foblets, M.-C., & Graziadei, M. (2025). Translation and the search for justice in contexts of religious and cultural diversity: A persistent and complex challenge. *International Journal for the Semiotics of Law – Revue internationale de Sémiotique juridique, 38*, 2547–2564. DOI: 10.1007/s11196-025-10356-y

Jerónimo, P. (2025). Legal translation and the challenges of overcoming language barriers in court practice: Evidence from Portuguese courts. *International Journal for the Semiotics of Law – Revue internationale de Sémiotique juridique, 38*, 2613–2638. DOI: 10.1007/s11196-025-10304-w

Uliasz, R. (2025). Cross-cultural and linguistic dynamics in the deterritorialization of legal concepts through international commercial contracts. *International Journal for the Semiotics of Law – Revue internationale de Sémiotique juridique, 38*, 1291–1313. DOI: 10.1007/s11196-024-10207-2

KEY TERMS AND DEFINITIONS

Accountability Opacity: The condition in which the chain of responsibility for interpretive choices in a translated legal text becomes diffuse and untraceable, distributed across model developers, training data, post-editors, and commissioning institutions. Distinct from the technical opacity often associated with the "black box" metaphor, accountability opacity concerns the absence of an identifiable human locus to which professional and legal responsibility can attach.

Algorithmic Mediation: The interposition of a computational system between source and target legal texts, such that the system actively shapes meaning rather than merely transmitting it. The term is preferred to "machine translation" because it foregrounds the interpretive and authoritative work performed by the algorithm, recognising that statistical prediction over tokens constitutes a form of meaning-making with discursive and legal consequences (Ziwei, 2025).

Critical Discourse Analysis (CDA): A discourse-analytic framework, developed principally by Fairclough (1992, 2003), which examines how texts encode and reproduce relations of power, ideology, and institutional authority. In the present chapter, CDA provides the apparatus for analysing how AI-produced legal translations may amplify the conceptual categories of dominant legal systems while obscuring those of minority ones.

Cross-Jurisdictional Discourse: The communicative space in which legal texts move between systems governed by distinct procedural traditions, evidentiary norms, and conceptual architectures. Translation in this space is never a purely linguistic operation but always also a jurisdictional one, requiring the reconstitution of meaning across legal cultures rather than the substitution of equivalents across languages (Cao, 2007).

Deontic Modality: The linguistic system by which obligation, permission, and prohibition are expressed. In legal texts, deontic choices, such as the distinction between shall, must, and may in English, or between يجب (yajib) and ينبغي (yanbaghi) in Arabic, are not stylistic but constitutive of legal effect: they determine whether a clause creates a binding duty, a permitted action, or a recommendation.

Genre (Legal): A conventionalized text type, such as a statute, contract, judgment, pleading, or treaty, whose rhetorical structure encodes the communicative purposes of a specific legal community. Following Bhatia (1993, 2004), legal genres are understood not as stylistic preferences but as constitutive features of legal validity: a text that fails to conform to its generic conventions may lack legal effect regardless of the clarity of its propositional content.

Legal Ambiguity: The range of interpretive indeterminacies that arise in legal texts. The chapter develops a fourfold taxonomy distinguishing lexical ambiguity (multiple word senses), syntactic ambiguity (multiple structural readings), pragmatic ambiguity (uncertain illocutionary force), and systemic ambiguity (the absence of conceptual equivalents across legal traditions). Each type generates distinctive translation challenges, and each is handled differently and, in the case of AI systems, typically concealed rather than resolved.

Legal Indeterminacy: The broader condition under which legal language is irreducibly open to interpretation. Three forms are distinguished in this chapter: vagueness (uncertainty in borderline applications of a term), ambiguity (the presence of two or more coherent interpretations), and open texture (the inability of legal rules, however carefully drafted, to anticipate every situation to which they will be applied). Open texture, following Hart (1961/2012), denotes a constitutive rather than incidental feature of legal language.

Systemic Functional Linguistics (SFL): A linguistic framework developed by Halliday and extended by Halliday and Matthiessen (2014), which analyses language as simultaneously serving three metafunctions: ideational (representing experience), interpersonal (enacting social relations), and textual (organizing discourse). SFL is particularly suited to the analysis of deontic modality in legal texts, since modal choices operate precisely at the intersection of representing legal states of affairs and enacting obligations between parties.

Chapter 9
A Comparative Analysis of Human and Machine Translation of Institutional and Honorific Expressions in the IMTFE Courtroom Records

Yeying Pan
http://orcid.org/0009-0007-1632-9803
Universiti Sains Malaysia, Malaysia & Zhejiang Yuexiu University, China

Mansour Amini
http://orcid.org/0000-0003-2149-4604
Universiti Sains Malaysia, Malaysia

Marlina Jamal
Universiti Sains Malaysia, Malaysia

ABSTRACT

This study aims to analyze the translation of institutional and honorific expressions in the courtroom records of the IMTFE from 5 and 6 August 1947. By analyzing the three texts – the English source text, the published Chinese translation, and the machine-translated Chinese version – the study intends to discuss the most salient types of such expressions and the degree to which the two Chinese versions pre-

DOI: 10.4018/979-8-3373-9179-3.ch009

serve their interpersonal meanings in terms of tenor and interpersonal equivalence. Results reveal that institutional role labels, historical official titles, and courtroom honorifics are among the most salient categories. It is also found that interpersonal meanings are generally better preserved in the published translation.

INTRODUCTION

Legal text translation is more than the process of transferring propositional meaning (Botezat, 2012; Chromá, 2014; Lin et al., 2023). In courtroom discourse, the meaning of the text can be expressed not only through content, but also through institutional roles, official titles, and honorific expressions. This is especially relevant for records of the International Military Tribunal for the Far East (IMTFE), also known as the Tokyo Trial. As a multilingual and extremely formal legal event, the IMTFE was defined by hierarchical structures, political authority, and socio-political control (Takeda, 2008). In such a context, linguistic choices could reflect negotiation processes, power relations, and politeness issues (Wu et al., 2026). One of the linguistic resources that was extensively used in such discourse was that of institutional and honorific expressions. These linguistic constructions could convey explicit information about judicial hierarchy, official positions, and interpersonal relations (Ozyumenko, 2023). Therefore, translation processes could affect the representation of these interpersonal relations and hierarchies in the target text.

Recent developments in machine translation technologies make it possible to employ machine translation as a tool for processing legal texts (Badah et al., 2025; Giampieri, 2023). Although machine translation systems can produce semantically intelligible outputs, legal-historical texts could present particular difficulties due to the specific characteristics of such linguistic constructions (Badah et al., 2025; Guzmán & Prieto Ramos, 2024; Kovács, 2022). The use of machine translation would not only change the wording of expressions in a legal-historical text but also the way in which they construct interpersonal meanings. Consequently, the comparison between the two versions of published translation (PT) and machine translation (MT) would allow to analyze not only wording, but also interpersonal meaning.

This paper approaches the issue of translating institutional and honorific expressions in courtrooms from the perspective of tenor and interpersonal equivalence. In the context of systemic-functional linguistics, the dimension of tenor is concerned with the interpersonal relations established in the course of linguistic communication (Halliday & Hasan, 1989; Hasan, 2020). Within the scope of this study, tenor will be examined by means of two dimensions – relative power and social distance. These two parameters are appropriate for the analysis of institutional and power relations in the context of highly regulated and formal court discourse (Fraser, 1990; Hale,

1997; Liu, 2008). From this point of view, the process of translation would not just change the wording, but also influence the interpersonal relations expressed in the source text (House, 1998; Liu, 2008).

Previous studies have shown that linguistic, power, interpreting, translating, and historical issues could emerge within the scope of courtroom discourse and its translation (Yang & Wang, 2021). Few studies have been devoted to the issue of translating institutional and honorific expressions in a courtroom and the maintenance of interpersonal meaning in this process. Moreover, fewer studies compare published translation and machine translation in relation to courtroom discourse and examine the preservation of interpersonal meanings. This gap is especially prominent when discussing IMTFE translations because the courtroom language is not only a product of procedural discourse but also a manifestation of historical hierarchy and formal interaction (Takeda, 2008; Wu et al., 2025a).

Against this background, the present study aims to focus on the IMTFE courtroom discourse from 5 and 6 August 1947. With the aid of the comparative analysis of the English source text, the published Chinese translation, and the machine-translated version, it seeks to analyze the rendering of institutional and honorific expressions and the preservation of their interpersonal meanings. In light of the above considerations, the following research questions arise:

RQ1: What are the most salient types of institutional and honorific expressions in the selected courtroom discourse?

RQ2: To what extent do the published translation (PT) and the machine translation (MT) preserve the interpersonal meanings encoded in these expressions in terms of relative power and social distance?

LITERATURE REVIEW

Courtroom Discourse as Institutionalized and Interpersonal Communication

Courtroom discourse has been repeatedly acknowledged as a highly institutionalized domain where participants engage in interactions with formal speech styles and unequal power relations (Uwen, 2023). Specifically, Uwen (2023) claims that courtroom discourse is not only an instrument of exchanging facts but also an instrument of enacting authority and hierarchy during interaction. Similar arguments are put forward by Ashurov (2025), who claims that legal discourse involves high level of formality and complex power relations. Moreover, Ashurov (2025) draws attention to the fact that linguistic choices made by courtroom participants are influenced by honorifics and other interpersonal resources. Khafaga's (2023) corpus-assisted critical discourse analysis of courtroom discourse further shows that lexical choices in legal settings may function as pragmatic meaning carriers rather than merely semantic units, performing functions such as confirmation, verification, uncertainty, and clarification. Yang & Wang (2021), in broader discussions of courtroom discourse and its translation, also emphasized that courtroom discourse has become an interdisciplinary subject representing different fields and the interaction between law, language, power, and ideology has become one of the core topics of courtroom discourse research focuses. In the Chinese context, Sun et al.'s (2025) study of Chinese courtroom discourse further shows that courtroom interaction is shaped by complex power dynamics and role assignments among participants. Their analysis indicates that attitudinal resources and courtroom metaphors are used strategically by discourse participants to negotiate authority, legitimacy, and evidential reliability, suggesting that courtroom discourse in the Chinese context is not merely informational but also deeply interpersonal and power-laden. Based on a corpus-based study of Chinese courtroom argumentation, Shi and O'Halloran (2025) show that courtroom interaction in China is shaped by the multimodal positioning of public prosecutors, defense lawyers, and defendants. These findings suggest that Chinese courtroom discourse is not only legally institutionalized but also deeply interpersonal, as courtroom participants use verbal and visual resources to negotiate role relations, authority, and legal-cultural values.

Tenor, Register, and Interpersonal Meaning in Translation

A further line of discussion that relates to the topic of the current research deals with the notions of tenor, register, and interpersonal meaning in the context of translation. Liu (2008) argues that tenor is one of the key dimensions that define translation because of its effect on representation of relations, roles, and attitudes in the target text. Xuan (2020) introduces the notion of equivalent tenor and suggests that the success of translation is determined not only by semantic correspondence but also by interpersonal equivalence. In a similar manner, Masykar et al. (2023) argue that register, including field, mode, and tenor, can help translators preserve ideational and interpersonal meanings across languages. Their discussion of tenor is particularly relevant to the translation of institutional and honorific expressions, as such expressions often encode social distance, politeness, and role relations that may not be directly transferable through literal lexical correspondence. From systemic-functional perspective, Fu (2016) studied Chinese-English translated and interpreted diplomatic discourse and demonstrated the importance of interpersonal meaning in translational activities. By comparing modal patterns in translated and interpreted political discourse, Fu (2016) shows that modality is not merely a grammatical feature but a resource for reproducing interpersonal connotations embedded in the source discourse. Register analysis has also been applied to translation quality assessment. Similarly, Chueasuai (2017) demonstrates the usefulness of SFL's interpersonal metafunction in analyzing the translation of power relations, demonstrating that interpersonal meaning can be realized through mood structures and tenor-related variables such as power, contact, and affective involvement. Yang (2019) argues that register, consisting of field, mode, and tenor, functions as an interface between the social system and the linguistic system and can help evaluate how social meanings are realized in translation. These studies suggest that tenor, register, and interpersonal meaning provide a useful analytical framework for examining how social relations, power, and interpersonal meanings are represented in translation.

Translation Challenges in IMTFE Courtroom Discourse

The IMTFE, or Tokyo Trial, has also received renewed scholarly and translational attention in recent years. Sokolsky (2022) notes that the trial has attracted new scholarly interest since the early 2000s after previously sealed archives were made public, which suggests the continuing relevance of IMTFE-related texts as historically and linguistically significant materials for translation research. Takeda (2007, 2008) studied interpreting procedures at the IMTFE and showed that the tribunal involved multiple languages and relied on interpreters, monitors, and language arbiters to handle disputes over translations and interpretations, indicating that IMTFE courtroom discourse was shaped by complex linguistic, institutional, and procedural constraints. Wu et al. (2025b) identify language style, proper nouns, institutions, military ranks, legal terms, and consistency as main challenges in IMTFE English-to-Chinese translation. It shows that institutions and military ranks cannot be transferred without considering context because they are historically embedded in language use. Furthermore, Wu et al. (2025a) demonstrate that modality shift can change stance and interpersonal force in courtroom translation. In other words, translated courtroom discourse differs from the source text not only in expressions but also in interpersonal meaning. Most relevant to the current research, Wu et al. (2026) emphasize the significance of hierarchy, power, and politeness in English-to-Chinese courtroom translation, highlighting the connection between courtroom translation and interpersonal relations and hierarchy.

Human and Machine Translation of Legal Discourse

A final relevant aspect of literature concerns the comparison between machine translation and human translation in legal texts. Vieira et al. (2021) conducted a study on machine translation in medical and legal settings and revealed that MT is increasingly used in high-risk contexts, including courtrooms, but its errors may have serious social and legal consequences. Their findings indicate that MT use in legal settings may affect immigration applications, court judgments, and the validity of evidence, suggesting that legal MT should be evaluated in relation to its real-world purpose rather than surface-level fluency alone. Kovács (2022) points out that although neural machine translation is able to produce legally correct texts, they differ from human translations in text cohesion and coherence. Similar conclusions are drawn by Guzmán and Prieto Ramos (2024) who claim that machine translation can achieve high levels of terminological adequacy but fail to ensure textual coherence. Al-Romany and Kadhim (2024) also found that human translation performed better than AI/machine translation in translating selected legal documents, particularly in terms of accuracy, legal effect, and the appropriate use of legal language. Moreover, Moneus and Sahari (2024) compared human and AI translation of legal texts and found that human translation, despite being less technologically advanced than AI-based translation, remains slightly superior in preserving legal effect, legal terminology, and contextual meaning. In contrast, by comparing human translations and post-edited NMT outputs of Greek-English property law texts, Sosoni et al. (2022) found no major differences in accuracy or fluency, but the post-edited versions contained more errors related to style and culture-specific references which indicates that legal machine translation should not be assessed only in terms of semantic accuracy, but also in terms of legal genre conventions, stylistic adequacy, and contextual appropriateness. In the Chinese context, Cui et al. (2023) compared human translation and post-editing in English-to-Chinese translation across different text types, including legal texts. Their experiment showed that post-editing generally involved less effort than human translation. However, legal texts showed a more complex pattern: students perceived greater effort in post-editing legal texts, and human translation received slightly higher scores than post-edited translation. The result suggests that legal discourse may reduce the efficiency advantage of machine translation because of its specialized terminology and complex syntactic structures. Moreover, Nan (2026) examines English-to-Chinese legal language translation from the levels of words, sentences, and discourse, arguing that legal translation requires attention not only to terminology but also to sentence structure and textual coherence and further proposes a multi-level knowledge-based neural machine translation model for improving English-to-Chinese legal translation quality.

As shown in the review of the literature, the courtroom discourse has received a considerable amount of scholarly attention in relation to institutional communication, power relations, tenor, and interpersonal meaning. Existing studies on IMTFE translation have also identified institutions, military ranks, legal terms, language style, modality, and consistency as important translation challenges. Studies on legal machine translation indicate that MT may perform relatively well in term of terminology but may still have difficulties in coherence, legal effect, style, and contextual appropriateness. However, several gaps still remain. First, while studies of courtroom discourse and tenor are abundant, few studies focus specifically on institutional and honorific expressions. Secondly, existing studies on IMTFE translation have identified institutions and military ranks as major translation problems, but they tend to treat these items mainly as terminological or historical accuracy issues. As a result, they overlook how such expressions encode interpersonal meaning, including relative power, status, authority, status, authority, politeness, and social distance among courtroom participants. Thirdly, few studies are dedicated to comparing published translation and machine translations of courtroom discourse with the focus on interpersonal meaning.

Theoretical Underpinning

The present study primarily draws upon the theoretical concept of tenor which refers to the interpersonal relations created in the discourse (Halliday & Hasan, 1989). As a supplementary evaluative concept, the principle of interpersonal equivalence is introduced (House, 1998). Tenor serves as the major analytical basis to analyze institutional and honorific expressions in courtroom discourse in the source text, whereas interpersonal equivalence will be applied as an evaluative tool to measure whether, and to what extent, those interpersonal relations are retained in the translation texts.

Tenor

In the systemic functional model, tenor constitutes one of the three elements, along with field and mode, of register (Halliday & Hasan, 1989). According to Halliday and Hasan (1989), register is an ensemble of meanings connected to a particular situational configuration and tenor is defined as the nature of the relations of the participants. Subsequent systemic functional research has reconsidered the concept of tenor with a broader and more socially grounded meaning. Hasan (2020) reconceptualizes tenor as interactant relations, emphasizing that interactant relations are socially constructed as well as grounded in social positioning and language conventions. From this perspective, tenor is not simply a matter of how two individuals speak to one another, but a contextual dimension through which socially organized relations are enacted in text. In addition, Hasan (2020) emphasizes that speaker and addressee constitute the most important role in text creation since they are the unique element that can control the text production process. This broad understanding of tenor is especially applicable to the case of courtroom discourse since courtroom discourse tends to be highly institutionalized and participant relations tend to be structured in terms of procedural roles, inequality in power and speech rights (Hale, 1997).

In the current study, tenor will be employed as the main analytical concept in the examination of institutional and honorific expressions in courtroom discourse. To be more specific, tenor will be operationalized into two dimensions, i.e., relative power and social distance. The dimensions of relative power and social distance are traditionally regarded as the two core dimensions influencing interpersonal interaction (Fraser, 1990). Relative power refers to the asymmetrical relationship between discourse participants in terms of authority, status, or the ability to impose one's will, and social distance concerns the degree of familiarity, solidarity, or interpersonal distance between them (Fraser, 1990). They are utilized to analyze the institutionalization of interpersonal relations in institutional and honorific expressions in the source text.

Interpersonal Equivalence

In the present study, the principle of interpersonal equivalence is selected as the supplement of the functional equivalence proposed by House (1998), which consists of ideational and interpersonal equivalences. According to House (1998), interpersonal equivalence should be comprehended not merely in terms of authorial stance transferred from the source text to the target text, but more broadly in terms of pragmatic and relational meanings contributing to the interpersonal function of a text (House, 1998). Therefore, the interpersonal equivalence discussed in the current study is about whether interpersonal values encoded in the source text are retained in the target text (House, 1998; Xuan, 2020).

In the present study, interpersonal equivalence is not treated as an independent analytical framework, but as an evaluative concept that complements the tenor analysis outlined above. More specifically, it is assessed through the two dimensions of tenor introduced before, namely relative power and social distance (Fraser, 1990). These two dimensions are particularly relevant because titles and honorifics can function as tenor-markers that reflect relations of power and distance between participants (Liu, 2008). Accordingly, the PT and MT are compared in terms of whether, and to what extent, they preserve the hierarchical relations and interpersonal distance encoded in the source text's institutional and honorific expressions. In this way, interpersonal equivalence functions as an evaluative bridge between the tenor analysis of the source text and the comparison of the two Chinese versions (House, 1998).

METHODOLOGY

Data Collection Procedure

The data for the current study are extracted from the official trial records of the International Military Tribunal for the Far East (IMTFE), also called the Tokyo Trial. To be more specific, it is Vol.21 of the first series which contains the proceedings of 5 August 1947 and 6 August 1947. The three versions of the same materials are included: the English source text, the published Chinese translation, and the Chinese translation produced by the popular DeepL translator. As a lending machine translation system, DeepL utilizes neural machine translation technology to provide accurate and fluent translations and is known for its high-quality translations (Hidalgo-Ternero, 2020; Naveen & Trojovský, 2024). Compared with Google translate, another widely used machine translation tool, DeepL is found to offer translation of better accuracy and readability (Bunga & Katemba, 2024; Yulianto & Supriatnaningsih, 2021). Those data were selected as they offer comparable bases for the examination of institutional and honorific expressions' translation.

Two hearing days were selected based on the following considerations. First, they belong to consecutive proceedings of the same volume, which helps maintain contextual continuity. Second, they contain a sufficient number of institutional and honorific expressions related to the present study. Third, since this study aims at small-scale qualitative analysis rather than corpus-based investigation, the selection of two hearing days constitutes an appropriate amount of data for the purpose of this study. Although two hearing days limit the range of expression types and does not allow broad generalization across the whole IMTFE corpus, the repeated occurrence of similar expressions within the selected data makes it possible to identify translation patterns and compare how the PT and MT handle interpersonal meanings.

Retrieval and Coding

The source data for this study were obtained through close reading of the English source text and its two translated Chinese versions, published translation and machine translation. Expressions that referred to institutional roles, official titles, and formal honorific forms were selected for analysis as they contributed to the construction of hierarchy, participant roles, and courtroom formalities. Each expression was first located in the English text, and then it was compared with its translations in the published version and the machine translation.

Coding was predominantly done in an inductive and category-based way. Categories emerged in the process of close reading, whereby the recurrent expression types were grouped based on what they referred to and how they performed in courtroom interaction. For the analysis, the selected expressions were coded into three categories: institutional role labels, historical official titles, and courtroom honorifics. Institutional role labels include procedural role labels that refer to officials' institutional roles in the hearing, such as presiding and supporting officials. Historical official titles include those referring to governmental or military officials whose titles are associated with a historical period and specific institution or department. Courtroom honorifics refer to institutional forms of addressing and honorifics used in interactions in the hearing room. Recurrent items were retained in the dataset not only to identify translation choices but also to observe the relative consistency of the two Chinese versions across repeated occurrences.

Data Analysis Procedure

Salient Types of Institutional and Honorific Expressions

The selected courtroom discourse shows that the institutional and honorific expressions identified in the two-day corpus can be grouped into three major categories: institutional role labels, historical official titles, and courtroom honorifics. As shown in Table 1, these categories are unevenly distributed in terms of both type and token frequency. Institutional role labels constitute the largest category, with 11 types and 357 tokens, accounting for 70.4% of all identified tokens. Historical official titles form the second category, with 12 types and 68 tokens, or 13.4% of the total. Courtroom honorifics contain the smallest number of types, with only 3 distinct expressions, but still account for 82 tokens, or 16.2% of the total. This distribution suggests that salience in the selected data is shaped not only by variety, but also by the repeated procedural and interactional use of a relatively small set of expressions.

The high token frequency of institutional role labels is closely related to the discourse structure of the trial record itself. These expressions recur because the transcript repeatedly identifies speakers, institutional sections, and courtroom functions as part of the procedural organization of the hearing. For example, throughout the proceedings, speaker turns are repeatedly marked by institutional labels such as *The President* and *Clerk of the Court*, which explains why this category dominates the corpus quantitatively. In other words, these expressions are frequent not simply because they denote institutional roles, but because the transcript as a genre relies on such labels to structure participation, indicate procedural authority, and maintain the formal organization of courtroom interaction (Hale, 1997).

Historical official titles, by contrast, are less dominant in raw frequency, but they are still highly salient because they cluster in the evidential core of the hearings. In the witness affidavit read on 5 August, titles such as *War Minister*, *Navy Minister*, *Prime Minister*, *Foreign Minister*, *Finance Minister*, *President of the Planning Board*,

Chief of the Army General Staff, and *Chief of the Naval General Staff* recur as the testimony reconstructs governmental decision-making, inter-ministerial discussion, and chains of command in wartime Japan. These titles are integral to the historical and political reconstruction undertaken in the proceedings, especially when the defense attempts to explain how economic planning, resource shortages, cabinet deliberation, and liaison conferences related to the decision for war. The salience of this category thus lies not only in the number of different titles identified, but also in their role in connecting the courtroom discourse to historically specific structures of political and military authority (Takeda, 2008).

Courtroom honorifics present a different distributional pattern. This category contains only three types: *Your Honor*, *Mr. President*, and *Honorable Justice*, but a relatively high token frequency of 82. This means that its salience derives not from lexical diversity, but from the repeated use of a very small set of conventionalized forms of address. The most striking example is *Your Honor*, which occurs 73 times in the selected corpus. This high frequency can be explained by the interactional structure of courtroom speech: counsel repeatedly addresses the bench while making submissions, answering judicial interventions, or clarifying the purpose of documentary evidence (Hale, 1997). On 5 August, for instance, *Your Honor* appears repeatedly in exchanges where *Mr. Logan* explains the relevance of the witness affidavit, responds to judicial questioning, and continues to argue that Japan had not planned or prepared for aggressive war. The recurrence of *Mr. President* similarly reflects direct address to the presiding judge at key points of examination and procedural exchange, while *Honorable Justice* appears in the formal description of tribunal members at the opening of the hearing. These forms are therefore few in type but high in token frequency because courtroom address is formulaic and institutionally regulated: the same honorifics are repeatedly used whenever participants orient themselves to judicial authority, deference, and courtroom decorum (Ashurov, 2025; Uwen, 2023).

It is also important to note that courtroom honorifics are defined relatively narrowly in the present study. Only conventionalized honorific forms of courtroom address were counted in this category, namely *Your Honor*, *Mr. President*, and *Honorable Justice*. Forms such as *Mr. Logan* and *Dr. Kiyose* were not included, even though they are formally marked, because their primary function in the transcript is speaker identification or personal title reference rather than the explicit marking of judicial deference or courtroom honorific address. This narrower definition helps explain why the category contains only three types while still yielding a high token frequency.

The distribution shown in Table 1 reflects the nature of the selected proceedings. On the one hand, the hearings are heavily structured by procedural and institutional organization, which explains the overwhelming frequency of institutional role labels. On the other hand, they are also deeply embedded in historical argumentation about governmental and military responsibility, which accounts for the prominence of historical official titles (Wu et al., 2025b). At the same time, the repeated use of a small number of courtroom honorifics shows that the interpersonal dimension of the hearings is strongly regulated through conventionalized forms of deference and judicial address (Liu, 2008). For this reason, the three categories identified in Table 1 do not merely represent different lexical groups; together, they capture the institutional, historical, and interpersonal dimensions of the courtroom discourse and therefore provide a sound basis for the subsequent comparison of the published translation and the machine-translated version.

Table 1. Distribution of institutional and honorific expressions in the selected data

Category	Types	Tokens	Percentage	Representative items
Institutional role labels	11	357	70.4%	Prosecution Section; Defense Section; Language Section, Clerk of the Court; Language Arbiter; The president
Historical official titles	12	68	13.4%	War Minister; Navy Minister; Prime Minister; Foreign Minister; Finance Minister
Courtroom honorifics	3	82	16.2%	Honorable Justice; Mr. President; Your Honor;
Total	28	507	100.0%	

Interpersonal Equivalence in the PT and the MT

Following the concept of tenor, this section examines whether the MT and the PT achieve interpersonal equivalence from the perspective of institutional role labels, historical official titles, and courtroom honorifics. As stated in the previous chapter, tenor is the dimension of discourse concerned with the enactment of interpersonal relations (Halliday, 1985). To test whether the interpersonal relations enacted in the source text have been reproduced in the translations, the current section utilizes the framework of relative power and social distance suggested by Fraser (1990).

Interpersonal Equivalence in Institutional Role Labels

This section aims to analyze the preservation of interpersonal equivalence in the translation of institutional role labels. Considering that the main purpose of institutional role labels is to highlight procedural authority, institutional position, and hierarchic relations within a courtroom discourse (Palashevskaya et al, 2017; Uwen, 2023), the analysis will focus on relative power. However, in some cases, it is also relevant to discuss the contribution of certain institutional role labels to social distance, particularly when it comes to formalized institutional distance in a courtroom setting.

In the selected proceedings of the IMTFE, various institutional role labels occur repeatedly throughout the entire transcript and reflect procedural organization. These role labels include *The President*, *Marshal of the Court*, *Clerk of the Court*, *Language Section, IMTFE*, and *Language Arbiter*. In fact, all these role labels represent the procedural positions and hierarchies within the hearing process. Therefore, when analyzing their translations into Chinese, it is important to consider whether the hierarchical relations encoded in the source text have been preserved in the target texts (Liu, 2008; Venuti, 2018).

As noted by Takeda (2008), during the IMTFE trial process, there was a three-tier hierarchy of linguists including interpreters, monitors, and the language arbitration board. In addition, the author emphasizes that the language arbitration board comprised the language arbiters appointed by the tribunal, whose function was to announce court decisions regarding any disputes about translations and interpretations in court (Takeda, 2008). In other words, it was not just an auxiliary language service provider but a formally established position within the judicial process with its own procedures and authority. In this sense, the translation of *Language Arbiter* as "语言裁定官" in the PT more accurately reflects the procedural authority and significance of the original role label, whereas the rendering of this term as "语言仲裁员" in the MT undermines its authority because it does not emphasize the judiciary aspect of the label.

Another institutional role label is *Language Section, IMTFE*. According to Takeda (2008), language section had a special supervisory role and coordinated the work of interpreters and monitors hired by the tribunal to fulfill the tribunal's language needs. Again, it was not just an auxiliary unit, but a formally organized body within the institutional structure of the tribunal. In this sense, the translation of *Language Section, IMTFE*, as "远东国际军事法庭语言部" in the PT is more effective because it specifies the hierarchical position of the institution and preserves its significance as an administrative entity. Conversely, the rendering of this role label as "IMTFE语言科" in the MT does not specify the nature and hierarchical level of the unit, and hence, is less adequate in terms of interpersonal equivalence. In Chinese court institutional nomenclature, internal bodies are commonly named with terms such as "庭", "局", "部", "处", "室", and "办公室", as reflected in the Supreme People's Court's official list of court institutions and its standardized English translations (Supreme People's Court, 2021). The term "科", although often used in general administrative institutions to render "section", is less typical in Chinese court contexts. Therefore, rendering Language Section, IMTFE as "语言科" also sounds less natural in a court-related institutional context.

The next interesting example is *The President*. It serves as an institutional label and is rendered as "主席," "法庭主席," and "裁判长" in the MT. In this case, the translation of "庭长" in the PT is more acceptable because it reflects the official position within the tribunal and it is more associated with Chinese judicial institutions (Supreme People's Court, 2021). Conversely, using "主席" does not emphasize the procedural aspect of the institution. "主席" is not appropriate in this courtroom context because "主席" is more commonly used for political, organizational, or meeting-related positions in Chinese. It does not reflect the conventional terminology of Chinese legal discourse. "裁判长" is also not appropriate in this context because it is not a conventional title in Chinese courtroom discourse. In contemporary Chinese, "裁判长" is more commonly associated with sports competitions, contests, or judging panels, where it refers to a chief referee or head judge (Lin & Wang, 2009). The inconsistency of the translation further weakens interpersonal equivalence because the lack of stability and specificity of the translated labels undermines the hierarchy encoded in the source text (Uwen, 2023).

Clerk of the Court is another good example that reflects relative power. The MT provides "法庭书记官" and the PT uses "法庭书记员." Both of these alternatives are correct and appropriate for a professional context. However, the use of "书记官" can imply that the role occupies a higher hierarchical position than "书记员." In this sense, the PT version of the label better preserves interpersonal equivalence, because it highlights the procedural position of the *Clerk of the Court*.

The role of *Marshal of the Court* also reflects relative power and social distance simultaneously. While the MT employs the label "法庭司仪", the PT uses "法庭执行官". In the context of the courtroom discourse, the term *Marshal of the Court* designates a formally specified procedural role associated with court management (Varga, 2020). From the perspective of register and textual function, "法庭司仪" shifts the role from a judicial-procedural setting to a ceremonial one, which weakens the social power of the original term (House, 2015). However, "执行官" more accurately translates the term in question, as it is compatible with judicial procedures and represents a formally established judicial position.

In addition to relative power, there are also some institutional role labels can be translated as reflecting the dimension of social distance. For instance, the MT renders *Prosecution Section* and *Defense Section* as "控方组成员" and "辩护组方面", while the PT uses "检方人员" and "辩方人员". Although all these versions are understandable, the second set of labels appears to better preserve the institutional dimension of the source texts. In fact, in judicial settings, "辩护组方面" has a more descriptive meaning, whereas "辩方人员" refers to the procedural and institutional aspects of court participation. Similarly, "检方人员" preserves the procedural and institutional significance better than "控方组成员" .

While discussing institutional role labels, it should be said that sometimes, the PT fails to achieve interpersonal equivalence, too. For instance, while translating *House of Peers*, the MT provides the correct rendering "贵族院", whereas the PT renders as "众议院". Obviously, in this case, the target text does not preserve the institutional dimension of the role label and distorts its hierarchical relation to other institutions within the system. From the perspective of legal and contextual adequacy, replacing House of Peers with "众议院" distorts the institutional hierarchy of the source legal-political system (Prieto Ramos, 2015). This example reveals that the achievement of interpersonal equivalence cannot rely solely on naturalness and the overall formal tone but also requires the accurate translation of the institution's hierarchy.

In most cases, the translation of institutional role labels should be based on the analysis of relative power, whereas the discussion of social distance may also become relevant in some examples. Most of the analyzed examples illustrate that the PT preserves interpersonal equivalence more effectively by representing institutional hierarchies.

Interpersonal Equivalence in Historical Official Titles

After examining institutional role labels, this section turns to historical official titles, another category in which interpersonal equivalence is closely linked to hierarchy, status, and institutional identity. This section investigates whether the MT and the PT preserve interpersonal equivalence in the translation of historical official titles. In this type of interpersonal function, the analysis focuses mostly on the representation of relative power. It should be noted that historical official titles in the selected data mostly encode ranks and offices in the complex administrative system of wartime Japan (Wu et al., 2025b). In some instances, historical official titles can also contribute to social distance, as they reflect historically established forms of social distancing from an authoritative and prestigious office.

The selected IMTFE texts contain historical official titles when the proceedings describe discussions during cabinet consultations and planning and apportioning of responsibilities. For instance, on 5 August, the testimony of the witnesses and further questioning relate to offices such as *War Minister*, *Navy Minister*, *Prime Minister*, *Foreign Minister*, *Finance Minister*, *President of the Planning Board*, *Chief of the Army General Staff*, and *Chief of the Naval General Staff*. The same titles appear again in connection with asking who attended the conference of 1 November 1941. These examples show that the titles in question are important institutional markers which help trace chains of authority, responsibility, and decision-making in the proceedings.

Based on the following analysis, the PT is generally more likely to preserve the relative power relations encoded in the historical official titles in the source text. For example, *Chief of the Army General Staff* is translated as "陆军参谋长" in the MT but as "陆军参谋总长" in the PT. Likewise, *Chief of the Naval General Staff* is translated as "海军参谋长" in the MT but as "海军参谋总长" in the PT. The character "总" in "参谋总长" is not a redundant modifier. In Chinese official and military titles, "总" indicates a higher-ranking or overarching position, suggesting that the office holder is the head of the general staff. In both cases, adding "总" in the translation helps better convey the higher institutional rank of the office holder. By contrast, the shorter title "参谋长" fails to reproduce the hierarchical nature of the office in question. Here the difference between the two translations cannot be explained solely with reference to vocabulary. Rather, it lies in representing interpersonal power encoded in the titles (Fraser, 1990).

Another case when the PT is more effective at reproducing relative power is the translation of *War Minister*, *Foreign Minister*, and *Finance Minister*. The titles in MT, "战争大臣," "外交大臣," and "财政大臣," are semantically understandable but less specific in terms of institutional rank. The corresponding titles in the PT, "陆军大臣," "外相," and "大藏大臣," better reflect the specificity of each of these offices. The translation of historical official titles should not be based solely on literal semantic correspondence but needs to reflect the institutional specificity and hierarchical status of the original title (Prieto Ramos, 2015). As can be seen from the above examples, historically specific titles are essential in the translation process, as they enable the representation of the relative power relations existing in the wartime Japanese state system (Wu et al., 2025b). Consequently, preserving the hierarchies of office in historical official titles results in better interpersonal equivalence in the target text.

The case of *President of the Planning Board* can serve as another illustration of the same issue. The MT presents this office as "计划委员会主席," whereas the PT uses "企划院总裁." In this case, the PT version has a higher degree of institutional specificity compared to the MT version. Indeed, "计划委员会主席" sounds like a more generic title and therefore fails to reflect the high ranking of this particular office. In this way, preserving the relative power of historically specific titles requires not only semantic accuracy but also attention to their institutional context, formal register, and historically established status (House, 2015; Prieto Ramos, 2015).

However, there are also examples when the published translation achieves interpersonal equivalence as a result of greater interpretative effort. Both *State Minister* and *Minister of State* in the source text are both translated as "国务大臣" in the MT, but as "商工大臣" (the minister responsible for commerce and industry) and "内阁大臣"(a cabinet minister) in the PT respectively. Such translation choices mean that the PT interprets the meaning of the English titles in the context of the

Japanese administration. In this case, the PT has a higher degree of specificity, and therefore better conveys the relative power of each of these titles. At the same time, the PT also reflects a higher degree of interpreter mediation. Therefore, translating historical official titles involves a delicate balance between tenor and formality.

Social distance may also occur in some cases in relation to historically specific titles. For example, "大藏大臣," "外相," or "参谋总长" could be considered socially distant compared to "财政大臣," "参谋长," and other less specific alternatives. Historical specific titles establish the institutional remoteness of their holders as part of the stratified administrative system of the wartime Japan. Therefore, in this case, social distance stems from the representation of relative power (Liu, 2008).

In conclusion, the PT better preserves interpersonal equivalence in the translation of historical official titles. First, this is achieved through better preservation of historically established offices. Second, the titles in the MT tend to be more generalized in this context, which undermines the representation of institutional authority. In this category, interpersonal equivalence depends on preserving historically specific relative power relations encoded in the titles.

Interpersonal Equivalence in Courtroom Honorifics

Beyond institutional labels, interpersonal relations in courtroom discourse are also constructed through honorific forms of address in courtroom interaction. This category consists of courtroom honorifics that are used in English judicial proceedings. To see whether the MT and the PT preserve the interpersonal equivalence in this category, this section analyzes the role of social distance and relative power in translating courtroom honorifics. The function of courtroom honorifics lies mostly in maintaining social distance because they represent the conventionalized way of addressing a person in order to emphasize formal institutional distance (Ashurov, 2025). However, courtroom honorifics also reflect relative power, as they imply the recognition of the superior judicial authority and the existence of an asymmetric relationship between judges and counsel (Ozyumenko, 2023).

As seen from the table above, there are only three courtroom honorifics used in English courtrooms: *Your Honor*, *Mr. President*, and *Honorable Justice*. However, they have a high token frequency in the two-day corpus examined in this paper. The salient feature is a low lexical variation because the recurrence of courtroom honorifics is motivated by the discursive structure of court proceedings, when counsel frequently address the bench during making submissions, responding to judicial interruptions, etc. (Uwen, 2023; Wodak, 1980).

One of the most frequently used honorifics is *Your Honor*. It is translated as "法官大人" in the MT and "法官阁下" in the PT. In this case, social distance becomes a crucial dimension, as *Your Honor* is the conventional courtroom form of address that implies recognition of judicial authority and maintenance of institutional distance between counsel and judge (Kryk-Kastovsky, 2010; Ozyumenko, 2023). Unlike English courtroom discourse, Chinese courtroom discourse does not have a fully equivalent fixed honorific corresponding to *Your Honor*; respect for judicial authority is more commonly expressed through institutional address forms, such as "审判长" or "法官". "法官大人" preserves the deferential force of the English honorific, but it sounds archaic and dramatized in modern Chinese. "法官阁下" is more formal, respectful and ceremonial in accordance with the interactional nature of courtroom discourse, yet it still sounds somewhat foreignized and is not a conventional address form in Chinese courtroom interaction. While "法官阁下" may be more acceptable than "法官大人" in preserving formality, both differ from the normal Chinese courtroom convention. Therefore, "法官大人" is considered to imply a lesser degree of recognition of relative power compared to "法官阁下," which is a more deferential form.

Similarly to *Your Honor*, in the case of *Mr. President*, the most important dimension becomes social distance, and relative power becomes a secondary one. *Mr. President* is the conventional courtroom honorific used to demonstrate respect to presiding judge (Ozyumenko, 2023). The MT renders it as "主席先生" and the PT renders it as "庭长先生". Comparing "主席先生" and "庭长先生," the latter is more closely associated with the courtroom context and therefore better reflects the institutional relationship between the speaker and the presiding judge. However, from the perspective of Chinese courtroom discourse, "审判长" would be a more conventional address form, because Chinese courtroom interaction usually expresses respect through procedural titles rather than honorific forms such as "先生." Although "庭长先生" is not the most conventional address form in Chinese courtroom discourse, it is still more appropriate than "主席先生" because "庭长" carries a clearer judicial-institutional meaning, whereas "主席" is more commonly associated with meetings, committees, or political and organizational positions, failing to maintain the institutional distance of the source text. At the same time, it also fails to convey the second dimension, as "庭长" identifies presiding judge much more precisely than "主席."

Honorable Justice presents a different case, as its translation differs greatly and suggests that the MT may better preserve the honorific nature of this expression. It is rendered as "法官阁下" in the MT and as "法官" in the PT. Unlike *Your Honor* and *Mr. President*, in this case it is obvious that MT preserves the overt marker of deference that can be seen in the phrase *Honorable Justice* (Ozyumenko, 2023). From the perspective of politeness and social distance, "法官阁下" creates a more pronounced institutional distance, while "法官" merely preserves the reference (Brown & Levinson, 1987). However, it does not mean that the PT fails entirely, as it may simply reflect the tendency toward the use of a more restrained Chinese documentary style. It is consistent with Chinese court terminology, where judicial authority is expressed through institutional titles such as "审判长" and "法官" (Supreme People's Court, 2021). Overall, in this case, the MT rendering may be regarded as more successful since it preserves the honorific force of *Honorable Justice* and this form, although is not a conventional address form in Chinese courtroom discourse, is consistent with the other translation of explicit markers, such as "庭长先生" and "法官阁下".

A simple descriptive count supports the qualitative analysis. Among the 20 expressions examined, the PT better preserves interpersonal equivalence in 18 cases (90%), while the machine-translated version performs better in 2 cases (10%). This tendency is particularly clear in historical official titles, where all 9 examples favor the PT.

DISCUSSION

Based on the analysis above, the first finding of the study is that relative power and social distance play unequal roles in all three categories. In institutional role labels and historical official titles, relative power becomes the primary dimension. The role labels in the English text are designed to identify institutional officeholders and place speakers and institutions within a hierarchy of authority. Specifically, expressions such as *The President*, *Clerk of the Court* and *Language Arbiter* indicate procedural authority within the court. In turn, titles such as *War Minister*, *Prime Minister*, *Chief of the Army General Staff*, and *President of the Planning Board* reflect historical responsibility outside the courtroom. Finally, in courtroom honorifics, social distance emerges as the dominating dimension. *Your Honor*, *Mr. President*, and *Honorable Justice* are used not to indicate institutional authority but for establishing respectful interaction and preserving formal distance in courtroom discourse (Al-Mamoory, 2022; Ashurov, 2025). Meanwhile, courtroom honorifics implicitly encode relative power, which recognizes the superior institutional role of a judge (Uwen, 2023).

Another discovery is that interpersonal equivalence in the present study is not achieved through lexical correspondence alone, but through faithful preservation of institutional relations. Indeed, the MT can deliver semantically clear translations, which however lack institutional specificity and precision. The problem manifests itself in phrases such as "语言仲裁员" (*Language Arbiter*), "计划委员会主席" (*President of the Planning Board*), or "海军参谋长" (*Chief of the Naval General Staff*). In all these cases, the meaning is recognizable, but the hierarchical nature of the original expression is lost due to the lack of lexical precision. In contrast, the PT often captures the institutional relation reflected in the source text by opting for

"语言裁定官," "企划院总裁," or "海军参谋总长." Therefore, the preservation of institutional relations and the accurate identification of the corresponding expressions seem to ensure the creation of equivalent interpersonal relations in translation (Liu, 2008; Ma & Wang, 2016).

Thirdly, the analysis of courtroom honorifics proves that interpersonal equivalence involves a balance between preserving deference and conforming to target-language courtroom conventions. In some cases, such as *Your Honor* and *Mr. President*, the PT successfully establishes conventionally formal relationships. However, in the case of *Honorable Justice*, the MT version "法官阁下" conveys deferential tone more explicitly of the source text than its PT alternative "法官". This does not mean that maximum explicitness should be treated as a general principle, since "法官阁下" is not a conventional address form in Chinese courtroom discourse. However, this example suggests that interpersonal equivalence in courtroom honorifics requires functional adequacy: the translator needs to preserve deference and formality while ensuring that the chosen expression remains credible within the target legal culture (Botezat, 2012).

The findings also reveal that the PT is more consistent in its handling of recurrent expressions. This is particularly important in a corpus such as the IMTFE proceedings, where certain role labels and honorific forms recur with high frequency and where consistency itself contributes to the stability of interpersonal meaning across the record. Considering the recurrent nature of certain role labels and honorifics, such as *The President* or *Your Honor*, the maintenance of interpersonal equivalence in IMTFE proceedings is closely connected to the stability of institutional terms. If role labels are rendered inconsistently, such as *The President* in MT, both lexical instability and loss of institutional coherence become inevitable. Therefore, consistency should also be seen as a dimension of interpersonal equivalence in institutional discourse (Lu et al., 2018).

Therefore, the study confirms that PT remains more advantageous than MT in the translation of interpersonal equivalence in legal-historical texts (Altakhaineh et al., 2025). Titles, role labels, and honorifics define the interpersonal relations between participants in a structured legal setting, playing a decisive role in the creation of interpersonal meaning. These findings align well with previous research in which the authors emphasize that legal discourse is distinguished by formal register, institutional roles, and power relations, and that institutions, military ranks, legal terms, and consistency are critical challenges for IMTFE translation (Wu et al., 2025b). Moreover, the results of this study prove that the value of analyzing the difference between MT and PT lies not only in identifying the strengths and weaknesses of each of the alternatives. Comparative analysis is an effective method for understanding how different versions reconstruct relative power and social distance. In this regard, interpersonal equivalence allows us to evaluate whether the tenor of courtroom discourse is preserved in translation.

However, it should also be noted that PT should not be automatically understood as a purely human translation. Since the published version may have involved MT followed by human post-editing, its better performance does not necessarily prove the general superiority of human translation over machine translation. The comparison suggests the importance of human-machine collaboration in translating legal-historical courtroom discourse. While raw MT can provide semantically understandable renderings, it often lacks sufficient sensitivity to institutional hierarchy, historical specificity, legal register, and interpersonal meaning (Killman, 2024). Human post-editing is therefore necessary to refine MT output, correct generic or misleading renderings, and restore the power relations and social distance encoded in the source text (Vieira, 2019). In this sense, the findings point not simply to the limitations of MT, but to the need for effective interaction between machine translation and human legal-historical expertise.

CONCLUSION

In conclusion, this study compared the original English text, the machine-translated Chinese version, and the published Chinese translation of the IMTFE courtroom records for 5 and 6 August 1947 with the focus on institutional and honorific expressions. Institutional role labels, historical official titles, and courtroom honorifics were analyzed in terms of tenor and interpersonal equivalence. It has been revealed that the PT generally manages to recreate the interpersonal equivalence more adequately, and the MT appears less adequate in terms of lexical stability, institutional specificity, and sensitivity to historical and legal register. In particular, the MT tends to render institutional titles and official positions in a more generic way, which may weaken the relative power, status, and social distance encoded in the source text. By contrast, the PT more often preserves the historically established nature of official titles and the procedural meanings of courtroom roles. However, the analysis also reveals that the PT is not always superior. As a result, the study proves that tenor and interpersonal equivalence are valuable theoretical constructs to analyze legal-historical texts and machine translation remains limited in translating historical specific terms, role labels, and honorifics. However, the data used in this study were limited to two hearing days of the IMTFE, and the MT output was generated using only one widely used MT system, DeepL. Future research could examine a larger corpus and compare MT outputs produced by different MT systems.

REFERENCES

Al-Mamoory, S. M. A. (2022). The sociolinguistics of honorifics in English courtroom interaction. *Humanities & Natural Sciences Journal*, *3*(2), 824–833. DOI: 10.53796/hnsj3245

Al-Romany, T. A. H., & Kadhim, M. J. (2024). Artificial intelligence impact on human translation: Legal texts as a case study. *International Journal of Linguistics. Literature and Translation*, *7*(5), 89–95. DOI: 10.32996/ijllt.2024.7.5.11

Altakhaineh, A. R. M., Alghathian, G. A., & Jarrah, M. M. (2025). A comparative study of accuracy in human vs. AI translation of legal documents into Arabic. *International Journal of Language & Law*, *14*, 63–80. DOI: 10.14762/jll.2025.063

Ashurov, B. S. (2025). Interpersonal style and politeness strategies in legal discourse.In Proceedings of the International Scientific and Practical Conference "Modern Philological Issues: Problems and Solutions" (pp. 14-18). DOI: 10.5281/zenodo.15371215

Badah, A. M., Khalaf, C. N., Dwaikat, F. J., & AlQbailat, N. (2025). The usage of artificial intelligence in legal translation: Bridging the gap between law and language. *Ampersand (Oxford, UK)*, *16*, 100248. DOI: 10.1016/j.amper.2025.100248

Botezat, O. (2012). The complexity of legal translation: Social and cultural bounds aspects. *Contemporary Readings in Law and Social Justice*, *4*(1), 641–647.

Brown, P., & Levinson, S. C. (1987). *Politeness: Some universals in language usage*. Cambridge university press. DOI: 10.1017/CBO9780511813085

Bunga, E. L. M., & Katemba, C. V. (2024). Comparing translation quality: Google Translate vs DeepL for foreign language to English. *Edusaintek: Jurnal Pendidikan, Sains dan Teknologi, 11*(3), 1147-1171. DOI: 10.47668/edusaintek.v11i3.1264

Chromá, M. (2014). Making sense in legal translation. *Semiotica, 201*(201). Advance online publication. DOI: 10.1515/sem-2014-0018

Chueasuai, P. (2017). The interpersonal metafunction and translation of power relations: A case study of fifty shades of grey. *MANUSYA: Journal of Humanities, 20*(3), 1-22. https://brill.com/view/journals/mnya/20/3/article-p1_1.xml

Cui, Y., Liu, X., & Cheng, Y. (2023). A comparative study on the effort of human translation and post-editing in relation to text types: An eye-tracking and key-logging experiment. *SAGE Open*, *13*(1), 1–15. DOI: 10.1177/21582440231155849

Fraser, B. (1990). Perspectives on politeness. *Journal of Pragmatics, 14*(2), 219–236. DOI: 10.1016/0378-2166(90)90081-N

Fu, R. (2016). Comparing modal patterns in Chinese-English interpreted and translated discourses in diplomatic setting: A systemic functional approach. *Babel. Revue internationale de la traduction/International Journal of Translation, 62*(1), 104-121. DOI: 10.1075/babel.62.1.06fu

Giampieri, P. (2023). *Legal machine translation explained: MT in legal contexts.* Cambridge Scholars Publishing.

Guzmán, D., & Prieto Ramos, F. (2024). Human and machine translation of legal terminology in international institutional settings: A case study. *De Europa:European and Global Studies Journal*, (special issue), 61–81.

Hale, S. (1997). The treatment of register variation in court interpreting. *The Translator, 3*(1), 39–54. DOI: 10.1080/13556509.1997.10798987

Halliday, M. A., & Hasan, R. (1989). *Language, context, and text: Aspects of language in a social-semiotic perspective.* Oxford University Press.

Hasan, R. (2020). Tenor: Rethinking interactant relations. *Language. Context and Text, 2*(2), 213–333. DOI: 10.1075/langct.00029.has

Hidalgo-Ternero, C. M. (2020). Google Translate vs. DeepL: Analysing neural machine translation performance under the challenge of phraseological variation. *Monographs in Translation and Interpreting*, (6), 154–177. DOI: 10.6035/MonTI.2020.ne6.5

House, J. (1998). Politeness and translation. In Hickey, L. (Ed.), *The pragmatics of translation* (pp. 54–71). Multilingual Matters. DOI: 10.21832/9781800417939-006

House, J. (2015). *Translation quality assessment: Past and present.* Routledge.

Khafaga, A. (2023). Strategic lexicalization in courtroom discourse: A corpus-assisted critical discourse analysis. *Cogent Arts & Humanities, 10*(1), 2217585. DOI: 10.1080/23311983.2023.2217585

Killman, J. (2024). Machine translation literacy in the legal translation context: A SWOT analysis perspective. *The Interpreter and Translator Trainer, 18*(2), 271–289. DOI: 10.1080/1750399X.2024.2344282

Kovács, T. (2022). Human and machine translation: A comparative analysis of neural machine-and human-translated EN-HU and HU-EN legal texts. *Porta Linguarum*, (1), 49–57. DOI: 10.48040/PL.2022.1.5

Kryk-Kastovsky, B. (2010). Power in Early Modern English courtroom discourse. In Tanskanen, S.-K., Helasvuo, M.-L., & Johansson, M. (Eds.), *Discourses in interaction* (pp. 153–172). John Benjamins., DOI: 10.1075/pbns.203.13kry

Lin, L., & Wang, X. (2009). Dui tiyu bisai zhong "caipan" yi ci fanyi de sikao [Reflections on the translation of the term "referee" in sports competitions]. *Journal of Sports Adult Education*, *25*(1), 40–42. http://dx.chinadoi.cn/10.3969/j.issn.1672-268X.2009.01.017

Lin, X., Afzaal, M., & Aldayel, H. S. (2023). Syntactic complexity in legal translated texts and the use of plain English: A corpus-based study. *Humanities & Social Sciences Communications*, *10*(1), 17. DOI: 10.1057/s41599-022-01485-x

Liu, Z. (2008). Translating tenor: With reference to the English versions of Hong Lou Meng. *Meta*, *53*(3), 528–548. DOI: 10.7202/019238ar

Lu, X., Kisselev, O., Yoon, J., & Amory, M. D. (2018). Investigating effects of criterial consistency, the diversity dimension, and threshold variation in formulaic language research. *International Journal of Corpus Linguistics*, *23*(2), 158–182. DOI: 10.1075/ijcl.16086.lu

Ma, Y., & Wang, B. (2016). A review of systemic functional translation studies from an interpersonal perspective. *International Forum of Teaching and Studies*, *12*(1), 36-42. https://americanscholarspress.us/journals/IFST/pdf/IFOTS-1-2016/v12n1-art5.pdf

Masykar, T., Nurrahmi, F., & Masykar, T. (2023). Systemic functional linguistics to preserve interpersonal and ideational meaning in English-Indonesian translation. *Journal of English Education and Teaching*, *7*(3), 560–572. DOI: 10.33369/jeet.7.3.560-572

Moneus, A. M., & Sahari, Y. (2024). Artificial intelligence and human translation: A contrastive study based on legal texts. *Heliyon*, *10*(6), e28106. DOI: 10.1016/j.heliyon.2024.e28106 PMID: 38524597

Nan, Y. (2026). Current English–Chinese legal language mutual translation based on the comparison of the three theoretical levels of words, sentences, and articles. *International Journal of Data Science and Analytics*, *22*(1), 43. DOI: 10.1007/s41060-025-01007-3

Naveen, P., & Trojovský, P. (2024). Overview and challenges of machine translation for contextually appropriate translations. *iScience*, *27*(10), 110878. DOI: 10.1016/j.isci.2024.110878 PMID: 39391737

Ozyumenko, V. I. (2023). Forms of address in courtroom discourse in Englishes of the "Inner Circle". In Baumgarten, N., & Vismans, R. (Eds.), *It's Different with You* (pp. 316–339). John Benjamins. DOI: 10.1075/tar.5.13ozy

Palashevskaya, I. V., Leontiev, V. V., & Kurchenkova, E. A. (2017). Status positions of courtroom discourse participants. In Proceedings of the 7th International Scientific and Practical Conference "Current issues of linguistics and didactics: The interdisciplinary approach in humanities"(CILDIAH 2017). Atlantis Press. DOI: 10.2991/cildiah-17.2017.36

Prieto Ramos, F. (2015). Quality assurance in legal translation: Evaluating process, competence and product in the pursuit of adequacy. *International Journal for the Semiotics of Law*, *28*(1), 11–30. DOI: 10.1007/s11196-014-9390-9

Shi, C., & O'Halloran, K. L. (2025). Constructing the prosecution-defense relationship through multimodal positioning: A corpus-based analysis of Chinese courtroom argumentation. *Social Semiotics*, •••, 1–23. DOI: 10.1080/10350330.2025.2546617

Sokolsky, A. (2022). Retranslating the Tokyo Trial: Shigemitsu Mamoru's Prison Diary. In *The Twelfth International Convention of Asia Scholars (ICAS 12)* (pp.674-682). Amsterdam University Press. DOI: 10.5117/9789048557820/ICAS.2022.078

Sosoni, V., O'Shea, J., & Stasimioti, M. (2022). Translating law: A comparison of human and post-edited translations from Greek to English. *Revista de Llengua i Dret*, (78), 92–120. DOI: 10.2436/rld.i78.2022.3704

Sun, Y., Zhu, X., & Liu, K. (2025). Judicial jigsaw and power dynamics: A cognitive-functional analysis of Chinese courtroom discourse. *International Journal of Legal Discourse*, *10*(1), 181–207. DOI: 10.1515/ijld-2025-2009

Supreme People's Court. (2021, July 22). *Renmin fayuan zuzhi jigou, zhiwu mingcheng, gongzuo changsuo yingyiwen[English translations of people's court institutions, titles, and workplaces]*. https://www.court.gov.cn/fabu/xiangqing/314981.html

Takeda, K. (2007). The making of an interpreter user. *International Journal of Interpretation and Translation*, *5*(1), 245–263. DOI: 10.1075/forum.5.1.11tak

Takeda, K. (2008). *Sociopolitical aspects of interpreting at the International Military Tribunal for the Far East (1946–1948)* [Doctoral dissertation, Universitat Rovira i Virgili]. https://open.unive.it/hitrade/books/TakedaSociopolitical.pdf

Uwen, G. (2023). Objection overruled: Language dynamics and power relations in courtroom interactions. *Language Matters (Pretoria)*, *54*(2), 21–41. DOI: 10.1080/10228195.2023.2229533

Varga, M. (2020). The role of linguistic impression management: The case of Hungarian courtroom discourses. *Corpus Pragmatics : International Journal of Corpus Linguistics and Pragmatics*, *4*(3), 381–400. DOI: 10.1007/s41701-020-00087-9

Venuti, L. (2018). *Rethinking Translation: Discourse, Subjectivity, Ideology*. Routledge. DOI: 10.4324/9780429432385

Vieira, L. N. (2019). Post-editing of machine translation. In O'Hagan, M. (Ed.), *The Routledge handbook of translation and technology* (pp. 319–336). Routledge., DOI: 10.4324/9781315311258-19

Vieira, L. N., O'Hagan, M., & O'Sullivan, C. (2021). Understanding the societal impacts of machine translation: A critical review of the literature on medical and legal use cases. *Information Communication and Society*, *24*(11), 1515–1532. DOI: 10.1080/1369118X.2020.1776370

Wodak, R. (1980). Discourse analysis and courtroom interaction. *Discourse Processes*, *3*(4), 369–380. DOI: 10.1080/01638538009544498

Wu, S., Amini, M., & Mahfoodh, O. H. A. (2025a). A Corpus-based analysis of modality shifts in English-to-Chinese courtroom translation. *Eurasian Journal of Applied Linguistics*, *11*(1), 152–166. https://ejal.info/menuscript/index.php/ejal/article/view/995/364

Wu, S., Amini, M., & Mahfoodh, O. H. A. (2025b). Exploring challenges and solutions in English-to-Chinese courtroom translation: Insights from the Tokyo Trial and implications for translator training. *SAGE Open*, *15*(4), 1–19. DOI: 10.1177/21582440251385865

Wu, S., Amini, M., & Wang, Y. (2026). Negotiating institutional hierarchy: Power, politeness, and meaning construction in English-to-Chinese courtroom translation. *SAGE Open*, *16*(1), 1–14. DOI: 10.1177/21582440261421582

Xuan, J.XUAN Junbin. (2020). Equivalent tenor in translation: A case study on Ophelia's Confession. *Sino-US English Teaching*, *17*(7), 211–216. DOI: 10.17265/1539-8072/2020.07.003

Yang, M., & Wang, M. (2021). A science mapping of studies on courtroom discourse with CiteSpace. *International Journal of Legal Discourse*, *6*(2), 291–322. DOI: 10.1515/ijld-2021-2057

Yang, N. (2019). The application of register analysis into translation quality assessment. *Theory and Practice in Language Studies*, *9*(12), 1550–1554. DOI: 10.17507/tpls.0912.11

Yulianto, A., & Supriatnaningsih, R. (2021). Google Translate vs. DeepL: A quantitative evaluation of close-language pair translation (French to English). *Asian Journal of English Language and Pedagogy*, *9*(2), 109–127. DOI: 10.37134/ajelp.vol9.2.9.2021

ADDITIONAL READING

Claridge, C., Jonsson, E., & Kytö, M. (2024). *Intensifiers in Late Modern English: A Sociopragmatic Approach to Courtroom Discourse*. Cambridge University Press. DOI: 10.1017/9781108560627

Giampieri, P. (2023). *Legal Machine Translation Explained: MT in Legal Contexts*. Cambridge Scholars Publishing.

Halliday, M. A. K. (1978). *Language as Social Semiotic: The Social Interpretation of Language and Meaning*. Edward Arnold.

Hassan, R., & Halliday, M. A. K. (1985). *Language, Context and Text: Aspects of Language in a Social-semiotic Perspective*. Deakin University Press.

Khafaga, A. (2023). Strategic lexicalization in courtroom discourse: A corpus-assisted critical discourse analysis. *Cogent Arts & Humanities*, *10*(1), 2217585. DOI: 10.1080/23311983.2023.2217585

Killman, J. (2024). Machine translation literacy in the legal translation context: A SWOT analysis perspective. *The Interpreter and Translator Trainer*, *18*(2), 271–289. DOI: 10.1080/1750399X.2024.2344282

Leech, G. N. (2014). *The Pragmatics of Politeness*. Oxford University Press. DOI: 10.1093/acprof:oso/9780195341386.001.0001

Munday, J. (2001). *Introducing Translation Studies: Theories and Applications*. Routledge.

Puurtinen, T. (1998). Tenor in literary translation. *Perspectives*, *6*(2), 159–173. DOI: 10.1080/0907676X.1998.9961333

Raven, B. H. (2008). The bases of power and the power/Interaction model of interpersonal influence. *Analyses of Social Issues and Public Policy (ASAP)*, *8*(1), 1–22. DOI: 10.1111/j.1530-2415.2008.00159.x

KEY TERMS AND DEFINITIONS

Courtroom Discourse: The specialized language and communication practices that occur within the legal setting of a courtroom.

Courtroom Honorifics: The respectful institutional forms of address used in interactions in courtroom settings to acknowledge the status and roles of participants, such as judges, lawyers, and witnesses.

Historical Official Titles: The governmental or military official titles that are associated with a historical period and specific institution or department.

Institutional Role Labels: The categorization and assignment roles within institutions, which are crucial for understanding and managing organizational structures and processes.

Interpersonal Equivalence: The preservation of social relationships and power dynamics between interlocutors in the source and target texts.

Machine Translation (MT): The translation from one language to another done by computerized systems without human assistance.

Tenor: The interpersonal function of language, enacting social relationships between discourse participants.

Chapter 10
Toward a Human-in-the-Loop Framework for AI-Assisted Legal Translation:
A Case Study in Deontic Modality

Mohammed H. Alaqad
http://orcid.org/0000-0002-9953-5763
Universiti Malaya, Malaysia

Gisele El Khoury
http://orcid.org/0009-0000-0673-7570
St. Lawrence University, USA

Lama Anwar AlAggad
http://orcid.org/0009-0001-1173-1242
Universiti Malaya, Malaysia

ABSTRACT

This chapter develops a human-in-the-loop framework for AI-assisted legal translation by examining how DeepL, GPT-4, and Claude render deontic modality in French, Arabic, and Malay commercial contracts translated into English. A corpus of twelve contractual segments was compared with translations by legal practitioners. The analysis identified three recurring problems: rendering obligations as descriptive rather than operative statements, weakening contractual prohibitions, and incompletely expressing entitlements. No system performed consistently across all language pairs and modal categories. In response, the chapter proposes a four-stage workflow covering jurisdictional and risk profiling, controlled AI drafting,

DOI: 10.4018/979-8-3373-9179-3.ch010

expert legal post-editing, and final validation. It also outlines required post-editor competencies and institutional measures for disclosure, audit trails, confidentiality, procurement, certification, and proportionate human review. The chapter concludes that AI can improve efficiency, but legally consequential decisions must remain under qualified human control.

INTRODUCTION

AI-assisted legal translation has moved rapidly from experimental use to routine incorporation into multilingual legal workflows. Law firms, corporate legal departments, arbitral institutions, courts, and public agencies increasingly use neural machine translation and large language models to produce first drafts, search terminology, compare versions, and accelerate the handling of high-volume documentation. Recent evaluations show that modern systems can produce highly fluent legal prose and, in some language pairs, perform competitively with conventional neural machine translation on broad measures of adequacy and readability (Briva-Iglesias et al., 2024; Bender et al., 2021; Giampieri, 2025; Moneus & Sahari, 2024). Fluency, however, does not establish that a target clause performs the same legal function as its source. A polished sentence can preserve the general proposition while changing the degree of obligation, the scope of a prohibition, the holder of a right, or the conditions under which a power may be exercised.

The companion chapter, "Algorithmic Mediation in Legal Translation: Discourse, Ambiguity, and Authority," develops the theoretical argument that legal translation involves the reconstruction of institutional meaning rather than the substitution of lexical equivalents. The present chapter does not repeat that theoretical discussion. It begins at the point where the companion chapter ends: the need to test a specific discourse-level risk and to convert the findings into an operational framework. Deontic modality is selected because it provides a focused diagnostic site. Contractual duties, permissions, prohibitions, entitlements, discretions, and conditions are routinely encoded through modal verbs, lexical predicates, tense choices, formulaic constructions, and clause architecture. Their translation therefore requires both linguistic interpretation and knowledge of target-system drafting practice (Cao, 2007; Šarčević, 1997).

The empirical literature supports caution but does not justify a blanket rejection of AI. Legal-domain studies report that automated systems can achieve useful levels of terminological consistency and can reduce editing effort, especially when the source is repetitive and the target convention is well represented in training data (Alwazna, 2024; Ive et al., 2020). At the same time, specialized evaluations identify errors in terminology, context management, omissions, and legally consequential word choices that may not be reflected adequately by sentence-level automatic metrics (Altakhaineh et al., 2025; ElFqih & Monti, 2024). Research on large-language-model post-editing likewise shows that LLMs can improve drafts while occasionally introducing unsupported or hallucinatory changes (Raunak et al., 2023). The relevant question is consequently not whether AI is universally accurate or inaccurate, but under what conditions its output can be integrated into a controlled legal translation process.

This chapter has three objectives. First, it presents an exploratory case study of twelve contract segments drawn from French, Arabic, and Malay legal materials and translated into English using three AI systems and a human legal reference. Second, it develops a risk-sensitive evaluation rubric that distinguishes linguistic acceptability from legal-functional adequacy. Third, it proposes a human-in-the-loop framework covering preparation, AI-assisted drafting, legal post-editing, quality assurance, certification, and institutional governance. The contribution is therefore empirical and procedural. It offers a limited but transparent test of deontic translation and then converts the observed risks into a workflow that can be implemented, audited, taught, and refined.

Four research questions guide the chapter: (1) How do DeepL, GPT-4, and Claude render obligation, prohibition, and entitlement formulae from French, Arabic, and Malay into English? (2) What recurrent divergences arise between AI outputs and the human legal reference? (3) Which divergences create low, medium, or high legal-functional risk? and (4) What human review stages and institutional controls are required to use AI-generated legal translations responsibly? The small corpus does not permit statistical generalization or claims that one system is categorically superior. It is designed instead as a diagnostic multiple-case study capable of identifying recurrent points of professional intervention (Alaqad, 2026).

Three terms are used in a deliberately operational sense. Algorithmic mediation refers to the intervention of a computational system between source and target legal texts. Deontic modality refers to linguistic resources that express duties, permissions, prohibitions, rights, powers, and recommendations. An operative formula is a conventional target-language construction selected to perform a legal function within a particular drafting environment. The term does not imply that only one wording can ever be valid. English-language contracts, for example, may use shall, must, agrees to, is required to, or the simple present under different institutional drafting policies. The evaluation therefore asks whether a translation is functionally appropriate, conventionally defensible, and internally consistent for its stated target context, rather than treating a single modal verb as universally mandatory (Garner & Kimble, 2024).

LITERATURE AND OPERATIONAL CONTEXT

AI Translation in Specialized Legal Workflows

Research on legal-domain machine translation has moved from general comparisons of human and machine output toward more differentiated questions about purpose, language pair, document genre, user expertise, and evaluation method. Briva-Iglesias et al. (2024) found that human assessors could rate LLM translations favourably even when automatic metrics preferred a conventional neural system, illustrating that metric choice affects conclusions. Ive et al. (2020), using a substantial post-editing dataset derived from European legal and institutional material, similarly showed that comparison with a single human reference may underestimate useful machine output. These studies caution against equating surface distance from a reference with legal error; multiple target formulations may be acceptable.

The opposite caution is equally important. Automatic scores and general fluency ratings may overlook a single substitution that changes the legal function of an entire clause. Alwazna's (2024) Arabic-English study demonstrates that a system can obtain a favourable edit-distance score while retaining a legally damaging terminological error. Moneus and Sahari (2024) also report persistent contrasts between AI and human legal translation despite major gains in general linguistic quality. ElFqih and Monti (2024) identify problems in the contextual and terminological treatment of Arabic legislative material by GPT-4 and Gemini. Taken together, these findings support multidimensional human evaluation in which legal effect, not merely lexical similarity, determines severity.

Recent studies have begun to examine AI legal translation in under-represented combinations and institutional environments. Altakhaineh et al. (2025) compare human and AI translation of legal documents into Arabic, while Badah et al. (2026) examine generative systems and student translators in legal tasks. Wright (2025) and Monjean-Decaudin (2025) consider AI-mediated translation in the multilingual legal order of the European Union, where efficiency must be balanced against legal certainty and institutional responsibility. This growing literature confirms that system performance is contingent: a tool that is adequate for informational translation may remain unsuitable for a certified, evidentiary, or contract-execution purpose without qualified review.

Post-Editing, Cognitive Risk, and Human Oversight

Post-editing is not a neutral final polish. It is a distinct cognitive activity shaped by the quality and apparent authority of the machine draft. Professional post-editors must identify errors, decide whether to repair or retranslate, manage consistency, and resist the tendency to accept a fluent proposal merely because it is already present. Guerberof-Arenas and Toral (2020) show that machine-assisted workflows can influence the resulting text and the reader's experience. Daems and Macken (2020) further demonstrate that revision and post-editing are related but not identical practices. These observations matter in legal translation because high fluency can reduce vigilance even where the remaining error is legally significant.

LLMs can themselves be used as post-editors. Raunak et al. (2023) report meaningful improvements when GPT-4 post-edits neural machine translation, but they also document hallucinated edits and therefore reject uncritical automation. Ki and Carpuat (2024) show that external error annotations can guide LLM post-editing, suggesting that structured feedback is more reliable than an unconstrained request to "improve" a translation. For legal practice, the implication is that AI-assisted revision should be bounded by explicit error categories, source-grounded instructions, and a human approval gate. A second model may help detect divergence, but it cannot replace the legally accountable reviewer.

International standards provide useful but incomplete foundations. ISO 17100:2015 distinguishes translation, revision, review, and final verification within a professional service process. ISO 18587:2017 specifies requirements for full post-editing of machine translation output and for post-editor competence. Neither standard was designed specifically for generative AI or for the jurisdictional consequences of modal choices in legal instruments. A current framework must therefore preserve their process discipline while adding AI-specific controls: model and prompt recording, data-security assessment, jurisdictional risk mapping, source-grounded verification, disclosure of tool use where required, and a named professional who accepts responsibility for the final target text.

Why Deontic Modality is an Appropriate Case-Study Variable

Deontic expressions are suitable for an exploratory case study because they are frequent, functionally important, and realized differently across languages and drafting traditions. English contracts use a mixture of modal verbs, lexical verbs, definitions, conditions, and performative constructions. French legal drafting often uses the present indicative, devoir, être tenu de, avoir le droit de, or ne pouvoir pas. Arabic may employ بجي, مزتلي, نيعتي, زوجي, ال زوجي, and قحي, each of which interacts with genre and jurisdiction. Malay legal texts use hendaklah, mesti, boleh, tidak boleh, berhak, and wajib, among other forms. A direct word-to-word map is therefore unsafe. The translator must identify the clause's function and select a target construction that is appropriate to the target instrument.

The chapter avoids a simplistic rule that shall is always stronger than must or that may not is necessarily unenforceable. Modern drafting authorities differ: some retain shall for contractual duties, while many plain-language policies prefer must or use the simple present. Courts interpret provisions in context rather than by applying a universal hierarchy of modal verbs. Accordingly, the analysis treats divergence from the human reference as a signal for legal review, not automatic proof of invalidity. A high-risk error exists when the output changes obligation into discretion, removes a negation, changes the obligated party, omits a condition, or creates an entitlement not supported by the source. A lower-risk issue exists when two formulations express the same function but differ in house style or conventional preference.

METHODOLOGY

Research Design

The study adopts an exploratory qualitative multiple-case design. Its purpose is diagnostic rather than predictive: it examines how three widely used AI systems handle selected modal constructions and identifies where expert intervention is required. This design is appropriate because legal-functional errors are not adequately represented by frequency alone. A single omission of not, a change of party, or a shift from permission to obligation can be more consequential than numerous stylistic deviations. The unit of analysis is therefore the legally operative clause or clause segment rather than the isolated token.

The corpus consists of twelve source segments: four French, four Arabic, and four Malay. All were translated into English. English model contracts and drafting guidance were used as target-context benchmarks, not as a fourth source-language subset. This clarification corrects the earlier formulation that could be read as twelve segments distributed across four source languages. The selected material represents service, sale, confidentiality, agency, construction, and related commercial contexts. Each segment contains at least one expression of obligation, prohibition, permission, entitlement, or conditional power.

Table 1. Corpus construction and sampling

Tier	Materials	Purpose	Selection criteria
1: Institutional parallel material	UN Parallel Corpus and publicly accessible bilingual legal materials	Identify aligned deontic constructions across English, French, and Arabic	Clear clause boundaries; identifiable modal function; public availability
2: Commercial contract material	UK model contracts, OHADA-related materials, Saudi and UAE commercial templates	Test operative language in recognizable commercial genres	Contractual use; deontic expression; sufficient context to identify parties and function
3: Malay legal material	Attorney General's Chambers materials, CIDB forms, standard-form construction material, reported legal usage	Include a hybrid and comparatively under-resourced legal-linguistic context	Publicly accessible text; commercial relevance; modal particle or entitlement formula

Purposive sampling was used because the objective was not to estimate the overall error rate of each system but to test legally salient constructions. The sample includes examples likely to expose cross-system mapping problems: French être tenu de, Arabic يجب and يحق, and Malay hendaklah and tidak boleh. Source segments were retained with enough co-text to identify the actor, action, object, and relevant condition. Personal and confidential data were excluded. Because the study relies on publicly accessible legal material and does not involve human participants as research subjects, no personal-data analysis was undertaken.

Systems, Translation Procedure, and Human Reference

Three systems were examined: DeepL, GPT-4, and Claude. They represent two different operational categories: a dedicated machine translation service and general-purpose generative language models. Each system received the same source segment under standard user-facing settings. The initial comparison used a direct translation instruction without supplying a bespoke glossary, because the study sought to observe baseline behaviour before the human-in-the-loop safeguards were introduced. Outputs were preserved without stylistic harmonization. The analysis is time-bound: cloud-based systems change continuously, and the findings should not be interpreted as permanent properties of a model family.

A human legal reference was prepared or validated by a practitioner with relevant legal-linguistic expertise. The reference functions as an informed target-context solution, not as the only theoretically possible translation. Where an AI version diverged from the reference, the divergence was evaluated for modal value, completeness, target drafting convention, and risk. This distinction is essential. Legal translation permits justified variation, and a different wording is not an error merely because it differs from the reference. The reviewer's task is to determine whether the alternative preserves the same legal relation and is defensible in the intended target context.

The original data record did not retain a reproducible model-build identifier for every cloud system. The revised chapter therefore does not claim exact replicability across future versions. Instead, it reports the procedure transparently, treats the outputs as a bounded snapshot, and incorporates model-version logging as a mandatory requirement in the proposed framework. Future replications should record access date, interface, subscription tier, model label, system instructions, full prompt, temperature or sampling controls where available, and any glossary or retrieval material supplied to the model.

Ethical, Confidentiality, and Data-Governance Considerations

Although the corpus uses publicly accessible material, the professional framework is designed for environments in which legal texts may contain confidential, privileged, commercially sensitive, or personal information. Tool selection therefore cannot be separated from data governance. Before uploading a document, the commissioning institution should determine where data are processed, whether prompts and outputs are retained, whether material may be used for model improvement, what contractual safeguards apply, and whether cross-border transfer restrictions are engaged. Consumer interfaces that are acceptable for public test clauses may be inappropriate for client documents. Enterprise controls, local deployment, redaction, or a prohibition on external processing may be required according to risk.

Professional consent and representation also matter. A client who commissions a certified or sworn translation may reasonably understand that a qualified person has exercised independent judgement over the text. Use of an AI drafting tool does not remove that responsibility. The reviewer must receive sufficient time and access to the complete source to perform a genuine bilingual review, and any statement describing the service must not imply a level of human production or verification that did not occur. The framework therefore treats transparency, competence, and truthful attestation as quality requirements rather than administrative additions.

The case study does not evaluate personal characteristics, legal outcomes, or confidential client files. Its ethical risk lies mainly in interpretation and overgeneralization. To reduce that risk, the revised analysis distinguishes observed textual divergence from proven legal invalidity, reports the corpus as exploratory, and identifies uncertainty where the complete instrument or jurisdiction-specific authority would be necessary. Future studies involving professional participants should obtain appropriate consent, protect client material, and ensure that productivity monitoring does not become intrusive workplace surveillance.

Table 2. Evaluation rubric

Dimension	Diagnostic question	Rating principle
Modal value	Does the target preserve obligation, permission, prohibition, entitlement, discretion, or recommendation?	Major error if the legal relation changes
Actor and scope	Are the obligated/entitled party, action, object, condition, exception, and temporal scope preserved?	Major error for changed party, omitted negation, exception, or condition
Operative conventionality	Is the wording defensible under the target instrument's drafting policy?	Minor to major depending on functional impact
Completeness	Has any legally meaningful element been omitted, added, or generalized?	Severity depends on effect on rights or duties
Instrument consistency	Is the modal choice consistent with definitions and connected clauses?	Minor if stylistic; major if inconsistent wording changes interpretation
Transparency and reviewability	Can the choice be traced to source wording, glossary, prompt, and reviewer decision?	Governance deficiency when traceability is absent

Errors were classified as low, medium, or high risk. Low-risk divergences concern style, capitalization, or a defensible alternative formula that preserves function. Medium-risk divergences create uncertainty, weaken instrument-level consistency, or depart from the declared drafting policy without clearly changing the legal relation. High-risk divergences change the modal category, omit a negation or condition, alter the relevant party, or introduce/remove a right or duty. The classifications are qualitative. No inter-rater reliability statistic is reported because the available dataset was evaluated through a single expert reference process; this is acknowledged as a limitation and converted into a recommendation for dual review in future research.

FINDINGS

Overview of Observed Performance

Across the twelve segments, all three systems produced grammatically fluent English. The principal differences appeared not in basic comprehensibility but in the relationship between source modality and target drafting convention. Three recurring patterns were identified: descriptive paraphrase in place of a preferred operative formula; variability in the rendering of prohibitions; and compression of entitlement constructions. The term pattern is used deliberately rather than error rate because the corpus is too small for robust system ranking.

Claude aligned most often with the human reference in the examples discussed below, particularly for prohibition and entitlement formulae. DeepL was frequently clear but tended to choose general descriptive English. GPT-4 often produced contextually plausible formulations but varied in its choice between shall, must, and descriptive predicates. These tendencies should not be generalized beyond the tested outputs. More importantly, no system demonstrated a stable capacity to explain why a particular modal construction was appropriate to the target jurisdiction or to flag when more than one drafting solution was possible.

Pattern 1: Descriptive Paraphrase and Operative Convention

Segment FR-02, drawn from an OHADA-related service agreement, contains the French formula est tenu de:

Table 3.

Version	Text
Source	Le prestataire est tenu de livrer les services conformément aux spécifications annexées.
DeepL	The service provider is required to deliver the services in accordance with the annexed specifications.
GPT-4	The service provider is required to deliver the services in accordance with the annexed specifications.
Claude	The service provider is required to deliver the services in accordance with the specifications set out in the Annex.
Human reference	The Service Provider shall deliver the Services in conformity with the specifications set out in the Annex.

All three AI outputs preserve the proposition that delivery is obligatory. The earlier draft characterized is required to as non-operative and therefore legally ineffective. That conclusion is too categorical. Is required to can express a binding obligation, and many target institutions might accept it. The analytically defensible finding is narrower: the systems produced a descriptive/passive formulation rather than the target drafting convention selected in the human reference. This is a register and functional-equivalence issue whose severity depends on the contract's drafting policy, surrounding clauses, governing law, and consistency. If the instrument systematically uses shall to allocate contractual duties, the mixed formula may create avoidable interpretive noise even if the duty remains intelligible.

The same issue appears in AR-01, where Arabic يجب was translated as must by the AI systems while the reference used shall. Must is not inherently weaker or stronger in every common-law environment. Many modern drafting guides prefer must precisely because it communicates obligation clearly. The review question is therefore whether must is consistent with the target contract and whether it could be confused with a condition precedent, an external legal requirement, or a drafting instruction. In MY-01, DeepL and Claude used shall for hendaklah, while GPT-4 used must. The outputs illustrate why a jurisdictional style sheet must precede translation: without a declared policy, evaluation can collapse into preference rather than functional analysis.

The pattern supports a central design principle of the framework. AI should not be asked simply to translate a contract "into English." It should be given the target jurisdiction, document purpose, intended legal effect, and approved modal policy. A controlled prompt might state that binding party obligations are to be rendered consistently with a specified model contract and that uncertain mappings must be flagged rather than normalized. The human reviewer then verifies that the chosen formula performs the intended function across the instrument.

Pattern 2: Variability in Prohibitions

Segment MY-03 contains the Malay construction tidak boleh in a standard-form construction context:

Table 4.

Version	Text
Source	Kontraktor tidak boleh menyerahkan atau memindahkan apa-apa bahagian kontrak ini tanpa kebenaran bertulis.
DeepL	The contractor may not assign or transfer any part of this contract without written permission.
GPT-4	The Contractor shall not assign or transfer any part of this Contract without written consent.
Claude	The Contractor shall not assign or transfer any part of this Contract without prior written consent.
Human reference	The Contractor shall not assign or transfer any part of this Contract without the prior written consent of the Employer.

The most important difference is not a universal hierarchy in which may not is always weak and shall not is always strong. Both constructions can express prohibition. The relevant issues are conventionality, scope, and completeness. The reference identifies the Employer as the person whose consent is required; the shortened source segment and some AI outputs render only written permission or consent. If the omitted actor is recoverable from surrounding text, the issue may be medium risk; if not, it may affect administration of the clause. Prior also narrows the temporal requirement and should be preserved when supported by the source or governing form.

In FR-03, the systems varied among under no circumstances may, may not, and shall not disclose. A formula such as under no circumstances may can be emphatic and legally clear, but it may not match the house style used elsewhere in the agreement. The human-in-the-loop task is therefore twofold: preserve the negative modal force and verify the prohibition's full scope, including actor, object, exceptions, consent mechanism, and survival period. This is more reliable than treating one English modal as intrinsically valid and another as invalid.

Prohibitions also present a known computational risk because negation can be omitted, displaced, or associated with the wrong constituent. A fluent clause may prohibit assignment without consent, prohibit only transfer, or imply that consent itself is forbidden. For that reason, every negative deontic construction should receive an automatic risk flag and a source-target alignment check. High-risk review is mandatory when negation, exception, or consent conditions differ.

Pattern 3: Entitlement Formulae and Correlative Duties

Segment AR-03 uses يحق to confer an agent's commission entitlement:

Table 5.

Version	Text
Source	يحق للوكيل الحصول على عمولة بنسبة عشرة بالمائة من قيمة كل صفقة مبرمة.
DeepL	The agent is entitled to a commission of ten percent of the value of each transaction concluded.
GPT-4	The agent is entitled to receive a commission of ten percent of the value of each concluded transaction.
Claude	The Agent shall be entitled to a commission of ten percent (10%) of the value of each transaction entered into.
Human reference	The Agent shall be entitled to a commission of ten percent (10%) of the value of each transaction entered into.

DeepL and GPT-4 used is entitled to; Claude and the reference used shall be entitled to. The earlier draft treated the first formulation as merely descriptive and potentially unenforceable. That claim is not sustainable without jurisdiction-specific authority. Is entitled to is commonly capable of expressing a present contractual right. Shall be entitled to may be preferred where the right arises in the future or upon satisfaction of a condition. The legal review must therefore examine timing, condition, correlative payment duty, and consistency with the contract's entitlement clauses rather than assuming that the presence of shall alone creates enforceability.

The example nevertheless reveals a genuine AI risk: systems may compress or expand the temporal and conditional structure of a right. An Arabic source may indicate that a party has a right, will acquire a right, may exercise a power, or is permitted to act. English target options such as is entitled to, shall be entitled to, may, has the right to, and is authorized to are not interchangeable in every context. If commission becomes due only after payment by the customer, the translation must preserve that trigger. A model that produces a smooth generic entitlement while omitting the condition creates a high-risk error even though the modal phrase itself appears professional.

Entitlements also illustrate the relationship between rights and duties. A clause granting the Agent a commission may imply or expressly impose a corresponding duty on the Principal to calculate and pay it. The post-editor must read connected payment, audit, termination, and dispute clauses to ensure that the translated right remains operational within the instrument. Sentence-level comparison is insufficient.

Table 6. Cross-case synthesis

Observed pattern	Typical AI behavior	Primary review question	Risk trigger
Obligation formula	Uses a fluent descriptive or alternative modal form	Does the formulation fit the declared target drafting policy and connected clauses?	Change from duty to condition, discretion, or recommendation
Prohibition	Varies among shall not, may not, cannot, and lexical negatives	Are negation, actor, exception, consent, and scope preserved?	Omitted/misattached negation or exception
Entitlement	Compresses present/ future right and sometimes omits trigger	When does the right arise and what correlative duty follows?	Omitted condition, changed holder, or invented right
Instrument consistency	Chooses different forms for similar source constructions	Is variation legally motivated or accidental?	Inconsistent allocation of duties or rights
Explanation/ uncertainty	Returns one confident version	Should alternative readings or a reviewer query be surfaced?	Ambiguous source silently normalized

The cross-case result is not that AI cannot translate modal language. In most examples, the systems conveyed the broad meaning. The result is that they did not reliably demonstrate target-system reasoning, instrument-level consistency, or uncertainty management. These are precisely the functions that a human-in-the-loop process must supply. The framework developed below therefore separates tasks that can be delegated—draft production, terminology retrieval, consistency scanning, alternative generation—from tasks that remain attached to accountable human judgement—legal-functional interpretation, risk classification, final wording, and certification.

A HUMAN-IN-THE-LOOP FRAMEWORK FOR AI-ASSISTED LEGAL TRANSLATION

Design Principles

The proposed framework is based on six principles. First, purpose precedes tool selection: an informational translation, internal working draft, due-diligence review, court filing, and certified contract translation require different assurance levels. Second, jurisdiction precedes wording: the target legal system and institutional drafting policy determine what counts as an appropriate operative formula. Third, the source remains authoritative: every AI intervention must be verifiable against the source and documented terminology. Fourth, risk determines review intensity: clauses that allocate rights, duties, liability, termination powers, remedies, governing law, confidentiality, or payment require enhanced review. Fifth, accountability must be named: a qualified person, not the software vendor or an abstract "human in the loop," approves the final text. Sixth, the process must be auditable: model, prompt, glossary, output, edits, reviewer, and approval decision should be recorded proportionately (Alaqad, 2026).

Human-in-the-loop should not mean that a person glances at an AI output after the substantive decisions have already been accepted. The human must have the authority, competence, time, and information needed to reject the draft, return to the source, request legal clarification, or translate a clause independently. A nominal review performed under unrealistic deadlines does not satisfy the framework. The model is therefore human-governed rather than merely human-present.

Phase 1: Commissioning, Risk Classification, and Jurisdictional Profiling

The process begins before translation. The commissioner records the document purpose, intended users, governing law, target jurisdiction, certification status, confidentiality level, and consequences of error. A risk class is then assigned. Class A covers low-stakes informational use with no direct legal effect. Class B covers internal legal work, negotiation drafts, and due-diligence material. Class C covers binding, evidentiary, regulated, or certified documents. Class C material requires full bilingual legal review and professional sign-off; it should not be released directly from an AI interface.

Jurisdictional profiling produces a short project brief. It identifies the source and targets legal traditions, contract genre, preferred drafting authority, modal policy, defined-term conventions, numbering style, and treatment of terms without direct equivalents. For the present case study, a French-to-English OHADA project might specify the selected English-law or international-contract model and how être tenu de, devoir, avoir le droit de, and ne pouvoir pas are normally handled. An Arabic-to-English GCC project should document whether English is an authoritative or convenience version and whether terms grounded in Islamic or domestic law require retention, glossing, or explanatory notes. A Malay-to-English project must account for the hybrid legal environment and the relationship between statutory Malay, English precedents, and sector-specific forms.

Risk mapping follows. The source is searched manually and computationally for obligation, prohibition, permission, entitlement, condition, exception, termination, indemnity, limitation, and dispute-resolution markers. Each occurrence is tagged with clause number, actor, action, beneficiary, trigger, exception, and cross-reference. This map directs attention during post-editing and creates a traceable checklist. It also prevents the common failure in which reviewers focus on terminology while overlooking a changed modal relation.

Phase 2: Controlled AI-Assisted Drafting

The AI system receives a bounded instruction rather than an open-ended request. The prompt identifies the translaxtion direction, document genre, intended target jurisdiction, approved glossary, modal policy, and requirement to preserve clause numbering and defined terms. It instructs the system not to add explanations inside the contract text and to flag uncertainty separately. Where confidentiality permits, relevant parallel clauses or an approved model contract may be supplied as retrieval material. The goal is constrained generation, not stylistic creativity.

A useful prompt architecture contains five elements: role, task, constraints, resources, and output format. For example, the system may be told to act as a legal translation drafting assistant; translate only the supplied clause; preserve every condition and negation; follow a glossary; use the project's approved obligation formula; and return both the translation and an uncertainty note. The prompt should prohibit invented citations, missing defined terms, and silent resolution of ambiguity. Because prompts themselves can alter output, they form part of the project record.

Multi-system comparison may be used selectively for high-risk clauses. Divergence among DeepL, GPT-4, Claude, or another approved system is not evidence that the majority version is correct. It is a triage signal. When outputs vary in modal category, actor, negation, or condition, the clause is escalated automatically. Conversely, agreement among systems does not eliminate review because shared training patterns can generate shared mistakes. The framework uses model agreement as workflow information, not as a substitute for legal judgement (Alaqad, 2026). e

Phase 3: Human Legal Post-Editing

Table 7.

Step	Purpose
1. Source reorientation	The post-editor reads the source clause and relevant surrounding provisions before reading the AI draft closely. This reduces anchoring and restores the source as the primary object of attention.
2. Modal-function analysis	The reviewer identifies whether the clause imposes a duty, prohibition, permission, entitlement, power, recommendation, condition, or exception, and records the relevant actor and trigger.
3. Target-form selection	The reviewer applies the jurisdictional style sheet and selects a defensible target formula. Where several forms are acceptable, consistency with the full instrument governs the choice.
4. Element-by-element alignment	Actor, action, object, beneficiary, timing, condition, exception, negation, cross-reference, and defined terms are checked against the source.
5. Connected-clause review	The clause is read with definitions, payment, termination, liability, and dispute provisions to ensure that rights and duties remain coherent across the document.
6. Independent challenge	For Class C material, a second qualified reviewer challenges high-risk choices and confirms that uncertainty has been resolved or disclosed.
7. Finalization and certification	Formatting, numbering, names, dates, amounts, and annex references are verified. A named professional approves the final text and records the scope of responsibility.

The framework distinguishes full post-editing from light post-editing. Light post-editing aims at intelligibility and may be suitable for Class A material. Full legal post-editing aims at functional equivalence, terminological consistency, target-genre conformity, and complete source-target correspondence. Class B and C documents require full post-editing. Certification is not a decorative final step; it is the point at which responsibility is attached to an identifiable professional under the applicable rules.

Phase 4: Quality Assurance, Audit Trail, and Release

Quality assurance combines automated and human checks. Automated checks can identify inconsistent defined terms, numbers, dates, missing segments, repeated clauses, and variation in modal wording. They cannot determine legal sufficiency. The human checklist therefore confirms the risk map, reviews every high-risk clause, verifies terminology against authoritative sources, and records unresolved issues. A release gate prevents delivery until mandatory items are complete.

The audit record should be proportionate rather than burdensome. At minimum, it contains the source version, target version, model and interface, access date, prompt, glossary, reviewer name and qualifications, review level, high-risk decisions, and approval date. For confidential work, the record also documents the data-processing basis and whether client material was uploaded to an external service. Auditability supports correction, accountability, procurement review, and future model evaluation.

Disclosure to clients should be governed by contract, professional rules, and institutional policy. The framework does not assume that every use of a spell-checker or terminology tool requires a prominent notice. It does require transparent disclosure when generative or machine translation materially produced the first draft of a binding or certified document, particularly where confidentiality, consent, or professional representation is implicated. The final attestation must accurately describe the human reviewer's work.

Table 8. Competency profile for legal AI post-editors

Competency	Required capability	Evidence in practice
Legal-linguistic competence	Interpret source legal function and select target-system wording	Explains modal choice with reference to source, governing context, and drafting policy
Comparative legal competence	Recognize non-equivalence across legal traditions	Flags concepts and formulae requiring adaptation, retention, or clarification
AI and data literacy	Understand model variability, prompting, hallucination, confidentiality, and logging	Uses bounded prompts, preserves records, and does not treat confidence as correctness
Post-editing and revision competence	Detect machine-specific errors and resist anchoring	Reorients to source, performs full bilingual checks, and retranslates when necessary
Instrument-level reading	Assess coherence across definitions and connected provisions	Checks rights, duties, exceptions, cross-references, and temporal triggers throughout document
Ethical and professional judgement	Determine review level, disclosure, escalation, and certification limits	Refuses unsupported sign-off and records unresolved legal questions

These competencies build on professional translation standards but add a distinct layer of AI governance. A linguistically strong translator without comparative legal knowledge may miss functional divergence. A lawyer without translation competence may overlook source-language nuance. An AI specialist without professional responsibility may optimize output without recognizing certification requirements. High-stakes legal post-editing therefore benefits from interdisciplinary teams or practitioners trained across these domains (Way, 2016; El-Farahaty, 2025).

IMPLEMENTATION SCENARIO AND FRAMEWORK VALIDATION

Worked Scenario: Arabic-English Agency Agreement

To show how the framework operates beyond the isolated examples, consider a hypothetical commission to translate a twenty-page Arabic agency agreement into English for negotiation between a UAE principal and an overseas agent. The agreement contains commission rights, exclusivity obligations, confidentiality restrictions, termination powers, audit rights, and governing-law provisions. The client requests a rapid English draft but also indicates that the English version may later be executed. Under the proposed model, the project cannot remain classified as a low-risk informational task merely because the immediate purpose is negotiation. Its likely progression to execution, its commercial value, and its allocation of payment and termination rights justify Class C controls from the outset.

During commissioning, the project manager records that UAE law governs, Arabic is the source and presumptively authoritative version, and English is intended initially for negotiation. A confidentiality assessment determines whether an external AI service may receive the unredacted text. The jurisdictional profile identifies recurrent Arabic expressions such as مزتلي, بجي, ال زوجي, زوجي, قحي, and ءاهنإ له قحي. It also sets a target policy: party obligations will use a consistent contractual form; permissions and discretions will be distinguished from entitlements; termination powers will preserve conditions and notice periods; and defined terms will remain unchanged throughout the document.

Risk mapping then identifies every clause involving commission calculation, payment date, set-off, exclusivity, assignment, confidentiality, termination, indemnity, liability limitation, audit, governing law, and dispute resolution. For each item, the map records the actor, beneficiary, action, trigger, exception, and related provision. The commission clause in AR-03 is therefore not reviewed in isolation. It is linked to clauses defining a completed transaction, receipt of customer payment, currency conversion, tax deduction, and post-termination commission. This connected view prevents a fluent translation of قحي from obscuring the event that actually causes the entitlement to arise.

In the controlled drafting phase, the model receives the approved glossary and is instructed to preserve all conditions, negations, percentages, cross-references, and defined terms. It is required to place uncertainty notes outside the translated clause. If two systems produce different translations of a termination provision—one using may terminate and another is entitled to terminate—the divergence is escalated. The post-editor does not decide by majority vote. The source construction, condition, notice requirement, and target drafting policy determine the final wording. If the Arabic remains ambiguous about whether termination is immediate or notice-dependent, the reviewer raises a query rather than silently selecting the more common English formula.

The first human review begins with source reorientation. The reviewer reads each high-risk Arabic provision and its surrounding clauses before examining the model's wording. The second review tests instrument-level coherence: a right granted in the commission clause must correspond to a payment obligation elsewhere; an assignment prohibition must use the same consent authority throughout; and a termination power must align with the survival clauses. Numbers, names, dates, defined terms, and annex references are checked separately because a legally accurate modal formulation can still fail through an incorrect percentage or cross-reference.

Before release, the audit package records the source version, tool and access date, prompt, glossary, initial AI draft, post-edited version, reviewer decisions, unresolved queries, and approval. If the English draft later becomes an execution version, the risk classification is revisited rather than assumed to remain unchanged. A final bilingual legal review is performed against the agreed Arabic text, and the responsible professional signs only after confirming the scope of review. This scenario illustrates that human-in-the-loop is a lifecycle process, not a single editing event.

Table 9. Decision matrix for review intensity

Document/use case	Illustrative risk class	Minimum human control	Release condition
Internal comprehension of a non-binding memo	A	Bilingual spot-check of terminology and material facts	Marked as informational; no certification
Negotiation draft or due-diligence material	B	Full post-editing of material clauses; targeted second review	Purpose and AI assistance recorded; unresolved issues disclosed
Commercial contract intended for signature	C	Full bilingual legal post-editing plus independent high-risk review	Named professional approval and complete audit record
Court, arbitral, regulatory, or certified submission	C	Jurisdiction-qualified review, formal verification, and applicable certification	Compliance with procedural and professional rules
Sensitive or privileged material	B or C	Approved secure environment or no external AI use	Data-governance authorization documented

Validation Plan for the Proposed Framework

The framework should be treated as a testable intervention rather than a finished universal standard. A suitable validation study would recruit professional legal translators and divide comparable contract segments among three conditions:

human translation from scratch, ordinary AI-assisted post-editing, and AI-assisted translation using the full framework. Participants would work with the same source materials, target brief, and time limits. Independent bilingual legal assessors, blinded to condition, would evaluate modal value, actor and scope, completeness, terminology, instrument coherence, and critical-error severity.

Outcome measures should include final quality, number of high-risk errors, time on task, number and type of edits, reviewer confidence, source consultation behaviour, and perceived cognitive effort. Process data could be collected through screen recording, keystroke logging, eye tracking, or retrospective interviews where ethically and practically appropriate. The central test is not whether the framework produces the most stylistically elegant text, but whether it lowers residual legal-functional risk without making the workflow unusably slow.

Validation should also examine calibration. Reviewers who are too distrustful may rewrite acceptable output unnecessarily, reducing efficiency, while reviewers who are too trusting may preserve subtle errors. The desired outcome is calibrated reliance: acceptance when the source-target relation is verified, correction when evidence supports it, and escalation when legal interpretation exceeds the translator's mandate. Repeated studies across Arabic-English, French-English, Malay-English, and reverse directions would reveal which controls are general and which must be localized.

Institutional pilots can complement laboratory studies. A law firm, court translation unit, or corporate legal department could implement the framework for a defined period and compare it with its previous workflow. Audit findings, client corrections, turnaround time, confidentiality incidents, and downstream disputes would provide practical evidence. Because serious legal errors are rare but consequential, near-miss reporting should be encouraged. A clause corrected before release is valuable evidence about a risk the system successfully controlled, not merely an editing inconvenience.

DISCUSSION

What the Case Study Demonstrates

The case study demonstrates that fluent AI output can be useful while remaining insufficiently self-validating. The systems generally recognized that the selected clauses involved duties, restrictions, or rights. Their divergence concerned how those functions were realized in the target contract and whether all elements of the legal relation were preserved. This is a more precise conclusion than claiming that AI uniformly mistranslates deontic modality. The systems can generate viable drafts;

they cannot independently establish that the draft is appropriate for the governing legal and institutional context.

The revised analysis also shows the danger of overclaiming legal consequences. A chapter about AI opacity should not replace machine certainty with scholarly certainty. Is required to, must, may not, is entitled to, and shall be entitled to can all be legally meaningful. Their interpretation depends on text, purpose, governing law, and drafting policy. The human reviewer's role is not to substitute a preferred word mechanically but to justify a formulation within the whole instrument. This nuanced position strengthens the chapter's central argument: legal translation requires accountable contextual judgement.

The findings align with broader evidence that legal-domain output should be evaluated through human, purpose-sensitive criteria. Automatic metrics can support benchmarking, but they do not assign severity according to legal effect (Alwazna, 2024; Briva-Iglesias et al., 2024). A one-word modal or negation error may be more serious than extensive stylistic editing. The rubric proposed here therefore prioritizes modal category, actor, scope, condition, and connected-clause coherence.

Implications for Professional Practice and Procurement

For practitioners, the framework shifts attention from choosing the "best" tool to designing a defensible process. Tool performance changes with model updates, prompts, language pairs, and document genres. Procurement based solely on price per word or general quality scores will not capture legal-functional risk. Commissioners should specify document class, required review level, post-editor qualifications, confidentiality controls, audit records, and liability allocation. Service providers should distinguish raw AI output, lightly edited informational translation, fully post-edited legal translation, and certified translation.

For law firms and in-house departments, the framework can be implemented through a standard operating procedure. Intake forms capture governing law and purpose; project templates contain jurisdictional glossaries; risk maps identify high-stakes clauses; approved prompts constrain drafting; and release checklists require bilingual review. Periodic audits can sample completed projects and compare error types, editing time, client corrections, and downstream incidents. Model choice may then be evidence-based and language-pair-specific rather than driven by reputation or convenience.

Confidentiality is a threshold issue. Commercial contracts may contain personal data, trade secrets, litigation strategy, and privileged communications. Institutions should assess whether the selected service stores prompts, uses inputs for training, transfers data across borders, or provides enterprise controls. Redaction, local deployment, contractual safeguards, or a prohibition on external AI may be necessary.

A human-in-the-loop framework that ignores data governance is incomplete even if its linguistic review is strong.

Implications for Pedagogy and Certification

Legal translation education should treat AI post-editing as a structured professional task rather than an informal shortcut. Students need controlled exercises in which fluent drafts contain modal, terminological, scope, and omission errors. Assessment should reward detection, explanation, source-based correction, and escalation, not merely the final wording. Comparative modules can require students to build jurisdictional style sheets for French-English, Arabic-English, and Malay-English projects and defend their choices before legal and translation specialists.

Training should also address cognitive bias. Students can compare independent translation with post-editing, review mislabeled human and machine outputs, and document how initial suggestions shape their choices. This develops source reorientation and calibrated trust. AI literacy should include prompt design, version logging, confidentiality, and the limits of automated metrics. Legal competence should include contract architecture, defined terms, conditions precedent, rights and remedies, and the difference between translating for information and producing an instrument intended to operate in the target system.

Professional bodies could create specialist continuing-development modules rather than assuming that general legal translation certification automatically covers AI-mediated workflows. Competence assessment may include an AI-generated contract containing hidden modal and scope errors, followed by a requirement to produce a corrected version and an audit note. Certification standards should make clear that the human signatory remains responsible for the final text regardless of the productivity tool used.

Table 10. Institutional governance criteria and performance indicators

Governance area	Minimum control	Example indicator
Purpose and risk	Classify every project before tool use	Percentage of projects with completed risk classification
Data governance	Approve tools for confidentiality and data-processing conditions	Number of unauthorized uploads or data incidents
Reproducibility	Record model, date, prompt, glossary, and source version	Percentage of Class C projects with complete audit records
Human review	Require qualified bilingual legal review for binding/certified texts	High-risk clauses independently checked

continued on following page

Table 10. Continued

Governance area	Minimum control	Example indicator
Quality	Track modal, omission, terminology, number, and cross-reference errors	Critical errors per 1,000 source words after post-editing
Efficiency	Measure time and cost without sacrificing error controls	Editing time by language pair and risk class
Accountability	Name final approver and escalation route	Percentage of releases with professional sign-off
Continuous improvement	Review errors and update glossaries/prompts	Corrective actions completed after quarterly audit

Performance indicators should not reward speed alone. A workflow that reduces turnaround time while increasing undetected high-risk errors is not successful. Institutions should track both productivity and residual risk, with special attention to errors discovered after delivery. The framework's effectiveness can be evaluated through controlled comparisons of human-only translation, AI-assisted translation under ordinary practice, and AI-assisted translation under the full protocol.

LIMITATIONS AND FUTURE RESEARCH

The study has several limitations. The corpus contains only twelve purposively selected segments and cannot support statistical claims about overall system accuracy. The examples are translated into English and focus on commercial contracts; results may differ in reverse directions and in statutes, judgments, pleadings, treaties, or administrative forms. The human reference represents an expert solution rather than an infallible gold standard. A larger study should use multiple independent legal translators, blind assessment, adjudication, and inter-rater agreement.

The cloud systems were examined during a bounded data-collection period, but exact build identifiers were not preserved consistently. This limits reproducibility and prevents claims about current model versions. Future studies should archive prompts and outputs with timestamps, model identifiers, parameter settings, and data-security conditions. They should test zero-shot translation, glossary-constrained prompting, retrieval-augmented generation, multi-agent review, and human-in-the-loop workflows under the same corpus and evaluation rubric.

The legal-effect analysis is necessarily cautious. Determining whether a wording changes enforceability may require jurisdiction-specific case law and the complete contract. Future interdisciplinary research should pair translation scholars with lawyers from each relevant jurisdiction and distinguish drafting preference, interpretive uncertainty, and demonstrable change in legal effect. Studies should also examine whether judges, lawyers, and clients perceive AI-generated modal formulations differently from human formulations.

Further research is especially needed for Malay and other under-resourced legal languages. Corpus development should include aligned authoritative texts, metadata on governing law and legal status, and annotations for deontic function, actor, condition, exception, and risk. The proposed framework should be field-tested with professional translators to measure editing time, cognitive effort, critical-error detection, trust calibration, and user acceptance. Longitudinal studies can determine whether model improvements reduce specific errors or merely shift them to less visible levels.

CONCLUSION

This chapter has extended the companion chapter by moving from theoretical diagnosis to empirical testing and procedural design. An exploratory comparison of DeepL, GPT-4, Claude, and a human legal reference across twelve French, Arabic, and Malay contract segments identified recurrent divergence in obligation, prohibition, and entitlement formulae. The systems produced useful and often fluent drafts, but they did not reliably supply the jurisdictional reasoning, instrument-level consistency, uncertainty signalling, and professional accountability required for high-stakes legal translation.

The revised analysis rejects two extremes. AI output should not be treated as autonomous legal translation, but every divergence from a preferred human formulation should not be declared legally invalid. Modal choices such as shall, must, may not, and is entitled to require contextual evaluation. The decisive questions are whether the target preserves the source legal relation, fits the target drafting policy, remains coherent across the instrument, and has been approved by a qualified professional.

The proposed human-in-the-loop framework responds through four connected phases: commissioning and risk mapping; controlled AI-assisted drafting; source-oriented human legal post-editing; and quality assurance, audit, and release. It adds a competency profile, governance controls, and measurable indicators. Its central principle is straightforward: AI may generate language, but legal authority must remain attached to identifiable human judgement. Responsible adoption therefore depends less on confidence in a particular model than on the strength of the process within which the model is used.

REFERENCES

Alaqad, M. H. (2026). Building excellence in conference interpreting in Malaysia: Training models, lifelong learning, and AI-driven career pathways. In Amini, M. (Ed.), *Enhancing quality in conference interpreting* (pp. 183–204). IGI Global Scientific Publishing., DOI: 10.4018/979-8-3373-3710-4.ch006

Altakhaineh, A. R. M., Alghathian, G. A., & Jarrah, M. M. (2025). A comparative study of accuracy in human vs. AI translation of legal documents into Arabic. *International Journal of Language & Law*, *14*, 63–80. DOI: 10.14762/jll.2025.063

Alwazna, R. Y. (2024). The use of automation in the rendition of certain articles of the Saudi Commercial Law into English: A post-editing-based comparison of five machine translation systems. *Frontiers in Artificial Intelligence*, *6*, 1282020. Advance online publication. DOI: 10.3389/frai.2023.1282020 PMID: 38282905

Badah, A. M., Khalaf, C. N., Dwaikat, F. J., & AlQbailat, N. M. (2026). The usage of artificial intelligence in legal translation: Bridging the gap between law and language. *Ampersand (Oxford, UK)*, *16*, 100248. Advance online publication. DOI: 10.1016/j.amper.2025.100248

Bender, E. M., Gebru, T., McMillan-Major, A., & Shmitchell, S. (2021). On the dangers of stochastic parrots: Can language models be too big? In *Proceedings of the 2021 ACM Conference on Fairness, Accountability, and Transparency* (pp. 610–623). Association for Computing Machinery. https://doi.org/DOI: 10.1145/3442188.3445922

Briva-Iglesias, V., Camargo, J., & Dogru, G. (2024). Large language models "ad referendum": How good are they at machine translation in the legal domain? *MonTI. Monografías de Traducción e Interpretación*, *16*(16), 57–90. DOI: 10.6035/MonTI.2024.16.02

Cao, D. (2007). *Translating law*. Multilingual Matters. DOI: 10.26034/cm.jostrans.2008.689

Daems, J., & Macken, L. (2020). Post-editing human translations and revising machine translations. In Koponen, M., Mossop, B., Robert, I. S., & Scocchera, G. (Eds.), *Translation revision and post-editing: Industry practices and cognitive processes* (pp. 50–70). Routledge., DOI: 10.4324/9781003096962-5

El-Farahaty, H. (2025). Integrating corpora and AI tools in the teaching, learning, and assessing of Arabic/English legal translation. *International Journal for the Semiotics of Law – Revue internationale de Sémiotique juridique, 38*, 2031–2060. https://doi.org/DOI: 10.1007/s11196-025-10281-0

ElFqih, K., & Monti, J. (2024). Large language models as legal translators of Arabic legislatives: Do ChatGPT and Gemini care for context and terminology? In *Proceedings of the 1st Workshop on Towards Ethical and Inclusive Conversational AI: Language Attitudes, Linguistic Diversity, and Language Rights* (pp. 111–122). Association for Computational Linguistics. DOI: 10.18653/v1/2024.arabicnlp-1.10

Garner, B. A., & Kimble, J. (2024). *Essentials for drafting clear legal rules*. Administrative Office of the United States Courts.

Giampieri, P. (2025). *Assessing the quality of AI and MT in legal translation*. Altre Modernità., DOI: 10.54103/2035-7680/28886

Guerberof-Arenas, A., & Toral, A. (2020). The impact of post-editing and machine translation on creativity and reading experience. *Translation Spaces*, *9*(2), 255–282. DOI: 10.1075/ts.20035.gue

International Organization for Standardization. (2015). *ISO 17100:2015 translation services—Requirements for translation services*. https://www.iso.org/standard/59149.html

International Organization for Standardization. (2017). *ISO 18587:2017 translation services—Post-editing of machine translation output—Requirements*. https://www.iso.org/standard/62970.html

Ive, J., Specia, L., Szoc, S., Vanallemeersch, T., Van den Bogaert, J., Farah, E., . . . Khalilov, M. (2020, May). A post-editing dataset in the legal domain: do we underestimate neural machine translation quality? In *Proceedings of the Twelfth Language Resources and Evaluation Conference* (pp. 3692-3697). https://aclanthology.org/2020.lrec-1.455/

Ki, D., & Carpuat, M. (2024). Guiding large language models to post-edit machine translation with error annotations. In *Findings of the Association for Computational Linguistics: NAACL 2024* (pp. 4253-4273). Association for Computational Linguistics. DOI: 10.18653/v1/2024.findings-naacl.265

Moneus, A. M. A., & Sahari, Y. (2024). Artificial intelligence and human translation: A contrastive study based on legal texts. *Heliyon*, *10*(6), e28106. Advance online publication. DOI: 10.1016/j.heliyon.2024.e28106 PMID: 38524597

Monjean-Decaudin, S. (2025). Les enjeux de l'intelligence artificielle pour la traduction juridique au sein de l'Union européenne: Observations générales du point de vue de la juritraductologie. *International Journal of Language & Law*, *14*, 194–203. DOI: 10.14762/jll.2025.194

Raunak, V., Sharaf, A., Wang, Y., Awadalla, H., & Menezes, A. (2023). Leveraging GPT-4 for automatic translation post-editing. In *Findings of the Association for Computational Linguistics: EMNLP 2023* (pp. 12009–12024). Association for Computational Linguistics. https://doi.org/DOI: 10.18653/v1/2023.findings-emnlp.804

Šarčević, S. (1997). *New approach to legal translation*. Kluwer Law International.

Way, C. (2016). The challenges and opportunities of legal translation and translator training in the 21st century. *International Journal of Communication, 10*, 1009–1029. https://ijoc.org/index.php/ijoc/article/view/3580

Wright, S. (2025). Artificial intelligence in legal translation at the Court of Justice of the European Union. *International Journal of Language & Law, 14*, 120–142. DOI: 10.14762/jll.2025.120

ADDITIONAL READING

Baaij, C. J. W. (2018). *Legal integration and language diversity: Rethinking translation in EU lawmaking*. Oxford University Press. DOI: 10.1093/oso/9780190680787.001.0001

Biel, Ł. (2014). *Lost in the Eurofog: The textual fit of translated law*. Peter Lang. DOI: 10.3726/978-3-653-03986-3

Bowker, L., & Buitrago Ciro, J. (2019). *Machine translation and global research: Towards improved machine translation literacy in the scholarly community*. Emerald Publishing.

Drugan, J. (2013). *Quality in professional translation: Assessment and improvement*. Bloomsbury Academic.

Foblets, M.-C., & Graziadei, M. (Eds.). (2025). *Legal translation, cultural diversity and the search for justice*. Springer.

Kenny, D. (Ed.). (2022). *Machine translation for everyone: Empowering users in the age of artificial intelligence*. Language Science Press.

Koehn, P. (2020). *Neural machine translation*. Cambridge University Press. DOI: 10.1017/9781108608480

O'Brien, S. (2022). Machine translation and cognition. In Kenny, D. (Ed.), *Machine translation for everyone* (pp. 309–324). Language Science Press.

Prieto Ramos, F. (Ed.). (2018). *Institutional translation for international governance: Enhancing quality in multilingual legal communication*. Bloomsbury Academic.

Tiersma, P. M. (1999). *Legal language*. University of Chicago Press. DOI: 10.7208/chicago/9780226854809.001.0001

KEY TERMS AND DEFINITIONS

Deontic Modality: The linguistic resources through which duties, permissions, prohibitions, entitlements, powers, and recommendations are expressed. In this chapter, modal value is evaluated together with actor, scope, condition, and target drafting convention.

Human-in-the-Loop Framework: A human-governed process in which AI may generate or assist a draft, but qualified professionals control risk classification, legal-functional interpretation, post-editing, quality assurance, and release.

Instrumental Translation: Translation that produces a target text functioning equivalently to the source text within the target legal system, as distinct from documentary translation, which renders what a source text says without reconstituting its operative effect. Legal translation belongs to the instrumental category.

Instrument-Level Verification: Review of a translated clause in relation to definitions, connected provisions, cross-references, and the overall allocation of rights and duties in the legal instrument.

Jurisdictional Profiling: Pre-translation documentation of governing law, target legal system, document purpose, drafting policy, terminology, certification requirements, and non-equivalent concepts.

Legal-Functional Adequacy: The degree to which a target formulation preserves the source legal relation and performs an appropriate function in the intended target context.

Operative Formula: A conventional linguistic construction used to realize a legal function in a specified drafting environment. It is a project- and jurisdiction-sensitive choice rather than a universally fixed word.

Post-Editing (Legal): The process of reviewing, correcting, and certifying a machine-generated translation to bring it into conformity with the discursive and normative requirements of the target legal system. Distinct from translation ab initio in both its cognitive demands and its professional ethics.

Risk Mapping: Identification and tagging of clauses involving duties, prohibitions, permissions, entitlements, conditions, exceptions, liability, remedies, or other consequences requiring enhanced review.

Source Reorientation: A post-editing technique in which the reviewer analyses the source and its legal function before accepting or modifying the machine proposal, reducing anchoring on fluent AI output.

Conclusion

The investigations compiled within Exploring Complexity in Legal Translation and Discourse Analysis collectively explore understanding and executing the transfer of legal meaning. Through empirical analysis and theoretical modeling, this volume has proven that legal translation cannot be isolated from the socio legal and discursive environments that produce it. The chapters have systematically dismantled the notion that linguistic fluency equates to legal accuracy, revealing instead a complex web of multimodal signals, institutional hierarchies, and performative obligations that must be meticulously preserved across linguistic borders.

A recurring revelation throughout this work is the inherent fragility of legal equivalence. Whether examining the nuanced honorifics of historical courtroom records or the dense conceptual frameworks of modern data protection laws, the contributors have highlighted the persistent gap between semantic correspondence and legal fidelity. The identification of implicit conceptual risks, particularly the phenomenon of false friends hidden beneath standardized terminology, serves as a critical warning for practitioners and policymakers. It underscores the reality that standardized dictionaries and glossaries are insufficient tools when separated from an understanding of statutory priority and jurisdictional context. The burden remains firmly on the translator to act as a comparative legal analyst, navigating divergent systems to protect the substantive rights enshrined within the source text.

Furthermore, this publication provides a critical intervention into the rapid proliferation of automated translation technologies. The collective findings clearly demonstrate that artificial intelligence, while highly efficient at processing syntax, currently lacks the capacity for true legal comprehension. The tendency of these systems to silently resolve ambiguities and reconstruct modal obligations presents a profound risk to institutional authority. By defining the algorithmic erosion of legal meaning, the research equips the academic community and the translation industry with the necessary vocabulary to advocate for responsible technological governance. The proposed diagnostic models and workflow frameworks offer a pragmatic path forward, establishing clear boundaries for machine involvement in legally consequential drafting.

Looking toward the future, the implications of this book extend far beyond the immediate sphere of translation studies. The demand for clear, accurate, and equitable legal communication will only intensify as global digital infrastructures expand. To meet this demand, the pedagogical strategies and institutional policies outlined in these chapters must be actively integrated into academic curricula and professional certification programs. Future legal translators must be trained not only as linguistic experts but as critical evaluators of algorithmic output, capable of identifying and correcting the discursive flattening caused by machine mediation.

Ultimately, Exploring Complexity in Legal Translation and Discourse Analysis serves as a rigorous defense of human agency in the administration of justice. It argues that the performative force of law, the very mechanism that binds societies together, requires the nuanced judgment and ethical oversight that only human professionals can provide. By bridging the gap between critical discourse theory and practical translation strategy, this volume empowers researchers, educators, and practitioners to safeguard the integrity of multilingual legal systems in an increasingly complex and automated world.

As we stand at the precipice of a new era in global communication, the discourse surrounding legal translation is no longer confined to human linguistic competence. The chapters within Exploring Complexity in Legal Translation and Discourse Analysis have charted a rigorous course through the intricate mechanisms of legal meaning, yet they also point toward a horizon dominated by rapid technological integration.

The advent of Large Language Models and Agentic AI has irreversibly altered the translation landscape. We are witnessing the rapid expansion of the Human Algorithm Interface in Translation, a space where computational efficiency frequently collides with the profound need for deontic precision. In this automated ecosystem, the risk of conceptual asymmetry is magnified. Algorithms, driven by statistical probability, often struggle to navigate the multimodal realities and nuanced source hierarchies inherent in complex legal frameworks.

This reality brings us to a critical juncture. The future of legal localization does not lie in the wholesale replacement of human cognitive labor, but rather in the deliberate cultivation of the Human Lead. As artificial intelligence systems assume greater roles in processing vast volumes of text, the human translator must evolve from a mere bilingual mediator into an expert post editor, a prompt literacy specialist, and a guardian of legal fidelity. The human must remain the ultimate arbiter of meaning, ensuring that the performative force of law is not diluted by algorithmic mediation.

Moving forward, our research and pedagogical frameworks must prioritize Multimodal Translation Studies and the complex realities of digital education ecosystems. We must equip the next generation of researchers and practitioners not only with advanced linguistic skills but with the technological agility required to govern artificial intelligence tools responsibly.

The discussions initiated in this volume are not endpoints but catalysts. They challenge us to continuously and critically evaluate how power, meaning, and authority are negotiated across languages and platforms. It is my hope that the frameworks and insights provided here will empower scholars and professionals to navigate the complexities of our multilingual world with both technological fluency and unwavering ethical resolve.

Mansour Amini

Universiti Sains Malaysia, Malaysia

Shuangjiao Wu

Zhejiang Yuexiu University, China

Qiufen Wang

Kashi University, China

Compilation of References

Abas, I. H., Rasli, A., Alipour, M., & Mustafa, F. (2026). AI and the Future of Translation: Trends and Challenges. In *Bridging Theory and Practice in Translation: Perspectives, Challenges, and Innovations* (pp. 243–284). IGI Global Scientific Publishing. DOI: 10.4018/979-8-3373-3705-0.ch008

Alaqad, M. H. (2026). Building excellence in conference interpreting in Malaysia: Training models, lifelong learning, and AI-driven career pathways. In Amini, M. (Ed.), *Enhancing quality in conference interpreting* (pp. 183–204). IGI Global Scientific Publishing., DOI: 10.4018/979-8-3373-3710-4.ch006

Alaqad, M. H., Amirdabbaghian, A., & Alhasani, H. (2026). Beyond the algorithm: Navigating ethics, quality, and accountability in AI-powered translation. In Larchen Costuchen, A., & Otaif, F. A. (Eds.), *AI bots in applied linguistics: Practice, policy, and creativity* (pp. 283–312). IGI Global Scientific Publishing., DOI: 10.4018/979-8-3373-6420-9.ch010

Alasmary, A. (2019). Lexical bundles in contract law texts: A corpus-based exploration and implications for legal education. *International Journal of English Linguistics*, *9*(2), 244–257. DOI: 10.5539/ijel.v9n2p244

Alavi, S. (2024). Challenges of lecturers in material selection to foster EFL university students' self-regulation. *LEARN Journal: Language Education and Acquisition Research Network, 17*(1), 514-537. Retrieved from https://so04.tci-thaijo.org/index.php/LEARN/article/view/270425

Alavi, S. (2026). Multimodality meets translation in TESOL: A scoping review of emerging pedagogies. In M. Amini. *Multimodality and Translation in Audiovisual Media* (pp. 249-288). IGI Global Scientific Publishing. DOI: 10.4018/979-8-3373-5717-1.ch009

Alavi, S., & Amini, M. (2026). Interdependencies of proficiency, motivation, and strategy: A quantitative study within a socio-cognitive framework for TESOL post-graduate curriculum design. *Community and Social Development Journal*, *27*(2), 115–127. DOI: 10.57260/csdj.2026.286722

Al-Mamoory, S. M. A. (2022). The sociolinguistics of honorifics in English court-room interaction. *Humanities & Natural Sciences Journal*, *3*(2), 824–833. DOI: 10.53796/hnsj3245

Al-Romany, T. A. H., & Kadhim, M. J. (2024). Artificial intelligence impact on human translation: Legal texts as a case study. *International Journal of Linguistics. Literature and Translation*, *7*(5), 89–95. DOI: 10.32996/ijllt.2024.7.5.11

Altakhaineh, A. R. M., Alghathian, G. A., & Jarrah, M. M. (2025). A comparative study of accuracy in human vs. AI translation of legal documents into Arabic. *International Journal of Language & Law*, *14*, 63–80. DOI: 10.14762/jll.2025.063

Altuwairesh, N. S., & AlGhamedi, N. A. (2025). Challenges & Solutions in Legal Translation Training: Translator Trainees' Perspectives. *Theory and Practice in Language Studies*, *15*(4), 1188–1195. DOI: 10.17507/tpls.1504.17

Alwazna, R. Y. (2018). Translation and legal terminology: Techniques for coping with the untranslatability of legal terms between Arabic and English. International Journal for the Semiotics of Law - Revue internationale de Sémiotique juridique, 32(1), 75-94. DOI: 10.1007/s11196-018-9580-y

Alwazna, R. Y. (2024). The use of automation in the rendition of certain articles of the Saudi Commercial Law into English: A post-editing-based comparison of five machine translation systems. *Frontiers in Artificial Intelligence*, *6*, 1282020. Advance online publication. DOI: 10.3389/frai.2023.1282020 PMID: 38282905

Ameen, K. S., Towfiq, T. A., Mousa, K. M., & Pooyanmehr, M. (2026). Judicial review of algorithmic administrative systems: Legality, evidence, and remedies in the smart city state. *Frontiers in Artificial Intelligence*, *9*, 1802986. Advance online publication. DOI: 10.3389/frai.2026.1802986 PMID: 42052213

Amini, M., Lee, K. F., Yiqiu, W., & Ravindran, L. (2026). Proposing a framework for ethical use of AI in academic writing based on a conceptual review: Implications for quality education. *Interactive Learning Environments*, *34*(3), 1394–1418. DOI: 10.1080/10494820.2025.2523382

Ashley, K. D. (2017). *Artificial intelligence and legal analytics: New tools for law practice in the digital age*. Cambridge University Press. DOI: 10.1017/9781316761380

Ashurov, B. S. (2025). Interpersonal style and politeness strategies in legal discourse.In Proceedings of the International Scientific and Practical Conference "Modern Philological Issues: Problems and Solutions" (pp. 14-18). DOI: 10.5281/zenodo.15371215

Austin, J. L. (1962). *How to do things with words*. Clarendon Press.

Azizah binti Harun & Ors. v. Pentadbir Tanah Kerian & Anor. (2025). *Alasan penghakiman* [Grounds of judgment]. Mahkamah Tinggi Malaya di Taiping, Perak. Saman Pemula No. AB-24NCVC-294-10/2024.

Baaij, C. J. (Ed.). (2012). *The role of legal translation in legal harmonization*. Kluwer Law International BV.

Baaij, C. J. W. (2012). The EU policy on institutional multilingualism: Between principles and practicality. *International Journal of Language & Law, 1*, 14–32. DOI: 10.14762/jll.2012.014

Badah, A. M., Khalaf, C. N., Dwaikat, F. J., & AlQbailat, N. (2025). The usage of artificial intelligence in legal translation: Bridging the gap between law and language. *Ampersand (Oxford, UK), 100248*. Advance online publication. DOI: 10.1016/j.amper.2025.100248

Bahdanau, D., Cho, K., & Bengio, Y. (2015). Neural machine translation by jointly learning to align and translate. In *Proceedings of the 3rd International Conference on Learning Representations (ICLR 2015)*. https://arxiv.org/abs/1409.0473

Bahdanau, D., Cho, K., & Bengio, Y. (2015, May 7–9). *Neural machine translation by jointly learning to align and translate. 3rd International Conference on Learning Representations (ICLR 2015)*, San Diego, CA, United States. https://arxiv.org/abs/1409.0473

Bajčić, M. (2014). Towards a terminological approach to translating European Contract Law. In Pasa, B., & Morra, L. (Eds.), *Translating the DCFR and drafting the CESL: a pragmatic perspective* (pp. 125–145). Seller European Law Publishers., DOI: 10.1515/9783866536067.125

Bajčić, M., & Basaneže, K. D. (2016). Towards the professionalization of legal translators and court interpreters in the EU: Introduction and overview. In Bajčić, M., & Basaneže, K. D. (Eds.), *Towards the professionalization of legal translators and court interpreters in the EU* (pp. 1–11). Cambridge Scholars Publishing.

Baker, M. (1993). Corpus linguistics and translation studies: Implications and applications. In Baker, M., Francis, G., & Tognini-Bonelli, E. (Eds.), *Text and technology: In honour of John Sinclair* (pp. 233–250). John Benjamins. DOI: 10.1075/z.64.15bak

Baker, M. (1995). Corpora in translation studies: An overview and some suggestions for future research. *International Journal of Translation Studies*, *7*(2), 223–243. DOI: 10.1075/target.7.2.03bak

Banakar, R., & Travers, M. (Eds.). (2005). *Theory and method in socio-legal research*. Hart Publishing.

Basu, S., Prakash, S., Barge, A. M., Jaiswal, S. D., Dash, A., Ghosh, S., & Mukherjee, A. (2025). Judging by appearances? Auditing and intervening vision-language models for bail prediction. *arXiv*. https://doi.org//arXiv.2510.00088DOI: 10.48550

Bender, E. M., Gebru, T., McMillan-Major, A., & Shmitchell, S. (2021, March 3–10). *On the dangers of stochastic parrots: Can language models be too big?* 2021 ACM Conference on Fairness, Accountability, and Transparency (ACM FAccT 2021), Virtual conference. DOI: 10.1145/3442188.3445922

Bengio, Y., Ducharme, R., Vincent, P., & Jauvin, C. (2003). A neural probabilistic language model. *Journal of Machine Learning Research*, *3*, 1137–1155. https://www.jmlr.org/papers/v3/bengio03a.html

Benjamin, R. (2024). *Viral Justice: How We Grow the World We Want*. Princeton University Press.

Bennett, K. (2019). The new iconicity: Challenges for translation theory and practice. *Translation Matters*, *1*(2), 1–8. DOI: 10.21747/21844585/tm1_2int

Bhashini. (n.d.). Retrieved May 17, 2026, from https://bhashini.gov.in/about-bhashini

Bhatia, V. K. (1983). Simplification v. easification—The case of legal texts1. *Applied Linguistics*, *4*(1), 42–54. DOI: 10.1093/applin/4.1.42

Bhatia, V. K. (1993). *Analysing genre: Language use in professional settings*. Longman.

Bhatia, V. K. (2004). Worlds of written discourse: A genre-based view. *Continuum.*

Bhatia, V. K. (2023). Designing English for legal communication programmes: Exploiting legislative genres. *International Journal for the Semiotics of Law*, *36*(4), 1883–1896. DOI: 10.1007/s11196-022-09968-5

Biber, D., Larsson, T., Hancock, G. R., Reppen, R., Staples, S., & Gray, B. (2025). Comparing theory-based models of grammatical complexity in student writing. *International Journal of Learner Corpus Research*, *11*(1), 145–177. DOI: 10.1075/ijlcr.23036.bib

Bidin, A. (1995). Issues in translation of legal texts in Malaysia. *Perspectives - Gerontological Nursing Association*, *3*(2), 205–213. DOI: 10.1080/0907676X.1995.9961261

Biel, Ł. (2008). Corpus assisted studies of legal language for translation purposes: Methodological and practical potential. In Kredens, K., & Goźdź-Roszkowski, S. (Eds.), *Language and the law: International outlooks* (pp. 21–38). Peter Lang.

Biel, Ł. (2014). The textual fit of translated EU law: A corpus-based study of deontic modality. *The Translator*, *20*(3), 332–355. DOI: 10.1080/13556509.2014.909675

Biel, Ł. (2016). Phraseology in legal translation: A corpus-based analysis of textual mapping in EU law. In *The Ashgate handbook of legal translation* (pp. 177–192). Routledge., DOI: 10.4324/9781315612706-13

Biel, Ł., & Engberg, J. (2013). Research models and methods in legal translation. *Linguistica Antverpiensia. New Series: Themes in Translation Studies*, *12*. Advance online publication. DOI: 10.52034/lanstts.v12i.316

Biel, L., & Kockaert, H. J. (2023). Introduction: Legal terminology. In Resi, R., & Steurs, F. (Eds.), *Handbook of Terminology* (pp. 1–14). John Benjamins Publishing Company., DOI: 10.1075/hot.3.int3

Biel, Ł., & Kockaert, H. J. (Eds.). (2023). Handbook of terminology: Vol. 3. *Legal terminology*. John Benjamins., DOI: 10.1075/hot.3

Bor, B., & Könczöl, M. (2019). Towards a semiotic theory of style in law: A Peircean approach. *International Journal of Law in Context*, *15*(3), 263–273. DOI: 10.1017/S1744552319000272

Botezat, O. (2012). The complexity of legal translation: Social and cultural bounds aspects. *Contemporary Readings in Law and Social Justice*, *4*(1), 641–647.

Bourdieu, P. (1977). *Outline of a Theory of Practice* (R. Nice, Trans.). Cambridge University Press. DOI: 10.1017/CBO9780511812507

Bourdieu, P. (1987). The force of law: Toward a sociology of the juridical field. *The Hastings Law Journal*, *38*(5), 814–853. https://repository.uclawsf.edu/hastings_law_journal/vol38/iss5/3

Breeze, R. (2015). Teaching the vocabulary of legal documents: a corpus-driven approach. *ESP Today, 3*(1), 44-63. https://www.esptodayjournal.org/pdf/current_issue/2015/3.%20RUTH%20BREEZE%20-%20full%20text.pdf

Breeze, R. (2021). Translating the principles of good governance: In search of accountability in Spanish and German. *International Journal of Legal Discourse*, *6*(1), 43–67. DOI: 10.1515/ijld-2021-2045

Brenner, J. E. (2015). Three aspects of information science in reality: Symmetry, semiotics and society. *Information (Basel)*, *6*(4), 750–772. DOI: 10.3390/info6040750

Briva-Iglesias, V., Doğru, G., & Cavalheiro Camargo, J. L. (2024). Large language models "ad referendum": How good are they at machine translation in the legal domain? *MonTI. Monografías de Traducción e Interpretación*, *16*(16), 75–107. DOI: 10.6035/MonTI.2024.16.02

Brown, P., & Levinson, S. C. (1987). *Politeness: Some universals in language usage*. Cambridge university press. DOI: 10.1017/CBO9780511813085

Brown, T., Mann, B., Ryder, N., Subbiah, M., Kaplan, J., Dhariwal, P., Neelakantan, A., Shyam, P., Sastry, G., Askell, A., Agarwal, S., Herbert-Voss, A., Krueger, G., Henighan, T., Child, R., Ramesh, A., Ziegler, D. M., Wu, J., Winter, C., & Amodei, D. (2020). Language models are few-shot learners. *Advances in Neural Information Processing Systems*, *33*, 1877–1901. DOI: 10.48550/arXiv.2005.14165

Bunga, E. L. M., & Katemba, C. V. (2024). Comparing translation quality: Google Translate vs DeepL for foreign language to English. *Edusaintek: Jurnal Pendidikan, Sains dan Teknologi, 11*(3), 1147-1171. DOI: 10.47668/edusaintek.v11i3.1264

Cacciaguidi-Fahy, S., & Mooney, A. (2009). The Promise of Legal Semiotics. *International Journal for the Semiotics of Law - Revue Internationale De Sémiotique Juridique, 22*(4), 381–386. DOI: 10.1007/s11196-009-9123-7

Candlin, C. N., Bhatia, V. K., & Jensen, C. H. (2002). Developing legal writing materials for English second language learners: Problems and perspectives. *English for Specific Purposes*, *21*(4), 299–320. DOI: 10.1016/S0889-4906(01)00029-1

Cao, D. (2010). Legal Translation. In Y. Gambier & L. Van Doorslaer (Eds.), Handbook of Translation Studies, Volume 1 (pp. 191-195). John Benjamins Publishing Company. DOI: 10.1075/hts.1.leg1

Cao, D. (2007). *Translating law* (Vol. 33). Multilingual Matters.

Cao, D. (2007). *Translating law*. Multilingual Matters. DOI: 10.26034/cm.jostrans.2008.689

Chalkidis, I., Fergadiotis, M., Malakasiotis, P., Aletras, N., & Androutsopoulos, I. (2020). LEGAL-BERT: The muppets straight out of law school. In *Findings of the Association for Computational Linguistics: EMNLP 2020* (pp. 2898–2904). *Association for Computational Linguistics*. https://doi.org/DOI: 10.18653/v1/2020.findings-emnlp.261

Chan, C. H. Y. (2020). *Legal translation and bilingual law drafting in Hong Kong: Challenges and interactions in Chinese regions*. Routledge., DOI: 10.4324/9780429443466

Che Mohd Faiz bin Che Zulkifle v. Pendakwa Raya. (2026). *Alasan penghakiman* [Grounds of judgment]. Mahkamah Tinggi Kuala Terengganu. Rayuan Jenayah No. TC-83D-42-01/2022.

Cheng, L., & Sin, K. K. (2008). Terminological equivalence in legal translation: A semiotic approach. *Semiotica, 2008*(172), 33–45. DOI: 10.1515/SEMI.2008.088

Chodkiewicz, C. (2004). Review of La Langue de La Common Law by Anne Wagner. *International Journal of Speech Language and the Law, 11*(1), 0146–158. DOI: 10.1558/ijsll.v11i1.150

Chromá, M. (2014). Making sense in legal translation. *Semiotica, 201*(201). Advance online publication. DOI: 10.1515/sem-2014-0018

Chueasuai, P. (2017). The interpersonal metafunction and translation of power relations: A case study of fifty shades of grey. *MANUSYA: Journal of Humanities, 20*(3), 1-22. https://brill.com/view/journals/mnya/20/3/article-p1_1.xml

Clay, E. (2026). Measuring divergence in migration-related terminology between EU legal discourse and press articles in English and French. *International Journal of Corpus Linguistics, 31*(1), 13–35. DOI: 10.1075/ijcl.25082.cla

Cosmulescu, A. M. (2021). A terminological perspective on legal translation. *Professional Communication and Translation Studies, 14*, 151–157. DOI: 10.59168/EPBG9565

Cotterrell, R. (1995). *Law's community: Legal theory in sociological perspective*. Clarendon Press.

Couldry, N., & Mejias, U. A. (2020). *The Costs of Connection: How Data Is Colonizing Human Life and Appropriating It for Capitalism*. Stanford University Press., DOI: 10.1515/9781503609754

Coulthard, M., & Johnson, A. (2007). *An introduction to forensic linguistics: Language in evidence*. Routledge. DOI: 10.4324/9780203969717

Cui, Y., Liu, X., & Cheng, Y. (2023). A comparative study on the effort of human translation and post-editing in relation to text types: An eye-tracking and key-logging experiment. *SAGE Open, 13*(1), 1–15. DOI: 10.1177/21582440231155849

Daems, J., & Macken, L. (2020). Post-editing human translations and revising machine translations. In Koponen, M., Mossop, B., Robert, I. S., & Scocchera, G. (Eds.), *Translation revision and post-editing: Industry practices and cognitive processes* (pp. 50–70). Routledge., DOI: 10.4324/9781003096962-5

Dahl, M., Magesh, V., Suzgun, M., & Ho, D. E. (2024). Large legal fictions: Profiling legal hallucinations in large language models. *The Journal of Legal Analysis*, *16*(1), 64–93. DOI: 10.1093/jla/laae003

DBP. (2026, February 5). Carian umum. Pusat Rujukan Persuratan Melayu @PRPM. https://prpm.dbp.gov.my/Cari1?keyword=conviction&d=382696&#LIHATSINI

De Gregorio, G., & Radu, R. (2022). Digital constitutionalism in the new era of Internet governance. *International Journal of Law and Information Technology*, *30*(1), 68–87. DOI: 10.1093/ijlit/eaac004

De Schutter, H. (2007). Language policy and political philosophy: On the emerging linguistic justice debate. *Language Problems and Language Planning*, *31*(1), 1–23. DOI: 10.1075/lplp.31.1.02des

Deacon, T. W., & Rączaszek-Leonardi, J. (2019). Abandoning the code metaphor is compatible with semiotic process. *The Behavioral and Brain Sciences*, *42*, e216. DOI: 10.1017/S0140525X19001419 PMID: 31775915

Debbarma, M. (2025). Linguistic Diversity and National Integration in India: Challenges, Policies and Pathways to Inclusivity. *Journal of Asian and African Studies*, *00219096251400655*, 00219096251400655. Advance online publication. DOI: 10.1177/00219096251400655

del Rey, J. T. (2019). The proper place of localization in translation curricula. In Sawyer, D.B., Austermühl, F., and Raído, V.,E. (Eds.), *The Evolving Curriculum in Interpreter and Translator Education. Stakeholder perspectives and voices* (pp. 229–258). John Benjamins Publishing. DOI: 10.1075/ata.xix.11tor

Demertzis, K., Rantos, K., Magafas, L., Skianis, C., & Iliadis, L. (2023). A Secure and Privacy-Preserving Blockchain-Based XAI-Justice System. *Information (Basel)*, *14*(9), 477. Advance online publication. DOI: 10.3390/info14090477

Department of Justice. (2012). *A guide to styles and practices*. https://www.doj.gov.hk/en/publications/pub20030011.html

Department of Justice. (2023). *Law Drafting Division: Chinese and English*. https://www.doj.gov.hk/en/about/orgchart_ldd_drafting_chi_eng.html

Doczekalska, A. (2023). *Legal terms, concepts and definitions in the transposition of EU law. Handbook of Terminology*. John Benjamins., DOI: 10.1075/hot.3.leg3

Douzinas, C., & Nead, L. (1999). *Law and the Image*. University of Chicago Press.

Drugan, J. (2013). *Quality in professional translation: Assessment and improvement*. Bloomsbury Academic. Cronin, M. (2003). *Translation and globalization*. Routledge.

Duan, M. (2024). A study of subtitle translation from the perspective of multimodal discourse analysis: A case of *My People, My Country. Journal of Social Sciences and Humanities*, *6*(10), 24–32. DOI: 10.53469/jssh.2024.6(10).05

Duan, Y. J. (2023). Legal text translation (E to C) under the guidance of Skopos Theory. *Open Journal of Modern Linguistics*, *13*(5), 581–586. DOI: 10.4236/ojml.2023.135035

Durant, A., & Davis, J. (2018). Linguistic analysis in trade mark law: Current approaches and new challenges. In L. Solan & P. Tiersma (Eds.), *The Oxford handbook of language and law* (pp. 287–320). https://doi.org/DOI: 10.1515/9781614514664-014

Dworkin, R. (1986). *Law's empire*. Harvard University Press.

Edwards, R. C. (1993). The legal fact as a work of art: Artificial intelligence and the pragmatics of legal interpretation [University of British Columbia]. DOI: 10.14288/1.0086106

El-Farahaty, H. (2025). Integrating corpora and AI tools in the teaching, learning, and assessing of Arabic/English legal translation. *International Journal for the Semiotics of Law – Revue internationale de Sémiotique juridique, 38*, 2031–2060. DOI: 10.1007/s11196-025-10281-0

ElFqih, K., & Monti, J. (2024). Large language models as legal translators of Arabic legislatives: Do ChatGPT and Gemini care for context and terminology? In *Proceedings of the 1st Workshop on Towards Ethical and Inclusive Conversational AI: Language Attitudes, Linguistic Diversity, and Language Rights* (pp. 111–122). Association for Computational Linguistics. DOI: 10.18653/v1/2024.arabicnlp-1.10

Endicott, T. A. O. (2000). *Vagueness in law*. Oxford University Press., DOI: 10.1093/acprof:oso/9780198268406.001.0001

Engberg, J. (2020). Comparative law for legal translation: Through multiple perspectives to multidimensional knowledge. International Journal for the Semiotics of Law - Revue internationale de Sémiotique juridique, 33, 263-282. DOI: 10.1007/s11196-020-09706-9

Engberg, J. (2021). Legal translation as communication of knowledge: On the creation of bridges. *Parallèles, 33*(1), 9–26.

European Union. (2015). *Joint Practical Guide for persons involved in the drafting of EU legislation.* https://eur-lex.europa.eu/content/techleg/EN-legislative-drafting-guide.pdf

European Union. (2023). *Interinstitutional Style Guide.* Home - Interinstitutional Style Guide - Publications Office of the EU

Faber, P. (2022). *Frame-based terminology. Theoretical linguistics research perspectives.* John Benjamins. DOI: 10.1075/tlrp.23

Fairclough, N. (1989). *Language and power.* Longman.

Fairclough, N. (1992). *Discourse and social change.* Polity Press.

Fairclough, N. (2003). *Analysing discourse: Textual analysis for social research.* Routledge. DOI: 10.4324/9780203697078

Farhan, A. K. (2022). Divergence in the translation of criminal law: A corpus assisted study of prohibition in Iraqi penal code and its English translation. *Ampersand (Oxford, UK), 10*, 100104. DOI: 10.1016/j.amper.2022.100104

Filipović, L. (2016). May vs. Might in native vs. non-native English: Implications for inference and judgement in legal and educational contexts. *Applied Linguistics Review*, *7*(2), 181–201. DOI: 10.1515/applirev-2016-0008

Fillmore, C. J. (1976). Frame semantics and the nature of language. *Annals of the New York Academy of Sciences, 280*(1), 20–32. DOI: 10.1111/j.1749-6632.1976.tb25467.x

Fontaine, L. (2013). *Analysing English grammar: A systemic functional introduction.* Cambridge University Press.

Foucault, M. (1972). *The archaeology of knowledge* (Sheridan Smith, A. M., Trans.). Pantheon Books. (Original work published 1969)

Frantsuzova, A. D. (2019). Communication failure in court interpreting within a linguosemiotic approach: A mismatch of expectations. In *Proceedings of the International Scientific and Practical Conference "Individual and Society in the Modern Geopolitical Environment"* (pp. 214–219). Atlantis Press. https://doi.org/ DOI: 10.2991/ismge-19.2019.38

Fraser, B. (1990). Perspectives on politeness. *Journal of Pragmatics, 14*(2), 219–236. DOI: 10.1016/0378-2166(90)90081-N

Fu, R. (2016). Comparing modal patterns in Chinese-English interpreted and translated discourses in diplomatic setting: A systemic functional approach. *Babel. Revue internationale de la traduction/International Journal of Translation, 62*(1), 104-121. DOI: 10.1075/babel.62.1.06fu

Garner, B. A., & Kimble, J. (2024). *Essentials for drafting clear legal rules*. Administrative Office of the United States Courts.

Garzone, G. (2001). Deontic modality and performativity in English legal texts. In Gotti, M., & Dossena, M. (Eds.), *Modality in specialized texts* (pp. 153–173). Peter Lang.

Gémar, J.-C. (2013). *Langage du droit et traduction*. Presses de l'Université de Montréal.

Gémar, J.-C. (2014). Catching the spirit of the law: From translation to co-drafting. In Glanert, S. (Ed.), *Comparative law: Engaging translation* (pp. 85–104). Routledge.

Giampieri, P. (2024). The use of AI in the translation of legal documents: A critical analysis. *trans-kom, 17*(2), 343–358. https://www.trans-kom.eu/bd17nr02/trans-kom_17_02_05_Giampieri_AI.20241128.pdf

Giampieri, P. (2023). *Legal machine translation explained: MT in legal contexts*. Cambridge Scholars Publishing.

Giampieri, P. (2025). *Assessing the quality of AI and MT in legal translation*. Altre Modernità., DOI: 10.54103/2035-7680/28886

Giampieri, P. (2025). Legal language and legal translation. In *Legal formulae: Exploring legal multi-words in English, Italian and French* (pp. 7–38). Springer Nature Switzerland.

Girón García, C. (2016). Teaching and learning EFL successfully through an online environment: An experimental study with "Legal English" students. *Journal of Electronics and Communication Engineering Research, 3*, 01-11. https://www.questjournals.org/jecer/papers/vol3-issue5/A350111.pdf

Goh, S. S., & Harjit Singh, D. S. (Eds.). (2015). Glosari Undang-undang jenayah Bahasa Inggeris-Bahasa Melayu. UTHM Publisher. https://publisher.uthm.edu.my/omp/index.php/penerbituthm/catalog/download/156/176/767?inline=1

Goodrich, P. (1998). Signs taken for wonders: Community, identity, and "A history of sumptuary law.". *Law & Social Inquiry, 23*(3), 707–728. DOI: 10.1086/492655

Gorlée, D. L. (2005). Hints and guesses: Legal modes of semio-logical reasoning. *Sign Systems Studies, 33*(2), 239–272. DOI: 10.12697/SSS.2005.33.2.01

Graziadei, M. (2024). Rodolfo Sacco's theoretical contribution to comparative law: A personal account. International Journal for the Semiotics of Law - Revue internationale de Sémiotique juridique, 37, 1471-1484. DOI: 10.1007/s11196-024-10128-0

Graziadei, M. (2025). Legal translation and the quest for authenticity. International Journal for the Semiotics of Law - Revue internationale de Sémiotique juridique, 38, 2565-2593. DOI: 10.1007/s11196-025-10283-y

Guerberof-Arenas, A., & Toral, A. (2020). The impact of post-editing and machine translation on creativity and reading experience. *Translation Spaces*, *9*(2), 255–282. DOI: 10.1075/ts.20035.gue

Guzmán, D., & Prieto Ramos, F. (2024). Human and machine translation of legal terminology in international institutional settings: A case study. *De Europa:European and Global Studies Journal*, (special issue), 61–81.

Hafner, C. A., & Candlin, C. N. (2007). Corpus tools as an affordance to learning in professional legal education. *Journal of English for Academic Purposes*, *6*(4), 303–318. DOI: 10.1016/j.jeap.2007.09.005

Hakimzadeh, S. (2020). Reclaiming the commons: Law, rhetoric, and C. S. Peirce's pragmatic philosophy. *Law, Culture and the Humanities*, *19*(3), 603–623. DOI: 10.1177/1743872120935934

Hale, S. (1997). The treatment of register variation in court interpreting. *The Translator*, *3*(1), 39–54. DOI: 10.1080/13556509.1997.10798987

Halliday, M. A. K. (1994). *An introduction to functional grammar* (2nd ed.). Arnold.

Halliday, M. A. K., & Matthiessen, C. M. I. M. (2013). *Halliday's introduction to functional grammar* (4th ed.). Routledge., DOI: 10.4324/9780203431269

Halliday, M. A., & Hasan, R. (1989). *Language, context, and text: Aspects of language in a social-semiotic perspective*. Oxford University Press.

Hamed, D. M., & Alqurashi, N. (2025). A corpus-driven study on legal translation challenges among Arab law students: Examining gender and academic level in applied legal linguistics. *Humanities & Social Sciences Communications*, *12*(1), 1–17. DOI: 10.1057/s41599-025-05451-1

Hansen, S. T. (2023). Exploiting and constructing legal ambiguity: UK arms exports to Saudi Arabia during the war in Yemen. *European Security*, *32*(4), 607–627. Advance online publication. DOI: 10.1080/09662839.2022.2144728

Hart, H. L. A. (1994). *The concept of law* (2nd ed.). Oxford University Press. (Original work published 1961)

Hart, H. L. A. (2012). *The Concept of Law*. OUP Oxford. DOI: 10.1093/he/9780199644704.001.0001

Hasan, R. (2020). Tenor: Rethinking interactant relations. *Language. Context and Text*, *2*(2), 213–333. DOI: 10.1075/langct.00029.has

Havelka, I. (2024). Interpreting intercepted communication: From talk to evidence. *The International Journal of Translation and Interpreting Research*, *16*(1), 17–37. DOI: 10.12807/ti.116201.2024.a02

Havnen, R. (2019). Multimodal and interactional aspects of sight translation – A critical review. *FITISPos-International Journal*, *6*(1), 91–106. DOI: 10.37536/FITISPos-IJ.2019.6.1.206

He, H., Amini, M., Ganapathy, M., & Lah, S. C. (2024). The application of Juliane House's translation quality assessment model in the English translation of Yu Hua's 'Yanre de xiatian.'. *Cogent Arts & Humanities*, *11*(1), 2386781. DOI: 10.1080/23311983.2024.2386781

Heimgärtner, R. (2026). Intercultural Design for Human-Centered AI Solutions. In *Handbook of Human-Centered Artificial Intelligence* (pp. 1–65). Springer., DOI: 10.1007/978-981-97-8440-0_77-2

Hellenic Data Protection Authority. (n.d.). *Annual reports*. https://www.dpa.gr/en/advanced-search/all?field_keywords=annual+reports

Heritier, P. (2023). Understanding legal semiotics. In *Research handbook on legal semiotics* (pp. 11–31). Edward Elgar Publishing., DOI: 10.4337/9781802207262.00010

Heylen, K., & Steurs, F. (2014). Translating legal and administrative language: How to deal with legal terms and their flexiblemeaning potential. *Turjuman Numero spécial octobre*, 96-146. https://revues.imist.ma/index.php/Turjuman/article/view/52714/27347

Hidalgo-Ternero, C. M. (2020). Google Translate vs. DeepL: Analysing neural machine translation performance under the challenge of phraseological variation. *Monographs in Translation and Interpreting*, (6), 154–177. DOI: 10.6035/MonTI.2020.ne6.5

Hildebrandt, M. (2015). *Smart Technologies and the End(s) of Law*. https://www.elgaronline.com/monobook/9781849808767.xml

Hisyamudin bin Ahmad v. Pendakwa Raya. (2020). [2020] 7 Malayan Law Journal 187 (High Court of Malaya, Johor Bahru). Ketua Pengarah Laut, Jabatan Laut Malaysia & Ors v. Straits Bunker & Trading Sdn Bhd & Anor. (2020). [2020] 7 Malayan Law Journal 71 (High Court of Malaya, Johor Bahru).

Hoffman, C. (2011). Using discourse analysis methodology to teach "Legal English." *International Journal of Law, Language & Discourse, 1*(1), 1-19. https://scholarship.law.georgetown.edu/cgi/viewcontent.cgi?article=2341&context=facpub

Hohfeld, W. N. (1919). *Fundamental legal conceptions as applied in judicial reasoning and other legal essays* (Cook, W. W., Ed.). Yale University Press., https://archive.org/details/fundamentallegal00hohfuoft

House, J. (1998). Politeness and translation. In Hickey, L. (Ed.), *The pragmatics of translation* (pp. 54–71). Multilingual Matters. DOI: 10.21832/9781800417939-006

House, J. (2015). *Translation quality assessment: Past and present*. Routledge.

Hsieh, H. P. (2018). Crossing Language Lines and Legal Tradition Lines—Legal Translation as an Economic Phenomenon. University College Cork. https://www.academia.edu/40008818/Crossing_Language_Lines_and_Legal_Tradition_Lines_Legal_Translation_as_an_Economic_Phenomenon

Huong, N. T., & Anh, V. T. (2024). The Application of ChatGPT in Translation Learning: A Case Study in Vietnam. *Journal of Institutional Research South East Asia, 23*(2), 224–245. https://www.seaairweb.info/journal/articles/JIRSEA_v23_n02/JIRSEA_v23_n02_Article12.pdf

Hutchinson, T. (2015). Doctrinal research: Researching the jury. In Watkins, D., & Burton, M. (Eds.), *Research methods in law* (2nd ed., pp. 7–31). Routledge.

Hyland, K. (2005). Metadiscourse: Exploring interaction in writing. *Continuum.*

Ibrahim, M. A. S., Abdalla, H. O. H., Idris, M. El. M., Eldouma, S., Abdallah, N. M. M., Taha, E. A. M., & Rushwan, I. M. H. (2025). The role of legal translation in ensuring fair trial rights for Arabic-speaking immigrants in U.S. courts. *Journal of Cultural Analysis and Social Change.* DOI: 10.64753/jcasc.v10i2.2215

International Organization for Standardization. (2015). *ISO 17100:2015 translation services—Requirements for translation services.* https://www.iso.org/standard/59149.html

International Organization for Standardization. (2017). *ISO 18587:2017 translation services—Post-editing of machine translation output—Requirements.* https://www.iso.org/standard/62970.html

Ive, J., Specia, L., Szoc, S., Vanallemeersch, T., Van den Bogaert, J., Farah, E., . . . Khalilov, M. (2020, May). A post-editing dataset in the legal domain: do we underestimate neural machine translation quality? In *Proceedings of the Twelfth Language Resources and Evaluation Conference* (pp. 3692-3697). https://aclanthology.org/2020.lrec-1.455/

Jackson, B. S. (1985). *Semiotics and legal theory*. Routledge & Kegan Paul.

Jackson, B. S. (1988). *Law, fact and narrative coherence*. Deborah Charles Publications.

Jones, R. H. (2012). Multimodal discourse analysis. In *The encyclopedia of applied linguistics*. Wiley-Blackwell., DOI: 10.1002/9781405198431.wbeal0813

Jopek-Bosiacka, A. (2023). *Definitions in law across legal cultures and jurisdictions. Handbook of terminology*. John Benjamins., https://www.jbe-platform.com/content/books/9789027249388-hot.3.def1

Joshi, P., Santy, S., Budhiraja, A., Bali, K., & Choudhury, M. (2020). The state and fate of linguistic diversity and inclusion in the NLP world. *Proceedings of the 58th Annual Meeting of the Association for Computational Linguistics*, 6282–6293. https://aclanthology.org/2020.acl-main.560

Kemp, J. (2022). *An investigation of the vocabulary representative of postgraduate International Law texts* (Doctoral dissertation, University of Leicester). DOI: 10.25392/Leicester.data.20317362

Kenny, D. (Ed.). (2022). *Machine translation for everyone: Empowering users in the age of artificial intelligence*. Language Science Press. DOI:DOI: 10.26034/cm.jostrans.2023.537

Kevelson, R. (1987). *Law and semiotics* (Vol. 1). Plenum Press., DOI: 10.1007/978-1-4613-0959-8_1

Kevelson, R. (1988). *The law as a system of signs*. Springer. DOI: 10.1007/978-1-4613-0911-6

Kevelson, R. (1996). *Pierce, science, signs* (Vol. 9). Peter Lang.

Khafaga, A. (2023). Strategic lexicalization in courtroom discourse: A corpus-assisted critical discourse analysis. *Cogent Arts & Humanities*, *10*(1), 2217585. DOI: 10.1080/23311983.2023.2217585

Khan, M. I.Mohammad Imran Khan. (2025). Impact of AI on legal and institutional translation: Issues and strategies. *International Journal of Translation and Interpretation Studies*, *5*(6), 1–15. DOI: 10.32996/ijtis.2025.5.6.1

Ki, D., & Carpuat, M. (2024). Guiding large language models to post-edit machine translation with error annotations. In *Findings of the Association for Computational Linguistics: NAACL 2024* (pp. 4253-4273). Association for Computational Linguistics. DOI: 10.18653/v1/2024.findings-naacl.265

Killman, J. (2024). Machine translation literacy in the legal translation context: A SWOT analysis perspective. *The Interpreter and Translator Trainer*, *18*(2), 271–289. DOI: 10.1080/1750399X.2024.2344282

Kim, N. Y. (2018). Chatbots and Korean EFL Students' English Vocabulary Learning. *Journal of Digital Convergence*, *16*(2), 1.

Kocbek, A. (2012). An integrated model for translating legal texts. Vertimo studijos, 5(5), 64-75. DOI: 10.15388/VertStud.2012.5.10560

Kocbek, A. (2015). The Decalogue of Legal Translation – Contracts in Intercultural Legal Communication. *CLINA*, *1*(1), 71–86.

Koehn, P. (2020). *Neural machine translation*. Cambridge University Press. DOI: 10.1017/9781108608480

Koteva, G. (2023). Dealing with legal terminology in the translation of business documents. *Научни трудове на УНСС, 2*(2), 137-154. DOI: 10.37075/RP.2023.2.10

Kothalawala, C., Kothalawala, T., & Pereira, S. S. (2023). *Move analysis of Sri Lankan legal letters of demand for teaching English for specific purposes*. ESP., DOI: 10.4038/ouslj.v18i1.7583

Kovács, T. (2022). Human and machine translation: A comparative analysis of neural machine-and human-translated EN-HU and HU-EN legal texts. *Porta Linguarum*, (1), 49–57. DOI: 10.48040/PL.2022.1.5

Kozhevnikov, V. V.Vladimir Valentinovich Kozhevnikov. (2022). Legal semiotics. *Matondang Journal*, *2*(1), 36–46. DOI: 10.33258/matondang.v2i1.807

Kress, G., & van Leeuwen, T. (2020). *Reading images: The grammar of visual design* (3rd ed.). Routledge., DOI: 10.4324/9781003099857

Krimpas, P. G. (2023). Semiotics in matters legal. *Punctum International Journal of Semiotics*, *9*(2), 241–245. DOI: 10.18680/hss.2023.0029

Kryk-Kastovsky, B. (2010). Power in Early Modern English courtroom discourse. In Tanskanen, S.-K., Helasvuo, M.-L., & Johansson, M. (Eds.), *Discourses in interaction* (pp. 153–172). John Benjamins., DOI: 10.1075/pbns.203.13kry

Kusik, P. (2024). Legal communication as a point of contact between legal translation and comparative law. *Journal of International Legal Communication*, *14*(3), 92–109. DOI: 10.32612/uw.27201643.2024.14.3.pp.92-109

Lai, J., Gan, W., Wu, J., Qi, Z., & Yu, P. S. (2024). Large language models in law: A survey. *AI Open*, *5*, 181–196. DOI: 10.1016/j.aiopen.2024.09.002

Lam, J., Chen, Y., Zulkernine, F., & Dahan, S. (2025). Legal text analytics for reasonable notice period prediction. *Journal of Computational and Cognitive Engineering*, *4*(3), 319–331. DOI: 10.47852/bonviewJCCE52024104

Latour, B. (2012). *We Have Never Been Modern*. Harvard University Press.

Legrand, P. (1996). How to compare now. *Legal Studies*, *16*(2), 232–242. DOI: 10.1111/j.1748-121X.1996.tb00005.x

Leung, J. H. C. (2026). *Digital Multilingualism and Platform Governance*. Elements in Forensic Linguistics., DOI: 10.1017/9781009263177

Lin, L., & Wang, X. (2009). Dui tiyu bisai zhong "caipan" yi ci fanyi de sikao [Reflections on the translation of the term "referee" in sports competitions]. *Journal of Sports Adult Education*, *25*(1), 40–42. http://dx.chinadoi.cn/10.3969/j.issn.1672-268X.2009.01.017

Lin, X., Afzaal, M., & Aldayel, H. S. (2023). Syntactic complexity in legal translated texts and the use of plain English: A corpus-based study. *Humanities & Social Sciences Communications*, *10*(1), 17. DOI: 10.1057/s41599-022-01485-x

Litvishko, O. M., Shiryaeva, T. A., Golubovskaya, E. A., & Mekeko, N. M. (2025). Why English Legal Discourse is Difficult to Understand. [IJAES]. *International Journal of Arabic-English Studies*, *25*(1), 403–430. DOI: 10.33806/ijaes.v25i1.675

Liu, Z. (2008). Translating tenor: With reference to the English versions of Hong Lou Meng. *Meta*, *53*(3), 528–548. DOI: 10.7202/019238ar

Lu, X., Kisselev, O., Yoon, J., & Amory, M. D. (2018). Investigating effects of criterial consistency, the diversity dimension, and threshold variation in formulaic language research. *International Journal of Corpus Linguistics*, *23*(2), 158–182. DOI: 10.1075/ijcl.16086.lu

Ma, Y., & Wang, B. (2016). A review of systemic functional translation studies from an interpersonal perspective. *International Forum of Teaching and Studies*, *12*(1), 36-42. https://americanscholarspress.us/journals/IFST/pdf/IFOTS-1-2016/v12n1-art5.pdf

Mackay, R. R. (2015). Multimodal legitimation: Selling Scottish independence. *Discourse & Society, 26*(3), 323–348. DOI: 10.1177/0957926514564737

Madsen, D. (1997). Towards a description of communication in the legal universe: Translation of legal texts and the Skopos theory. *Fachsprache (1990), 19*(1-2), 17-27.

Malayan Law Journal (MLJ) Articles and Cases

Manning, C. D., & Schütze, H. (1999). *Foundations of statistical natural language processing*. MIT Press.

Marín, M. J., & Fernández Toledo, P. (2015). The influence of cognates on the acquisition of legal terminology: Help or hindrance? A corpus assisted study. *Procedia: Social and Behavioral Sciences, 198*, 320–329. DOI: 10.1016/j.sbspro.2015.07.450

Martindale, M. J., & Carpuat, M. (2018). Fluency over adequacy: A pilot study in measuring MT quality for post-editing. In *Proceedings of the 13th Conference of the Association for Machine Translation in the Americas* (pp. 113–124). Association for Machine Translation in the Americas.

Masykar, T., Nurrahmi, F., & Masykar, T. (2023). Systemic functional linguistics to preserve interpersonal and ideational meaning in English-Indonesian translation. *Journal of English Education and Teaching, 7*(3), 560–572. DOI: 10.33369/jeet.7.3.560-572

Matoesian, G., & Gilbert, K. E. (2018). Let the fingers do the talking: Language, gesture and power in closing argument. In Leung, J. H. C., & Durant, A. (Eds.), *Meaning and power in the language of law* (pp. 137–163). Cambridge University Press., DOI: 10.1017/9781316285756.007

Mattila, H. E. S. (2006). *Comparative legal linguistics*. Ashgate.

Matulewska, A. (2019). Legal and LSP Linguistics and Translation: Asian Languages' Perspectives. *International Journal for the Semiotics of Law - Revue Internationale De Sémiotique Juridique, 32*(1), 1–11. DOI: 10.1007/s11196-019-09602-x

McConville, M., & Chui, W. H. (Eds.). (2017). *Research methods for law*. Edinburgh University Press. DOI: 10.1515/9781474404259

McEwan, C. (2008). Postcolonialism and Development. *Postcolonialism and Development*, 1–354. DOI: 10.4324/9780203887387

Meenal, T. S., & Govindarajan, P. (2023). The challenges of using machine translation while translating Polysemous words. *Studies in Media and Communication, 11*(2), 63–67. DOI: 10.11114/smc.v11i2.5944

Mendonca, M. (2021). *Access denied: Exploring web accessibility standards and their implications for users with cognitive impairments* [Master's thesis, Toronto Metropolitan University]. https://doi.org/DOI: 10.32920/ryerson.14655063.v1

Mittelstadt, B. D., Allo, P., Taddeo, M., Wachter, S., & Floridi, L. (2016). The ethics of algorithms: Mapping the debate. *Big Data & Society*, *3*(2), 1–21. DOI: 10.1177/2053951716679679

Mokhtar, H. S. (1983). Undang-undang Malaysia Akta 32 Akta Bahasa 1963/67. Percetakan Negara, Kuala Lumpur. https://eseminar.dbp.gov.my

Moneus, A. M., & Sahari, Y. (2024). Artificial intelligence and human translation: A contrastive study based on legal texts. *Heliyon*, *10*(6), e28106. DOI: 10.1016/j.heliyon.2024.e28106 PMID: 38524597

Monjean-Decaudin, S. (2025). Les enjeux de l'intelligence artificielle pour la traduction juridique au sein de l'Union européenne: Observations générales du point de vue de la juritraductologie. *International Journal of Language & Law*, *14*, 194–203. DOI: 10.14762/jll.2025.194

Monzó-Nebot, E., & Mellinger, C. D. (2022). Language policies for social justice—Translation, interpreting, and access. *Just. Journal of Language Rights & Minorities. Revista de Drets Lingüístics i Minories*, *1*(1–2), 15–35.

Mustafa 'Afifi Ab Halim, Mohd Mahyeddin Mohd Salleh, Rezki Perdani Sawai, Nurhafizah Muhd Shukor, Dini Farhana Baharuddin, Joki Perdani Sawai, & Abd Halim Mohd Hussin. (2013). Bayi yang dibuang: Hak dan kedudukan bayi di sisi undang-undang. Malayan Law Journal, 5, i–xii.

Nan, Y. (2026). Current English–Chinese legal language mutual translation based on the comparison of the three theoretical levels of words, sentences, and articles. *International Journal of Data Science and Analytics*, *22*(1), 1–13. DOI: 10.1007/s41060-025-01007-3

Naveen, P., & Trojovský, P. (2024). Overview and challenges of machine translation for contextually appropriate translations. *iScience*, *27*(10), 110878. DOI: 10.1016/j.isci.2024.110878 PMID: 39391737

Nicolini, D., Reinecke, J., & Ismail, M. A. (2021). *You're grounded! Toward a theory of enactive legitimation, materiality and practice. Research in the Sociology of Organizations*. Emerald Publishing Limited., DOI: 10.1108/S0733-558X20200000071004

Nie, T., Sun, J., & Ma, W. (2025). Exploring the roles of large language models in reshaping transportation systems: A survey, framework, and roadmap. *Artificial Intelligence for Transportation*, *1*, 100003. DOI: 10.1016/j.ait.2025.100003

Nikioporietz, S., Kulish, L., Magas, L., Melnik, M., & Piddubchak, S. (2024). Utilizing the semiotic model to enhance semantic adequacy in translation processes. *Вісник науки та освіти, 3*(21), 47–62. https://doi.org/DOI: 10.52058/2786-6165-2024-3(21)-47-62

Niu, J., & Jiang, Y. (2024). Does simplification hold true for machine translations? A corpus-based analysis of lexical diversity in text varieties across genres. *Humanities & Social Sciences Communications*, *11*(1), 480. Advance online publication. DOI: 10.1057/s41599-024-02986-7

Noble, S. U. (2018). *Algorithms of oppression: How search engines reinforce racism* (pp. xv, 229). New York University Press.

Northcott, J. (2008). Language education for law professionals. In Gibbons, J., & Turell, M. T. (Eds.), *Dimensions of forensic linguistics* (pp. 27–46). John Benjamins. DOI: 10.1075/aals.5.04nor

Northcott, J. (2013). Teaching legal English: Contexts and cases. In Paltridge, B., & Starfield, S. (Eds.), *The handbook of English for specific purposes* (pp. 471–487). Wiley-Blackwell.

Nöth, W. (2021). Linguistics and semiotics in the framework of sciences in general. *Cahiers du Centre de Linguistique et des Sciences du Langage, 65*, 29–50. https://doi.org/DOI: 10.26034/la.cdclsl.2021.1360

Novak, M. (2021). Visual as multi-modal argumentation in law. *Bratislava Law Review*, *5*(1), 91–110. DOI: 10.46282/blr.2021.5.1.187

Novelli, C., Bongiovanni, G., & Sartor, G. (2022). A conceptual framework for legal personality and its application to AI. *Jurisprudence*, *13*(2), 194–219. DOI: 10.1080/20403313.2021.2010936

Novikova, E. R., Polyakov, O. G., & Hausmann-Ushkova, N. V. (2020). Teaching English to law students by means of discourse analysis on the basis of C. Hoffman's comprehensive approach. *Pedagogy. Theory into Practice*, *5*(5), 652–657. DOI: 10.30853/ped200166

Olteanu, A., & Ongstad, S. (2024). Utterance-genre-lifeworld and sign-habit-Umwelt compared. *Biosemiotics*, *17*(2), 523–546. DOI: 10.1007/s12304-024-09561-2

Olurotimi, T. S. (2022). Semiotics: A transdisciplinary quest for meaning. *International Journal of Linguistics. Literature and Translation*, *5*(8), 117–124. DOI: 10.32996/ijllt.2022.5.8.14

Open, A. I. (2026). *ChatGPT (May 2026 version) [Large language model].* https://chat.openai.com

Orozco, M., & Sánchez-Gijón, P. (2011). New resources for legal translators. *Perspectives, 19*(1), 25–44. DOI: 10.1080/09076761003784979

Oxford University Press. (n.d.). *Oxford English dictionary*. In *OED Online*. Retrieved April 20, 2026, from https://www.oed.com

Ozyumenko, V. I. (2023). Forms of address in courtroom discourse in Englishes of the "Inner Circle". In Baumgarten, N., & Vismans, R. (Eds.), *It's Different with You* (pp. 316–339). John Benjamins. DOI: 10.1075/tar.5.13ozy

Palashevskaya, I. V., Leontiev, V. V., & Kurchenkova, E. A. (2017). Status positions of courtroom discourse participants. In Proceedings of the 7th International Scientific and Practical Conference "Current issues of linguistics and didactics: The interdisciplinary approach in humanities"(CILDIAH 2017). Atlantis Press. DOI: 10.2991/cildiah-17.2017.36

Park, J. "The Multidimensional Prospects for L2 English Legal Writing" (2014). Open Access Theses. 363. https://docs.lib.purdue.edu/open_access_theses/363

Pasquale, F. (2015). *The black box society: The secret algorithms that control money and information*. Harvard University Press. DOI: 10.4159/harvard.9780674736061

Pasquale, F. (2019). A Rule of Persons, Not Machines: The Limits of Legal Automation. *The George Washington Law Review*, *87*(1), 1–55.

Pau, C. C. (2017). *Localization as multimodal-cultural translation: A comparative case study* [Master's thesis, Nanyang Technological University]. https://doi.org/ DOI: 10.32657/10356/72421

Pavliuk, N. (2023). A potential of legal terminology to be translated: The case of "regulation" translated into Ukrainian. *International Journal for the Semiotics of Law-Revue internationale de Sémiotique juridique, 36*(6), 2429-2454. DOI: 10.1007/s11196-023-10034-x

Pendakwa Raya lwn Mohd Jairulnizam bin Mohd Nordin dan satu lagi. (2020). [2020] 7 *Malayan Law Journal* 103 (Mahkamah Tinggi Malaya, Taiping).

Pendakwa Raya v. Akhil Mursyid bin Nor Hisham & Anor. (2026). *Alasan penghakiman* [Grounds of judgment]. Mahkamah Majistret Kota Bharu, Kelantan. Kes Tangkap No. DA-83RS-135-08/2023.

Pendakwa Raya v. Aliff Syukri bin Kamarzaman. (2026). *Alasan penghakiman* [Unpublished grounds of judgment]. Mahkamah Sesyen Sepang, Selangor. Kes No. BK-63-(11,12,13,14)-10/2022.

Pendakwa Raya v. Aminuddin bin Jusoh @ Yusof. (2026). *Alasan penghakiman* [Grounds of judgment]. Mahkamah Majistret Kuala Berang, Terengganu. Kes Tangkap No. TE-82JS-1-07/2021.

Pendakwa Raya v. Firdaus Rizal bin Abdul Manan. (2026). *Alasan penghakiman* [Grounds of judgment]. Mahkamah Sesyen Teluk Intan, Perak. Kes Jenayah No. AC-62K-1-02/2023 & Ors.

Pendakwa Raya v. Hazmi Ruzaini bin Azlihudin. (2026). *Alasan penghakiman* [Grounds of judgment]. Mahkamah Sesyen Sepang, Selangor. Kes Jenayah No. BK-62D-100-10/2025.

Pendakwa Raya v. Ibrahim bin Harun. (2026). *Alasan penghakiman* [Grounds of judgment]. Mahkamah Tinggi Malaya di Temerloh, Pahang. Perbicaraan Jenayah No. CB-45A-07-02/2022.

Pendakwa Raya v. Ku Mahamad Isa bin Jaafar. (2026). *Alasan penghakiman* [Grounds of judgment]. Mahkamah Majistret Kuala Kangsar, Perak. Kes Jenayah No. AG-83RS-6-01/2026.

Pendakwa Raya v. Ku Mahamad Isa bin Jaafar. (2026). *Alasan penghakiman* [Grounds of judgment]. Mahkamah Majistret Lenggong, Perak. Kes Jenayah No. AR-83RS-2-01/2026.

Pendakwa Raya v. Mohamad Sukry bin Wahab & Muhammad Hafiszan bin Naser. (2026). *Alasan penghakiman* [Grounds of judgment]. Mahkamah Sesyen Sepang, Selangor. Perbicaraan Jenayah No. BK-63ES-1-07/2022.

Pendakwa Raya v. Mohamad Zakir Husim bin Mohd Alwi. (2026). *Alasan penghakiman.* Mahkamah Sesyen Kuala Pilah, Negeri Sembilan. Kes Tangkap No. NB-62D-222-10/2023.

Pendakwa Raya v. Mohd Nazuli bin Mohd Nazari. (2026). *Alasan penghakiman* [Grounds of judgment]. Mahkamah Sesyen Jenayah (2) Alor Setar, Kedah. Kes Jenayah No. KA-61R-2-01/2022.

Pendakwa Raya v. Mustapha bin Ibrahim. (2026). *Alasan penghakiman* [Grounds of judgment]. Mahkamah Tinggi Malaya di Kota Bharu, Kelantan. Rayuan Jenayah No. DA-41S-1-01/2025.

Pendakwa Raya v. Sarimah binti Abdul Rahman. (2026). *Alasan penghakiman* [Grounds of judgment]. Mahkamah Majistret Melaka. Kes Saman No. MA-85-138-05/2024.

Pendakwa Raya v. Syed Akmar bin Syed Othman. (2026). *Alasan penghakiman* [Grounds of judgment]. Mahkamah Majistret Kangar, Perlis. Kes Jenayah No. RA-83D-408-02/2023.

Pendakwa Raya v. Tee Wei Xuan. (2026, January 30). *Alasan penghakiman* [Unpublished grounds of judgment]. Mahkamah Sesyen Jenayah 10, Wilayah Persekutuan Kuala Lumpur. Kes Tangkap No. WA-62K-269-12/2025.

Pendakwa Raya v. Viknshpran a/l Batu Malai. (2026). *Alasan penghakiman* [Grounds of judgment]. Mahkamah Majistret Teluk Intan, Perak. Kes Tangkap No. AC-83D-1448-11/2025.

Peruzzo, K. (2023). *Legal terms that travel: Constraints to presenting national legal terminology to international audiences. Handbook of terminology*. John Benjamins., DOI: 10.1075/hot.3.leg1

Peters, T. D. (2020). Daredevil as legal emblem. *Law. Technology and Humans, 2*(2), 198–226. DOI: 10.5204/lthj.1656

Phillvin Guachin v. Pendakwa Raya. (2026). *Grounds of judgment.* Mahkamah Tinggi Johor Bahru, Johor. Usul No. JA-44-39-10/2025.

Pisulińska, J. (2021). Wincenty Zakrzewski o roli Kościoła w dziejach Polski. *Klio Polska*, (13), 103–122.

Piszcz, A., & Sierocka, H. (2020). The Role of Culture in Legal Languages, Legal Interpretation and Legal Translation. *International Journal for the Semiotics of Law, 33*(3), 533–542. DOI: 10.1007/s11196-020-09760-3 PMID: 33214737

Pitkäsalo, E., & Kalliomaa-Puha, L. (2019). Democratizing access to justice: The comic contract as intersemiotic translation. *Translation Matters, 1*(2), 30–42. DOI: 10.21747/21844585/tm1_2a2

Pontrandolfo, G., & Peruzzo, K. (2017). Legal translation and interpreting: between old and new theoretical, discursive and professional perspectives. *International journal of legal discourse, 2*(2), 171-176.

Pontrandolfo, G. (2023). The importance of being patterned: Old and new perspectives on legal phraseology. In *Handbook of terminology* (pp. 124–150). John Benjamins. DOI: 10.1075/hot.3.imp1

Powell, R., & Saw, T. G. (2021). Multilingual legal practice and law student internships in Malaysia. *World Englishes*, *42*(3), 579–592. DOI: 10.1111/weng.12570

Prathap, S., & Kabaleeswaran, D. (2025). *The construction of identities and resistance through film narratives*. Sociology Lens., DOI: 10.1111/johs.70013

Prieto Ramos, F. (2011). Developing legal translation competence: An integrative process-oriented approach. *Comparative Legilinguistics*, *5*(1), 7–22. DOI: 10.14746/cl.2020.41.1

Prieto Ramos, F. (2014). Legal translation studies as interdiscipline: Scope and evolution. *Meta*, *59*(2), 260–277. DOI: 10.7202/1027475ar

Prieto Ramos, F. (2015). Quality assurance in legal translation: Evaluating process, competence and product in the pursuit of adequacy. *International Journal for the Semiotics of Law*, *28*(1), 11–30. DOI: 10.1007/s11196-014-9390-9

Prieto Ramos, F. (2020). Translation at International Organizations: The Legal and Linguistic Hierarchies of Multilingualism. In Ji, M., & Laviosa, S. (Eds.), *The Oxford Handbook of Translation and Social Practices* (pp. 455–477). Oxford University Press., DOI: 10.1093/oxfordhb/9780190067205.013.13

Prieto Ramos, F., & Cerutti, G. (2021). Terminology as a source of difficulty in translating international legal discourses: An empirical cross-genre study. *International Journal of Legal Discourse*, *6*(2), 155–179. DOI: 10.1515/ijld-2021-2052

Prieto Ramos, F., & Cerutti, G. (2023). Terminological hybridity in institutional legal translation: A corpus-driven analysis of key genres of EU and international law. *Terminology*, *29*(1), 45–77. DOI: 10.1075/term.21047.pri

Prieto-Ramos, F. (2017). Global law as translated text: Mapping institutional legal translation. *Tilburg Law Review*, *22*(1–2), 185–214. DOI: 10.1163/22112596-02201009

Public Prosecutor v. Mohd Idham bin Mokhtar. (2026). *Grounds of judgment*. Sessions Court Johor Bahru. Criminal Case Nos. JA-61R-24-12/2021 & JA-61R-9-06/2022.

Quinci, C., & Pontrandolfo, G. (2023). *Testing neural machine translation against different levels of specialisation: An exploratory investigation across legal genres and languages. trans-kom, 16*(1), 174–209. trans-kom article

Ramalingam, S., Sabaruddin, J. S., & Dhanapal, S. (2022). The language of justice in Malaysian courts: The law and the reality. *IIUM Law Journal*, *30*(2), 23–48. DOI: 10.31436/iiumlj.v30i2.758

Rashid, B. N. (2023). Multimodality in the courtroom in American and British criminal cases. *IJPS, 16*(1), 1–8. DOI: 10.37648/ijps.v16i01.001 PMID: 36998925

Raunak, V., Sharaf, A., Wang, Y., Awadalla, H., & Menezes, A. (2023). Leveraging GPT-4 for automatic translation post-editing. In *Findings of the Association for Computational Linguistics: EMNLP 2023* (pp. 12009–12024). Association for Computational Linguistics. https://doi.org/DOI: 10.18653/v1/2023.findings-emnlp.804

Reifman, D. (2022). Canonicity as a defining feature of legal and religious discourse. In *The Cambridge handbook of law and humanities* (pp. 151–170). https://doi.org/ DOI: 10.1017/9781108760997.007

Reisberg, L. (2018). Interpretation of undefined legal concepts and fulfilling of legal gaps in Juri Lotman's semiotic framework. *Juridica International*, *27*, 3–11. DOI: 10.12697/JI.2018.27.01

Rivas Ginel, M. I., & Moorkens, J. (2025). Translators' trust and distrust in the times of GenAI. *Translation Studies*, *18*(2), 283–299. DOI: 10.1080/14781700.2025.2507594

Sacco, R. (1991). Legal formants: A dynamic approach to comparative law (Installment II of II). *The American Journal of Comparative Law*, *39*(2), 343–401. DOI: 10.2307/840784

Santos, B. D. S. (2009). Democratizar a democracia: os caminhos da democracia participativa. In *Democratizar a democracia: os caminhos da democracia participativa* (pp. 678-678).

Šarčević, S. (1997). *New approach to legal translation*. Kluwer Law International B.V.

Šarčević, S. (2012). *Challenges to the legal translator. The Oxford handbook of language and law*. Oxford University Press., DOI: 10.1093/oxfordhb/9780199572120.013.0014

Schauer, F. (1991). *Playing by the rules: A philosophical examination of rule-based decision-making in law and in life*. Clarendon Press.

Scott, J. (2017). Legal translation – a multidimensional endeavour. *Comparative Legilinguistics*, *32*, 37–66. DOI: 10.14746/cl.2017.32.2

Searle, J. R. (1969). *Speech acts: An essay in the philosophy of language*. Cambridge University Press. DOI: 10.1017/CBO9781139173438

Serttaş, A., Gürkan, H., & Dere, G. (2025). Synthetic Social Alienation: The Role of Algorithm-Driven Content in Shaping Digital Discourse and User Perspectives. *Journalism and Media*, *6*(3), 149. Advance online publication. DOI: 10.3390/journalmedia6030149

Shamonina, G., & Kostova, B. (2025). Pravnite tsennosti kato kulturno-znachimi orientiri v obuchenieto po chuzhd ezik na studenti-yuristi [Legal values as culturally significant landmarks in foreign language training of law students]. *Chuzhdoezikovo Obuchenie, 51*(4). Advance online publication. DOI: 10.53656/for2025-04-07

Shi, C., & O'Halloran, K. L. (2025). Constructing the prosecution-defense relationship through multimodal positioning: A corpus-based analysis of Chinese courtroom argumentation. *Social Semiotics*, •••, 1–23. DOI: 10.1080/10350330.2025.2546617

Sierocka, H. (2014). *Curriculum development for legal English programs.* Cambridge Scholars Publishing.

Silk, A. (2019). Theories of vagueness and theories of law. *Legal Theory, 25*(2), 132–152. DOI: 10.1017/S1352325219000028

Sokolsky, A. (2022). Retranslating the Tokyo Trial: Shigemitsu Mamoru's Prison Diary. In *The Twelfth International Convention of Asia Scholars (ICAS 12)* (pp.674-682). Amsterdam University Press. DOI: 10.5117/9789048557820/ICAS.2022.078

Solan, L. M. (1993). *The language of judges.* University of Chicago Press. DOI: 10.7208/chicago/9780226767895.001.0001

Sopjani, V., & Hamiti, V. (2022). Challenges in the translation of legal texts: The case in Kosovo. *Comparative Legilinguistics, 52*, 351–380. DOI: 10.14746/cl.52.2022.15

Sosoni, V., O'Shea, J., & Stasimioti, M. (2022). Translating law: A comparison of human and post-edited translations from Greek to English. *Revista de Llengua i Dret*, (78), 92–120. DOI: 10.2436/rld.i78.2022.3704

Stiefenhofer, P., Gergerlioğlu, U., & Deniz, C. (2025). *Delegating authority to algorithms: Legitimacy and public values in European tax administrations.* Philosophy and Realistic Reflection., DOI: 10.55121/prr.v3i1.757

Stubbs, M. (2001). *Words and phrases: Corpus studies of lexical semantics.* John Wiley & Sons.

Sulaiman, M. Z., Zainudin, I. S., & Haroon, H. (2024). Pemprofesionalan Amalan Terjemahan Dan Kejurubahasaan Di Malaysia: Satu Tinjauan Awal (The professionalisation of translation and interpreting practice in Malaysia: A preliminary study). *GEMA Online Journal of Language Studies, 24*(4), 387–409. DOI: 10.17576/gema-2024-2404-21

Sun, X., & Chen, X. (2024). Review of legal terminology translation research. *International Journal of Education and Humanities, 17*(3), 343–348. DOI: 10.54097/1zy4e144

Sun, Y., Zhu, X., & Liu, K. (2025). Judicial jigsaw and power dynamics: A cognitive-functional analysis of Chinese courtroom discourse. *International Journal of Legal Discourse, 10*(1), 181–207. DOI: 10.1515/ijld-2025-2009

Supreme People's Court. (2021, July 22). *Renmin fayuan zuzhi jigou, zhiwu mingcheng, gongzuo changsuo yingyiwen[English translations of people's court institutions, titles, and workplaces].* https://www.court.gov.cn/fabu/xiangqing/314981.html

Surden, H. (2014). Machine learning and law. *Washington Law Review (Seattle, Wash.), 89*(1), 87–115.

Svitych, O. (2026). Blind transparency: A critical discourse analysis of the EU AI Act. *Critical Policy Studies, 20*(1), 127–143. DOI: 10.1080/19460171.2025.2496193

Swales, J. M. (1990). *Genre analysis.* Cambridge university press., DOI: 10.1075/z.184.513swa

Syameel, D. (2025a, April 28). 1.HONORIFICS TEST 1 [Ms Word]. Malaysian Institute of Translation and Books.

Syameel, D. (2025b, April 28). 2. Hierarchy of Sources [Ms Word]. Malaysian Institute of Translation and Books.

Syameel, D. (2025c, April 28). 3. LEGAL TERMS/PHRASES [Ms Word]. Malaysian Institute of Translation and Books.

Szarkowska, A. (2010). Between text and image: Updating research in screen translation. *International Journal of Translation Studies, 22*(2), 363–368. DOI: 10.1075/target.22.2.11sza

Tabrizi, H. H., & House, J. (2025). Moving beyond conventional tests: Performance assessment as an alternative for evaluating students' academic translations. *Contrastive Pragmatics, 6*(3), 608–639. https://brill.com/view/journals/jocp/6/3/article-p608_5.xml

Takeda, K. (2008). *Sociopolitical aspects of interpreting at the International Military Tribunal for the Far East (1946–1948)* [Doctoral dissertation, Universitat Rovira i Virgili]. https://open.unive.it/hitrade/books/TakedaSociopolitical.pdf

Takeda, K. (2007). The making of an interpreter user. *International Journal of Interpretation and Translation, 5*(1), 245–263. DOI: 10.1075/forum.5.1.11tak

Tamanaha, B. Z. (2001). *A general jurisprudence of law and society.* Oxford University Press. DOI: 10.1093/acprof:oso/9780199244676.001.0001

Termorshuizen-Arts, M. (2008). Legal Semantics: A contribution to the methodology of legal comparison, jurisprudence and legal translation (S. Kahn, Trans.). Willem-Jan and René van der Wolf. https://www.researchgate.net/publication/275462781_Legal_semantics_A_contribution_to_the_methodology_of_legal_comparison_jurisprudence_and_legal_translation#fullTextFileContent

Tessuto, G. (2011). Nationalising English legal language pedagogy in L2 genre-based writing: Legal problem question in the UK loci of law. Implications and challenges for the pluricentricity of a legal English pedagogy. *ESP Across Cultures*, *8*, 7–28. DOI: 10.1016/j.esp.2011.05.001

Thapa, S., Shiwakoti, S., Shah, S. B., Adhikari, S., Veeramani, H., Nasim, M., & Naseem, U. (2025). Large language models (LLM) in computational social science: Prospects, current state, and challenges. *Social Network Analysis and Mining*, *15*(1), 4. DOI: 10.1007/s13278-025-01428-9

Tiersma, P. M. (1999). *Legal Language*. University of Chicago Press. DOI: 10.7208/chicago/9780226854809.001.0001

Tiersma, P., Solan, L., Ainsworth, J., Shuy, R. W., Tiersma, P., Solan, L., Ainsworth, J., & Shuy, R. W. (Eds.). (2015). *Speaking of Language and Law: Conversations on the Work of Peter Tiersma*. Oxford University Press.

Torresi, I. (2013). *The photographic image: Truth or sign?* Springer., DOI: 10.1007/978-90-481-9322-6_6

Turaeva, U. (2020). Characteristics, Methods, and Challenges Of Translating Law Terminology. JournalNX—A Multidisciplinary Peer-Reviewed Journal, 6(11), 312-316.

Uwen, G. (2023). Objection overruled: Language dynamics and power relations in courtroom interactions. *Language Matters (Pretoria)*, *54*(2), 21–41. DOI: 10.1080/10228195.2023.2229533

Van Hoecke, M. (Ed.). (2011). *Methodologies of legal research: Which kind of method for what kind of discipline?* Hart Publishing.

van Kolfschooten, H., Goosen, S., van Oirschot, J., Schouten, B., Vajda, I., & Willems, L. (2025). Legal, ethical, and policy challenges of artificial intelligence translation tools in healthcare. *Discover Public Health*, *22*(1), 904. DOI: 10.1186/s12982-025-01277-z PMID: 41487681

Van Parijs, P. (2011). *Linguistic Justice for Europe and for the World*. Oxford University Press. DOI: 10.1093/acprof:osobl/9780199208876.001.0001

Varga, M. (2020). The role of linguistic impression management: The case of Hungarian courtroom discourses. *Corpus Pragmatics : International Journal of Corpus Linguistics and Pragmatics*, *4*(3), 381–400. DOI: 10.1007/s41701-020-00087-9

Vaswani, A., Shazeer, N., Parmar, N., Uszkoreit, J., Jones, L., Gomez, A. N., Kaiser, Ł., & Polosukhin, I. (2017, December 4–9). *Attention is all you need* [Paper presentation]. *31st Conference on Neural Information Processing Systems (NIPS 2017)*, Long Beach, CA, United States. DOI: 10.48550/arXiv.1706.03762

Venuti, L. (1995). *The translator's invisibility: A history of translation*. Routledge.

Venuti, L. (2018). *Rethinking Translation: Discourse, Subjectivity, Ideology*. Routledge. DOI: 10.4324/9780429432385

Vieira, L. N. (2019). Post-editing of machine translation. In O'Hagan, M. (Ed.), *The Routledge handbook of translation and technology* (pp. 319–336). Routledge., DOI: 10.4324/9781315311258-19

Vieira, L. N., O'Hagan, M., & O'Sullivan, C. (2021). Understanding the societal impacts of machine translation: A critical review of the literature on medical and legal use cases. *Information Communication and Society*, *24*(11), 1515–1532. DOI: 10.1080/1369118X.2020.1776370

Volansky, V., Ordan, N., & Wintner, S. (2015). On the features of translationese. *Digital Scholarship in the Humanities*, *30*(1), 98–118. DOI: 10.1093/llc/fqt031

von Wright, G. H. (1951). Deontic logic. *Mind; A Quarterly Review of Psychology and Philosophy*, *60*(237), 1–15. DOI: 10.1093/mind/LX.237.1

Voskanyan, R. (2018). Legal English: Lexical competence and curriculum design. *The ESP Journal, SI-2*, 57–73. Advance online publication. DOI: 10.46991/AFA/2026.SI-2.57

Wa Thiong'o, N. (1998). Decolonising the mind. *Diogenes*, *46*(184), 101–104. DOI: 10.1177/039219219804618409

Wachter, S., Mittelstadt, B., & Russell, C. (2024). Do large language models have a legal duty to tell the truth? *Royal Society Open Science*, *11*(8), 240197. Advance online publication. DOI: 10.1098/rsos.240197 PMID: 39113763

Wagner, A., & Marusek, S. (2025). Law without roots: Mapping the rhizomatic turn in legal thought and practice. *Undecidabilities and Law*, *5*(5), 9–13. DOI: 10.14195/2184-9781_5_0

Wan Mahmud, W. A. (2026, Jan 7). Asas penterjemahan teks Undang-undang [PPT].

Wang, H. (2017). Multimodal discourse of criminal courtroom discourses. *ICPEL Proceedings*. https://doi.org/DOI: 10.2991/icpel-17.2017.56

Wang, Q., Amini, M., & Tan, D. A. L. (2025). Strategies, errors, and challenges in translating Culture-Specific Items in Chinese-English literary works: A systematic review. *JURNAL ARBITRER, 12*(2), 259–273. https://arbitrer.fib.unand.ac.id/index.php/arbitrer/article/view/591

Wang, C., Yin, Y., & Hu, H. (2026). The rise of algorithmic governance and the dual revolution: Applications, challenges, and governance of artificial intelligence in public administration. *Technology in Society*, *86*, 103264. DOI: 10.1016/j.techsoc.2026.103264

Wang, Q., Amini, M., Yang, C., & He, Q. (2026). Translating Culture-Specific Items in The True Story of Ah Q: A comparative evaluation of GPT-4o, KIMI, and Google Translate under multimodal prompts. *SAGE Open*, *16*(1), 21582440251412225. Advance online publication. DOI: 10.1177/21582440251412225

Wang, Q., Wang, Y., Amini, M., Xian, M., & Fu, Z. (2026). Quality assessment of Tibetan–Chinese poetry translation: Integrating automated metrics and qualitative insights through a cross-system comparison of dedicated NMT engines and a prompted LLM. *Language Resources and Evaluation*, *60*(2), 42. Advance online publication. DOI: 10.1007/s10579-026-09918-8

Wan, S. Y. C., Abu Bakar, A., Amini, M., & Rafik-Galea, S. (2018). Problems and solutions in English translations of Malay short stories. *The Journal of Social Sciences Research*, *6*(Special Issue), 1158–1166. https://arpgweb.com/pdf-files/spi6.3.2.1158.1166.pdf

Way, C. (2016). The challenges and opportunities of legal translation and translator training in the 21st century. *International Journal of Communication*, *10*, 1009–1029. https://ijoc.org/index.php/ijoc/article/view/3580

Winner, L. (1980). Do Artifacts Have Politics? *Daedalus*, *109*(1), 121–136.

Wodak, R. (1980). Discourse analysis and courtroom interaction. *Discourse Processes*, *3*(4), 369–380. DOI: 10.1080/01638538009544498

Wright, S. (2025). Artificial intelligence in legal translation at the Court of Justice of the European Union. *International Journal of Language & Law*, *14*, 120–142. DOI: 10.14762/jll.2025.120

Wu, S., Amini, M., & Mahfoodh, O. H. A. (2026). Exploring translators' perceptions of translation decisions in courtroom translation. *International Journal for the Semiotics of Law-Revue internationale de Sémiotique juridique, 39*(1), 319-339. DOI: 10.1007/s11196-025-10274-z

Wu, S., Amini, M., & Mahfoodh, O. H. A. (2025). A corpus assisted analysis of modality shifts in English-to-Chinese courtroom translation. *Eurasian Journal of Applied Linguistics, 11*(1), 152–166. https://files.eric.ed.gov/fulltext/EJ1474997.pdf

Wu, S., Amini, M., & Mahfoodh, O. H. A. (2025a). A corpus-based analysis of modality shifts in English-to-Chinese courtroom translation. *Eurasian Journal of Applied Linguistics, 11*(1), 152–166. https://ejal.info/menuscript/index.php/ejal/article/view/995/364

Wu, S., Amini, M., & Mahfoodh, O. H. A. (2025a). A Corpus-based analysis of modality shifts in English-to-Chinese courtroom translation. *Eurasian Journal of Applied Linguistics, 11*(1), 152–166. https://ejal.info/menuscript/index.php/ejal/article/view/995/364

Wu, S., Amini, M., & Mahfoodh, O. H. A. (2025b). Exploring challenges and solutions in English-to-Chinese courtroom translation: Insights from the Tokyo Trial and implications for translator training. *SAGE Open, 15*(4). Advance online publication. DOI: 10.1177/21582440251385865

Wu, S., Amini, M., & Mahfoodh, O. H. A. (2026). Unveiling certainty and doubt: A systemic functional exploration of epistemic modality in courtroom discourse. *International Journal for the Semiotics of Law, 39*(2), 501–522. DOI: 10.1007/s11196-025-10321-9

Wu, S., Amini, M., & Wang, Y. (2026). Negotiating institutional hierarchy: Power, politeness, and meaning construction in English-to-Chinese courtroom translation. *SAGE Open, 16*(1), 1–14. DOI: 10.1177/21582440261421582

Xu, Y. (2020). *Second Language Writing Complexity in Academic Legal Discourse: Development and Assessment under a Curricular Lens*. Linguistics. hdl.handle.net/10822/1060758

Xuan, J.XUAN Junbin. (2020). Equivalent tenor in translation: A case study on Ophelia's Confession. *Sino-US English Teaching, 17*(7), 211–216. DOI: 10.17265/1539-8072/2020.07.003

Xu, W., Geluso, K., & Staples, D. (2023). Navigating complexity in plain English: A longitudinal analysis of syntactic and lexical complexity development in L2 legal writing. *Journal of Second Language Writing*, *62*, 101059. Advance online publication. DOI: 10.1016/j.jslw.2023.101059

Yang, M., & Wang, M. (2021). A science mapping of studies on courtroom discourse with CiteSpace. *International Journal of Legal Discourse*, *6*(2), 291–322. DOI: 10.1515/ijld-2021-2057

Yang, N. (2019). The application of register analysis into translation quality assessment. *Theory and Practice in Language Studies*, *9*(12), 1550–1554. DOI: 10.17507/tpls.0912.11

Yulianto, A., & Supriatnaningsih, R. (2021). Google Translate vs. DeepL: A quantitative evaluation of close-language pair translation (French to English). *Asian Journal of English Language and Pedagogy*, *9*(2), 109–127. DOI: 10.37134/ajelp.vol9.2.9.2021

Zhou, X., & Hu, C. (2024). A review of research on correspondence and processing of legal terminology in legal translation. *International Journal of Education and Humanities*, *16*(2), 290–295. DOI: 10.54097/t5cbrj67

Ziwei, C. (2025). *AI translation and data ownership: Ethical conflicts, legal risks, and translator agency in the algorithmic era. The Frontiers of Society*. Science and Technology., DOI: 10.25236/FSST.2025.070702

Zuboff, S. (2020). L'âge du capitalisme de surveillance. *Le combat pour un avenir humain face aux nouvelles frontières du pouvoir*.

Zweigert, K., & Kötz, H. (1983). An Introduction to Comparative Law (3rd ed.). Oxford University Press. Malaysian Court Judgments (Alasan Penghakiman / Grounds of Judgment)

About the Contributors

Mansour Amini is an interdisciplinary researcher and senior lecturer at the School of Languages, Literacies, and Translation, Universiti Sains Malaysia (USM). He holds a Diploma in Mathematics and Physics, a B.A. in English Language and Literature, an M.A. in English Language Teaching, and a Ph.D. in Translation Studies. Dr. Amini has published several academic articles, books, chapters, and reviews in Education and Translation Studies. He serves as the editorial board member for several academic journals and has conducted workshops on research writing and methodology.

Shuangjiao Wu has a Phd in Translation. Her main area of research is legal discourse and translation. Formely she served as the Head of Department of Translation and Interpreting (School of English Studies) at Zhejiang Yuexiu University, Shaoxing, China.

Qiufen Wang is a senior lecturer and has a Phd in translation. Her areas of research include translation, education, and culture.

***

Imelda Abas is a trained scholar and teacher currently based at Shinawatra University (SIU), Bangkok. With a background in Applied Linguistics (PhD and MA, Universiti Utara Malaysia) and English Literature (BA, Hasanuddin University), she brings extensive experience in higher education, research mentoring, and accessible teaching practices. Her work focuses on making complex ideas clear and practical for diverse students, whether through mentoring students on dissertations, guiding faculty on institutional reporting, or designing engaging classroom activities.

Lama Alaggad is a master candidate at the department of Shariah Law at the Academy of Islamic Studies, University of Malaya, Malaysia

Mohammed Al-Aqad is a distinguished Assistant Professor and Researcher at the Faculty of Languages and Linguistics at the University of Malaya, Malaysia. He is a resident scholar at Hashim Sani Centre for Palestine Studies, University of Malaya, Malaysia. He specializes in translation and interpreting studies, AI and applied linguistics, bringing over 15 years of academic & industrial experience to his role. Dr. Alaqad has been an invited speaker and presenter at more than 50 international conferences and events, and he has authored numerous research papers and books. He is also the founder and CEO of the Asian Federation of Translators and Interpreters, Malaysia.

Maryam Alipour (Ph.D) is an English language lecturer at Language and General Education Centre Shinawatra University Thailand. She holds a Doctor of Arts in English Language Studies from Universiti Kebangsaan Malaysia (UKM) in 2021. She completed her Master of Arts in English Language Studies at Universiti Kebangsaan Malaysia (UKM) in 2012. She received her Bachelor of Arts in English Translation at Islamic Azad University of Shiraz. She has published journal articles and a book chapter. Maryam speaks three languages, namely Persian, English and Arabic.

Ebraiek Aljheme is a Libyan scholar and translator specialising in English language, applied linguistics, and legal discourse studies. He holds a Master's degree in Applied Linguistics from Universiti Utara Malaysia (2011) and a Bachelor's degree in English Language from Sebha University (2005). Ebrayek has extensive academic and professional experience, serving as Head of the English Language Department at Sebha Open University (2022–2026) and previously at the College of Languages (2018–2019). He has lectured in English language and translation since 2007, with teaching roles spanning Sebha University's Law College, medical schools, and specialised training programs for the Libyan Oil Corporation. His expertise includes legal translation, English for specific purposes, and multimodal literacy in law.

Sanjana Bharadwaj is a doctoral researcher in Law at NALSAR University of Law, Hyderabad, where she has been pursuing her Ph.D on the aspect of 'Linguistic Genocide in India'. She holds an LL.M. from NALSAR University of Law, with a strong academic foundation in constitutional law, international law, and governance studies. Her research engages with critical issues at the intersection of law, language, identity, and global justice. She has contributed to Scopus-indexed scholarship, including work on linguistic rights and minority protections, as well as constitutional responses to humanitarian crises such as the Rohingya issue. Her publication in the Journal of Asian and African Studies examines the concept of linguistic genocide and its implications within Indian legal frameworks, while her work in Novum Jus critically analyses constitutional failures in India and Myanmar. In addition to her research, she has served as an editor for academic volumes including Reimagining Constitutionalism in the Indian Context and Technology, AI & Law, reflecting her engagement with contemporary debates in constitutional theory and legal technology. Her work adopts an interdisciplinary and critical approach, contributing to emerging scholarship on rights, governance, and structural inequality.

Kranti Deshmukh is the Principal and Associate Professor of Law. She holds B.A., LL.B., and LL.M. degrees, has qualified the UGC-NET, and earned her Ph.D. in Law with a thesis titled "Maintenance of Internal Security in India: Contemporary Challenges and Legal Perspectives." Her academic interests include Constitutional Law, Family Law, Intellectual Property Law, and Research Methodology. Dr. Deshmukh has made significant contributions to legal scholarship through her research and publications in reputed peer-reviewed and indexed journals. Her work spans critical areas such as internal security, human rights, constitutional freedoms, and emerging legal challenges. Her notable publications include studies on criminal justice and internal security, freedom of religion and equality with reference to the Uniform Civil Code, sedition laws under Section 124 IPC, and the development of the right to privacy in India. She has also written on contemporary issues such as women and crime, terrorism and human rights, and consumer disputes in the medical sector, reflecting her interdisciplinary engagement with law and society.

Gisele El Khoury is the director of the Language Resource Center and an Arabic Instructor in the Department of World Languages, Cultures & Media at St. Lawrence University (SLU), where she has taught since the Fall of 2006 and has published several articles in her field.

Malini Ganapathy is a lecturer at the School of Languages, Literacies and Translation, Universiti Sains Malaysia, Penang. She has a Certificate of Education (TESL), B.A. (Hons.) in English Language and Literature Studies, M.A. and Ph.D in Applied Linguistics from Universiti Sains Malaysia. She has 18 years of teaching experience at secondary schools, prior to joining Universiti Sains Malaysia in 2014. Her research interests include English Language Teaching (ELT), Literacy (Multiliteracies, Multimodality, New Literacies) and Writing. She has published numerous research articles focusing on her area of research, both in international and local journals.

Rahul Gangurde is an Assistant Professor of Law at Government Law College, Mumbai. He holds both his Master's degree and Ph.D. in Law from Savitribai Phule Pune University, Pune, India. His doctoral research focuses on the right to health, with particular emphasis on structural inequalities, regulatory gaps, and the evolving dynamics of healthcare governance in India. His academic contributions are reflected in Scopus-indexed publications that critically engage with themes such as the regularity of healthcare practices, the commercialization of healthcare and education, and the broader intersections of law, governance, and social justice. His research adopts an interdisciplinary approach, examining how institutional and policy frameworks shape access, equity, and accountability in the Global South. In addition to his scholarly work, he is actively involved in teaching, mentoring, and academic writing, with a commitment to advancing critical legal scholarship and inclusive legal education.

Marlina Jamal is a Senior Lecturer at the School of Languages, Literacies and Translation, Universiti Sains Malaysia, Penang. She possesses a Bachelor's Degree in BLL from Universiti of Malaya, Master of Arts (MA) from Universiti Sains Malaysia and a Doctoral Degree (Ph.D) in Critical Discourse Analysis from Universiti Sains Malaysia. She has a vast experience of teaching tertiary education in both public and private institutions. Her area of specialization is Critical Discourse Analysis. Her areas of research includes discourse analysis, stylistics, forensic linguistics, gender studies and pure linguistics.

Shatha Jarrah is a Phd candidate in Translation at the School of Languages, Literacies and Translation, Universiti Sains Malaysia, Penang, Malaysia. Her area of research is AI in Translation and Education. She has published several peer-reviewed journal articles and presented at the international conferences.

Gehan Khaled is a Phd candidate in Translation at the School of Languages, Literacies and Translation, Universiti Sains Malaysia, Penang, Malaysia. Her area of research is AI in Translation and Education. She has conducted several research projects.

Yoke Lian Lau graduated from Universiti Malaya in 2009 with a Master of Modern Language and Mokpo National University Korea with a Master of Arts in 2011. In addition, she earned a Bachelor of Arts from Universiti Malaya in 2006 and a certificate in Korean Language and Culture from Chongju University. Presently, she holds the position of lecturer at Universiti Malaysia Sabah's Centre for the Promotion of Knowledge and Language Learning. The scope of her research encompasses translations, AI, Chinese learning and teaching, Chinese languages, and linguistics.

Yeying Pan is a Phd candidate at the School of Languages, Literacies and Translation, Universiti Sains Malaysia. She has published several articles on translation. Currently, she is an Associate Professor at Zhejiang Yuexiu University, China.

Lina Sidgi is a lecturer in Applied Linguistics specializing in foreign / second language learning. She focuses on educational technology in teaching and learning, with particular interest in academic speaking, writing development and innovative pedagogical practices.

Chen Yang is a PhD candidate at the School of Languages, Literacies and Translation, Universiti Sains Malaysia. She has published several research articles in the literary translation area.

Index

A

C

D

E

F

M

N

P

S

T

www.ingramcontent.com/pod-product-compliance
Lightning Source LLC
LaVergne TN
LVHW080907300926
849162LV00003B/593